Biblical Essays IV

BOOKS BY JAMES D. QUIGGLE

DOCTRINAL SERIES

Biblical History
Adam and Eve, a Biography and Theology
Angelology, a True History of Angels

Essays
Biblical Essays
Biblical Essays II
Biblical Essays III
Biblical Essays IV

Marriage and Family
Marriage and Family: A Biblical Perspective
Biblical Homosexuality
A Biblical Response to Same-gender Marriage

Doctrinal and Practical Christianity
First Steps, Becoming a Follower of Jesus Christ
Thirty-Six Essentials of the Christian Faith
The Literal Hermeneutic, Explained and Illustrated
Christian Living and Doctrine
Spiritual Gifts
Why Christians Should Not Tithe

Dispensational Theology
A Primer On Dispensationalism
Understanding Dispensational Theology
Dispensational Eschatology, An Explanation and Defense of the Doctrine
Antichrist, His Genealogy, Kingdom, and Religion

God and Man
God's Choices, Doctrines of Foreordination, Election, Predestination
God Became Incarnate
Life, Death, Eternity
Did Jesus Go To Hell?

COMMENTARY SERIES

The Old Testament
A Private Commentary on the Bible: Judges
A Private Commentary on the Book of Ruth
A Private Commentary on the Bible: Esther
A Private Commentary on the Bible: Song of Solomon
A Private Commentary on the Bible: Daniel
A Private Commentary on the Bible: Jonah
A Private Commentary on the Bible: Habakkuk

A Private Commentary on the Bible: Haggai

The New Testament

The Gospels
A Private Commentary on the Bible: Matthew's Gospel
A Private Commentary on the Bible: Mark's Gospel
A Private Commentary on the Bible: John 1–12
A Private Commentary on the Bible: John 13–21
(John's Gospel is also in a one volume edition)

The Parables and Miracles of Jesus Christ
The Passion and Resurrection of Jesus the Christ
The Christmas Story, As Told By God

Pauline Letters
A Private Commentary on the Bible: Galatians
A Private Commentary on the Bible: Ephesians
A Private Commentary on the Bible: Philippians
A Private Commentary on the Bible: Colossians
A Private Commentary on the Bible: Thessalonians
A Private Commentary on the Bible: Philemon

General Letters
A Private Commentary on the Book of Hebrews
A Private Commentary on the Bible: James
A Private Commentary on the Bible: 1 Peter
A Private Commentary on the Bible: 2 Peter
A Private Commentary on the Bible: John's Epistles
A Private Commentary on the Bible: Jude

Revelation
The Epistle of Jesus to the Church

REFERENCE SERIES

Dictionary of Doctrinal Words
Translation of Select Bible Books (Old And New Testament)
Old and New Testament Chronology (Also in individual volumes: Old
Testament Chronology; New Testament Chronology)

TRACTS

A Human Person: Is the Unborn Life a Person?
Biblical Marriage
How Can I Know I am A Christian?
Now That I am A Christian
Thirty-Six Essentials of the Christian Faith
What is a Pastor? / Why is My Pastor Eating the Sheep?
(All tracts are in Kindle format and cost $0.99)

Visit me at https://www.facebook.com/BooksOfQ

Biblical Essays IV

James D. Quiggle

Copyright Page

Biblical Essays IV

This print edition of *Biblical Essays IV* contains the same content as the digital editions of this work.

Table of Contents

Abbreviations

AD ... Anno Domini (In the year of the Lord [since Christ was born])
BC ... Bello Christo (Before Christ [was born])
ca. ... about (an approximate date) (Latin: circa)
cf. ... compare (Latin: confer)
e.g. ... for example (Latin: exempli gratia)
etc. ... and so forth, and so on (Latin: et cetera)
Ibid ... in the same place (referring to the source cited in the previous entry) (Latin: ibidem)
i.e. ... that is (Latin: id est)
NPNF ... Nicene and Post-Nicene Fathers
LXX ... Septuagint (Greek translation of the Old Testament completed ca. 130 BC)
n. ... note (referring to a footnote or endnote in the work cited)
s. v. ... under the word (Latin: sub verbo)
v. ... verse
vv. ... verses

Preface

Four years, four volumes, and 451 essays on a wide number of biblical topics has brought the Biblical Essays series to a close. This is the final volume in the series. I have written about many biblical topics, some more than once throughout the series. I have greatly enjoyed writing this series of essays. I trust you, the reader, have found a blessing and benefit in reading.

The Spiritual Gift of Bible Teacher

The Spirit-given ability to understand and explain doctrine in a practical way to show others its sense and relevance; knowledge: insight to understand complex spiritual truths above and beyond the ability of the average Christian; prophecy: the ability to explain complex spiritual truths in a way the average Christian can grasp.

The spiritual gift of teaching is the ability to combine knowledge and prophecy to communicate doctrine in a way that reveals its meaning and significance to the average Christian, in such a way that he or she can understand it and make use of it in their daily life.

The skills associated with this gift are:

Is able to present truth in a logical, systematic way

Validates truth by checking out the facts

Loves to do study and research

Enjoys word studies

Prefers to use biblical illustrations rather than life illustrations

Gets upset when Scripture is used out of context

Feels concerned that truth be established in every situation

Is more objective than subjective

Easily develops a large vocabulary

Emphasizes the facts and accuracy of words

Checks out the source of knowledge of others who teach

Prefers teaching believers to engaging in evangelism

Feels Bible study is foundational to the operation of all gifts

Solves problems by starting with scriptural principles

Is intellectually sharp

Is self-disciplined

Is emotionally controlled

Has only a select circle of friends

Has strong convictions and opinions based on investigation of facts

Believes truth has the intrinsic ability to produce change

Focuses on changing lives by helping others understand the Bible better

Scriptures associated with this gift are:

1 Corinthians 12:7–11; 2 Chronicles 1:7–12; Colossians 2:2–3; 2 Corinthians 11:6; Daniel 2:20–21; Proverbs 2:6; Proverbs 9:10; Psalms 119:66; Jeremiah 3:15; Ephesians 4:11–16; Romans 12:6–8; 1 Corinthians 12:28–31; Hebrews 5:12–14; Acts 18:24–28

Most Christians have one or more of those characteristics. But if you read this and said, "All of those characteristics describe me!" then here are the steps by which you determine if that assumption is valid.

There is an inward calling by the Holy Spirit to a certain ministry or ministries (the average Christian usually tries more than one before finding the one).

There will be opportunities to use the gift *and* to improve the gift.

There will be positive feedback from others who recognize the gift at work in you.

There will be feedback you see in lives positively affected by your use of the gift.

One more thing. The spiritual gift of Bible teacher is an optimistic gift. Of course, no one is optimistic all the time, but the gift continuously infuses optimism into the Bible teacher's spirit. The one with the gift genuinely believes as an article of his or her faith that if I can just explain it better, if I can find the right words, if I can reason and discuss to the best of my ability, then the truth once explained will be convincing and change lives and opinions.

And that optimistic confidence is what keeps the Bible teacher active and teaching despite all discouragements, insults, desertions, depressions, and persecutions.

Bible Teacher: an irrepressible motivation to instruct others in the things which the Divine will has revealed to them (John Owen).

I know, because I have been given the spiritual gift Bible Teacher.

Live In The Land

This year I will publish five books on the Bible and begin a fifth. People have asked, "How do you write so fast?" The answer is, I have lived in the land a long time, and taken many journeys throughout its breadth and length, met its people, and understand its stories and what they teach. What seems to an observer "so fast" is the laborious accumulation of knowledge and understanding, the result of forty-seven years of living in and exploring the land of which I write, the Bible.

When a person is first taught a task, he does it slowly. With experience he does it more quickly. When a person takes his first walk or first drive into an unknown place, he does so slowly and cautiously. But with experience he does so comfortably. I have lived in the Bible for forty-seven years (this May 19). I have published fifty-three books on the Bible, half of which are commentaries on OT and NT books. I have lived and travelled in the land.

The land that is the Bible is no longer unfamiliar to me. I have met the Author. I know the geography and the topography, the people and the cities, the stories and the teachings. When I apply what I learned to create an explanation, an interpretation—a travel guide for others—so much is familiar, which helps me understand the unfamiliar. The Holy Spirit made me a Bible teacher, and has given me grace to improve and use that gift.

Diligent effort to improve what I have been given has resulted in detailed explanations for others as I teach through writing. Earlier this month I published a commentary on the Thessalonians letters. When I came to live in Thessalonians I had already lived in Ephesians, Philippians, Colossians, and Philemon, from 2012 to 2020. I knew the lay of the land; I had lived where Paul had lived; I already had an understanding of the people and the teachings. And then, having lived in Ephesians, Philippians, Colossians, 1 & 2 Thessalonians, and Philemon I went to live in Galatians.

So the journey, the writing of books, is not "so fast" as it seems. The commentary on the Galatian letter was begun in October with the translation, completed in February with the interpretation, and still must be edited. The journey that resulted in a book on the thirty-six essentials of the faith, to be published next month, was begun in 1974 with a little book my pastor gave me, "What is Sin? What is Virtue?" Each volume of "Biblical Essays" is the work of a year, out of the experience of a lifetime spent living in the Bible.

This month I began translating the Greek text of Luke's Gospel. I will begin the commentary in June. I am very familiar with Gospel Land, having created commentaries on Matthew, Mark, and John (2014–2019). Actually, Matthew was begun in 2008, when I taught for a year in a Bible Institute in Reno, NV. Behind every book is a long history of living in the Bible.

The purpose of this little essay is not to promote myself or my work. I teach because I must; I write because the Holy Spirit made me a writer so I could teach. The purpose of this essay is to say to you, "there is no substitute for the long journey that brings knowledge, there is no substitute for the hard work that results in understanding."

When I was young I thought I could take a shortcut by reading many theology books and commentaries. But all I did was fill my head with facts about places that I had never visited, about a land I saw from a distance. Yes, I am saying that while it is useful to read a commentary on Bible books and doctrines, mine or another's, they are only a guide to the land, not a substitute for the experience of walking and living in the land. Those "travel guides" are created by those who have walked the length and breadth of the land. Use them to guide you on your own journey, not as a novel to excite you about lands you never visit. Live in the land.

Zealous For Truth

"He that is not zealous against error, is not likely to be zealous for truth." —J. C. Ryle

"Hold fast to the good." — Paul the Apostle, 1 Thessalonians 5:21.

In the constant struggle to represent and defend the many truths of our faith, where do we draw the line between zealous and not so zealous? What truths of Christianity are we to hold fast, and which should we surrender?

There is a sharp line between truth and error, a knife's edge formed and sharpened by God's character. God is "a God of truth and without injustice," Deuteronomy 32:4. The believer is to "serve God in truth with all your heart," 1 Samuel 12:24; to "live our manner of life before God in truth," 1 Kings 2:4. God desires truth as a necessary part of our being, Psalm 51:6. God's truth—the nature of God as truth—is as everlasting as his love and mercy, Psalm 105:5. Because God is truth, his saved people are to be "fellow workers for the truth," 3 John 8.

How important is truth? God beget us as his saved people "by the word of truth," James 1:18. "God's word is truth," John 17:17, and by that same word the believer is set apart from sin and dedicated to God—sanctified—by truth, John 17:17.

Is it not, then, a strange thing to seek harmony and fellowship and peace at the cost of truth? Truth in its essential nature is divisive: there is truth; there is error. "The person knowing God listens to us. The person who is not of God does not listen to us. From this we know the Spirit of truth and the spirit of error," 1 John 4:6. Where there is darkness there is no light; where there is error there is no truth. Darkness is the absence of light, error the absence of truth.

There are no partial truths, no half-truths, no admixture of error with truth and truth be truth still. If, as is the case, the origin and source of truth is God, is God partly true and partly false? Are we justified in holding truth by one hand and error by the other as we walk through this life? Is it okay to be less zealous for some truths in Scripture than for others; to hold fast to some but not all?

In the realm of our Christian profession we have divided truth. Some is essential and some not as essential. There is a right place for this peculiar view of truth. Not all recognize truth as well or as easily as others, and the enemy of our souls uses this fact to divide brethren. That one says, 'This is truth," but another says, "No, that is error."

From the beginning of our Christian faith men and women of faith have asked one another, "What are the truths that are essential to define Christianity as the biblical, apostolic faith?" What are those particular truths, which when missing or denied from our profession, cause Christianity to stop being biblical, apostolic Christianity?" And so men and women of like precious faith have agreed that some truths are "essential" to define the profession of Christianity, and some truths are not as essential to define our mutual faith as biblical, apostolic Christianity.

The problem is, once we have divided our profession of faith into essential and non-essential truths, we forget to be zealous for all truths against error. We chastise the one who defends all truth with equal passion and vigor. Should some faithful apologist dare to defend a "non-essential truth" with same passion, vigor, and conviction as an "essential truth," then he or she is "majoring on the minors," elevating the non-essential, lacking proportion, being divisive, creating dissent, disrupting the harmony of fellowship among brethren.

Brethren, this ought not to be. Truth by its very nature is divisive, and therefore defending truth will be divisive. Should truth divide between fellows, well that is the natural effect of truth. While it is good and proper to define some truths as essential to our profession of faith, to agree on the "without which nothing" of our faith, it is equally good and equally proper to proclaim and defend against error all the truths of our faith, whether categorized as "essential," or "non-essential."

As Mr. Ryle said, "He that is not zealous against error, is not likely to be zealous for truth." By allowing—by silencing those who would defend all truth some truths are left to the rending and tearing of error. By not "holding fast" to all the truth of Scripture, our most precious faith has suffered at the hands of error.

Here is an essential of the faith: truth is a unity. Truth is like a diamond: one gem with many facets. Truth is like a web, pluck one strand and others respond. Truth is a relational database where changing one bit of data produces a ripple effect through other bits of data, changing some, deleting others. In a great house there are many doors by which one may enter. Leave even the least, most unimportant, seldom used door unlocked and error will sneak into the house, threatening the whole of the house of truth.

"He that is not zealous against error, is not likely to be zealous for truth." Brethren, even if we disagree on some truths, we must continue to defend truth. In the analogy of truth as a diamond, the believer must take care to polish all the facets, else the diamond, the truth, is marred, and then, as this facet, and another, and another cease to sparkle and shine, truth ceases to be that brilliant gem from the God of truth that gave birth to our faith and sanctifies us in that faith.

John Bunyan spoke of "Mr. Valiant-for-Truth" in the Pilgrim's Progress, who wielded the sword of truth against all enemies of the truth. Let us not be as some who "are not valiant for the truth on the earth," Jeremiah 9:3. Let us always be valiant for truth, each and every truth, with sword drawn, blood on our face, our clothing disheveled, our limbs tired from the work of defending the truth, but our heart and mind and soul always passionate in its defense.

Mark 4:26–29, The Parable of the Growing Seed

At the time this essay is being written, I have begun work on a new book, *The Parables and Miracles of Jesus the Christ* (now published, May, 2020). Here is a little something from the book.

Translation Mark 4:26–29.

26 And he said, "In this manner is the kingdom of God: as a man should cast the seed upon the earth, 27 and should sleep and rise, night and day, and the seed should sprout and grow, he knows not how. 28 The earth of itself brings forth fruit. First a stalk, then a head, then abundant grain in the head. 29 Then when the grain is ready, he immediately sends the sickle, for the harvest has come."

Translation Note.

In v. 28 I have taken wheat as Christ's example: "First a stalk, then a head, then abundant grain in the head." The Greek vocabulary fits wheat better than corn. Older versions used the example of corn, e.g., the KJV, "first the blade, then the ear, after that the full corn in the ear." Corn, or more properly "maize," was first domesticated in what is now Mexico about 8,700 years ago. What we think of as corn was not known in biblical times and places. Older versions, such as the 1611 KJV, suited the translation to their readers European culture, because ancient middle eastern agriculture culture was not well known or understood.

Exposition

In the preceding parable of the sower, Mark 4:3–9, the key to understanding is sowing the seed, not the reaction of the soils to the seed. The seed is the Word of God, 4:14. People, as represented by the four kinds of soils, respond to the seed according to their nature. Of course, we know from other scriptures there is more to salvation than proclaiming the Word. But parables do not teach doctrine, and they do not illustrate every aspect of doctrine. A parable is designed to teach one point. The one point in both sower-seed parables is not salvation. The point of both parables is the believer is to be faithful in sowing the seed no matter what the result.

The parable in 4:26–29 appears only in Mark's Gospel. The key to this parable is in 4:27, the farmer does not know how the seed sprouts and grows. Unlike the soils parable, whose focus is sowing the seed, the focus of this parable is the seed itself. The seed itself has life. The farmer does not need to know how the seed grows. His role is to sow the seed. If the seed is sown the seed will grow. But the one point of this parable is not that the seed will grow—we know from the soils parable that not all seed planted will be fruitful. The one point of the parable is the farmer is responsible to sow the seed, because it is the seed, not the farmer, that has life and produces results.

In plainer terms, the believer is responsible to proclaim the Word of God. God will see to the results. The power of God is in the Word of God because God has given his Word spiritual power. We are to proclaim the Word. God's Word will accomplish every purpose he has planned for it to accomplish.

A believer plants the Word through evangelism, personal testimony, etc. Like broadcast sowing, the Word falls where it will. Some falls on good soil and produces salvation. But the believer does not know on what kind of soil the Word will fall, and he is not to concern himself with the nature of the soils on which he has sown the seed. The believer will see some seed grow to fruition, but he himself is not the cause of that growth. Pulling in metaphors from other scriptures, some believers plant and others water, but God alone gives the increase (1 Corinthians 3:6). "The wind blows where it pleases, and you hear its sound, but do not know from where it comes and where it goes. So is everyone having been born of the spirit" (John 3:8).

Both of the sower-seed parables describe the mystery form of the kingdom, which is the visible New Testament church between the two advents as composed of both saved and unsaved—the New Testament church as it appears to the world. The parable in Mark 4:26–29 of the growing seed focuses on the Spiritual Kingdom between the two advents—genuine believers in the New Testament church throughout the world.

The worldwide community of genuine believers grows as the Holy Spirit sends believers to sow and water the world with the Word. God alone gives the increase as he chooses. The believer sees the seed grow: a stalk, then a head, then abundant grain in the head, at which point Jesus sends a believer to harvest the saved soul.

Jesus' Miracles: Literal or Fictional?

There are two ways of understanding the miracles of Jesus.

The first is the presupposition that miracles are a violation of natural laws and conclude there is no such thing as a miracle, therefore Jesus did not perform miracles.

The second way of understanding miracles is to admit a miracle is a violation of natural laws, for the simple reason "a miracle is an exceptional activity of God in the material realm, not explainable by man's understanding of the physical laws governing creation, brought about by the immediate efficiency or simple volition of God" [Quiggle, *Dictionary*].

The second is the true, biblical supposition. God created the physical laws of this present universe. As their creator he is not bound by those laws, but may change them at any time to suit his sovereign purpose. That God is able to change the physical laws of this current universe is apparent from two facts.

Fact one, miracles occur in the Old and New Testaments. There is no proof to the contrary, simply disbelief. Fact two, God will destroy this present universe, 2 Peter 3:10–13; Revelation 20:11; 21:1, and create a new universe with different physical laws.

Proof of those new physical laws for a new heaven and earth? The New Jerusalem that will sit on the new earth is 1,500 miles on each side and 1,325 miles high. Outer space begins at fifty miles above the earth's surface in this current creation. The international space station orbits at 254 miles above the earth's surface in this current creation. A large structure extending 1,275 miles into space is an impossibility in this current creation. Truly the new heaven and earth will have different physical laws.

Miracles, then, are the genuine activity of the God-man in the New Testament, the work of omnipotent deity. How to interpret miracles? The same way the rest of the Bible is interpreted: the Literal hermeneutic consistently applied to every scripture. Here is what "literal interpretation" means in relation to interpreting miracles:

> The literal hermeneutic understands the words and language used by the human authors of the Bible in the normal and plain sense of words and language as used in everyday conversation and writing.
>
> Understanding words in their plain and normal sense means all words in all languages have a semantic content and range that

reflects the historical-cultural background of the original writer and reader.

Understanding words in their plain and normal sense means that languages also communicate meaning through well-defined rules of vocabulary, grammar, and syntax.

If an interpretation invests an author's words with a meaning other than the plain and normal meaning of their use in the language in which he is communicating, then it is not a literal interpretation, but is an allegorical or spiritual interpretation: an abstract distortion of the meaning of the text dependent on the interpreter's imagination, not the biblical writer's truth-intention.

Considering the above propositions, a "literal" hermeneutic determines the biblical author's intended meaning (his truth-intention) through the normal and plain sense of the words and language he used. To discover the author's truth-intention the "literal" method applies historical, cultural, contextual, grammatical, lexical, syntactical, theological, genre, and doctrinal analysis to the author's text.

The purpose of the miracles also supports a literal interpretation. The people of Israel had been taught in their long history and through the Scripture record of that history, to identify God at work through the miraculous things he accomplished.

God did not and does not continuously do miraculous works. In fact, a miracle is a rare event in the Scripture record. But God keeps pointing to past miracles to validate his presence and message. To a new generation about to enter the Land, God pointed to the miracles at the Red Sea, Deuteronomy 11:4, to identify himself as the same God who had rescued their fathers. He reminded them again to trust him for their future as they were about to enter the promised land, Joshua 4:23. Nehemiah, at 9:9, pointed to the event at the Red Sea as an encouragement to the immigrant Jews who had come to the land from Babylon. The Writer of Hebrews reminded his Hebrew Christian readers of the event, as an encouragement to persevere in the kind of faith that inherits the promises.

So, too, Israel was taught in the Scripture record to identify their messiah through the miracles that would validate him as the "anointed" (Psalm 2:2), which in Hebrew is *māshîah*. The clearest example is in Matthew 11:2–6.

'Now John, having heard in the prison the works of the Christ, sent two of his disciples, 3 said to him, "Are you the Coming One, or are we to look for another?" 4 And answering Jesus said to them, "Go and tell to John what you hear and see: 5 blind see, and lame walk, lepers are cleansed, and deaf hear, and dead are raised, and poor have good news proclaimed. 6 And blessed is he who may not be offended in me.'"

John Baptist was the herald of Messiah-King. A correct understanding of the gospel record is necessary to distinguish between Messiah as king and Messiah as redeemer. The Jews were expecting the king, not the redeemer. Messiah-King is clearly revealed in Psalm 2. Messiah-Redeemer is as clearly revealed in Isaiah 53, when one applies the New Testament revelation of Jesus the Christ. The Jews in Jesus' day didn't understand Isaiah 53 applied to the man most knew as Jesus of Nazareth, and his followers believed to be the promised Messiah. They were looking for Messiah-King.

So, too, John Baptist, who was expecting Messiah-King to purge Israel of sinners and free Israel of gentile domination. We can forgive John. He was at a low moment in his life, in prison instead of living in Messiah's Davidic Kingdom (2 Samuel 7:13, 16; Psalm 2). So he questioned the evidence he had been given, John 1:33–34, and asked for clarification.

When John Baptist heard about the works Jesus was doing, he sent two of his disciples to question Jesus. John had proclaimed a King who would judge the people and establish his kingdom according to certain Old Testament messianic prophecies.

Jesus responds by pointing John to the messianic signs he had performed, implicitly referring to Isaiah 35:5–6; 61:1. John had preached that the messiah would judge sinners—burn up the chaff. When John heard that Jesus was consorting with prostitutes, tax-collectors, lepers, etc., this seemed to be very un-messianic behavior. In answer Jesus pointed John to Isaiah's prophecies of messiah preaching of the good news to the poor. What Jesus was doing was exactly what Isaiah said the messiah would do.

Jesus' answer to John, pointing him to literal works, tells us to interpret the miracles literally. Jesus actually, literally turned water into wine, healed the blind and lame, raised the dead, stilled the storm, and did other exceptional activities of God in the material realm, not explainable by man's understanding of the physical laws governing creation, brought about by the immediate efficiency or simple volition of God.

Water Into Wine, John 2:1-11

Oínos (the only Greek word for "wine") throughout the ancient world was normally diluted 3 parts water to 1 part wine. The alcoholic content before diluting was less than the modern beer (which is about 5% by volume). A person simply could not drink sufficient quantities of diluted *oínos* in one sitting to become drunk.

> Facts: Wine vinegar, which is soured *oínos*, was in the ancient world, and is today, 5%–6% alcohol by volume, and in the ancient world was diluted and used as a beverage. There are wine-making techniques used by the ancients and today that can produce wine of 12% to 16% alcohol by volume; and it was normally diluted. Higher percentages of alcohol in assorted modern beverages are achieved through distillation, which was invented in the 1800s.

There are seven Hebrew words describing beverages made from various fruits (usually grapes), both alcoholic and non-alcoholic. The ancient world knew and used 5 methods to preserve fruit juices without fermentation. Reducing the volume of non-fermented grape juice by boiling was the easiest and most popular. Water was added after boiling to produce the *oínos*. Grape juice will not ferment after boiling.

The Hebrew word *yayin* represents grape juice, fermented or not. The Hebrew word *tirosh* was "wine, new wine, sweet wine" usually used in a good sense, which would indicate not fermented.

Because all *oínos* was diluted at least 3:1 prior to drinking, it really doesn't matter if the wine Jesus made at the wedding in Cana was *yayin* or *tirosh*. My preference for this event is Jesus made non-fermented *yayin;* what we would identify as freshly squeezed grape juice.

The most important word in the passage is *methúskō*, John 2:10. Some translate *methúskō* as "well-drunk," which others have misused to mean to "make drunk," thereby (somehow) insisting Jesus made alcoholic wine after everyone was drunk. The KJV/NKJV "well-drunk," the NIV "too much to drink," and the NLT "a lot to drink," have the same problem. The cultural fact of dilution prevents that interpretation, and the fact dilution was universally used indicates the ancients in general disapproved of drunkenness. The word *methúskō* within the cultural context means "drink freely," HCSB/CSB, YLT, ASV, ESV, JQT.

The *oínos* Jesus made at the wedding was refreshing, not intoxicating. No one at the wedding was drunk.

How old was Jesus when he died?

Jesus was born between 7–5 BC. He died in AD 33. There is no year zero between BC and AD. Jesus was 38–40 when he died. (7 BC + AD 33 = 40; 6 BC + AD 33 = 39; 5 BC + AD 33 = 38.)

Why then do people say Jesus was 33 years of age when he died? Wasn't Jesus born AD 1? Short answer: No.

Longer answer. If BC means "Before Christ" (Bello Christo), and AD means "in the year of our Lord" (Anno Domini), then why wasn't Jesus born in 1 BC or AD 1?

In the ancient world the passing of years was calculated from some significant event. Usually that event was the accession of a king to the throne. So in one country it might be the year 27 of this king, and in another country it might be the year 33 of that king. On the other hand, the Jewish year is the number of years since the creation (sort of) according to Jewish views of the creation days.

In the Roman Empire, the years were calculated from the founding of the city of Rome. The Latin phrase is *Anno Urbis Conditae*, abbreviated AUC. The years AUC ran from March to March. Jesus was born in a certain year AUC, and died in a certain year AUC.

In AD 525, Pope St. John I assigned Dionysius Exiguus, a Roman Catholic scholar and theologian, to create a new calendar based on the birth of Christ. Exiguus knew from Scripture Jesus was born before Herod died. Using the best historical information available, he determined Herod died in April 754 AUC. Exiguus believed there was only a very short time between Jesus' birth and Herod's death. So his calendar, which is our calendar, began in the year 754 AUC, which he renamed the year AD 1. Exiguus's calendar divided history into BC and AD. We have been counting the years from 754 AUC/AD 1 ever since, backwards into BC, forward into AD. This year is the year AD 2020, or the year 2774 AUC.

However, centuries after Exiguus created the BC–AD calendar, historians discovered Herod actually died in 750 AUC. By that time every historical event from past to present was arranged according to the monk's BC–AD calendar. Rather than change every historical date, historians adjusted the date of Christ's birth to somewhere between 7–5 BC. I believe 5 BC is the most likely, based on historical information in Luke's gospel, 1:5; 2:2; 3:1.

So, don't let anyone tell you Jesus was 33 years of age when he died, but be prepared to give a long explanation.

Lucan Parable 7:41–50

Translation

41 "There were two debtors to a certain creditor. The one owed five hundred denarii, and the other fifty. 42 They having nothing with which to pay, he forgave both. Therefore which of them will love him more?" 43 Answering, Simon said, "I suppose that one whom he forgave the most." And he said to him, "You have rightly judged." 44 And having turned to the woman, he said to Simon, "Do you see this woman? I entered into your house, you gave no water for my feet. But she with her tears wet my feet, and with her hair wiped them." 45 You did not give me a kiss. But she has not stopped kissing my feet from when I came in. You did not anoint my head with oil. But she anointed my feet with scented oil. 47 Therefore I say to you, her many sins have been forgiven, because she loved much. But to whom little is forgiven, little he loves." 48 And he said to her, "Your sins have been forgiven." 49 And those reclining began to say within themselves, "Who is this who even forgives sins?" 50 Then he said to the woman, "You faith has saved you. Go into peace."

Exposition

The context for this parable is Luke 7:36–40. The point of the parable is not gratitude but forgiveness. Jesus was invited, and attended, a dinner party at the house of a Pharisee named Simon. Somehow, a woman who was known as a sinner got into the house.

Now, the identification, "sinner," had particular meaning in the culture of first century rabbinical Judaism. A sinner was someone who did not rigorously keep the law (John 7:34), or was born with some disease (John 9:1, 34), or had a disapproved vocation or lifestyle (Luke 5:30; 15:2). In practical terms, if you fit into one of these categories, you were a sinner.

In the theology of the day, the sinner did not possess the righteousness necessary to enter the kingdom. The righteous (as they defined themselves) were looking forward to entering the Kingdom of God at the resurrection. So the thought of a sinner possessing the necessary righteousness for entry into the kingdom was ludicrous in the theology of the day.

Spiritual salvation of the soul was not part of the picture. Salvation was possessing the righteousness necessary to enter Messiah's Kingdom. That righteousness was gained by living according to the Law. Forgiveness of sins was given by God to those who had made themselves righteous through obedience to the law. The more exacting the obedience, the greater the righteousness, the greater the assurance of entry into the kingdom. It was a thoroughly works-based soteriology.

(In contrast, biblical soteriology, in both the Old Testament and the New Testament is always saved by God's grace through the believer's faith in God and God's testimony of the way of salvation, as historically revealed in the progressive revelation of truth.)

In terms of the parable, Simon the Pharisee would see himself as the debtor with little to be forgiven, and someone with less righteousness with much to be forgiven. That the woman could be the second debtor in the parable did not cross his mind, because she had no righteousness.

The point of the parable, then, is not that the sinner with the most forgiven will love more than the sinner with little forgiven, although that perception is true. People tend to think of sin in terms of its consequences in their culture, not in relation to the judicial penalty. The penalty of any sin is spiritual death. Whether it is the theft of a pencil from the office, or the theft of a life through kidnapping or murder, the penalty is the same: spiritual death. We tend to think of murder as requiring more forgiveness than theft, because the first has greater consequences than the latter (and God punishes the unsaved according to the consequences of their works, Revelation 20:12, which is why the books of works are opened). But in terms of forgiveness, each sinner has the same "amount" of forgiveness: every sin is forgiven, the death penalty thereby remitted.

The Lord adapts his lesson to the understanding of his listeners. Simon the Pharisee could not imagine the woman was susceptible to forgiveness. The comparison of the two debtors is used to impress on Simon the greatness and grace of forgiveness, because he also thinks in terms of consequences—her sins are too great to be forgiven. But she was forgiven, and that is the point of the parable: the fact of forgiveness when there is no merit for forgiveness. The secondary lesson is the authority of Jesus to forgive sins.

The Parable of the Good Samaritan

The parable is found at Luke 10:30–37, the context of this parable is Luke 10:25–29. The purpose of this parable was to answer the question posed at Luke 10:29, "And who is my neighbor." This question was asked because a certain man, an expert in the Mosaic Law (in modern terms, a PhD in theology), had asked what he might do to inherit eternal life. The man was thinking how he might obey the Law to ensure his place in the coming kingdom. Undoubtedly he already thought he was righteous. He was asking someone he recognized as a fellow teacher of the Law to validate his righteousness.

Jesus asked the man to answer his own question. And so he did, quoting Deuteronomy 6:5 (HCSB, as it appears in Luke), "Love the Lord your God with all your heart, with all your soul, with all your strength, and with all your mind," and Leviticus 19:18 (HCSB, as it appears in Luke), "and your neighbor as yourself." Jesus agreed: "Do this and you will live.

But the problem with the righteousness according to the Law—righteousness gained by good works—is you can never be certain you have done enough good works to earn the righteousness that inherits eternal life. So the man, "wanting to justify himself," asked, "And who is my neighbor."

The parable envisions up a likely circumstance. The setting is the road that, literally, went down in elevation from Jerusalem on the mountain to Jericho in the valley. The straight line distance is about sixteen miles, but the road winds and turns so the walking distance is about eighteen miles. The traveler begins in Jerusalem at 1200' above MSL (mean sea level) and ends at Jericho at -2000' below MSL.

The road was heavily travelled, and so it was also infested with thieves. Few walked the road alone, but in small groups and caravans for security in numbers. However, for the purpose of the lesson the parable is teaching, all the characters in the story are walking the road alone.

A man is walking alone on the road from Jerusalem to Jericho, is attacked, beaten half dead, robbed, and left to die. Three men also walking the road come to where he is laying. Two are men who believe their place in the kingdom is assured by their righteousness—and others believe the same about them, including the teacher of the Law whom Jesus is answering with this parable. Jesus chose the most respected people in society, a priest, and a Levite.

But their righteousness is deficit. These two men of the Law pass by the injured man. Undoubtedly many of those listening felt this was the correct action. Stopping to help the injured man might expose the person to an attack by the thieves; the wisest course is to pass by. Or those passing by might properly assume the man at the side of the road is a beggar whose companions beat, robbed, and left, and therefore not worthy of help from a righteous man. Giving a little money to a beggar was one thing, the fulfillment of a minor part of the law. No one would stop to physically render aid to a beggar on the streets of Jerusalem. So why stop here on the road?

The fulcrum on which the parable turns and makes its point is the question, "And who is my neighbor." In one sense, every Israelite was the neighbor of every other Israelite, as they were all descendants of one man. But in the Greco-Roman culture of the times, a neighbor was someone who was a member of one's family. Family took care of family and no one else. The Jews were out of step with the larger Greco-Roman culture in that they engaged in what we would think of as charitable giving for widows, orphans, and to a lesser degree, beggars.

So there was no specific Law requiring the priest and Levite to help the injured man, and there was no cultural reason to help him. Everyone listening would have thought the priest and Levite, being important and righteous men, had acted prudently and righteously.

The third person in this drama is a Samaritan. No Jew considered a Samaritan to be a brother or a neighbor. Their ancient history, conquered by the Assyrians and intermarriage with them, had religiously defiled them, made them more gentile than Jew, and even the average Jew avoided contact. The most righteous Jews would not even travel through Samaria, but either take the coastal road, or more likely the road running between Jericho to Scythopolis—not on the west side of the Jordan River, but on the east side of the Jordan, through Perea. The crowd probably let out a collective gasp when Jesus said the Samaritan had compassion. Who would suspect a Samaritan had the capacity for compassion? But he did, and he helped the man, going above and beyond the expectations of the culture.

Jesus asked the teacher of the Law, "Which of these three seems to you to have been a neighbor?" The man could not bring himself to say the word, "Samaritan," saying instead "The one having shown compassion toward him." Then comes the one point the parable is making: "You go and do the same." You, Mr. righteous Teacher of the Law, you go and be like the Samaritan if you would inherit eternal life. The Scripture does not tell us the man's reaction, but I believe he was disappointed and disgusted, but also troubled in his self-righteousness, because the truth was obvious: the Law viewed anyone in need as a neighbor.

And that is the great truth taught in this parable, the truth that transcends its cultural setting and declares the principle, what does it mean to love.

> Love is a choice of the will to actively seek the best good for another person, without expectation of recompense, reciprocity, or recognition for one's self, and without consideration of merit or demerit in the one so loved. [Quiggle, *Dictionary.*]

A "neighbor" is someone in need toward whom you have the ability and opportunity to help—toward whom you can express love. No one can help everyone at all times, but love recognizes when ability and opportunity are able to take action to help.

How God Answers Prayer

God answers prayer in many ways for five reasons.

No. You are asking amiss that you may spend it on your pleasures (James 4:3). I will never give you these things. Stop asking.

No. You are asking for something you may have, but what you are asking for is not right for you, at least not now. I love you too much to give you what you are requesting.

Yes, if you insist. I want you to understand this thing you want so desperately is not the best for you, so you become wise and stop wanting to have it.

Yes. Here is what you have requested. Use it wisely.

Yes, and here is more for you to use wisely.

Here is what we must learn about prayer. Ask in faith for the things God has promised. Receive by faith whatever God gives. Receive a "Yes" or "No" with equal praise and thankfulness.

Hebrews 10:19, "Therefore, brothers, having confidence for entering the holy places by the blood of Jesus,"

Hebrews 10:19 says the Christian has confidence to enter into the "holy places," through the propitiation of God made by Jesus Christ on the cross (the meaning of, "the blood of Jesus.")

The word I have translated "holy places" in 10:19 is *hágios*. Many versions do not translate *hágios* but rather interpret it for the reader as "holiest, most holy place, sanctuary, or heavenly sanctuary."

But in 10:19 *hágios* is used as an adjective, not a noun, so substituting those interpretations for the proper translation is not appropriate. The interpretation robs the believer of a precious truth (which I will explain below). The adjective refers to things or places that are holy. Because the believer is entering, the best interpretation is "holy places" (which the YLT, ASV, NASB, and ESV recognize).

The Writer is not referring to an earthly or a heavenly temple in 10:19–22. There is no physical temple the believer must enter to be in the presence of God, and there is no literal temple or sanctuary in heaven. A temple/sanctuary in heaven is used in Hebrews as a metaphor for the immediate presence of God, e.g., 9:24.

What, then, does the Writer mean when he says the believer is able with confidence to enter into the holy places? In the same way the burning bush was a holy place because God manifested himself, and the inner sanctuary of the temple was a holy place because God manifested himself, even so whatever time and place in the world the believer in this mortal life enters into the presence of God through prayer or devotion or service for the sake of Christ, that is a "holy place," because God is manifesting himself in the believer's life.

The precious truth obscured by interpreting *hágios* for the reader is the believer is always at all times and in all places in this mortal life able to enter into the presence of God, because prayer or devotion or service for the sake of Christ is the presence of God in this mortal life.

(In a very real and genuine sense the believer him or herself is a holy place, because God is indwelling the believer's soul. Hence the constant Scripture exhortations to be holy, live righteously, pray upon every appropriate occasion, and do all things to the glory of God.)

This, of course, is part of the Hebrews Writer's theme of "better than." The New Testament believer's relationship with God in Christ is better than the Old Testament believer's relationship with God through the Law and the Temple. (And we may add better than any relationship where a moral code, or a building, or a priest, or laws and regulations, or wine and wafers, or a cross, amulet, pendant, or anything else, acts as a mediator between a believer and God.)

"For you have need of perseverance, so that, having done the will of God, you may receive the promise."

The miss-characterization of Hebrews 11 as, "Heroes of the Faith," or, "The Hall of Faith," has cheated generations of Christians out understanding, and applying, the genuine purpose of the chapter. Those people are not pictures in a historical museum for us to walk through and admire each in turn, then having left, leave them behind.

When we read the Old Testament, those people we read about in the Old Testament are not random selections out of Israel's history. Each was selected, by the Holy Spirit through the writer, to communicate something, good or bad, about a relationship with God and life with, or without, faith. As Paul says, Romans 15:4, the things written before were written for our learning. We learn how to live a godly life, or how not to live, by walking a moment in their shoes.

So also the Old Testament people in Hebrews 11 were selected for a purpose. The chapter was written as an illustration 10:36, "you have need of perseverance . . . so that . . . you may receive the promise." Each person illustrates some aspect of perseverance in living for God. Some died because of their perseverance and some lived in their perseverance.

And here is the key, the reason, chapter 11 was written: although none literally received the promise, each by faith received the promise; you, Christian, go and live likewise. You, Christian, have the promise of a returning Lord. Most of you will not literally receive the promise during your lifetime; but all of you are able to receive the promise by faith.

For example, Abraham received the promise, 6:15, but Abraham did not receive the promise, 11:39. Literally Abraham, and all who are in Hebrews 11, is still waiting for the promise to be fulfilled. But by faith he and all the rest did receive the promise.

That is why chapter 11:1 defines faith in a certain way. "Now faith is the title deed of the things of which we are assured, the objective evidence of the things not yet seen."

The word I translated "title deed" is *hupóstasis*, the real presence. Jesus, Hebrews 1:3, is the *hupóstasis*, the visible real presence/ essence/substance of God in the universe: to see Jesus was and is to see God. In the context of 3:14; 11:1 *hupóstasis* could be translated "title deed." A title deed describes real property, such as land, a home, or a car. When one legitimately possesses the title deed, then he holds physical proof of possession of the property. Therefore, in 3:14; 11:1 *hupóstasis* refers to that certain reality in which one's faith is resting.

The word I translated "assured" is *elpízō*, which means to expect with desire. The word I translated "objective evidence" is *élegchos*, which may mean subjective or objective evidence. But as it is in parallel with *hupóstasis*, then *élegchos* must mean objective evidence.

The origin and source of the kind of faith the Hebrews Writer is speaking of at 11:1 is God alone. A title deed, objective kind of faith originates in God: he makes the soul alive and gives conviction. The spiritual realities of the promises of God cannot in or of themselves be sensually or rationally perceived within the limitations of our material existence. But through objective faith these spiritual realities can be perceived as though literally present.

An objective faith is itself the reality of the spiritual presence of the things hoped for and not seen. Faith does not *make* these things real to the believer, for that would be persuasion, a subjective reality. Faith itself *is* the objective reality of the things hoped for and not seen. Faith in the soul is the *hupóstasis*, the objective presence/essence/substance, of the spiritual realities the believer is certain to receive: the title deed. The promises will be received through persevering in life by means of that kind of faith (10:36). Just as Jesus Christ is the real presence of the Spirit-being God, a person's faith is the real presence of spiritual realities hoped for and not seen.

When one has faith in the certainty of the promises, one has certainty he will receive the promises, because that kind of faith—the conviction given only by God—is itself the real presence of the promises. Faith itself is the continuing objective presence of the reality of the promises. That quality of faith creates perseverance.

And that is the true meaning of Hebrews 11. They persevered in the kind of faith that inherits the promises, because they knew with absolute, Holy Spirit given conviction, that God always keeps his promises. This is not a matter of human perception, nor is it a matter of feeling persuaded. I objectively know God keeps his promises, because the spiritual reality of the matter has been revealed to me by God.

Yes, a personal rational comprehension of Scripture is essential to perseverance, because God has created us to be rational beings whose choices are supported by reason. There is a difference, however, between being certain because of experience, and having experience validated by the certainty of faith. The certainty of faith validates our experiences as genuine or false. The certainty of faith causes us to make the choice to persevere and informs us when the practice of our faith, perseverance, is based upon spiritual reality.

Thus, in 11:1, in response to 10:36, the Writer is not talking about the choice to persevere, he is addressing the basis for perseverance. Faith itself is the objective presence of spiritual reality. Faith itself is the objective demonstration of the spiritual reality of the things not seen. Because the believer has that presence of a God-given objective kind of faith, he/she perseveres.

"For you have need of perseverance, which is obtained through the reality of the objective faith given by God, so that, having done the will of God, you may receive the promise."

Hermeneutics: From the Warning to the Flood

I want to do a little exercise in interpretation, literacy, and paying attention. The subject is, "How much time passed between God's warning to Noah about the flood and the occurrence of the flood?" Many will say 120 years, based on Genesis 6:3. But, that is not what Genesis 6:3 says, and that is not what the facts teach.

Genesis 6:3 is God setting a limit on human lifespan. "My Spirit shall not strive with man forever . . . yet his days shall be 120 years." And so it was, as a little biblical and secular research will show, human lifespan decreased after the flood. Since about the time of Jacob no one has lived past 120 years (and if I have missed someone, a longer lifespan is notable because so exceptional). God had given each human being hundreds of years of physical life prior to the flood, and the result was, 6:5, "the wickedness of human beings was great in the earth." God in mercy limited human lifespan and thereby human wickedness.

So, back to the question, how long between the announcement of the flood and the occurrence of the flood? The Scripture tells us—if we pay attention. In Genesis 5:32 (NKJV), "Noah was 500 years old, and Noah beget Shem, Ham, and Japeth." And again, Genesis 6:9–10 (NKJV), "This is the genealogy of Noah. Noah was a just man, perfect in his generations. Noah walked with God. And Noah begot three sons: Shem, Ham, and Japheth." Then God tells Noah he will destroy humankind, Genesis 6:13. But the warning came before the three boys were born.

Two more pieces of evidence. The flood came in the 600th year of Noah's life, Genesis 7:11. The flood waters were upon the earth 371 days (one year, six days), Genesis 7:11 with 8:13–14.

Last piece of evidence: Genesis 11:10 says Shem, the first listed and therefore probably the oldest of Noah's three sons, was 100 years old when he fathered Arphaxad, two years after the flood, which had lasted a year.

Shem, the oldest, was ninety-seven when the flood came. Ham was probably ninety-five and Japeth ninety-three (approximate ages) when the flood came.

Noah apparently thought the times before God gave his warning of judgment to come were so bad he did not want to bring children into the world. God's warning of judgment gave him hope, and he fathered three sons, who married three women, before the flood.

Summing up, Noah was warned during or just after the 500th year of his life. He then fathered three sons who, unless they were triplets, were born about ninety-seven, ninety-five, and ninety-three years before the flood, respectively. The flood came in the 600th year of Noah's life. Shem was 100 when he fathered Arphaxad, two years after the flood, which had lasted a year, so he was ninety-seven when the flood came. So the maximum amount of time between the warning and the flood was 100 years, perhaps a year or two less.

Interpretation requires gathering and weighing all the available facts, not just one verse. If you want to know and understand the Bible, this is the kind of hard work you have to do, comparing Scripture with Scripture.

The Origin and Source of Saving Faith

When I say the unsaved human being cannot initiate saving faith, and that the origin and source of saving faith is God, I believe I am repeating what God has said. Ephesians 2:8–9, "For by grace you are having been saved, through faith, and that not of yourselves. Of God the gift, not of works so that no one should boast." (My translation.)

But to say faith is the result of God's gift is just making a label. Let's look at the ingredients.

The first ingredient is grace, which in Ephesians 2:8 is prevenient grace. All soteriological views that recognize God's grace as essential to salvation recognize God gives grace in advance of saving faith. This is known as prevenient grace.

There are several views of when God gives prevenient grace, and the effectiveness of prevenient grace. But, these may be summarized into two.

> One, God universally gives every sinful human being the grace necessary to overcome their sin and personally, without further action by God, be able to choose to initiate saving faith, or choose not to initiate saving faith.
>
> Or, Two, God brings into the life of specific individuals, at a specific moment in time, the grace necessary to change the spiritual boundary of their human nature, so the person is able to receive and act on the saving faith given by God.

The first view, with a refinement here and there (for the statement is a summary) is the Arminian view. The second conforms to the Calvinistic—or as I would say—to the biblical view.

The next ingredient is unsaved human nature. Those holding to the Arminian view of prevenient grace, view sin as less than debilitating because of the universal prevenient grace given to every sinner. Those holding to the biblical (oops, Calvinistic) view of prevenient grace, view sin as completely debilitating, which means in fine, sin affects every aspect of human nature.

Sin, by the way, is a principle of rebellion against God in human nature. Sin is said to dominate the will, not as some invincible overlord, but as an innate part of human nature constructively working with all the other attributes of human nature to persuasively incline the will to choose an act of sinning. The sinner freely chooses sinning because his/her will is of itself always inclined to choose sinning, and as being rebellious and disobedient toward God never desires to change its inclination to choose sinning to rebel against God, disobey his commandments, and seek a path in life apart from God.

Every person conceived into the world is under the dominion of sin (Genesis 5:3; Romans 5:12), which is why God must give his prevenient grace for salvation to take place. Both Arminian and Calvinistic soteriology agree without prevenient grace, no salvation.

Now, we can see the difference. The Arminian soteriology says every sinful human being has been given the capability to initiate saving faith, or not, as he or she may choose—human beings are the origin and source of saving faith. The Calvinistic soteriology says the total debilitating effect of sin prevents the sinful human being from initiating saving faith until God gives, specifically to those whom he has chosen, his gift of prevenient grace and faith, which always results in salvation—God is the origin and source of saving faith.

But, we have two other ingredients to consider: free will and sinful human nature. Free will is one of the most misunderstood attributes of human nature. The word "free" conjures notions of license without limits or responsibility. Nothing could be further from the biblical truth.

Human nature has boundaries, physical, moral, spiritual. Those boundaries are like a fence. You can do whatever you want inside the fence. You can vigorously flap your arms, but you cannot fly by flapping your arms: physical boundaries. You can lie or tell the truth, moral boundaries. The spiritual boundary is, you cannot be saved without God's prevenient grace, because you are always in rebellion against God without his prevenient grace.

The Arminian view says God changes the spiritual boundary of the human nature of every sinner coming into the world by giving every sinner prevenient grace (three methods have been proposed: hearing the gospel; God indiscriminately drawing all; Christ's atoning work on the cross) so any sinner is able to act so as to save him or herself by initiating saving faith, or not, as each chooses.

The Calvinistic view—and again I would argue it is the biblical view—says God changes the spiritual boundary of the human nature of one person at a time, as he gives that person according to his sovereign purpose his gift of grace-faith-salvation. God changes the spiritual boundary of a particular sinner's human nature, by his gift of prevenient grace (Ephesians 2:8), not to give the sinner the ability to save him or herself, but so the sinner is able to receive and use the gift of faith God's gift has also given, Ephesians 2:8.

And those are the ingredients behind the label. The spiritual boundary of unsaved human nature is limited by sin to constant rebellion against God. God gives prevenient grace to change that boundary so salvation may (Arminian) or will (Calvinistic) take place.

Depending on your soteriology, either every sinner may or may not use God's prevenient grace to initiate saving faith and save him or herself. Or God's act of giving prevenient grace is given to specific sinners so as to change the spiritual boundary of their unsaved human nature to receive and use God's gift of faith.

So when I say God is the origin and source of saving faith, all that I have said above describes the ingredients behind that label.

The Boundaries of Free Will

Human free will is not the source and origin of saving faith. But in all other aspects of life, free will is part of God's design of human nature—the moral authority to make choices.

The "will" may be defined (as W.G.T. Shedd, *Dogmatic Theology*, has defined it) as "that voluntary power of human nature which determines the continuous movement of the soul toward its ultimate reason for living, according to those principles of life [attributes] which together make up human nature."

More simply, the will is the decision-making faculty of the soul, the synergistic effect of all the attributes in human nature working together to determine the person's path in life.

Free will and volition are synonyms. But like all synonyms the two are not quite the same. "Volition" is individual acts of the will. So the "will" chooses the general direction of life, whereas "volitions" are the individual choices in life that conform to that general direction. An illustration: If I make a journey from Texas to Las Vegas, NV, as I have done many times, the I-40 highway is the will, and a side trip to visit Meteor Crater along the way is a volition. The side trip has not changed the general direction, it is a response to a choice made within the boundaries of the general direction.

Whether viewed as the "will" or as "volition," the "will" is the decision making faculty of the soul, whether as to the general course of life, or the individual decisions of living. I freely choose to travel to Las Vegas, as influenced by external and internal motivations, and I freely choose to visit Meteor Crater, as influenced by external and internal motivations.

I am, therefore, as the one making the choices, responsible, and accountable, and liable for my choices and the consequences arising from my choices. There is no just reward or just punishment without liability for one's choices. There is no accountability without responsibility, there is no liability without accountability—each depends on the moral ability to freely make choices.

Some people view free will as unencumbered by any external influences, but only God has that kind of free will. All sentient beings exercise free will: choices made within the boundaries of their physical, moral, and spiritual nature. Even God makes choices in agreement with his nature.

A formal definition: Free will is the moral authority God designed into his sentient creatures to make choices within the physical, moral, and spiritual boundaries of their nature, as further influenced by internal and external motivations and consequences.

Without the moral authority to make choices, God cannot justly hold his sentient creatures (human, angel) accountable for their wrong choices (acts of sinning), or reward them for their right choices (acts of righteousness).

What does it mean free will acts within the physical, moral, and spiritual boundaries of human nature? Well, can you decide to flap your arms and fly to the mini-market to get a candy bar? No, there is a physical boundary: you can decide to flap your arms, and you can decide to buy a candy bar, but you cannot decide to fly by flapping your arms. Do you tell the truth; do you lie? The moral boundary of human nature is flexible enough to allow both. But the moral boundary in sinners weighs telling the truth or telling a lie on the scales of self-interest, and therein lies the moral boundary. The sin attribute has reprioritized the attributes of human nature to serve self, not God, and therein lies the moral and spiritual boundaries of the unsaved sinner.

Can a sinner initiate saving faith without God's grace? No, the sin attribute continuously disposes the sinner to rebel against God and reject his salvation, and that is the spiritual boundary. One cannot choose to be saved without God giving his gift of grace-faith-salvation. All biblically based theologies—Arminian, Reformed, Dispensational—believe an individual's salvation begins with God's grace, Ephesians 2:8. (How that grace is received and used is the issue between Arminian and Reformed/Dispensational soteriology.)

The unsaved sinner chooses to commit acts of sinning. Some will say, "Oh, the sinner is dead." Yes, but he/she is spiritually dead not physically dead, and thereby morally and spiritually disposed to rebel against God and reject God's salvation. Spiritually dead means separated from communion with God, separated from that eternal life that comes from God, and lacking understanding of the spiritual things of God. But the sinner is very much spiritually active: he/she actively makes the spiritual choice to rebel against God and reject God's salvation. Free will cannot make a person spiritually alive, because of the boundary formed by sin's dominion in unsaved human nature.

In the matter of salvation, God works with the free will he designed into humankind. God's gift of grace-faith-salvation (Ephesians 2:8) changes the spiritual boundary in human nature—the boundary of sin's dominion—by enlivening the soul's faculty of spiritual perception to comprehend the issues of sin, the Savior, and salvation. In terms the Reformers and Puritans used, God makes the sinner willing to exercise saving faith. God's grace is not irresistible because it overcomes all resistance, God's grace is irresistible because it effects a change in the spiritual boundary of human nature, resulting in the complete cooperation of the sinner receiving God's grace.

So we see God alone is the origin and source of saving faith. But salvation requires the sinner who has received God's gift to exercise saving faith, that is clear from the repeated exhortations to believe and be saved, an act of choice. These apparently contradictory truths are complementary: they combine to produce salvation.

Now, someone out there will say, "No, if God's grace and man's choice are complementary, that is synergism not monergism, but salvation is monergistic—all of God." Let's take a calming breath and re-read the premise: God alone is the origin and source of saving faith: monergism. The exercise of saving faith is the sinner's response to God's gift of grace-faith-salvation.

Charles Spurgeon addressed faith both as man's duty to believe and as the gift of God, in his sermon "Faith and Regeneration" (*Metropolitan Tabernacle*, # 979, March 5th, 1871), In summarizing his argument he said:

> Brethren be willing to see both sides of the shield of truth. Rise above the babyhood which cannot believe two doctrines until it sees the connecting link. Have you not two eyes, man? Must you needs put one of them out in order to see clearly? Is it impossible to you to use a spiritual stereoscope, and look at two views of truth until they melt into one, and that one becomes more real and actual because it is made up of two? Many men refuse to see more than one side of a doctrine, and persistently fight against anything which is not on its very surface consistent with their own idea. In the present case I do not find it difficult to believe faith to be at the same time the duty of man and the gift of God; and if others cannot accept the two truths, I am not responsible for their rejection of them; my duty is performed when I have honestly borne witness to them.

Salvation requires God's gift and the sinner's exercise of saving faith. What is the exercise of saving faith? It is the personal appropriation of truth to satisfy the spiritual need for salvation, a spiritual need felt by the sinner because God's gift of grace has changed the spiritual boundary.

A sinner is not enabled to believe, he or she is convicted

through the work of God the Holy Spirit of the truth of personal sin, the judicial guilt and punishment of sin, the need for salvation by faith not works, and the all-sufficiency of the propitiation made by Jesus Christ the Savior required to save his or her soul. On the basis of that conviction, the sinner personally appropriates these truths to satisfy his or her spiritual need for salvation. That personal appropriation of truth to satisfy the spiritual need for salvation is the exercise of saving faith. [Quiggle, *Dictionary.*]

Let me summarize the essential points of the discussion.

Free will is the moral authority to make choices, a moral authority God designed into human nature, exercised in both saved and unsaved according to the physical, moral, and spiritual boundaries of their human nature.

If the sinner is not the one making the choice to commit an act of sinning, who made that choice? If the sinner is not the one making the choice to commit an act of sinning, then he or she cannot justly be held accountable, responsible, or liable to a just punishment for the sin.

Saving faith is: the result of God giving his gift; the choice to exercise saving faith is the duty of the sinner; the ability to make that choice and exercise saving faith is the result of God's gift of grace-faith-salvation changing the spiritual boundary in the sinner's human nature.

For by grace are you saved, it is the gift of God. Believe on the Lord Jesus Christ and you will be saved.

God's Testimony As To Salvation

An extract from my work in progress, "Thirty-six Essentials of the Christian Faith, The Doctrines Briefly Explained."

God did not reveal everything at one time, but over time God's revelation was completed. As God said through Isaiah 28:10 (ESV), "For it is precept upon precept, precept upon precept, line upon line, line upon line, here a little, there a little." That is how God revealed himself over time.

God revealing himself over time is known as the "doctrine of progressive revelation." Each succeeding age of humankind knew a little more of God's purpose, his plans to fulfill his purpose, and his processes to accomplish those plans.

Today, with God's completed revelation, the Bible, in hand, we are able to put together all that God has revealed of his purpose, plans and processes. In relation to salvation, the completed revelation tells us a sinner was, is, and always will be saved by God's grace through the sinner's faith in God, through God's historically current testimony as given in the progressive revelation of truth.

Perhaps more simply, looking at the span of time from Adam to the completed revelation (the Bible we have had since apostolic times), before the revelation was completed a person could not know what God had not yet revealed, but as the revelation progressed a person was responsible to act on what God had revealed.

Each age prior to this New Testament age responded to God's current historical testimony as to the way of salvation, known as the content of faith. Enoch's content of faith was to live the manner of life prescribed by God: he believed and walked with God. The content of Noah's faith was judgment is coming, get into the ark to be saved. The content of Abraham's faith was the promise of the land to him and his descendants through an heir from his own body.

The content of faith under the Mosaic Law was faith in God and his testimony that repentance of sin with confession of sin and a proper sacrifice for sin would result in forgiveness of sin. Simply bringing a sacrifice did not save; one must have faith, prompted and accepted by God's grace, in order to be saved.

It was impossible (that is, not as Reformed soteriology teaches) the Old Testament peoples could have as the object of their faith the incarnate, crucified Son, the Lamb of God, because the revelation was in progress in the Old Testament. For example, the revelation Jesus Christ is the Lamb of God was given by John Baptist (John 1:29), so not known prior to that revelation.

In this New Testament age the revelation is completed. Salvation occurs when a sinner repents of his or her sins and believes on Christ as their Savior, Acts 2:38; 3:19–20; 11:18; Romans 3:22–26; 10:9–10, 13; Galatians 3:22; 1 Peter 1:21; 1 John 3:23.

Lordship Salvation Considered

A repeat from *Biblical Essays III*, with additional information from Ryrie's review of the doctrine.

If one reads MacArthur's book, *The Gospel According to Jesus* (Zondervan, 1988), one sees the intent is to help God create a pure church in the world, that is, one composed only of believers. To do that, MacArthur argues a commitment to obedience to Christ as Master is a precondition to salvation. I am putting this in my own words, because MacArthur was very careful not to state this precondition so baldly. For example,

> A person must trust Jesus Christ as his Savior from sin and must also commit himself to Christ as Lord [by which MacArthur means Master, not God] of his life, submitting to his sovereign authority. (*The Gospel*, chapter 1, under the heading, "Wrongly Dividing the Word," 3rd paragraph, last sentence.)

> There are many today who hear the truth of Christ and immediately respond like the son who said he would obey but did not. Their positive response to Jesus will not save them." (*The Gospel*, last paragraph, chapter 15.)

> The subject [of an evangelism training film] instructed youth workers *not* to tell unsaved young people they must obey Christ, given Him their hearts, surrender their lives, repent of their sins, submit to his Lordship, or follow him." (*The Gospel*, chapter 16, 3rd paragraph, emphasis MacArthur.)

> Those who want to eliminate the lordship of Jesus from the gospel message insinuate that it is heresy equal to Galatian legalism to demand that sinners forsake their sins, commit themselves to Christ, obey his commands, and surrender to him." (*The Gospel*, Appendix 2, first sentence. MacArthur is referencing Ryrie, *Balancing the Christian Life*, p. 170.)

MacArthur's requirement for a commitment to obedience by the sinner as a precondition for salvation is often confused as a works-based salvation; it isn't. But it is another gospel.

Here is the reasoned conclusion of a top-notch theologian, Charles C. Ryrie, after reading MacArthur's book. "Lordship salvation: The teaching that to be saved a person must not only trust Jesus as Savior but also as the Lord of his life, submitting (or at least being willing to submit) his life to His sovereign authority." [Ryrie, "So Great Salvation," 156.]

Neither MacArthur nor any in his camp or under his influence have denied that Ryrie's definition accurately describes MacArthur's doctrine of salvation. They cannot, for that is his doctrine.

MacArthur is not a good expositor; a reading of any of his NT commentaries reveals old interpretations long ago corrected, and exegesis that fails to consider all the available context; a sweet tasting morsel for immature Christians. His failure in Lordship salvation is twofold. One, he fails to consider the influence of the sin attribute in unsaved human nature. The sinner is incapable of making a commitment to obedience prior to salvation. Only the regenerated, born-again nature is capable of such a commitment. The gift of God (Ephesians 2:8) enlivens spiritual perception and initiates saving faith. Regeneration follows.

Two, he fails to consider the process of spiritual maturity. The newly-saved believer grows in grace, knowledge, and understanding—is directed by the Scripture to grow. The Holy Spirit is too wise to require all sinning stop at the moment of salvation and complete obedience commence. But in MacArthur's world, the lack of complete obedience is a sign the person is unsaved. One would think the fact Scripture acknowledges that believer's do fail to obey, and why they fail to obey (e.g., 1 John 1:8–10) would have had some impact on MacArthur's thesis. Sadly, no. First John 1:8, 10 are not mentioned or considered in MacArthur's book, and 1 John 1:9 mentioned only in the context of "a progressive, life-long process of repentance" (*The Gospel*, chapter 15, "What is Repentance," last paragraph). Sadly, that insight does not apply to those MacArthur thinks must be unsaved. For MacArthur, salvation requires "the intent to serve to [sic] God." (*The Gospel*, chapter 15, "What is Repentance," 2nd paragraph), as part of salvation.

MacArthur wants what Christ said was not going to happen: a visible church composed only of believers. Christ makes clear, in a number of parables (e.g., Wheat and Darnell; Mustard Seed, Leaven), that the New Testament church is a mixed multitude of saved who are immature, maturing, and mature in the faith; unsaved responding to the gospel; and the unsaved. The apostles make clear—through many exhortations to live a righteous life; to forsake sinning, to repent and confess acts of sinning—that the New Testament church as it is in the world is a mixed multitude.

MacArthur may loudly proclaim "salvation by grace through faith," but to the exercise of simple volitional saving faith he adds a commitment to obedience to Christ as Master. That is what makes MacArthur's "Lordship Salvation" another gospel.

I Love Responding to Silly Memes

The Latest: a drawing of Noah's Ark, caption, "The Ark was designed to hold as many as were going to be saved from God's wrath—no more."

No, Scripture states Noah was a "preacher of righteousness" to his generation. Scripture never states a limit on who could come into the ark.

The Genuine doctrine: The ark was designed to hold as many as would come, unlimited atonement; it held only those whom God invited, Genesis 7:1, limited redemption.

An explanation. First, let us agree we have taken a literal thing and by interpretive alchemy transposed it into an illustration of two doctrines: the sufficiency of Christ's propitiation (atonement) toward God; the efficiency of Christ's propitiation in redemption of sinners.

An illustration is not designed or intended to teach doctrine, but to reveal some aspect of doctrine. An illustration is like an arrow: aimed at one point. In this case, we have aimed one arrow at two points, so we have already complicated our illustration.

Regardless, we can say in this illustration that the ark was large enough to hold all who might choose to enter. If we say otherwise, then we are saying God sent Noah as a preacher of righteousness to tell a lie. For what would Noah have preached but the message he himself had been given: judgment is coming, get into the ark to be delivered from judgment. As far as Noah or anyone else, including you and me, knew/knows, the ark was designed by God to be large enough to hold more than the eight people it eventually did deliver from judgment.

Second, we may also say God did not take any action to prevent any from entering. There is never any indication in the Bible that God's choice of whom to deliver from judgment excludes those not chosen. (A simple word study of the appropriate words will affirm that conclusion.) The deliverance of the eight was made certain by God's choice. No one else was prevented from entering prior to that moment when God sealed the eight into the ark. Everyone, anyone, who heard the invitation from Noah could have positively responded with the expectation of deliverance, and found room in the ark. Nothing in Scripture states or implies otherwise.

Therefore, in this illustration, the first target at which our illustrative arrow is aimed is the capacity of the ark. Nothing we know from Scripture indicates the capacity of the ark was limited to eight human beings, but rather the message preached indicated the capacity to deliver any who might choose to enter.

Let us consider this from the point of view of the seven people who went with Noah into the ark. The only person who heard God speak was Noah. Everyone else who got into the ark, Noah's wife, their three children (we only know of three), and their three wives, got into the ark because they heard Noah's testimony. The made a choice, the same choice available to everyone else hearing Noah's message.

The second target of our illustrative arrow is the fact of deliverance from judgment. Any might have responded, but only those whom God invited did respond. The deliverance was limited to eight.

Because we are attempting to use the ark illustrate the sufficiency of Christ's propitiation, then the Scripture presentation of the seemingly unlimited capacity of the ark to deliver as many as might believe illustrates the sufficiency of Christ's propitiation. We can say with the Synod of Dort that Christ's propitiation was sufficient for all—all the sins of the whole world, 1 John 2:2. (Second Head of Doctrine, Article 3.)

And, because we are attempting to use the ark illustrate the redemption of sinners, then the Scripture presentation that none but those whom God invited entered the ark indicates the efficiency of Christ's propitiation. We can say with the Synod of Dort Christ's propitiation was efficient only for the elect. (Second Head of Doctrine, Article 8.)

In the illustration: the ark's capacity was not limited to eight people: unlimited propitiation (atonement); and the ark became the deliverance for eight people chosen by God: limited redemption.

God Cares About Sin

Recently I was asked, "Did God not care about sin prior to giving the Ten Commandments? Moses murdered someone but God did not punish, or even say anything."

God did care about sin prior to giving the Ten Commandments. Adam and the Woman disobeyed God, and as a result of their sin their relationship with God was changed, and they were expelled from Paradise, Genesis 3:16–24, which had many consequences. Cain murdered Able, and God's justice was to exile him from his family home to wander the earth, Genesis 4:9–14. (But God set a mark on him so none would exact personal vengeance.)

Yet it is also true we do not always see God taking immediate action against an act of sinning. Lamech is an example, he murdered, Genesis 4:23, but we do not see any immediate consequences. However, just because we are not told God disapproved, or are not told God took action, that does not mean God approved, and it does not mean God did not take action. Just because the Bible reports somebody thought it, said it, did it, or believed it doesn't mean God approved it. Just because the Bible reports the facts does not mean God accepted the wrong.

God often acts in mercy, which has two aspects: delaying deserved justice; or relieving distress. When we look to Genesis 6:5, the wickedness of humankind, we see God had mercy for a long time toward sins. The whole earth, in a matter of a few thousand years, had become evil, with just a few exceptions. Ultimately God acted in justice and destroyed humankind from the earth through the worldwide flood, saving only eight people. God cared about sin.

God made a law against murder for the people after the flood, which includes you and me. Genesis 9:6, "Whoever sheds man's blood, by man shall his blood be shed." Most Bible students mark this moment as the beginning of human government on the earth (after the flood). The word "blood" is often used in the Bible as a euphemism for death. In this case, a wrongful death, "shed man's blood," which is to say, premeditated murder.

There are several biblical principles that respond to this question. The first is, God's moral values are based in God's immutable (unchanging) holy and righteous character. God is always holy and righteous. God's moral values are who he is, his essence. Whether we see those moral values in action, or not, they are always present and always active, and they never change.

One of God's moral values is, premeditated murder is wrong, because human beings were made in God's image, giving all human beings value. God requires justice against the murderer, Genesis 9:6, "because in God's image God made humankind."

Other moral values that relate to this question are God's longsuffering with evil because of his mercy. God gives human beings many opportunities to repent so he does not need to act in justice against sin. I am glad for that particular moral value. God put up with me, delaying deserved punishment for twenty-two years before I believed on Jesus Christ and was saved. God still has mercy toward me, because I still, even as a believer, commit an occasional act of sinning. God, instead of immediately punishing me, acts in mercy, convicts me of my sinning, and gives me time to come to him in confession and repentance, 1 John 1:9. God acts that way toward all whom he has saved.

We see other examples of God punishing sin before Moses. Sodom and Gomorrah come to mind, Genesis 19:24. But the Bible does not focus on punishment, but on God's relationship with his saved people. So we do not always see God acting against sin. The times of punishment reported in the Bible are enough for us to know God acts against sin, because God's moral values never change. Sin is always wrong, and sin always receives punishment. If not in the here and now of this mortal life, then after death, for those who are unsaved.

For the saved, Christ received their punishment. Christ fully paid the penalty of sin to God for all the believer's past, present, and future sins. That God did exact punishment for the believer's sins shows us God's moral values never change. The believer can be forgiven because the punishment for his sins has been paid by Christ.

As to Moses specifically, God in mercy delayed punishment, and Moses later became a believer in God. The punishment due his sins was fully paid for by Christ. Praise God for his mercy toward Moses!

"Did God not care about sin prior to giving the Ten Commandments?" I believe when we look at God's character and his actions we see God did care about sin prior to giving Moses and Israel the Law, which begins with the Ten commandments.

We see in those examples of punishment for sin in the days before Moses, that God's moral values never change. Because of that fact there is always a payday someday, a day of reckoning and accountability for every human being, either personally, or though faith in Christ.

We see God acts in mercy and longsuffering, and it is good for us that he does, for who would survive if God immediately punished every sin? We just have to have faith God always acts properly, even when we cannot see it.

We must have faith God sovereignly has mercy on whom he will have mercy (Romans 9:15; Exodus 33:15), by grace forgives whom he will, and in justice punishes the guilty who despise his grace. The God of all the earth always does right (Genesis 18:25).

Hermeneutics: Philippians 1:12–13

Translation: 12 Now I want you to know, brothers, that the things concerning me have really served to the advancement of the gospel, 13 so my imprisonment in Christ has become apparent to all the palace guard, and to all the rest.

Exposition

In 1:12–26 Paul seems to be responding to his friends' concerns for his health and safety, no doubt communicated by Epaphroditus. Whereas most people would respond with a list of physical problems, his answer is about his spiritual condition.

Paul's imprisonment had not slowed his proclamation of the gospel. In the whole history of Christianity neither imprisonment nor persecution has stopped the proclamation of the gospel. Both are God-given opportunities to proclaim salvation in Christ. Different circumstances, different audience, but the same message for all.

Paul's imprisonment was typical for a Roman citizen with the means to support himself. He was, Acts 28:30, living in "his own rented house." He was watched by, perhaps chained to, a soldier—rather, many soldiers as the days passed and the duty rotated among the soldiers responsible to keep him secured. That is why "my imprisonment in Christ has become apparent to all the palace guard."

Paul has identified fully with Christ. He does not say, "my imprisonment for Christ's sake," but "my imprisonment in Christ." In his letter to the Colossians he expands on this idea. At 1:24 he wrote, "Now I rejoice in my sufferings for your sake, and I make good what is lacking of the afflictions for Christ in my flesh for the sake of his body, which is the church."

What he means is this. The believer, who is a "little Christ" (a "Christian"), continues to suffer the world's hatred against Christ, because the believer represents Christ to the world. Christ has "overcome the world," but "in the world you will have tribulation," John 16:33. The afflictions Christ suffered from worldlings continue to be suffered by his saved people. Christ is absent from the world, but his people represent him and therefore suffer the persecution and tribulation the world would place on him if he were here.

If Christ were here, he would continue to suffer affliction from the world. The believer suffers afflictions from the world because he/she is Christ' representative. The "lack of afflictions" Paul speaks of is not suffering for the sake of salvation, but the afflictions yet to be suffered for Christ's sake. [Quiggle, *Colossians*, 101.]

Paul is saying to the Philippians that he represents Christ in his imprisonment—that Christ would be the one in chains if he was physically present, but not being physically present Paul is in chains in his place; and Christ is in chains through Paul. This is encouraging, for where the believer is persecuted for Christ's sake, Christ is there being persecuted with the believer.

The identification between Christ and his saved people is so complete, that they are spiritually one. What is done for the believer, it is as though done for Christ. What is done to the believer, it is as though done to Christ. Be encouraged, Christ knows your state in the world, he is there with you.

Thoughts on Philippians 3:2

The Judaizers Paul speaks about in his letters, (e.g., Philippians 3:2) were Christians of Hebrew descent who believed Christians of gentile descent must do some works of the Mosaic Law in order to be genuine Christians. Those troublers of the church are no longer with us, but the spirit of their doctrine—it takes good works to make the Christian acceptable to God—haven't gone away, they are just wearing different clothes and new name tags.

The genuine Christian must always remember he/she already stands on the holy ground all other religions are trying to gain through their good works: a relationship with God. All others do good works trying to gain good standing with God, whether for salvation, or blessing, or to maintain salvation.

The appeal of doing good works to gain a righteous standing with God is strong and ever tempting. Even genuine Christians succumb to the temptation, by measuring themselves and their brothers and sisters by the number or quality of good works, both theirs and that of others.

But the standard by which God measures the Christian is his or her likeness to Christ. As the apostle John said (1 John 2:6), "The person claiming to abide in Christ is obligated, even as Christ lived his life, also himself to behave in the same manner." Not in doing the same works (for we don't have the same mission), but in the same attitude of dependence upon and submission to God's will and providence.

The genuine Christian does good works just because he/she is in a relationship with God; because such is pleasing to God and accomplishes his will, which is the desire of all genuine believers.

"I pursue toward the goal for the prize of the heavenly calling of God in Christ Jesus."

The identity of this "heavenly calling" has been debated for centuries. Most believe the prize is, "the eschatological consummation of what is already his in Christ" [Fee, *Philippians*, 348]. In other words, residence in heaven with Christ.

But that interpretation seems unlikely. The believer is nowhere exhorted to pursue heaven, or physical death, or rapture, one of which must take place if the, "prize of the heavenly calling," is only realized in, "the eschatological consummation of what is already his in Christ."

The believer is not called to go to heaven, he/she is already going to heaven. The destination ending the believer's journey through life is certain: he has his ticket in hand, there are no stops along the way. The believer is called to be like Christ and live for Christ during his/her journey through this life. John puts it this way, saying, because the believer knows he/she is going to heaven, that knowledge causes him and her to be, "constantly purifying himself just as Christ is pure," 1 John 3:3. To be like Christ today, so as to live for Christ today and tomorrow.

The goal of the Christian life is always today, because the far tomorrow is always certain. If one lives for Christ today, then he/she will always be prepared for all their tomorrows, including the "eschatological consummation" to this life. The full possession and enjoyment of all the believer's possessions in Christ is assured. The task is to possesses one's possessions in Christ as fully as possible today, in this life: to live for Christ and to be like Christ; to become spiritually mature. Being like Christ today is the "prize of the heavenly calling of God in Christ Jesus." That prize must be pursued every today.

What Paul is speaking of, which he introduces in 3:11, is not heaven, but is the essential tension of the Christian life: the balance between the positional and experiential aspects of salvation. This is the balance we see in the perseverance of the saints. God himself maintains the believer's salvation, and the believer is to work out his/her salvation. God gives the grace of perseverance and the believer must use God's grace to persevere. God has declared the believer righteous and holy, and the believer is constantly exhorted to live righteously and to be holy.

Thus, in 3:11, Paul says one of his goals is to be "conformed to Christ's death." To be conformed to Christ's death is to reckon one's self as raised to newness of life and no longer under the dominion of sin—dead to sin; see Romans 6:1–14. Then, with a slight turn of the phrase, Paul changes the point of view from dead to sin to resurrected to new life from the dead. Just as Christ spiritually died to sin, so too Paul's goal is to spiritually die to sin. Just as Christ physically died and was physically resurrected, so too Paul will physically die and be physically resurrected.

The prize, therefore, stated another way, is spiritual maturity in this mortal life: attaining and practicing that mindset which leaves the sins of the past behind and lives in the present by being like Christ—in submission to and dependence upon God—so as to live for the sake of Christ in the world. The Christian lives with two horizons in view. There is the near horizon of today, and there is the far horizon of the ending of this mortal life which begins the next. Arrival at the far horizon is assured, it is the near horizon that requires our constant attention. Live for Christ today and you will always be prepared for all your tomorrows.

Philippians 3:15, "as many as are mature should be of this mindset." Paul knows the members of a local church are individuals, some of whom are mature, others gaining maturity, some struggling, and others just beginning. Whatever maturity one has attained, 3:16, practice that, and pursue more. Through deliberately and habitually living the Christian life, one will over time mature into the habitual practice of the Christian life. That is a prize worth pursuing.

The Image of Christ

Every saved person, Old Testament and New Testament, will be conformed to the image of Christ.

Humankind, in the person of Adam, was created in the "image and likeness" of God, Genesis 1:26. That image and likeness may be categorized under three general headings: moral, intellectual, and spiritual.

> *Moral:* Holiness; Sanctification; Righteousness; Justice; Mercy; Faithfulness
>
> *Intellectual:* Personality; Will; Volition; Veracity; Knowledge; Wisdom
>
> *Spiritual:* Love; Compassion; Goodness; Kindness; Longsuffering; Mercy

Mercy is listed in both the moral and spiritual columns because mercy may delay justice, a moral quality, or relieve suffering, a spiritual quality.

The image and likeness of God are the communicable properties and attributes of God. Some of God's attributes are not communicable, meaning they belong to God alone. For example, omniscience, omnipotence, omnipresence, sovereignty, self-existence, etc.

Man in God's image is man's soul fashioned according to God's communicable attributes in finite measure, in a greater or lesser degree, depending on the attribute in question. Stated a little differently, the pattern God used to create man's soul were his communicable attributes in a measure suitable to a finite creature. For example, man is not the standard of truth (veracity) but has the capacity for truthfulness. Man was given dominion, but his dominion is not from himself and does not correspond to God's sovereignty, which is incommunicable. [The above from Quiggle, *Adam and Eve, A Biography and Theology*.]

The decree of God that established the believer's conformity to Jesus Christ is known as "predestination." The decree of predestination is often confused with the decree of election. Here is the difference between election and predestination [Quiggle, *Dictionary*].

> Election. The choice of a sovereign God (Ephesians 1:4), 1) to give the gift of grace-faith-salvation to effect the salvation of some sinners (Ephesians 2:8), and 2) to take no action, positive or negative, to either effect or deny salvation to other sinners

(Romans 10:13; Revelation 22:17). The decree of election includes all means necessary to effectuate salvation in those elected.

Predestination. God's decree to conform the believer to be like Christ according to certain aspects of Christ's spiritual character and physical form (Romans 8:29–30; 1 John 3:2), and to place the believer in the legal position of God's son and heir (Ephesians 1:5, 11), so that the believer has an inheritance from God and is God's heritage.

Election concerns the salvation of the sinner. Predestination concerns the character and inheritance of the believer: to be like Christ, Romans 8:29.

The Christian is saved, "created in Christ Jesus," (Ephesians 2:8) to be Christ-like. Sin reprioritized the attributes of human nature—God's image and likeness in humankind—to serve self not God. Salvation reprioritizes human nature to serve God not self. The Holy Spirit trains the believer to be like Christ, think like Christ, and respond like Christ.

The essence of Christ-likeness is Jesus Christ depended upon God to keep him in the world and provide for him, and submitted to the authority of the Father to accomplish his mission in the world. So too the believer in Christ. For the believer in Christ, these characteristics may be summed in four words: worship, fellowship, service, and obedience. When these four aspects of the believer's life are like Christ, that is spirituality. [Quiggle, *Dictionary*.]

Spirituality. Biblical spirituality is both a state and an action. The Christian's state is sanctified in Christ: set apart from sin and dedicated to God. The Christian's action is to live sanctified in the world: to practice righteous living so as to continue in worship, fellowship, obedience, and service to Christ.

Another way to define spirituality is spiritual maturity: consistently cooperating with the influence of the Word of God and the power of the Holy Spirit to change every aspect of one's life to be more like Christ. Developing the believer to be spiritual and mature is what the Holy Spirit does when he acts to conform the believer to be like Christ.

Christ likeness is not instantaneous upon salvation. The several actions that take place when the believer is saved and "born-again" are the beginning of conformity to Christ. Overcoming the influence of the sin attribute is the process of becoming like Christ.

God, for reasons that seemed good to him, leaves the sin attribute resident in the saved, born-again human nature, 1 John 1:8. One reason is suggested at 2 Corinthians 12:9 (ESV), "my grace is sufficient for you, for my power is made perfect in weakness."

Being saved and born-again gives the believer the spiritual power to overcome the influence and temptations from the sin attribute. The believer habitually says "No" to temptations and enforces the decision. Occasionally, the believer agrees with a temptation and commits an act of sinning, 1 John 1:10. The believer then confesses and repents, 1 John 1:9.

The more spiritual-mature the believer becomes, the more his or her manner of living is like Christ. As the believer matures in Christ, he begins to sin less; he/she never becomes sinless in this mortal life. The believer does sin less and less as the Holy Spirit conforms him or her to be more like Christ. He/she says "No" more frequently to temptation and acts of sinning.

One measure of spiritual maturity-conformity to Christ, is abiding in Christ.

> 1 John 2:6, The person claiming to abide in him is obligated, even as he lived his life, also himself to behave in the same manner.

> 1 John 3:9, Every person who has been born from God does not habitually practice sin, because his seed abides in him, and he is not able to habitually sin, because from God he is born.

Whoever abides in Christ is not able to habitually sin. The opposite must be true: whoever is not abiding in him does sin. Therefore an occasion of sinning is inversely related to the habit of abiding. Sinning is habitual when not abiding; not sinning is habitual when abiding.

> Augustine, In so far as he [the believer] abideth in Him [Christ], in so far sinneth not.

The key to being Christ-like is abiding in Christ. When the believer is abiding in Christ he/she is not committing acts of sinning. During those times when a believer is not abiding, he/she is committing acts of sinning. The conclusion is that not sinning is as habitual as abiding, acts of sinning are as occasional as not abiding.

To abide in Christ is to habitually order one's behavior so as to maintain moral purity and purity of faith. To abide in Christ is to behave in the same manner as Christ. To abide in Christ is to be like Christ, because it is Christ-likeness God most enjoys.

To be like Christ is to believe the doctrine Christ believed, to be submissive to and dependent on the Father as Christ was, and to do the works one is given to do, as Christ did the works he was given to do. Not the same works, because the believer doe s not have the same mission as Christ, but to do the works one is given in the same manner as Christ did his works: in dependence upon and submission to God.

That is what it means to be in the image of Christ. Conforming the believer to be like Christ is a work of the Holy Spirit known as "experiential sanctification."

Enoch A Type of the Rapture?

Is Enoch, Genesis 5:21–23, a type of the rapture of the New Testament church? Some think so, drawing an analogy between Enoch and the Rapture.

Let us biblically consider the analogy between Enoch and the rapture of the New Testament church. Enoch was translated into heaven because he walked with God. He lived a manner of life (walk) pleasing to God, and as a reward was removed to heaven (and as a mercy, for in being translated that righteous man did not have to endure another 600 years of the world's increasing sinfulness). He would have died before the flood, an important point, had God allowed him to continue on the earth.

If Enoch's translation into heaven is a picture of the rapture of the New Testament church, then only those believers whose lives are pleasing to God will be removed into heaven. That "he pleased God" was the condition for his translation into heaven, even as those who support this analogy will state, quoting Hebrews 11:5.

This analogy between Enoch and the Rapture is nothing less than the "Partial Rapture" theory, which states, members of the New Testament church are raptured as they become pleasing to God, meaning some believers will not endure the Tribulation, but others will endure the Tribulation, until they have suffered enough to be pleasing.

Let us apply the author's analogy to another man of the times who pleased God. Noah, Genesis 6:9, "Noah walked with God." But Noah wasn't translated out of the world. Noah, who was safe in the ark, nevertheless endured through the time of God's wrath against the world, a "Tribulation" of worldwide proportions. Does that mean Noah is a type of the rapture of the New Testament church? If so, then the New Testament church will endure through the Tribulation and be raptured at the end, a post-tribulational rapture.

I reject this analogy. The entire living New Testament church will be raptured out of the world prior to the Tribulation, whether living pleasing to God, or not. It is the propitiation of Christ to God for all the believer's sins, not a pleasing manner of life, that ensures the removal of all New Testament church at the same time: a pre-Tribulation rapture.

Enoch illustrates a partial rapture, but others were also walking pleasing to God: a whole chapter of believers pleasing to God, but God did not translate them. So there is not a Partial rapture, not a Post-tribulation rapture. The Bible student must beware of analogies built on one expression or phrase that doesn't consider the entire biblical context, but manipulates that context to support a pre-determined theory.

The Rapture-as-Jewish-wedding

This essay was first published in the *Evangelical Dispensational Quarterly Journal,* September, 2020, vol. 4, Num 2, published by the Scofield Biblical Institute.

One of the latest and most well-known theologians to use the "rapture-as-Jewish-wedding" illustration is Dr. Arnold Fruchtenbaum, *The Footsteps of the Messiah: D, The Marriage of the Lamb*. Dr. Fruchtenbaum has done great service to the New Testament church and Dispensationalism. But in this he is mistaken. This essay is explains the reasons this illustration is wrong.

Introduction

Explaining the rapture of the New Testament church by analogy to a Jewish betrothal-wedding has gained in popularity. The essential elements are:

> After a Jewish betrothal, the analogy claims the bridegroom left to prepare a place for his fiancé and himself to live as husband and wife.

> This long separation afforded the fiancé time to gather her trousseau and prepare for married life.

> After a long time the groom returns, marries his betrothed, and then takes her to the new home he prepared.

> Christ left, is preparing a place, and is returning to receive the New Testament church to himself at the rapture. Therefore the rapture is like a Jewish betrothal-wedding.

Does the comparison of the rapture with a Jewish betrothal-wedding conform to what the Bible presents about the New Testament church and the rapture of the New Testament church? No. The rapture as Jewish betrothal-wedding is an allegorical interpretation of certain Scriptures and misuse of historical-cultural information that fails to conform to the proper use of the Literal hermeneutic.

The Literal hermeneutic requires understanding Scripture within the historical-cultural context of the biblical setting, and an interpretation of the scriptures that considers the literary context in which those scriptures are set. The Literal hermeneutic also has definite rules concerning the proper interpretation and use of figures of speech. The purpose of this essay is to show the rapture as Jewish betrothal-wedding does not meet the high standards of the Literal hermeneutic.

Let me pause and say the rapture of the New Testament church is a biblical fact. How do we know? The Literal hermeneutic teaches the removal of the New Testament church from the world by Christ at some yet-future date. The fact of the rapture is found by comparing Scripture with Scripture: John 14:2–3; 1 Thessalonians 4:13–17; Revelation 3:10. The fact of the rapture is not in doubt, only the allegorical rapture as Jewish betrothal-wedding is disputed. Now to the argument.

Historical-Cultural Information

What historical-cultural information is used to support the rapture as Jewish betrothal-wedding ? Usually it is data similar to that found in the *Jewish Encyclopedia*.

> After the lapse of a certain period from the time of betrothal (twelve months if the bride was a virgin and a minor, and thirty days if she was an adult or a widow; Sefaria, *Ketubot*, 57b), during which the bride could prepare her trousseau, the marriage proper was celebrated. This was attended with the ceremony of home-taking (*liḳḳuḥin* or *nissu'in*) and isolation of the bridal pair in the bridal chamber (*ḥuppah*). From that time they became husband and wife, even if there was no cohabitation. Various ceremonies attended the act of marriage (see Marriage Ceremony). An important feature was the handing over of the marriage contract (*ketubah*) to the bride. In later times the two stages of marriage were combined, a custom universally followed at the present time. [http://www.jewishencyclopedia.com/articles/10435-marriage-laws]

The problem with this data? It does not meet the requirement of the Literal hermeneutic. The marriage custom described is a 6th century AD Jewish custom, not a 1st century AD custom. The above quote is from the *Babylonian Talmud*, written ca. AD 450–550.

There is historical-cultural data more close to the time of Jesus. The *Mishnah* was compiled ca. 200 BC–AD 200, and therefore is more likely to be the betrothal-wedding rules Christ would have referred to— if Christ had proposed a rapture as Jewish betrothal-wedding analogy. However, the *Mishnah* knows nothing of a mandatory waiting period between betrothal and marriage. The word "betrothal" occurs seventeen times in the *Mishnah* [General Index]. The *Mishnah* has many varied rules about betrothal (see tractate, *Kiddushin*), but none present any kind of mandatory waiting period between betrothal and marriage.

When we turn to the tractate on marriage, *Ketuboth*, the *Mishnah* does say, "After the husband has demanded her, a virgin is granted twelve months wherein to provide for herself; and like as [such time] is granted to the woman so it is granted to the man to provide for himself. And a widow [is granted] thirty days" [m. *Ketuboth*, 5.2]. The waiting period was not mandatory, and need not continue for twelve months.

Under what we assume, from the *Mishnah*, was current Jewish law in 1st century Israel, a young woman could be betrothed when she was twelve years and one day old. The law reads, "A man may give his daughter in betrothal while she is still in her girlhood" [m., *Kiddushin*, 2.1]. The translation "girlhood" is the Hebrew *na'ărâ*, defined as twelve years and a day old or older, unmarried but marriageable. (A woman who had reached her majority was described as *bogereth*.) The fact a twelve year old could be betrothed was probably the reason the *Mishnah* allowed, but did not require, a twelve month period to elapse between betrothal and marriage. Puberty was more likely at thirteen than at twelve.

Summing up. During the time Jesus walked the earth, it seems likely twelve months was allowed between betrothal and marriage, if the girl was a virgin. But not if the woman was a widow. The twelve month period can only be declared, "seems likely," because the historical document Mishnah was compiled between 200 BC–AD 200, a sufficient span of time to cast doubt on when that particular custom came into existence. The waiting period between the two stages of marriage, betrothal and wedding, was not mandatory.

The custom outlined in the *Babylonian Talmud, Ketubot*, 57b, is from the 6th century AD. But, let us note the *Babylonian Talmud* also did not mandate twelve months elapse from betrothal to marriage: "a virgin is given twelve months to prepare for her marriage." The reason is most likely for her to complete puberty; to go from *na'ărâ* to *bogereth*. For example, "Rabbi Zeira said: It was taught in the *Tosefta, Ketubot*, 5:1, (The *Tofseta* is from the same time period as the *Mishnah*) with regard to a minor girl: Either she or her father may delay the wedding until she has reached majority" [*Babylonian Talmud, Ketubot*, 57b]. "Rabbi Abba bar Levi said, "One may not finalize an agreement to marry a minor girl in order to marry her while she is still a minor, but one may finalize an agreement to marry a minor girl in order to marry her when she becomes an adult woman" [*Babylonian Talmud, Ketubot*, 57b]. "Rabbi Huna said, "If she has reached her majority, even for just one day, and then she is betrothed, she is given her thirty days to prepare for her wedding, like a widow, since prior to reaching adulthood she presumably had already prepared everything needed for her marriage" [*Babylonian Talmud, Ketubot*, 57b].

The Rabbis interpreted the grant of twelve months to apply to those who had been betrothed at the age of twelve years. To make a general application of that rule to Christ and the New Testament church seems unwarranted.

Conclusion: the 6th century historical source used as the basis for the rapture as Jewish betrothal-wedding analogy is not only not the historically current law in the time of Jesus, but also had a limited application.

Scriptures

There are several biblical issues with the rapture as Jewish betrothal-wedding analogy. The first is, we don't know that much about Jewish betrothal-wedding customs in first century Israel. All our knowledge assumes the rules in the *Mishnah* were in use during Jesus' earthly ministry. The gospels have nothing to say about the relationship between betrothal and marriage—are not the gospels the primary source for the rapture-wedding analogy? Either Jesus put his departure and return for the church in terms of a Jewish betrothal-wedding, or he did not. The Scriptures say he did not.

There is no mention of betrothal customs in the gospels, meaning Jesus had nothing to say about betrothal. We see one mention of a betrothal in the gospels: Mary was betrothed to Joseph, Luke 1:27. Jesus did not describe his relationship with his church as a betrothal. Jesus did not use or refer to what we know of betrothal customs as stated in the then historically current document, the *Mishnah*.

Did Jesus speak about the act of marriage following a betrothal? Or perhaps the period of time between a betrothal and marriage? No. Jesus said marriage was between a man and a woman, Matthew 19:5; Mark 10:8–9. That's it, nothing more (he did speak about divorce). Jesus did not refer to his relationship with the New Testament church as a betrothal or a marriage.

The "rapture-Jewish wedding" analogy depends on the answer to a simple question: Do the Scriptures present Jesus the Christ as betrothed to the New Testament church? The answer may be developed from several points of view. First point of view: the relationship between Christ and the New Testament church is created by what is known as the New Covenant.

The New covenant is first stated in Jeremiah 31:31–33. The covenant promises YHWH will, "put My law in their [those of national ethnic Israel who are members of the covenant] minds, and write it on their hearts; and I will be their God, and they shall be My people. No more shall every man teach his neighbor, and every man his brother, saying, 'Know the Lord,' for they all shall know Me, from the least of them to the greatest of them, says the Lord. For I will forgive their iniquity, and their sin I will remember no more."

The New Covenant in Jeremiah is yet-future for Israel, "behold, the days are coming." (As a Dispensationalist I believe the New covenant for Israel waits for the Millennial Kingdom.) The key fact in relation to this discussion is the New Covenant is not a marriage covenant. YHWH does say Israel broke the Mosaic covenant, "though I was a husband to them," but the Mosaic covenant is nowhere described as a marriage covenant.

The word "husband" in Jeremiah 31:32 cannot have been used in a literal sense. YHWH is not a man that he should marry. Nor does the New covenant refer to betrothal or marriage. The word "husband" is used figuratively of the fidelity YHWH showed toward Israel, even though Israel was faithless and broke the Mosaic Covenant. One of the rules for interpreting a figure of speech is, "A figure of speech is not used to teach the literal thing on which it is based." YHWH illustrating his Mosaic covenant relationship with Israel as a husband is not being used to teach YHWH is literally a husband to Israel.

Excursus: Figures of Speech

I believe it necessary at this point to divert from the main topic discuss the proper use and interpretation of biblical figures of speech. There are five unbreakable, unalterable, unchanging rules for figures of speech:

> A figure of speech is a comparison (by example or analogy) of one thing with another that clarifies some aspect of the thing being illustrated by the figure of speech.

> A figure of speech does not teach doctrine. A figure of speech clarifies what is being taught for the purpose of helping the

understanding.

A figure of speech clarifies one aspect, not all aspects, of the thing being illustrated.

A figure of speech is based in something literal and is intended to teach something literal.

A figure of speech does not teach the literal thing on which it is based.

The rule that is of interest to the rapture as Jewish betrothal-wedding analogy is the last, "A figure of speech does not teach the literal thing on which it is based."

The use of marriage is a biblical figure of speech designed to communicate the idea of spiritual fidelity, and nothing more. In relation to the figure of speech, "YHWH as husband to Israel" (or the more common, "Israel as wife of YHWH"), the Mosaic covenant, which was the covenant at the time Jeremiah wrote, was not a marriage covenant. God and the people of Israel did not become one-flesh.

The figurative use of marriage was created by God through his prophets to communicate the nation Israel, as a whole, was religiously unfaithful to YHWH; hence the corresponding use of adultery to describe Israel's idolatry. Only false gods marry—ask the Egyptians, the Greeks, the Romans, the Mormons. The one true God does not present himself as married literally or metaphorically, because "God is not a man." Marriage as a metaphor or illustration does not teach God is literally married, but that Israel was spiritually unfaithful.

Let us examine the use of fire, a well-known figure of speech. Literal fire destroys, and literal fire cleanses. A literal fire will consume a building. A literal fire will purge impurities from ore (smelting). From these two literal uses of literal fire the scriptures teach two literal meanings: judging the unsaved and cleansing the saved. For example, absolutely no one properly using the Literal hermeneutic will interpret, e.g., Isaiah 30:27, "And His [YHWH's] tongue is like a burning fire," to mean YHWH's tongue is literally burning up Assyria. YHWH will destroy Assyria, as a fire destroys a building. The imagery is the word of God in the mouth of God pronouncing judgment on the enemy of God.

No one properly using the Literal hermeneutic will interpret Revelation 1:16, a sharp two-edged sword comes out of Christ's mouth, to mean Christ walks around with a sword coming out of his mouth. Nor will the interpreter say it means Christ's tongue is metaphorically razor sharp like a sword and metaphorically cuts the listener. The two edged sword is a figure of speech used as an illustration of the Word of God at work in the believer and the world, Hebrews 4:12, revealing and convicting. This figure of speech as used in Revelation represents the Word of God in the mouth of God accomplishing the will of God. The interpretation, when all aspects of Christ's visual appearance are considered, is Christ the high priest come to judge his people, Revelation 2, 3, and God the righteous Judge coming to judge the world, Revelation 6–19, compare 19:15, "From His mouth comes a sharp sword, so that with it He may strike down the nations."

Is the New Testament church the Bride of Christ?

Israel was not literally the wife of YHWH under the Mosaic covenant, and will not literally be the wife of YHWH under the yet-future New covenant. Even so, the New Testament church is never presented as literally the bride or wife of Christ. The New Testament church has a New covenant with Christ. Some believe it is a current application of YHWH's yet-future, Jeremiah 31:31–34, New covenant with Israel. Others, like myself, believe Christ's covenant with the New Testament church is similar to YHWH's New covenant with Israel, but independent of it, being a covenant between Christ and the New Testament church. The conditions of Christ's New covenant with the New Testament church are similar to that of YHWH with Israel, Hebrews 10:16–17. Two similar but independent covenants for two separate people groups to accomplish the same end for both people groups.

Regardless of which view one takes, just like YHWH's New covenant with Israel is not a marriage contract, even so Christ's New covenant with the New Testament church is not a marriage contract. It is a covenant promising salvation and regeneration—a covenant of redemption.

There is no place in the New Testament where Christ's covenant relationship with his church is described in terms of a betrothal or marriage. But someone somewhere will point to New Testament use of marriage to make the opposite case (as does the rapture-wedding analogy). Let's take a look.

There are two literal weddings in the New Testament. One is the wedding at Cana, John 2, a marriage celebration. At this stage of Jesus' public ministry, he is announcing "the Kingdom of Heaven is at hand." Jesus' activities at the Cana wedding are in relation to his messianic mission to Israel. Wine is used as a figure of joy in Messiah's

Kingdom, e.g., Jeremiah 31:12; Hosea 14:7; Amos 9:13–14.

A wedding is not a prominent Old Testament messianic theme, but marriage is occasionally used as a figure of speech of the relationship between Messiah and national ethnic Israel. See Isaiah 54:1; 62:4; Jeremiah 3:14; Hosea 2:19–20. Jesus used marriage as a figure of speech to describe his messianic relationship with Israel at Matthew 22:1–4; 25:1–3. But in no place does Jesus use marriage to describe his relationship with the New Testament church.

The second marriage in the New Testament is that between Joseph and Mary. In this marriage story, Mary leaves the village after the betrothal, for three months, Joseph stays behind, and when Mary returns she receives Joseph as her husband. Nothing in this betrothal-marriage supports the "rapture-Jewish wedding" theory.

Other gospel references to Jewish weddings are not literal weddings. In John 3, John Baptist uses marriage figuratively to describe his decreasing importance in the proclamation of the messianic kingdom: the groomsman becomes less important when the bridegroom arrives. Applying the Literal hermeneutic, which views the historical-cultural aspects of the passage, no one hearing the Baptist describe Christ as a bridegroom would have thought of the non-existent New Testament church. If Christ was being presented by the Baptist as a literal bridegroom—which he was not—then two observations: one, the moment is not about betrothal, nor returning for the bride, but is about the marriage ceremony; two, the bride would have been national ethnic Israel, not the non-existent New Testament church. But, the figure was not about betrothal or marriage, but John Baptist. A figure of speech does not teach the literal thing on which it is based.

Matthew 9:15–17 (parallels Mark 2:19; Luke 5:34) uses "bridegroom" in a figurative manner. The point of the parable is Mosaic Judaism was not part of the coming kingdom of national ethnic Israel under the Messiah. The message at this early stage of Jesus' ministry is about the promised Davidic-Messianic kingdom, because the kingdom is still being proclaimed. As with the Baptist's use of the figure, the moment is not about betrothal, nor returning for the bride; and if a bride was in view (which it is not) the bride would have been national ethnic Israel, not the non-existent New Testament church. The "bridegroom taken away" is a reference to the coming crucifixion. No mention is made of a return. Nor can the figure be about Christ ascending into heaven, else he would have condemned the New

Testament church to perpetual mourning until his return.

Matthew 25 uses a bridegroom as an element of a parable. Before continuing, a few words about interpreting a parable.

> A parable is a story—a word picture or an illustration—told to teach a single point. A parable is usually built with something literal (a farmer sowing seed, a man giving a banquet), but may also use figures of speech, idioms, slang, symbols, or types. Like a symbol, a parable is always based in something literal and always teaches something literal. The intent of a parable is not to describe every aspect of doctrine, but only to illustrate one point. Before trying to interpret a parable, look for the reason for telling the parable, and there you will usually find the one, single, main point the parable is teaching. Do not try to interpret all the parts that were used to build the parable. The parts are the cart and horse that carries the one main point. [Quiggle, *Literal Hermeneutic*, 36.]

> Whenever any interpreter seeks an elaboration of meaning in a parable, and commences to find meaning in far more points than the parable can hope to make, that interpreter has returned to the reprehensible method of allegorizing the parables. [Ramm, 279.]

The point of the parable of Matthew 9:15–17 is national ethnic Israel's preparedness for Messiah. Here the timing is the second advent, not the rapture. In the parable the marriage ceremony has already taken place, the husband is bringing his wife to his home. No rapture, no waiting period, no betrothal are in this parable. But the point is not the marriage. The returning husband and wife are simply an element on which the story is built, part of the cart and horse carrying the message. The point of the parable is, will Israel be prepared when Messiah returns to establish the kingdom? At the very most, (although it is not wise to interpret the individual elements of a parable) the wife in this parable is the New Testament church, which returns with Christ at the second advent. This parable has nothing do to with the rapture of the New Testament church.

No verse in the Four Gospels teaches the rapture is like a Jewish wedding.

But let us assume the point for a moment. A Jewish marriage consisted of two stages, betrothal and wedding. In the scenario imagined by the analogy, Christ paid the purchase price for the New Testament church, left, and is coming back for the wedding.

Let's take a moment to more closely examine the idea Christ purchased the church. In a Jewish betrothal the prospective groom often gave money establish the betrothal, "By three means is the woman acquired . . . She is acquired by money, or by writ, or by intercourse" [m. *Kiddushin*, 1.1]. Acts 20:28 reads in a few versions, "the church of God which he purchased with his own blood." However, the word translated "purchased" in the KJV, ASV, NKJV, HCSB, *peripoiéō*, means "to acquire" [Zodhiates. s. v. "4046"], not purchase. The verse is properly translated (and with a little paraphrasing), "the church of God which Christ acquired through his propitiatory death." (The word blood in this verse is a euphemism for death.) Christ's death propitiated God for sin, 1 John 2:2, Romans 3:25. The merit of the propitiatory death is applied to sinners through the decree of election (Ephesians 1:4) and the gift of God (Ephesians 2:8).

That salvation of the soul effected by the gift of God is a completed salvation. We know this for two reasons. One, the soul of every saved sinner is regenerated, born-again. Two, every physically dead sinner goes to heaven to be in God's presence, and is certain to experience reunification with the resurrected physical body.

The problem with the rapture as Jewish betrothal-wedding analogy is salvation in the analogy corresponds to the betrothal stage. The consequence of salvation as betrothal is an incomplete salvation. A Jewish marriage consisted of two stages: betrothal, then wedding. One without the other was incomplete. The betrothed woman was not a wife. The Jewish betrothal laws treated her legally as a wife in one aspect only: the betrothal could only be dissolved by a divorce.

This is a very troubling aspect of the analogy. Christ on the cross propitiated God for the sins of the world, 1 John 2:2; Romans 3:25. The merit of that propitiation is applied through the degree of election by the gift of God (Ephesians 2:8) to effect the complete redemption of the soul. We know the redemption of the soul is complete because the soul is regenerated, born-again. If the soul is waiting for the wedding, then salvation lacks something to make it complete.

But the fact of the regeneration and the believer in heaven upon physical death deny that salvation is incomplete. If salvation is incomplete, then the saved could not go into heaven, for there is no sin in God's presence. That implies some sort of purgatory until salvation is completed—God forbid.

Regeneration indicates salvation is not like a betrothal waiting for the wedding, but is a completed salvation. That condition of born-again-regenerated applies equally to the Old Testament saved sinner, who will not be raptured. As one of the Puritans said (a truth apparently not known today), "It is absolutely necessary that all should be new born . . . no age, no time excludes it" [Charnock, 12]. The redemption of the soul is complete, and viewed as completed, even though the body remains to be redeemed, Ephesians 1:14, through resurrection. Just as the Old Testament saints were not waiting for their salvation to be completed, even so the New Testament saints are not waiting for a wedding to complete their salvation. The rapture as Jewish betrothal-wedding analogy implicitly distorts the completed nature of salvation.

Eschatology

The analogy depends on a certain eschatology. The eschatology of the Synoptics is not applicable to the rapture as Jewish betrothal-wedding theme. That eschatology is the Tribulation, the second advent ending the Tribulation, and the consequent Davidic-Messianic-Millennial Kingdom. As Pentecost stated,

> [A] fourth view suggests that verses 4–8 outline the first half of the tribulation and verses 9-26 describe the second half of the week . . . Consistency of interpretation would seem to eliminate any application of this portion of Scripture to the church or the church age. Inasmuch as the Lord is dealing with the prophetic program for Israel . . . The parallelism between verses 4-8 and Revelation 6 seems to indicate that the first half of the Tribulation is here described. [Pentecost, 278.]

Pentecost quotes Arno C. Gaebelein and E. Schuyler English in support [Pentecost, 279]. This must also have been Pentecost's view, for he speaks approvingly.

The eschatology in John's gospel only seems applicable to the analogy. The only eschatology in John's Gospel is at 14:2–3. There Jesus states, "In my Father's house are many abiding places; but if not I would have said that to you. I go to prepare a place for you. And when I should go and prepare a place for you, I am coming again and will receive you to myself; that where I am, you may be also."

That is the only gospel reference to the rapture. But let us be careful not to add to what Jesus said. Jesus did not say, "Just like a bridegroom leaving to prepare a place for his bride, so I go to prepare a place for you," etc. There is no mention of a betrothal or a wedding. The only way to find a reference to Jewish marriage (betrothal plus wedding) in the eschatology of the gospels is to bring it with you so you can "discover" it there.

Bride of Christ?

Jesus never names the New Testament church as his bride. Jesus never describes his return for the New Testament church in terms of a Jewish betrothal-wedding. In fact, the New Testament view of the church is quite different from that of a bride:

> John 10:27, "my sheep."

> Hebrews 2:10, "having brought many sons to glory."

> Hebrews 2:11, "he is not ashamed to call them brothers."

> Hebrews 2:13, "Look, I and the children whom God has given to me."

I hear the objection, "what about the bride of Christ in Ephesians 5?" Tell me, show me, where in Ephesians 5 is the New Testament church named as a bride? Ephesians 5:22–33 is about existing marriage, not betrothal, not leaving and returning, not about the rapture. Only marriage is in view. Let's look:

> Just as Christ is the head of the church, so the husband is head of the wife, v. 23.

> Just as the church is subject to Christ, so the wife is subject to the husband, v. 34.

> Just as Christ loves the church, so the husband is to love the wife, v. 25.

The members of the New Testament church are, "members of Christ's body," v. 30. That is spiritual union through the indwelling Holy Spirit. In a figure of speech it is marriage, but it is not literal marriage and it is not betrothal. Nowhere in Ephesians does Paul state the New Testament church is the wife or bride of Christ. The word "bride" never appears. Two verses might seem to imply the church is the wife of Christ.

One verse that may seem to speak of a marriage yet to occur is Ephesians 5:27. "In order than he should present to himself the church in glory, not having spot or wrinkle or any of such things, but that it should be holy and without blemish." That is not marriage, because in marriage the groom does not present his bride to himself. What this is, is explained in 5:25–26, "The husbands are to love their wives, even just as Christ loved the church and gave up himself for her, so that he might sanctify her, having cleansed her by the washing of water with the Word." That is redemption, not marriage. Christ presents the church to himself through his actions of redemption and sanctification. In 5:27 neither betrothal nor wedding are mentioned or in view. In 5:26–27 the comparison is "love" not betrothal or wedding.

Paul quoting Genesis 2:24 at Ephesians 5:31 may seem to imply a marital relationship between Christ and the church. Even if one accepts that interpretation, the quote is not about betrothal, a bride, a wedding, or a rapture, but the character of the husband-wife marital relationship. The point of quoting Genesis 2:24 in Ephesians 5 is unity, fidelity, loyalty. Submit to your husband's headship as the church submits to Christ. Love your wife as Christ loves the church. Nourish and cherish your wife as Christ does the church. The point is the character of the relationship between husband and wife is to be of the same character as the relationship between Christ and the New Testament church. Not betrothal, not bride, not wife, but love, respect, and care for one another.

Looking to Genesis 2:24, the New Testament church is not literally Christ's flesh and bones. Just as the husband and wife are not literally "one flesh." The sinner leaves his old life and transfers his loyalty to Christ. The husband leaves his old life and transfers his loyalty to the wife. The husband's loyalty prior to marriage was to his parents. In marriage the husband transfers that loyalty to his wife, just as she transfers her loyalty to her husband. That is what "one flesh means": the union between husband and wife is created by an exclusive loyalty contract. "Marriage," and "wife," and "bride" (if it occurred in the passage), when used as a figure of speech in relation to God, is always about unity, loyalty, and fidelity.

Someone somewhere looks to the Lamb's wedding supper at Revelation 19:7. The "Lamb's wife" is only the New Testament church if you import that concept into the passage and then "discover" it there. What is more likely is the "Lamb's wife" is all the saved in both Testaments, from Adam to the end of the Tribulation. Christ is about to return to the earth to establish the Davidic-Messianic kingdom promised to national ethnic Israel. That act will be the consummation of all the Old Testament kingdom promises, not promises to the New

Testament church. The New Testament church participates in the Kingdom as joint-heirs with Christ, Romans 8:17. The "lamb's wife" in Revelation 19:7 is the eschatological kingdom and its members.

Conclusion

The rapture as Jewish betrothal-wedding is an allegorical interpretation created by overlaying that analogy on top of certain scriptures in order to support a doctrine decided beforehand. Here is the thesis:

> The New Testament portrays the Church as the Bride of Christ in Ephesians 5:22-33 (Paul even quotes Genesis 2:24 as the union at the Parousia of the Bridegroom in v.31!); cf. Romans 7:4; 2 Corinthians 11:2; James 4:4. In the opening verses of John 14, the marriage covenant is confirmed. Paul continually reminds us of the purchase price and the covenant by which we, the Bride, are set apart, or sanctified.
> [https://www.khouse.org/articles/2003/449/?fbclid=IwAR3b tcTBTO2iZDOnU82MwyL5-ZYoZRDBQxDHpALSeWgkeOilBxXEv5Q9xOg]

No, the New Testament church is never identified by Paul as a bride or wife of Christ. Genesis 2:24 is about the exclusive loyalty covenant that is marriage. No New Testament scripture ever creates a marriage contract between the New Testament church and Christ. Christ did not pay a "purchase price" for the church, he propitiated God so God could act redemptively toward sinners, acquiring the church through his propitiatory death. The opening verses of John 14 say nothing about betrothal, or marriage, or a wedding. Like most allegorical interpretations, this view manipulates the Scriptures to "discover" the doctrine decided upon beforehand.

Is Jesus returning for the New Testament church in an event named in the Greek text of 1 Thessalonians 4:17 the *hárpazō*, the "catching away," and in the Latin text the *raptuare*, the rapture. Yes. How do we know? John 14:2–3; 1 Thessalonians 4:13–17; Revelation 3:10. Does the rapture correspond to a 4th century AD description of the two aspects of Jewish marriage as practiced in the 6th century AD? No. Does the New Testament teach the rapture is like a Jewish betrothal-wedding? No. Does the Bible ever identify the New Testament church as the bride of Christ? No. Step away from the allegorical interpretive method; don't play with it, it will only hurt you.

TRANSLATION: 6 Be anxious about not even one thing or person, but in everything by prayer and petition on behalf of yourself and others, with thanksgiving, make your requests known to God. 7 And the peace of God surpassing all understanding will guard your hearts and your minds in Christ Jesus.

TRANSLATION NOTE:

The words "thing or person," attached to "not even one" are my interpretative translation of the conditional negative *mḗ*, to correspond to *en pás*, "in everything."

EXPOSITION

If, as should be the case, the believer is always in agreement with God's will (the quality of joy as complacency with God's will in any circumstance), then the believer should not experience anxiety when confronted with the circumstances of the world.

The word translated "anxious" is *merimnáō*, "to be troubled, be anxious about" [Zodhiates, s. v. "3309"]. Anxiety is "mental distress or uneasiness because of fear of danger or misfortune" [Dictionary.com, s. v. "anxious"]. The word translated "not even one," is *mḗ*, the conditional negative [Zodhiates, s. v. "3361"], (as opposed to *ou*, the absolute negative). Paul says anxiety may happen as one encounters the circumstances of the world, but the believer is to overcome anxiety through being satisfied and compliant with the Lord's will, whatever the outward circumstances might be.

Instead of anxiety, commit yourself to prayer, petition, and thanksgiving. The interaction between "prayer" and "petition" indicates "prayer" in this verse is not the activity of "asking" one normally associates with the word "prayer." The word translated "prayer" is *proseuchḗ*, prayer, or metonymically the place of prayer [Zodhiates, s. v. "4335"]. The words, "petition on behalf of yourself and others," are a translation of *déēsis*, "to make known a particular need, especially for oneself" [Zodhiates, s. v. "1162"]. Inherent in the word *déēsis* is the act known as "intercession" for others.

Paul advises both *proseuchḗ* and *déēsis*, "prayer and petition," on behalf of yourself and others. We may look at this in two ways. One way is, *proseuchḗ* is indicating the act of prayer in general and *déēsis* is indicating the particular objects of prayer, oneself and others.

Or, one may understand the combined use of *proseuchḗ* and

déēsis as indicating *proseuchḗ* is being used in the sense of that act of worship in which the believer comes to God in submission and dependence, and *déēsis* indicates the requests one is making during the act of worship through prayer.

In interpreting, one must consider both context and vocabulary. Contextually, Paul has not left the theme of joy as willing submission to God's will, which is itself an act of worship. In regard to vocabulary, Paul might have used *proseúchomai*, the word for the act of praying [Zodhiates, s. v. "4336"], but instead he used *proseuchḗ*. Based on these two considerations, it seems to me Paul advises worship and petition (for oneself and others), in response to circumstances that might lead to anxiety.

Paul's advice, then, is to replace anxiety with submission to God and dependence upon God through worship. Then make your requests for assistance from God by supplication for oneself and intercession on behalf of others. An interpretive translation: "in everything through worship and by petition, on behalf of yourself and others, with thanksgiving, make your requests known to God."

"With thanksgiving." A comment by John Davenant (1572–1641) in his commentary on Colossians (at 2:7), comes to mind, (paraphrasing): True faith does not exist with ingratitude. Gratitude is justly required by God from his saved people in acknowledgment for his mercies [Davenant, 386–387]. The exhortation to give thanks to God occurs forty times in the Scripture. An act of thanksgiving to God is mentioned thirty-two times. Giving thanks to God is mentioned another seventy-five times. God does require his people worship him through the act of giving thanks. To give thanks is not a requirement to receive, but is an act of praise and worship to him who alone is able to answer our petitions.

When the believer is not anxious about even one thing or person, it is because he/she practices joy as an act of worship, and petitions God for needs, and gives praise to God in thanksgiving. The believer in active communion with God has God's peace in the world. The peace of God is like a calm lake without a ripple. The world throws the rocks of trouble and trial and persecution into lake, which disappear with nary a ripple to disturb the calm and peace—the lack of "mental distress or uneasiness because of fear of danger or misfortune"—that God gives his saved people.

Paul is not speaking of the peace that comes when the sinner is reconciled to God through salvation. He is speaking of that sense of calm and quiet that is undisturbed by the circumstances of the world. That kind of peace given by God "surpasses all understanding." Paul does not mean the peace God gives to his people cannot be understood. He means those who practice anxiety cannot understand God's peace.

The worldling believes it is impossible to be calm and quiet when your world is collapsing into ruin and destruction. The believer calmly waits for God to act on his or her behalf, by accepting the circumstances as God's will. He/she quietly approaches God in submission and dependence, giving praise, making petition, returning thanksgiving for blessings already received and about to be received. The circumstances may not be relieved, but the peace of God will prevail in the believer's soul throughout the evil times. Thereby the believer is guarded against the anxiety created by the world.

Exercising Godly Love

If there is any one biblical word as misunderstood by the Christian community as "love" I have yet to find it.

Godly, biblical, Christian love is not based in the sentiment—feelings, emotions, affections—also known as "love." Feelings, emotions, and affections can develop from the exercise of godly love, but are not required to exercise godly love.

What is godly love? Definition: the *agápē* kind of love, genuine biblical godly love, is a choice of the will to actively seek the best good for another person, without expectation of recompense, reciprocity, or recognition for one's self, and without consideration of merit or demerit in the one so loved.

This is the love God has for man and his saved people are to exercise toward others. This love is expressed in the covenant and salvific relationships God has with his saved people. This is the love that causes God's saved people to pay attention to and care for the spiritual and physical well-being of others, within and outside their faith community.

Genuine biblical godly love is not the sentiment, the affection, also known as love, which is based on having something in common with another person. The exercise of godly love does not require having anything in common. God has nothing in common with the unsaved sinner. God is kind because it is his nature to be kind. He seeks the best good for his creature man because it is his nature, his love, to seek the best good.

The exercise of godly love in doing good to others may or may not be accompanied by feelings of compassion or mercy. Godly love is not dependent on feelings. Although sentiment may develop during its exercise, godly love begins as a decision, not an emotional feeling, and does not require sentiment for its exercise. Godly love is the obligation to do right, as God defines what is right.

How do I know these things? 1 John 4:10, "In this is love, not that we have loved God, but that he loved us, and [because of this love] sent his Son, a propitiation concerning our sins." When God loved us, we were morally disgusting to God, an abomination, fit only for eternal punishment, automatically repugnant to God's holiness, separate and separated from God.

God loved us when we were unsaved sinners, when we had nothing in common with God whereby he might have affection toward us. He loved us by being good. He loved us by being merciful—delaying deserved justice, and reliving deserved misery. He loved us by taking action to bring us into a salvific relationship with himself in Christ.

God's love then, toward sinners, is threefold. One, God acts in goodness toward his creation, as the natural expression of his nature. That goodness keeps the earth spinning, the sun shining, the seasons arriving, and our material needs provided.

Second, God acted in love by sending Christ to propitiate God for all sins, 1 John 2:2; Romans 3:25. The infinite merit of that propitiation is sufficient for all. Three, God acts in love by bringing some sinners into a salvific relationship with himself through Jesus Christ, and by not preventing any sinner from coming to him through faith in Christ. Because just as his love is not based in sentiment, neither is his hate. Just as his love is a decision, not an emotion, so is his holiness, and his justice. That is good for us, because none are good enough apart from Christ to merit God's affections.

Those three actions, my friends—his goodness, his propitiation, and his election—are the decisions of God's will, not his affections. They are the exercise of godly love toward those who are unlovable, without merit.

The saved person has the affection of God because he/she is now by salvation, and through being conformed by the Holy Spirit, more and more like the person God truly loves, his Son. He has affection for his Son, for all who love the Son, and for all who are like the Son.

But for the unsaved sinner, God has no affection. God will separate himself from the unsaved sinner for eternity. As others have said, God casts the sinner into the lake of fire, not the sin.

The best good a Christian may do for a sinner—love!—is to tell them they are a sinner subject to God's wrath and Christ is able to save them from their sins and give them eternal life. There are many ways to make an opportunity to give that salvation message—food, shelter, medical aid, emotional comfort, other physical aid—many ways—and using those ways are a genuine expression of godly love, because it asks for nothing in return, and gives in the face of positive demerit.

Godly love is freely given even without giving a gospel message, through giving needed physical aid and comfort, because the one who loves has made a decision to help. The exercise of godly love is not more complicated than a decision. Am I to love my neighbor? My neighbor is the one who has a need and I have been given the means and opportunity to meet that need. Using the opportunity through the means to meet the need is love. In that we can be loving toward those who have no consciousness of their sins, no repentance for their sins, who despise God and his saved people, by giving the gospel and providing physical aid, that they might know God and his love.

But make no mistake. The Christian is not required to have affection for those who have no consciousness of their sins, no repentance for their sins, who despise God and his saved people. God doesn't. God seeks the best good of the unsaved sinner through the gospel and through his providence that provides material needs. That decision by God is godly love, the kind of love the Christian is to have toward the world.

Godly love does not overlook the unsaved sinner's sins; nor make excuses for their sins. Neither should the Christian. Godly love confronts the sinner with the accusation of his or her sins and the proclamation of the risen Christ the only Savior.

God always does what is right. The ethic of the Christian's exercise of godly love may be summed in the words, "Do right."

So when someone posts on social media, or speaks in a sermon, or a Bible study, or on TV, or whatever, that a Christian is to love the anarchists of the world currently trying to tear down freedom and laws and faith, we are indeed to love them, by telling them openly and truthfully that they are wrong, and with the same openness and truth telling them how to get right through the gospel. That is the true exercise of genuine godly love.

The exercise of godly love is a little different toward one's fellow believer's in Christ. An *agápē* kind of love means that one is willing to experience self-sacrifice for the benefit of the person loved. This love causes the believer to be long suffering toward a fellow believer, to treat him or her kindly, and actively seek the welfare of the one loved, the best good for his or her sake alone, without seeking any return for one's self, without jealousy or pride or vanity, bearing all things, believing all things, hoping all things, and enduring all things which achieve the goal of *agápē* toward the one loved. This love is to be pure, i.e., without ulterior motive, and in its application it is to be earnest, constant, and fervent. Only this love will hold the Christian community together in the face of persecution.

Interpreting the Symbolic

Understanding when a word in Scripture is to be understood literally or as symbol or illustration can be difficult (for which see Virkler, *Hermeneutics*). Interpreting those symbols and illustrations is easier, but does require a bit of imagination and a lot of common sense. Habakkuk (my latest writing project) provides some good examples.

TRANSLATION Habakkuk 1:7–8, "Awesome and fearful he is—his justice and dignity proceed from himself. 8 And his horses—swifter than leopards, sharper than wolves of the night. And their horsemen spring about, and their horsemen come from afar. They fly as the vulture that hastens to eat.

EXPOSITION

The Chaldeans were not, "awesome and fearful," in a good sense, as is God. The meaning of 1:7 may be summed in single modern word: arrogance. The Bible's negative view of "pride" sets the reader's expectations. The Babylonians were prideful and arrogant because of overwhelming confidence in themselves. They were, they believed, destined to be the rightful rulers of the world. They were the arbiters of justice and dignity. All others would bow to their power, authority, and laws.

The Babylonians did have the military power to enforce their will, and from their power they believed they had the authority. They believed their gods had given them the world. But YHWH was the one who had given them temporary authority and the power to use that authority. YHWH gives as he sees fit, to accomplish his plans and purpose, and YHWH takes away, as he sees fit, to accomplish his plans and purpose.

The military strength of the Babylonians is exampled in their calvary. Horses and horsemen are used here in a metonymy for all their military might. Their horses are powerful, 1:8, through the comparison with leopards. The ancient Semitic world knew of leopards, but not cheetahs, so the leopard is used as the example of speed for the purpose of violence. The leopard quickly runs down his prey, captures it, and does with it as he wants. So too the Babylonians would quickly accomplish both their and YHWH's objectives.

The environs of the ancient Middle East were home to wild animals not present today. For example, lions, mentioned from the times of Jacob (Genesis 49:9) and Samson (Judges 14:5), were still present in the times of Habakkuk and Daniel (Daniel 6:16). Isaiah 11:6, and his contemporary Hosea 5:14, speak of leopards, as does Habakkuk's contemporaries, Jeremiah 5:6; 13:23; Daniel 7:6. The missionary William Thomson speaks of leopards living in the Middle East, ca. 1855–1880 [Thomson, *Land and Book*, 1:224; 2:305, 441, 450, 591, 594, 603].

"Sharper than wolves of the night." The word "sharper" is usually translated "fierce," but the Hebrew word is *hādad*, "be sharp, keen" [Harris, s. v. "605"]. The translation "sharpness" brings with it the idea of injury from the sharp teeth and claws of the wolf. The word "night," *'ereb* [Harris, s. v. "1689b"] means "evening, night." The setting of the sun brings its own fears because the dangers of the world have become hidden under darkness, from which they may strike without warning. There is no defense against the wolf attacking in the darkness. Even so there would be no defense against the Babylonians.

As noted above, the word "horsemen" is used, like the word "horses," as a metonymy for military might. The words "spring about" indicate the energy and activity of that army in conquering all foes. The Babylonians were determined to conquer and rule what they understood as the known world. The reasons were both pride and economic. Conquered territories paid tribute (taxes) to the Empire, and bowed under the rule of the current King. That they "come from afar" means great distance is not safety.

The final metaphor is, "they fly as the vulture that hastens to eat." We cannot apply what we know of winged carrion eaters today (vultures, eagles, other birds), to what Habakkuk said over 2,600 years ago.

The bible speaks observationally, phenomenally. People observed the carrion eater hastening across the sky to its meal. Nor should we interpret the illustration beyond the one point it was intended to make. The point is the speed at which the Babylonians were moving as they conquered Mesopotamia. Just as distance was not safety, so also time was not safety. God's judgment against unrighteous Israel was coming and no one and nothing could hinder or stop it.

Selecting A Local Church

Recently, my wife said she would like to visit a church in our home town (we currently attend a church in another town, where we used to live). My first question was, "What are their doctrines?"

This particular local church is affiliated with SBC, but that really doesn't matter pro or con. Attending (over the past 46+ years) thirteen churches in five denominations in two countries has taught me affiliation is only one indicator of soundness, and not the most critical. Church affiliations, and associations, and national conventions are like a pair of worn-out old shoes you keep long past their usefulness, because they still feel comfortable. A local church should be evaluated on its own merits: their doctrine, their practice, their preaching and teaching programs.

In decades past I would have attended one Sunday or Wednesday and asked for a copy of the church's doctrinal statement. But the Internet makes this necessary task much easier; at least it should.

So, I went to the church's web site. Sadly, this church has followed the disturbing trend of not revealing its doctrine. I've heard all the reasons. They are all worldly marketing solutions to attract visitors. None are biblical. Truth does not hide its light, and neither do those who are of the light. But the world constantly intrudes into the church.

There was a generic "Core Values" tab at the home page, which was all practice, not doctrine, that almost any local church claiming to be baptistic in nature might have posted. Not very useful. "Baptist" these days is a big tent that encompasses every thing from biblical to heretical.

So I sent the pastor an email, with a statement of the Core Values that guide our Christian lives (a bit more detailed than their generic statement), and the doctrines we believe, a comprehensive and detailed statement, with Scripture. I asked if our core values and doctrine would be compatible with the local church he leads. That was yesterday afternoon. Now awaiting a reply. (Update: never received a reply.)

Friends, Do Not select a local church without knowing their doctrine. It does not really matter how wonderful their programs seem to be. Biblical worship, fellowship, service, obedience, and unity always, always, always emerges based on doctrine and practice, never vice versa. If the doctrine is not right, the practice is not right. Be discerning, ask, walk away if they won't tell.

Are Statues Idolatry?

I just had someone ask me if statues of religious figures are idols. Thought I would share my answer.

There are two biblical principles to consider. The first is the principle of worship. God is really very clear throughout the Bible that he alone is to receive worship. Looking specifically at the Ten commandments, God says in the first commandment, Exodus 20:3, "You shall have no other gods before me." The second commandment, Exodus 20:4, 5, develops from the first. "You shall not make for yourself a carved image . . . you shall not bow down to them or serve them."

From these two precepts—worship only God; do not make a representation of God or any god(s)—we can derive several principles. Worship God only. Do not worship God through any kind of representation: statue, painting, drawing, photograph, etc.

We can also derive this principle: a representation of a person or thing does not break the commandment if that representation is not being worshiped or worship is not occurring through that representation. For example, a statue of Jesus, or Buddha, or Mary of Nazareth. But the problem is, people do worship, or worship through, statutes and other representations.

A statue is only a piece of art, *if there is no worship to it or through it*. For example, Siddhartha Gautama, who became known as "the Buddha," is dead. He was and remains just a human being. It is wrong people use a statue Buddha for worship, but without worship it is just a statue. The same is true for Mary of Nazareth, or Paul the apostle, or Moses. It there is no worship to it or through it, then it is just a person someone is trying to honor with a statue or painting or drawing. A statue or painting or drawing of Jesus, or any religious figure, can just be a way of honoring that person.

Paul deals with this issue of worship to or through things. This involves the second biblical principle: do not do something you believe God has said is wrong. This brings us to Romans 14; 1 Corinthians 8. Paul was discussing what had become a critical issue for first century believers. The question was, should a believer eat meat that had been sacrificed to idols?

A little historical background is necessary. Much of the meat sold in the butcher shop had first been offered in a gentile temple to one of the gentile gods. After the sacrifice and offering, a butcher shop bought the meat from the temple and sold the meat in the market place. Undoubtedly some gentiles believed that meat offered to an idol was more blessed than other meat. The believed that because they believed the idol represented one of their gods.

Some Christians believed it was wrong to eat meat that had been offered to an idol. Other Christians said it was alright, because an idol is nothing. Paul said in 1 Corinthians 8:4 (ESV), "Therefore, as to the eating of food offered to idols, we know an idol has no real existence, and that there is no God but one."

But Paul also recognized some believers did not think that way. Of those believers Paul said, 1 Corinthians 8:7 (ESV), "not all possess this knowledge [idols are nothing, 8:4]. But some, through former association with idols, eat food as really offered to an idol, and their conscience, being weak, is defiled."

Paul's conclusion was this: it was okay to eat meat offered to idols, but don't eat if it would make your bother in the Lord stumble in his or her faith.

> 1 Corinthians 8:9–13 (ESV), "But take care that this right of yours does not somehow become a stumbling block to the weak. For if anyone sees you who have knowledge eating in an idol's temple, will he not be encouraged, if his conscience is weak, to eat food offered to idols? And so by your knowledge this weak person is destroyed, the brother for whom Christ died. Thus, sinning against your brothers and wounding their conscience when it is weak, you sin against Christ. Therefore, if food makes my brother stumble, I will never eat meat, lest I make my brother stumble."

When discussing this same issue a year or so later in his letter to Rome, Paul repeated what he has said to the Corinthians. Romans 14:21 (ESV), "It is good not to eat meat or drink wine or do anything that causes your brother to stumble," a summary of 14:14–20. And then Paul added something that applies to this "are statues idols" issue.

> Romans 14:22–23 (ESV), "The faith that you have, keep between yourself and God. Blessed is the one who has no reason to pass judgment on himself for what he approves. 23 But whoever has doubts is condemned if he eats, because the eating is not from faith. For whatever does not proceed from faith is sin."

What Paul says in 14:23 directly applies to the statue question. If we believe God has forbidden a thing—whether it is right or wrong in itself—and we do that thing, then by doing it we are questioning God's authority; and rebellion is sin.

I know in myself that a statue of a religious figure is nothing; it is a mere work of art. I don't have one in my house because others I know would be spiritually offended if they saw it in my house. I have a reputation as a Bible scholar and committed believer. I do have small statues of animals in my house, because I appreciate those representations as artistic.

So the biblical response is this: 1) will other believers be spiritually offended by viewing art incorporating a religious figure—what is your reputation as a believer? And 2), what do you believe about statues—is the representation of a religious figure idolatry, or is it nothing, a mere work of art, as long as there is no worship going on?

"It is biblical to use a representation of a religious figure as a piece of art." Answer. Yes, no problem, as long as no believer would be spiritually offended by it and their faith made weak, and as long as there is no worship directed to it or through it, and as long as it does not violate what you believe God has said about such representations.

The Problem of evil, or "Why does God allow evil?"

The reason God allows evil is found in the creation of humankind. When God created Adam, he designed humankind to possess and use the moral authority to make choices; what most identify as "free will." Evil exists because of free will. Human beings are not pre-programmed soulless automatons, but are free agents responsible for their choices.

God has respect for what he created. God allows human beings to exercise their free will, even when that use results in wrong choices. God is a just God who has told humankind the right choices and warns against the wrong choices. He has given humankind moral standards so right and wrong may be discerned. God rewards the right, warns against the wrong, and punishes the wrong. Evil exists because human beings are sinners freely making wrong choices.

Without the authority to make choices, there would not be accountability for those choices. If no accountability, they no responsibility and no liability. Without accountability and responsibility there is not just liability to punishment. Human beings are liable to punishment for their wrong choices. Therefore human beings are responsible and accountable to God for their choices, indicating God gave them the moral authority to make choices: free will.

Could God stop all wrong choices? Of course. Let's begin with you. What, you don't need God to stop you from making choices, you just want God to prevent others from making wrong choices? But there are none good, Romans 3:12; Psalm 14:1, and that includes you. God gives you and every other human being the moral authority and responsibility to make right choices. That moral authority must include the possibility of wrong choices, otherwise it is not free will.

So, what is free will? Free will, or freely made choices, is the moral authority to make choices within the physical, moral, and spiritual boundaries of human nature, as further influenced by internal and external motivations and consequences.

A few examples. I put my five year old grandson into my backyard and he can do whatever he wants to do, in the back yard. He cannot leave the yard to wander off down the street after the ice cream truck. A person might choose to flap his arms and fly to the grocery store. The physical boundary of human nature permits flapping one's arms, but not flying. A person might choose to tell the truth or lie. The moral boundary of human nature allows either choice. The sinner cannot choose to initiate saving faith because the spiritual boundary set by the sin attribute prevents that choice through its unceasing rebellion against God.

The will is not neutrally suspended between good and evil, but is inclined toward one or the other by the several attributes of human nature. In the case of unsaved human beings, the will is inclined toward sin because of the principle of evil, the sin attribute, that became part of human nature following Adam's sin and propagation. Free choice or freely made choices means choices made within the context of the will as circumscribed by the nature of the sentient being—whether human, holy angel, or fallen angel—making the choice.

The boundaries of human nature are its attributes as created by God, corrupted by sin, and in the case of the saved, regenerated by salvation. The inclination of sinner is to rebel against God and disobey his commandments, thereby effectively persuading human beings to choose their path in life apart from God. In the case of the unsaved, free will means choices made within the context of the will as circumscribed by their sinful human nature. The unsaved human being is unable to overcome the influence of the sin attribute without God's gift of grace-faith-salvation.

Sin is an attribute of fallen human nature, a principle or attribute of evil that motivates human beings to rebel against God, disobey his commandments, and seek a path in life apart from God. Sin has authority (dominion, rule) over the sinner, not as some invincible overlord, but as an innate part of human nature constructively working with all the other attributes of human nature to persuasively incline the will to choose an act of sinning. The evil attribute sin influences every other attribute with the inclination to sin, and in that sense sin can be said to dominate the will. The sinner freely chooses sinning because his will is of itself always inclined to choose sinning, and as being rebellious and disobedient toward God never desires to change its inclination to choose sinning to rebel against God, disobey his commandments, and seek a path in life apart from God.

Free will, like liberty or freedom, isn't a license to think or do anything I want. Free will is the capability to make decisions within the boundaries of the attributes and characteristics of human nature. Its source is the moral authority God gave human beings when he designed human nature. Its limits are the physical, mental, and moral attributes of the person. The sinner freely chooses to sin; the believer freely chooses to deny temptation. Both are decisions made within the limits imposed by the human nature of sinner or saint. Both are responsible to make right choices, which responsibility means both are accountable and liable for the choices they do make.

The sinner freely chooses to sin. His/her choice is conditioned by the moral and spiritual boundaries set by the sin attribute in his or her human nature. Without that freely made choice there is no responsibility, accountability, or liability. When we deny that free exercise of the will, we have denied God made humankind with the power to choose, the moral authority to exercise choice, the responsibility to choose rightly, and the accountability and liability for every freely made choice. When we deny the free exercise of will, we have proclaimed God made human beings soulless automatons that merely dance on the strings of some master puppeteer.

The sinner freely chooses to sin. The believer freely chooses to deny temptation. Both are decisions made within the limits imposed by the boundaries of the human nature of sinner or saint. Only God is able to overcome the sin attribute and turn a sinner into saved, and conform the saved to the likeness of Christ.

God allows evil because he has respect for the free will he created, thereby allowing all his sentient creatures, human and angel, to exercise that faculty. There will be a day of accounting for every human being for the choices he/she has made.

The Problem of Suffering

Why does God not take action—why is God silent—when the wicked practice their wickedness and swallow the righteous (Habakkuk 1:13)? This question has been echoed by the righteous in every age. The most basic answers are: to glorify God; to be purged from indwelling sin and love of the world; to be purged of independence from God; to testify of the grace and salvation of God.

Why believers suffer.

> Because life happens. The physical and moral laws of the universe are not suspended for the believer.

> Because of circumstances. Believers suffer when the world they are in suffers. God makes his rain, fires, floods, and storms to fall on the just as well as the unjust. Believers endure and suffer with an attitude of joy whatever God brings upon the world.

> Because of the world. This is by two means. One, by sin in the world sowing its seed and reaping its fruit. God allows sin to have its painful effect both as to punishment and natural consequences and as a goad to seek salvation in him alone. Secondly, believers suffer from sinners directly attacking the believer for his or her faith.

> To wean believers from the world. Whether one is newly saved or a maturing believer, the flesh is part of this world and struggles to remain at home in the world. The new believer must learn, grow, and mature in his or her faith to deny the world and the flesh. Misery in the world reveals to the believer this world is not home and has nothing to offer the godly soul.

> To wean believers from their flesh. The nature of sin is rebellion against God: a selfish, self-centered independence. When faced with doubts and decisions, the first instinct, an instinct generated by the corruption of sin, is to rely upon self and not God. One sees the opposite in the mature believer. He/she will always turn to God for guidance, approval, and power. Misery in the world teaches the believer to live according to God's values, by God's spiritual empowerment.

> To increase reliance and dependence on God. One effect of a trial is to replace dependence on the world and the flesh with

dependence on God. This is how Jesus lived, with complete dependence and reliance upon God for all things in his life, including trials. This is how every believer should live.

To glorify God. Although believers suffer in common with the world, it is how they suffer, endure, and overcome that glorifies God. When the believer turns to God for guidance, approval, and power in times of trouble, he is not acting like the world; and, therefore, the weak human vessel is filled with the strength of God manifesting his glory to all creatures.

To draw sinners to saving faith. If in the suffering a believer glorifies God, then in that suffering the Holy Spirit may use the believer to testify to the lost about the salvation found only through faith in God and God's testimony.

Believers suffer that they may not be condemned with the world. God addresses acts of sin committed by the believer in this life because for the believer there is no sin, guilt of sin, or punishment for sin in the next life. Here and now believers are plagued by an indwelling sin nature, they do suffer defeat by its temptations and do commit acts of sin. God cannot have fellowship with sin. He chastises and cleanses the believer from acts of sin so that fellowship may remain.

Believers suffer in order that unrepentant sinners may receive the greater punishment. This may be difficult to accept, but those who reject salvation continue in sin and reap to themselves judgment. Job 21:30, "For the wicked are reserved for the day of doom; they shall be brought out on the day of wrath." God is just in that the unrighteous, having chosen their lot in this present world, find their fulfillment in this world and have no place in the world to come.

God uses the problems believers encounter in the world. Through them the believer may evaluate his or her faith; make a course-correction in one's manner of living; turn further away from sin; or act to mature one's faith. The believer should count it all joy that he or she is being weaned from the world and made fit for heavenly things.

Two Questions

My wife's book (a small group Bible study), titled, *What Does it Mean to Be Counted Worthy* (by Linda Marie Quiggle), asks many pertinent, soul searching questions. These are two of those questions, and my response. Your response may differ.

"Does it get easier to let God mold you as time passes and you mature?"

> Yes. That is the natural consequence of maturity. The process of maturing is more difficult for a time because that is part of the maturation process—we kick against the goads, then submit to the requirements. We begin small and grow tall. As one matures the habits of righteousness also mature. As time goes by, as more and more of you fits into God's mold (the likeness of Christ), God has a little less work to do to mold you into the likeness of Christ.

"Is God asking more of you now than He was 1 year, 5 years, 10 years ago?"

> When one is small, his or her reach is short. As one grows tall, one's reach lengthens. As our reach—our perception and understanding—increases, it seems as if God is asking more of us. But what has happened is we are recognizes more of what God has been asking of us from the beginning. As our perception of all God asks increases, the resulting maturity slowly encompasses all God asks, and that maturity makes us better able to do all God requires.

God does not ask us to attain to more than we are capable of doing, he makes us able to do all that he asks. With Augustine [Schaff, *NPNF* 1:153; *Confessions*, 10.29.40] we understand God gives to us what he commands of us. While God always requires us to do all that he asks, God understands his saved people are creatures of time and circumstances. As we walk along our life path, God prepares us in the present step to be able to do that which is required in the next step. Ephesians 2:10, he has prepared beforehand works for us to do. And if the works are prepared for us beforehand, we may have complete confidence God will always prepare us before we reach a work he has prepared beforehand. We are always being prepared, and thereby are always being made able to accomplish what God requires of us, as we live our life through our times and circumstances.

In response to the question, "Is God asking more of you now than He was," from the perspective of our time-bound existence, it seems as if God is asking more of us as we mature. What is happening is as our reach increases, we are able to grasp, and do, more of what God has always required of us.

What God asks of his saved people neither increases nor diminishes. Believers are always supposed to live according to God's moral values, principles, and precepts. As we spiritually mature, we become more aware of those values, principles, and precepts, and begin to live by them. God's requirements haven't changed, the believer has changed. Believers are always supposed to persevere in the faith by faith. Believers are always supposed to positively respond to duty and responsibility. Believers are always supposed to do the works God has prepared beforehand. The way in which these things work out during our lifetime change with increasing maturity, ever-changing circumstances, and the diverse opportunities for service provided by the Holy Spirit.

What is your response?

Worship in the Midst of Suffering

At Habakkuk 3:2, the prophet wrote, "YHWH I have heard your report. I worship." That simple declaration, I worship, is meaningful within his current circumstances.

Habakkuk wrote in the early years of the Babylonian Empire. The Babylonians had ended the Assyrian Empire and chased Egypt out of the Middle East, ca. 605 BC. They had put Jerusalem under tribute and deported the best of its citizens (Daniel 1:1–4). About twenty years later, 587/586 BC, Jerusalem rebelled, again, and the Babylonians destroyed Jerusalem, razed the temple, and deported more Hebrews to Babylon. It is in the midst of those last events that Habakkuk wrote, "I worship."

Habakkuk had first complained, about 609 BC, to YHWH about the unrighteous in Israel, 1:2–4. When was YHWH going to exact justice upon the unrighteous. YHWH had responded, he would bring the Babylonians (Chaldeans) to punish the unrighteous, 1:5–11. That had happened ca. 605 BC.

Time passes, about twenty years. Habakkuk complains again, 1:12–2:1. When would YHWH exact justice upon the Babylonians? YHWH answered, 2:2–20. Habakkuk's second compliant, and YHWH's answer, was most likely as Habakkuk and others were forcibly marched to Babylon after the destruction of Jerusalem. The righteous were suffering because the unrighteous had been punished. When would YHWH act?

After YHWH reveals he will punish the Babylonians, Habakkuk says, "I worship." We can easily understand Habakkuk worships because the nation that just destroyed his nation will be punished. But we miss something if we fail to understand Habakkuk's, "I worship," was as he was forcibly marched to Babylon city. We miss something valuable and magnificent if we fail to see that in the midst of the destruction of his homeland and the captivity of his people Habakkuk says, "I worship." We miss something if we fail to understand the righteous suffer when the unrighteous are punished. We miss a valuable lesson if we fail to understand the righteous worship in the midst of their suffering.

The history of God's saved people throughout the ages is plain. When God punishes the unrighteous, his saved people living among the unrighteous also suffer from the punishment inflicted on the unrighteous. What is important is God is not punishing the righteous, and will sustain the righteous throughout their troubles. The rain falls on the just and unjust. The same sunshine that ripens the fruit of the just also ripens the fruit of the unjust. The floods that destroy the fields of the unjust also flood the fields of the just. The unrighteous are punished; the righteous endure through the circumstances.

The righteous do not always suffer directly. Noah and his family did not suffer the flood, but rather its consequences, for which, and in which, God amply provided for their safety and needs. Many in Israel did not suffer the destruction of Jerusalem and razing of the temple, because they had already been deported to Babylon. The New Testament church will not suffer the Tribulation (a pretribulation rapture). Those saved during the Tribulation will endure the consequences of God's judgment against the earth-dwellers, the unsaved, but God will bless and provide for them, as he always does for his people in times of trouble. They will be made able to persevere, through life and a martyr's death.

What makes the difference between the righteous and unrighteous in difficult circumstances is their attitude and God's abiding providence working for the good of his saved people. The righteous trust and worship; the unrighteous complain and sin. God always has a purpose in allowing his saved people to suffer. (I addressed reasons for suffering in a previous essay, "The Problem of Suffering").

God works in ways we sometimes fail to comprehend. When God sent his people Israel into captivity—both the righteous and the unrighteous—it was a blessing that burdened the unsaved, but protected YHWH's saved people. The economy of Israel was devastated, Jerusalem destroyed, their temple razed, the land occupied by gentiles. God gave the land, and his saved people, a rest.

> 2 Chronicles 36:20–21 (HCSB), Those who escaped from the sword he deported to Babylon, and they became servants to him and his sons until the rise of the Persian kingdom. This fulfilled the word of the Lord through Jeremiah [25:11] and the land enjoyed its Sabbath rest all the days of the desolation until 70 years were fulfilled.

In the Mosaic Law, the land was to lie fallow every seven years, Leviticus 25:2–7, a Sabbath rest. Israel had failed to follow that requirement of the law, thereby incurring the penalty.

> Leviticus 26:24, 32–35, (NKJV), "And after all this, if you do not obey me . . . I will bring the land to desolation, and your

enemies who dwell in it shall be astonished at it. I will scatter you among the nations and draw out a sword after you; your land shall be desolate and your cities waste. Then the land shall enjoy its sabbaths as long as it lies desolate and you are in your enemies' land; then the land shall rest and enjoy its sabbaths. As long as it lies desolate it shall rest— for the time it did not rest on your sabbaths when you dwelt in it."

God provided for his righteous ones in their captivity.

Jeremiah 29:4–7 (ESV), "Thus says the Lord of hosts, the God of Israel, to all the exiles whom I have sent into exile from Jerusalem to Babylon: Build houses and live in them; plant gardens and eat their produce. Take wives and have sons and daughters; take wives for your sons, and give your daughters in marriage, that they may bear sons and daughters; multiply there, and do not decrease. But seek the welfare of the city where I have sent you into exile, and pray to the Lord on its behalf, for in its welfare you will find your welfare."

Although the righteous endured suffering when the unrighteous majority were punished, God provided for his saved people in, by, and through their captivity.

God also gave them hope. Jeremiah 25:10 expressed that hope directly. "For thus says the Lord: After seventy years are completed at Babylon, I will visit you and perform My good word toward you, and cause you to return to this place" (NKJV).

Habakkuk expresses that hope in this manner: "YHWH, revive your work in the midst of the years." YHWH's work is his covenant relationship with his saved people. When the covenant was broken, its penalty provisions were activated. When the penalty was completed, its blessing provisions were activated. Habakkuk knew, and therefore prayed for, the restoration of Israel per the Mosaic covenant; and if he knew Jeremiah's prophesies, then he also prayed per God's promises through Jeremiah.

Thus, Habakkuk also prays, "in wrath remember mercy." Difficult times lay ahead. Mercy was needed. Mercy has two aspects. One is the delay of deserved justice. That time had passed for Israel. God delays justice to give his people time for repentance. God delays justice to bring salvation to sinners.

The second aspect of mercy is relieving misery. This is what Habakkuk prays for from YHWH. In the midst of their deserved punishment, please act to relieve the misery experienced by your people Israel. This aspect is expressed at Jeremiah 29:4–7. In the context of the preceding sentence, the relief of misery must also include the fulfillment of the promised restoration of the people to the land. That is Jeremiah 25:10.

God never forgets his saved people. They should never forget him. In the midst of suffering, persecution, troubles, and what often seems like unfair and unjust treatment, be like Habakkuk: "I worship."

(Adapted from my book, *A Private Commentary on the Bible: Habakkuk*, Amazon/KDP, 2019.)

Why is KJV-Only bigotry?

KJV-Only doctrine says God only works through the KJV to save sinners. That doctrine denies the possibility of salvation to those who don't speak or understand KJV English. That is heresy against God and bigotry against those not using the KJV.

KJV-Only doctrine says God only works through a translation into another language that has been made from the KJV English translation. That doctrine denies the possibility of salvation to those not using such a translation. That is heresy against God and bigotry against those not using the KJV.

KJV-Only doctrine says a certain group of ancient biblical texts copied from the originals (the autographs), popularly known as the Textus Receptus, that those copies were inspired by God and thereby preserved the autographs without error.

Therefore, says KJV-Only doctrine, any translation made from any other biblical text but the Textus Receptus is not an inspired Bible. That is false doctrine, because not supported by any biblical text, including the Textus Receptus. That is bigotry against those using a translation not made from the Textus Receptus.

Setting aside the ridiculous arguments of the KJV-Only movement—which I have studied in depth and read their leading proponents (a tiresome task)—it is blasphemy to say God cannot work through *any* Bible translation to save sinners and teach his people to live righteous lives.

That is why KJV-Only is heresy, and bigotry. And KJV-Only is blasphemy, for it slanders God by limiting his sovereign authority to accomplish his will as seems best to him.

I don't care what version or translation or language in which you read and study the Bible. God has the sovereign authority to work his will through even the worst translations. But take care you do not exclude a Bible version or translation or language in which God has given his Bible to others to read and study. Not because of me, but because God will hold you accountable.

The KJV-Only Cult-Like Devotion

KJV-Only is a cult, or more accurately, cult-like. When I say a "cult" I am not using the word in its technical sense, but of the cult-like devotion KJV-Only has toward this one translation. If the KJV were a person, its members would truly be in a cult.

Still, if we consider the KJV translation as their leader the group has many characteristics of a cult:

> The group displays excessively zealous and unquestioning commitment to its leader, in this case, the KJV translation.

> Questioning, doubt, and dissent are discouraged or even punished

> The group claims a special, exalted status for its leader, the KJV.

> The group has a polarized, us-versus-them mentality, which may cause conflict with others not of the same belief.

> The leader, the KJV translation, is not held accountable to any authorities.

> The group teaches or implies that its supposedly exalted ends justify whatever means it deems necessary to maintain its beliefs.

> Subservience to the leader.

> The group is preoccupied with bringing in new members.

> Members are encouraged or required to live and/or socialize only with other group members.

> The most loyal members (the "true believers") feel there can be no life outside the context of the group.

Not technically a cult, but certainly cult-like devotion.

A Question From A KJV-Only

I shared the essay on the cult-like devotion of the KJV-Only on my Facebook pages, which generated a lot more heat than light from KJV-Only devotees. But I did finally receive a reasonable question from one of the KJV-Only followers.

Question "Can you show a copy of an inerrant bible that you believe?"

Before answering, a little background. The foundation for my answer is about 500 years of investigation into the thousands of OT plus NT manuscripts (copies) of the autographs (the original writing from the hand of the Bible writer). A science developed over those centuries, the science of textual criticism, with well-defined rules, worked out from vast experience in examining the manuscripts and identifying typical scribal errors: misspelling, word order, a word left out, added, or repeated, and that occasional scribe who imported a verse form one place into another.

Errors in a manuscript are called "variants." Though the centuries of manuscript comparison about 400,000 variants have been discovered. That sounds like a lot, but when you consider a variant is often an alphabet character—a mis5pelled word—it if not much at all. There are 183 characters in that last sentence. One word is misspelled, a .5% error.

Of the 400,000 variants (mostly spelling and word order), only 1% are important: 400. Of those 400 variants, only 50 are important to the meaning of a sentence, and none of those 50 affect any doctrine.

Here is my answer to the question, "Can you show a copy of an inerrant bible that you believe?"

Only the autographs of Scripture were inspired and inerrant. Copies and translations of God's Word are not inspired or inerrant.

God has protected the copies and translations of his Word in such a manner that in every practical way the Scripture we have today is sufficient as the guide and rule of personal faith and practice.

By comparing the thousands of manuscript copies with one another, we see the autographs were so preserved in the copies by God's providence as to accurately reflect the autograph. Comparison of over ten thousand New Testament manuscripts through the science of textual criticism has allowed the original text to be reconstructed to what is believed to be more than 99 percent accuracy.

"The vast majority of variant readings concern grammatical details that do not significantly affect the meaning of the text" [Henry A.

Virkler and Karelynne Gerber Ayayo, "Hermeneutics: Principles and Processes of Biblical Interpretation" (2nd ed. Grand Rapids, MI: Baker Academic, 2007), 35].

"The variant readings about which any doubt remains among textual critics of the New Testament affect no material question of historic fact or of Christian faith and practice" [F. F. Bruce, "The New Testament Documents, Are They Reliable" (1943. 5th ed. Grand Rapids, MI: William B. Eerdmans Publishing Company, 1960), 19–20].

God preserved his word such that copies descended from the autographs are sufficient as the rule and guide of faith and practice. In every respect the Bible Christians possess today is an authentic, accurate, and credible reproduction of the autographs.

[Copyright 2021, James D. Quiggle, "Thirty-Six Essentials of the Christian Faith," a manuscript in progress at the time of this writing, February 2021.]

Is the Unsaved Sinner's Free Will Dead?

If Free Will is dead, as some propose, then it is not enslaved, because slaves respond to commands, they are not dead. Or, if Free Will is a slave without choice, as other propose, then God unjustly holds all sinners accountable for their sins. For if the will is a slave, then the choice to sin is made by another and forced on the slave.

The biblical fact is humankind was created with the moral authority to choose. "Free Will is the moral authority to make choices within the physical, moral, and spiritual boundaries of human nature." That moral authority, Free Will, remains today, reprioritized by Adam's act of sinning to serve self, not God.

Setting aside various proofs for the freely made choices (examine your day, they are obvious), and the physical and moral limitations to choice (also obvious), and looking only at the unsaved person, his/her spiritual choices are made within the boundary set by the sin attribute in human nature. That boundary is continuous, unrelenting rebellion against God and his commandments.

Sin has authority (dominion, rule) over the sinner, not as some invincible overlord, but as an innate part of human nature constructively working with all the other attributes of human nature to persuasively incline the will to choose an act of sinning. The evil attribute sin influences every other attribute with the inclination to sin, and in that sense sin can be said to dominate the will. The sinner freely chooses sinning because his will is of itself always inclined to choose sinning, and as being rebellious and disobedient toward God never desires to change its inclination to choose sinning to rebel against God, disobey his commandments, and seek a path in life apart from God.

Therefore the unsaved sinner always freely chooses to rebel against God and disobey his commandments. Because his/her choices to sin are the freely made expression of his/her nature, God justly holds the unsaved sinner accountable, responsible, and liable for his/her choices to commit acts of sinning. God justly punishes the sinner for his or her sin.

The effect of the sin attribute in relation to salvation is the unsaved sinner is unwilling and unable to initiate saving faith. That action is outside the spiritual boundary of his unsaved human nature, a boundary set by the sin attribute. God must give his gift of grace-faith-salvation (Eph. 2:8) to effect a change in the unsaved sinner's nature and thereby initiate saving faith in the sinner. An unsaved sinner who receives God's gift will (in every case) respond by freely choosing to exercise saving faith. God gives his gift (Ephesians 2:8), according to his decree of election (Ephesians 1:4), to apply the merit of Christ's propitiation (1 John 2:2; Romans 3:25), to the unsaved sinner's spiritual need.

Free will is not the license to do whatever you may want to do. A simple example using the limits of your physical nature. You may try to choose to flap your arms and fly, but the physical limits of your human nature will only allow the choice to flap your arms. Every freely made choice responds to the limits of the physical, moral, and spiritual aspects of human nature. All choices made within those limits are freely made choices. So as you stand there furiously flapping your arms up and down in an attempt to fly, don't lie to yourself and deny either your free will, or that free will always come with limits.

Free will is a biblical doctrine. The choices of the unsaved will are limited by the sin attribute, requiring God's gift of grace-faith-salvation in order to be saved.

Don't Do *Porneía*

First Thessalonians 4:3-5a. 3 For this is the will of God, your sanctification: you are to abstain from sexual immorality. 4 Each of you is to know how to control his or her sexuality in holiness and honor, 5 not in the passion of lust . . . (my translation).

The word I have translated "sexual immorality" is *porneía*. Many think of this word only in terms of sexual intercourse outside the context of marriage—fornication. But when used literally the word means any kind of sexual immorality, not just sexual intercourse.

The Greek *porneía*, and the corresponding Hebrew *zānâ*, when used literally, mean any illicit sexual activity. (Illicit: not permitted for moral or ethical reasons.) The times and cultures and peoples (Hebrews and gentiles) within which the Bible was written possessed erotic literature, visual depictions of nudity and sexual activity, practiced sexual activity with minors, practiced homosexuality, practiced prostitution, and practiced heterosexuality outside the context of marriage. All these actions are comprehended under the Old Testament term *zānâ* and the New Testament term *porneía*.

The meaning has not changed with the advent of modern means of communication, production, and distribution of illicit sexual activity. Any kind of sexual attraction or sexual activity that occurs outside the context of biblical heterosexual marriage—whether in person, in print, or displayed for public view in any kind of media, electronic or otherwise, is sexual immorality. Sexual immorality is also the public display via any media of heterosexual sexual activities by married couples. Any kind of heterosexual sexual activity occurring within the context of marriage which is publicly displayed through various media is sexual immorality.

Illicit sexual activity is defined by the biblical view of marriage. Marriage is the union of one male with one female in a permanent, monogamous, heterosexual relationship joined together by an exclusive loyalty covenant that commits them to each other and none else.

In greater detail, marriage is an exclusive loyalty covenant between one man and one woman—what the Bible describes as a one-flesh relationship. The terms and conditions of the exclusive loyalty covenant require the man and woman commit their physical, emotional, and spiritual being to the benefit and enjoyment of one another and none else. The marriage covenant does not exclude friendly relationships with others, but it does exclude commitments, especially sexual and emotional commitments, that are of the same order as those composing the marriage relationship.

In every culture that has ever existed or currently exists, marriage, including a biblical marriage, requires a suitable public declaration that, "we are married." In the Greco-Roman culture the apostle Paul lived in, marriage could be as simple as two people declaring to friends and family they wanted to be married [Cohick, 29, 102–103].

So a biblical marriage is accurately defined as,

> The union of one male with one female in a permanent, monogamous, heterosexual relationship joined together by an exclusive loyalty covenant that commits them to each other and none else, solemnized by a culturally suitable public declaration of that exclusive loyalty commitment.

Only a biblical marriage is moral and ethical marriage. Sexual activity is licit (morally and ethically acceptable) only in a biblical marriage.

Having sexual intercourse does not make a marriage. "Living together" is not a biblical marriage. A "common-law marriage" is a worldly legal default but it is not a biblical marriage. A civil marriage is, in the world's perspective, a relationship consisting of cohabitation and sexual intimacy between two persons that is legally recognized by civil authority as a marriage covenant—a definition that allows same-gender marriage, which disqualifies the civil definition of marriage from being biblical marriage.

Any kind of sexual activity—physical, visual, audio, audio-visual—that is not within the context of biblical marriage is *porneía*, no matter how acceptable to worldly culture, morality, and ethics. That includes a heterosexual marriage sharing its sexual activities with the world, or a few close friends. A Biblical marriage is between "one" male and "one" female, not many.

Christians are to abstain [not do] *porneía*, Acts 15:20, 29. The Christian's body is "not for *porneía*, 1 Corinthians 6:13. Christians are to run away from *porneía*, 1 Corinthians 6:18. Christians are to avoid *porneía*, 1 Corinthians 7:2. (I begin to see a pattern of required behavior.) Christians practicing *porneía* are to repent (stop) their *porneía*, 2 Corinthians 12:21. The event or practice of *porneía* is not to be named (is not to occur) among Christians, Ephesians 5:3. Christians are to put to death thoughts of *porneía*, Colossians 3:5. Christians are to abstain [not do] *porneía*, 1 Thessalonians 4:3.

If you are, about-to-be-but-are-not-yet, married, don't commit *porneía*. Marriage requires "a culturally suitable public declaration of the exclusive loyalty commitment."

If you are having casual sex, "hook-ups" for sex, or whatever the current slang might be, you are committing *porneía*. If you are dating and committing *porneía*, stop. If you are living together without marriage, stop. The power of human sexuality was designed by God to strengthen the marriage commitment. When misused sexual activity will create a false commitment, a false bond.

If you are committing *porneía*, stop. If you have a sexual addiction to *porneía*, seek help. This part of your life also needs to be conformed to Christ. As a believer, trust in Christ to give you the spiritual authority to say "No," and enforce that commitment. Seek the counsel and help that Christ makes available through others.

Malachi 3:8, Will a Man Rob God?

"Will man rob God? Yet you are robbing me. But you say, 'How have we robbed you?' In your tithes and contributions." (ESV)

How could a man rob God? YHWH was the owner of the land he gave to Israel, Leviticus 23:23. The Israelites were tenants on YHWH's land. Therefore Israel owed YHWH a tithe as rent for the land, Leviticus 27:30–33, "all the tithe of the land . . . is YHWH's." "Concerning the tithe of the herd or flock . . . shall be holy to YHWH." When the people of Israel did not tithe, then they retained for their own use something that belonged to God, which is robbery.

Often, too often, well-meaning Bible students impose on the New Testament church the requirement for a tithe, 10%, citing Malachi 3:8. It is tempting to say this is the most famous New Testament verse on tithing (although that honor may have to go to 3:10).

Let's look at Malachi 3:8. The first question of interpretation is always, "What is the context?" YHWH, the God of Israel is speaking to his covenant people Israel. YHWH states Israel has violated a provision of the Mosaic Covenant. Israel has failed to give God the tithes and contributions required by the Mosaic Law. So the next question is, what was a contribution and what was a tithe?

Oddly enough, those using this verse to support tithing never mention the "contributions" (but Paul does, as I will show later) This is the Hebrew word *teruma*. The word refers to various altar offerings, materials to maintain the building (Ex 25:2–3), the half-shekel atonement (Ex 30:13), etc. Any non-tithe religious offering. In the Book of Malachi, God said the people were not making sacrificial offerings, were not giving to maintain the physical property of the temple, and other required non-tithe giving, so they were robbing God of the *teruma*.

The "tithe" was food, nothing else. There were four tithes, each 10%.

> First Tithe was when farmer/rancher gave 10% of grains, fruits, nuts, flocks, and herds to the Levites, who were a special class of people God created out of the tribe of Levi to help the priests and maintain the tabernacle and later the temple. The First Tithe was only given eight out of twelve months—when there was a harvest and after weaning young sheep, goats, cattle, or oxen.

> Second Tithe was from the Levites to the priests, 10% of the

grains, fruits, nuts they had received from the farmer; no animals.

Third Tithe was the festival tithe, which the farmer/rancher gave to himself a tithe of his produce so he and his family would have something to eat in Jerusalem at the three mandatory festivals in the year.

Fourth Tithe was the third year tithe for the poor, given to the local village elders, which was 10% of whatever was left over in the barn at the end of the year (the growing- harvest-First Tithe year). This tithe was also grains, fruits, nuts.

Some simple and logical conclusions may be made. The tithe was intended to feed the Levites (first tithe), be one part of the food supply for the priests (second tithe; the *teruma* were the other part), support individual worship at the mandatory feasts (third tithe), and help feed the poor (fourth tithe; the poor could also glean the fields year-round).

The priests did not tithe. To whom would they tithe? They were, literally, at the top of the food chain. So Malachi 3:8 does not apply to the priests, because not being obligated to tithe, they could not rob God of his tithes.

The Levites tithed to the priests from the first tithe, but the New Testament church does not have a class of Levites—every Christian is a priest. Every Christian a priest also means there is no class or group in the New Testament church corresponding to the Hebrew farmer/rancher, who gave first tithe to the Levites and third tithe to himself—every Christian is a priest.

What is also obvious is, if you were not a farmer/rancher or Levite you could not tithe, you were not obligated to make a tithe, and therefore you could not rob God of the tithe. That is why YHWH also mentioned the *teruma*, which all were obligated to give. And, also obvious, the tithe was not year-round. There were eight months of harvest. There were eight months of tithing—another reason the *teruma* were important.

So, looking at tithing in relation to the New Testament church.

The New Testament church has no land, so none owe rent to God.

All New Testament believers are priests, so none are obligated to give a tithe.

No New Testament believer is a Levite, so none are obligated to give a tithe.

While there are farmers and ranchers in the New Testament church, there are no Levites for them to tithe to, so not obligated to give a tithe. Those in the New Testament church who are not farmers or ranchers never had an obligation to tithe.

There are no mandatory festivals in the New Testament church, so there is no obligation to give a tithe to one's self.

The requirement to help the poor is established in the New Testament without reference to a tithe.

Conclusion: there is no rational, logical, biblical, scriptural reason for a New Testament believer to tithe.

When we compare the tithing requirements of the Mosaic Law to the New Testament church, we discover no New Testament church believer is able to rob God of a tithe. Conclusion? Malachi 3:8 is not a New Testament verse, and cannot be rationally stretched to apply to the New Testament church. No one in the New Testament church is able to rob God of a tithe.

What about Malachi 3:10? "Bring the full tithes into the storehouse, that there may be food in my house" (ESV). God was not speaking metaphorically. King Hezekiah, 696–686 BC (Malachi was written ca. 435–400 BC), had set aside certain rooms in the buildings around the temple, part of the temple "campus," to store the food tithe given the Levites. The temple of the New Testament church is each individual believer, not a building. Besides, as we have seen, no New Testament church believer is obligated to tithe. No food, no storehouse, no tithe.

What is New Testament giving? Paul has a great explanation in 1 Corinthians 9:1–14. I do not have space to speak to all of that passage. But take a look at 9:13 and 9:14. Paul says, 9:14, Christ has commanded those who preach the gospel should live from the gospel. Paul has already given the principle in 9:7–10. He gets specific in 9:13. There, without using the Hebrew word, he speaks of the *teruma*, the contributions, specifically the animals sacrificed on the altar, to enforce his conclusion at 9:14. He could have spoken of the Levites' tithe to the priests, but he speaks of the *teruma* as showing the Christian he/she has an obligation to provide for the maintenance those who preach the gospel. Only in failing to make the New Testament equivalent of the *teruma* can a New Testament believer rob God. But not by not tithing, which no New Testament believer is obligated to do.

If you are convicted to give 10%, then do it. Give whatever amount the Holy Spirit convicts you to give. Ask him, trust him, he will guide you. Giving is as much an obligation as paying the bills, feeding and sheltering your family, saving for emergencies, and any other legal obligation—and the amount you give must not prevent you from satisfying all your other obligations. Proportionate giving is a New Testament principle: adjust your giving as income or obligations rise and fall. Whatever amount you are convicted to give, be consistent, be regular, be faithful. I can tell you that whether you regularly give a penny or regularly give a thousand dollars the Holy Spirit will test your faithfulness. Be faithful. Giving is a Christian responsibility.

The Defining Qualities of the Christian Life.

Faith: inwardly believing the testimony of God through the infallible conviction given by the Holy Spirit, and outwardly acting through the power given by the Holy Spirit to conform one's thoughts and actions to that conviction.

Love: a choice of the will to actively seek the best good for another person, without expectation of recompense, reciprocity, or recognition for one's self, and without consideration of merit or demerit in the one so loved.

Hope: the assurance the believer has in the promises of God; the assurance that the thing promised will be received; hope always refers to the thing embraced in hope, not to the basis or character of hope. Genuine hope perseveres to the receipt of the things hoped for.

Worship of God. The primary duty of the creature. The expression of love for God, devotion to God, and dedication to God. Genuine worship is the suitable appreciation of God's Person and works. Worship is based upon a spiritual apprehension of the worth of God, which is given by the Spirit to the born-again believer. Genuine worship comes from faith through a personal relationship with God in Jesus Christ. To worship is to "bend the knee," i.e., to submit to God as superior, to confess to God his worth, to proclaim to God, "I am dependent on you," and to express devotion and affection for him as God. Praise and worship admit to all present that this God is the one true God, and that those who praise and worship him are his people, chosen by him, saved by him, given by and through him an overwhelming salvation that secures eternal blessedness in him.

Obedience toward God. The second duty of the creature. The willing and voluntary acceptance of one's responsibility to conform to God's will in all things. Obedience is the key that turns on every spiritual power. Obedience is faith in exercise, responding to the divine will, directed by the divine authority, energized by divine power. In the Old and New Testaments the Hebrew and Greek words translated "obey" literally mean "to hear," so "obedience" means "an active response to something one hears." To hear God's word is to obey God's word. Worship is the first duty of the creature; obedience the second.

Fellowship with God. The first privilege of the creature. Friendship through mutual delight in things held in common. The things we have in common with God are our devotion to Christ, our commitment to manifest God's glory, our willingness to serve, and our submission to duty, i.e., our obedience to him. Fellowship with God is a form of worship. Fellowship with God is when God enjoys our presence within his presence and we are counted as his friend. Fellowship is by holiness in one's heart and mind and righteous actions in one's Christian life. Fellowship with God incorporates fellowship with Christ, which is friendship through mutual delight in Christ through things held in common. The things in common are: his crucifixion-resurrection and our salvation, his commandments and our obedience, his sovereignty and our worship, his love and our devotion. To have fellowship with Christ is first to be "in Christ" and then to be "like Christ."

Service for God. The second privilege of the creature and third duty. To be God's servant. To work for God. To accomplish God's good works. To actively look for and act upon the works God prepared beforehand for the believer to accomplish, by living the Christian life doing God's good works. To use and improve the spiritual gifts given by the Holy Spirit, with the intent to edify the New Testament church both corporately and individually, through the opportunities provided by the Holy Spirit. To use the opportunities provided by the Holy Spirit to pay attention to and care for the spiritual and physical well-being of others. To practice godly love through good works.

Godliness. God living and active in humanity, humanity acting and living according to God's values. Godliness is when the believer's thought, will, and action, his or her manner of life, conforms to the moral, holy, and righteous standard set by God's own character. In simpler terms, to be Christ-like. Godliness arises out of the new nature birthed by the Holy Spirit. God takes delight in those whose character and actions reflect his character and actions. God's character defines the worth of the actions performed by all beings: they are godly or ungodly. God takes delight in those whose character and actions reflect his character and actions. Godliness is not naturally generated by the believing soul, but depends on the work of the Holy Spirit through the grace he gives to all believers to live a godly life pleasing to God. While it is true a life of faith is the product of God's grace, it is also true that a lot of personal effort must be expended in order to live a godly and righteous life. There is a cost to living a life of faith: denying the temptations of sin in the mind and flesh; alienation from the world and worldly practices; separation from sinning and sinners engaged in sin; caution in one's relationships with sinners.

Read Church History

There are so many lessons for us in church history. In recent church history, the Protestant Reformation and the Roman Catholic church (RCC) counter-reformation is dated 1517–1648. Yes, there was a counter-reformation in which several countries reverted back to Roman Catholicism.

The Diet of Worms—in the German language the "W" is pronounced as a "V"; Worms was a German city; a "Diet" was a formal assembly of deliberation. The Diet of Worms was Luther's final break with the RCC, in 1521. Zwingli broke away from RCC 1525. Luther translated the New Testament into German 1522, the Old Testament in 1534. Calvin's break with RCC was ca. 1530. The *Institutes* were published 1536 in Latin, 1541 in French.

The English Church broke from the RCC in 1534 over a political issue, not religious issues, becoming the Church of England, which was in essence the English version of the Roman Catholic Church.

The English Thirty-Nine Articles of the Church of England, in which the Reformation principles and doctrines were expressed, was approved 1571. The Thirty-Nine were preceded by the Ten Articles in 1536, and after 1536 by five revisions that developed into the 1571 Thirty-Nine Articles.

It was a busy half-century from 1517 to 1571.

The Church of England was a long time adopting the Reformer's doctrine, and still did not wash away all of RCC (and still hasn't). Which is why the Baptists were birthed by the Puritan Separatists of the Church of England in 1611 (General Baptists), and 1638 (Particular Baptists) in England, and in American in 1639, evolving into General and Particular Baptists.

The Baptist denominations were founded by English Puritans. The Puritans came out of the Church of England, which separated from the Roman Catholic church in AD 1534 over a political issue (The Pope would not grant the King of England a divorce). The Puritans were divided into two main groups. The Congregationalists and the Separatists. Both groups were troubled by remnants of Roman Catholicism within the Church of England. The Congregational Puritans believed they should try to work for change within the Church of England. The Separatists believed they should completely separate from the Church of England.

In 1611 or 1612, the Puritans Thomas Helwys, John Murton, and their followers, all who were Puritan Separatists, organized the very first English Baptist church. They were known as "General Baptists " Another group of Puritan Separatists, led by John Spilsbury, organized the Particular Baptist church in England in 1638.

In 1639, in Providence Rhode Island, Roger Williams, a Puritan Separatist, organized the very first American Baptist church, although the church at Newport may have been the first Baptist church in America.

The Baptist church did not begin in biblical times, it was not founded by the apostles. The Baptist church did come out of the Protestant Reformation, indirectly, through Puritan reformers in the Church of England.

The Baptists were well established when Wesley founded the English Methodist church 100 years later in 1739, and the American Methodists in 1784.

The Dissenters, who were various groups of Christians—some were heretical, some not—predate the Roman Catholic Church (dated AD 590 by most historians), from the time of Tertullian (b. AD 160), and were never part of the RCC or its predecessors. Some of the most recognizable names of the Dissenters during the Reformation are the Swiss Anabaptists, founded by Zwingli in 1525, the Hutterites (1536) and Mennonites (1525).

And that is today's history lesson, a brief overview of Reformation highlights. Today's points? 1) Ecclesiastical harmony (1,000 years of Roman Catholicism) does not always lead to doctrinal purity. 2) Denominations can be useful in distinguishing between biblical and non-biblical doctrines. 3) As we see similar things happening today (e.g., the SBC drifting into modernism) we know God always raises up someone—many someones—to champion the truth.

Source: Earle, E. Cairns, *Christianity Through the Centuries* (3rd ed., Zondervan, 1996), 331, 362.

What is Election?

Some may not know what election is, others many not understand, and many may have heard only a distorted view of election. Here is a brief explanation. First a definition.

> Election. The choice of a sovereign God, 1) to give the gift of grace-faith-salvation to effect the salvation of some sinners, and 2) to take no action, positive or negative, to either effect or deny salvation to other sinners. The decree of election includes all means necessary to effectuate salvation in those elected. [Quiggle, *Dictionary*.]

The Greek word translated "he chose" (most versions) in Ephesians 1:4 is *eklégō* [Zodhiates, s. v. "1586"]. The word means "to select, to choose," and is translated choose, chose, chosen, or elect in twenty-two verses. This word, as used by the Greeks and Romans, and as used by the New Testament writers, does not necessarily imply an adverse or negative action toward those not chosen. Nor, as used by the New Testament writers in regard to election to salvation, does this word imply something meritorious in those chosen, or something undesirable in those not chosen. When used with regard to salvation, *eklégō* simply means God made a choice. [Quiggle, *God's Choices*, 17.]

God, before he created anything, saw all human beings as sinners. In the foreordaining acts of God to sovereignly make a universe according to his purpose in creating, God created a sinless human being, Adam. God chose to allow Adam to choose his path in life. The choices available to Adam were continued submission and obedience to God's authority, Genesis 2:17, or rebellion against God. Adam chose rebellion, Genesis 3:6. The principle of rebellion against God is known as "sin." Adam's disobedience to God's commandment added the principle of rebellion, sin, as an attribute of his human nature, permanently changing Adam from sinless to sinner.

Adam was the seminal and legal representative of his descendants: his sin became their sin. Seminally his sin became their sin because Adam's sin changed his human nature, adding the principle of rebellion against God. When Adam procreated, his sinful nature was inherited by his descendants, Genesis 5:3. Thus, Romans 5:12, sin entered the world through one man's sin and spread to all human beings, so that all in Adam die, 1 Corinthians 15:22. Legally, Adam was the representative of his race, the legal head because the seminal head. The judicial guilt of Adam's sin was imputed to his descendants. (Just as the righteousness of Christ is imputed to those who are his "descendants," not physically, but those who believe on him for salvation.)

God, then, in the process of his foreordaining choices, saw all human beings—the descendants of Adam— as sinners because of Adam's sin. God sovereignly chose to save some sinners, justly leaving the rest as he found them. God never says why he made an electing choice, nor the reasons for the choice, nor the reasons for his particular choices (which individuals he would elect). God, with all his attributes acting in union and harmony, chose to establish a covenant relationship with some sinners, and bring them into that covenant through salvation. God made a decision of his will, not an emotional decision. God's decision toward the non-elect to leave them as he found them, in their sin, was also not an emotional decision, but a decision of his will that, like the decision to elect some, would fulfill his purpose in creating.

God's love and mercy in election was his decision to seek the best good for some sinners, without expectation of recompense or reciprocity, and without consideration of their merit (they had none) or demerit, 1 John 4:10. He made this decision without favoritism toward the elect. Those God elected were chosen in love and mercy (Ephesians 1:4; 2:4) to be saved, sanctified, and adopted, to the praise of his glory. That same love does not prevent any non-elect from choosing to come to God through faith in God's testimony concerning salvation to believe and be saved.

Because election does not prejudice God against the non-elect, God would, in fact, act savingly toward any non-elect if they did choose to seek him and come to him for salvation. But their desire for their sin persuades them to make the choice to reject God.

Sin is an attribute of fallen human nature, a principle or attribute of evil that motivates human beings to rebel against God, disobey his commandments, and seek a path in life apart from God. Sin has authority (dominion, rule) over the sinner, not as some invincible overlord, but as an innate part of human nature constructively working with all the other attributes of human nature to persuasively incline the will to choose an act of sinning.

The evil attribute sin influences every other attribute with the inclination to sin, and in that sense sin can be said to dominate the will. The sinner freely chooses sinning because his will is of itself always inclined to choose sinning, and as being rebellious and disobedient toward God never desires to change its inclination to choose sinning to rebel against God, disobey his commandments, and seek a path in life apart from God.

The propitiation (atonement) Christ made on the cross for sin completely satisfied God's justice for the crime of sin, all sin, 1 John 2:2; Romans 3:25. Propitiation (atonement) powers redemption, but propitiation is not redemption. Propitiation is directed toward God to satisfy God's justice for the crime of sin. God's justice being satisfied, God could act righteously to redeem sinners according to his sovereign choices. Christ's propitiation powers redemption through Election, Ephesians 1:4, and God's gift, Ephesians 2:8.

God, for reasons suitable to his purpose in creating, reasons known only to himself, acted sovereignly to choose to redeem some sinners (election, Ephesians 1:4) by applying the merit of Christ's propitiation, through his gift of grace-faith-salvation (Ephesians 2:8) to their spiritual need, thereby regenerating their soul, leading to the sinner's exercise of faith, and the forgiveness of sins. Election guarantees the salvation of the elect, but neither helps nor hinders the non-elect, who could be saved, if they would freely choose to be saved. But the desire of the non-elect for their sin is so powerful they do not choose to be saved. Thus the necessity of God's gift of grace-faith-salvation to effect faith and salvation in the sinner.

> An illustration of election. The river of sinful humankind is justly racing toward the waterfall of death emptying into the lake of eternal fire; God reaches into the river and saves many; he prevents no one from swimming to the safety of the heavenly shore; he puts his saved people on the shore encouraging all to believe on Christ and be saved; he saves all that come to him by faith in his testimony of salvation.

A complete explanation of foreordination and election may be found in my book, "*God's Choices, the Doctrines of Foreordination, Election, and Predestination.*"

Textual Issues

Have you seen the meme comparing the KJV with another version, to point out "missing" words or phrases or sentences? Don't be fooled.

The words that seem to be missing are not missing from the New Testament. They are in other gospels. As the New Testament autographs were copied, and the copies were copied, over and over again, some scribes, not being well-regulated or supervised, thought they needed, on their own authority, to make the gospel accounts harmonize with one another. So these scribes imported a word or phrase or sentence from a verse in one gospel into a verse in a different gospel where the context was similar.

Diligent comparison of the, literally, thousands of ancient New Testament manuscripts in Greek and other languages show where that sort of thing happened. Translators coming after the 1611 KJV had greater access to more manuscripts, and believed it was their duty to present accurate manuscripts to the public. Don't let the KJV-Only error affect your confidence in the Bible translation you use.

The science of textual criticism weighs all sorts of evidence as to which manuscripts and readings are most likely to reflect the original apostolic text: the autograph. The many manuscripts of the Book of Revelation are the most difficult.

The Western manuscripts, are older and have greater consistency in their readings. The Byzantine manuscripts are not as old, but there are many more of them, but not as consistent in their readings. The newer versions of the Bible (e.g., NIV, HSSB, ESV) usually give the reading of Western texts because they are the older texts. The older versions of the Bible (KJV and its offspring, NKJV) usually give the reading of the Byzantine texts, because they are the more numerous texts, and because the Western texts were not discovered until after the older translations were made.

Let's take the case of Revelation 8:13. The Western texts read "eagle," and the Byzantine texts, read "angel." Those favoring "eagle" note the eagle is a carrion bird, and the woes relate to the destruction of God's enemies. Those favoring "angel" note all the other announcements are made by angels. The reader and the translator must make a choice based on what seems to him or her the strongest textual, contextual, and biblical evidence.

Here is why I believe the better reading is "angel." (From my book, *The Epistle of Jesus to the Church, A Commentary on the Revelation*, 260).

All the messages of judgment (in Revelation) are delivered by angels. There are no Scripture parallels of an eagle or any animal announcing judgment.

The fourth living creature (4:7) was not an eagle but was "like a flying eagle." In 12:14 "eagles wings" are a simile, not a literal eagle. There are no eagles in heaven.

An eagle was an abomination under the law, Leviticus 11:13.

An eagle was symbolic of the rapidity and rapaciousness of the pagan nations, Deuteronomy 28:49; Habakkuk 1:8.

An eagle was a symbol of apostasy, Hosea 8:1.

The interpretation of any one verse must always be the context of the entire Scripture (see below), because "the scriptures explain themselves" (A.W. Pink's last words, [Murray, 182]). The text that agrees with the whole of Scripture reads, "an angel," not an eagle.

(Supporting Scripture: Leviticus 11:13; Deuteronomy 14:12; 28:49; 32:11; Job 9:26; 39:27; Proverbs 23:5; 30:19; Jeremiah 48:40; 49:16; 49:22; Ezekiel 1:10; 10:14; 17:3; 17:7; Hosea 8:1; Obadiah 4; Micah 1:16; Habakkuk 1:8; Revelation 4:7; 12:14.)

All the differences altogether in all the 25,000 New Testament manuscripts do not affect the integrity of the biblical text. There are 3,116,480 characters (alphabet characters) in the New Testament, there are 807,370 words. There are 400,000 variants—places where an alphabet character is different, a word is different, or the word order is different (Greek, unlike English, is not a word order language).

Of the 400,000, only 400 affect the sense of a passage, such as Revelation 8:13, and of those, only fifty are actually important. Revelation 8:13 is not among the fifty because it is the message that is important, not the means of delivery.

In any case, no variant of any kind affects any doctrine, no variation in word order affects the meaning of a sentence (because word endings determine subject-verb association). Spelling differences seldom affect meaning. For example, the difference in spelling by one Greek alphabet character makes the text of Revelation 1:5 read washed or loosed.

In every way that is important and necessary for faith and practice, the New Testament texts as we have them accurately reflect the originals. Translation variations are more important than manuscript variations.

Salvation First

The worldly philosophy is work hard to change yourself so you are worthy to follow Christ.

The biblical philosophy is the closer one follows Christ, something only the saved can do, the more he is changed by that relationship and denies himself.

The biblical precept is, Mark 8:34, "If any person desires to come after me, let him deny himself, and let him take up his cross, and let him follow me."

The cross is always a symbol of sacrifice and death. Not the death of the self, the "I," but the death of sinful desires and deeds. Only the born-again believer has the spiritual nature and power to make the choice to deny sinful desires and deeds.

A person follows Christ because saved, not to become saved. The person following Christ puts his sinful desires and deeds on the cross.

The marriage commitment makes a good analogy. One does not deny others to make the marriage commitment, one makes the commitment and that marriage commitment by its very nature denies others.

Marriage is an exclusive loyalty covenant between one man and one woman—what the Bible describes as a one-flesh relationship.

The terms and conditions of the exclusive loyalty covenant require the man and woman commit their physical, emotional, and spiritual being to the benefit and enjoyment of one another and none else.

The marriage covenant does not exclude friendly relationships with others, but it does exclude commitments, especially sexual and emotional commitments, that are of the same order as those composing the marriage relationship.

The world always reverses the biblical order of things. If one enters into the marriage commitment on the basis of denying others, then that commitment is only as enduring as the desire to continue denying others. But when one makes a genuine exclusive loyalty marriage commitment with another, then the source of the denial of others is that commitment, and so the marriage endures.

The nature of a biblical marriage is such a man and a woman do turn their backs on other men and women, because of that prior commitment with one another. In relation to following Christ, the analogy is, just as a person must be born again in order to follow Christ and deny himself, even so the one who has made the exclusive loyalty marriage commitment with another will follow their spouse and deny other men and women.

In the Bible, marriage is the commitment that makes denial possible. In the Bible, it is salvation that makes following and denial possible.

Unlimited Propitiation, Limited Redemption

A lengthy technical discussion for those with an interest in the subject.

> Proposition: Propitiation is not redemption. The merit has to be applied. God applies the merit of Christ's propitiation according to election through his gift of grace-faith-salvation. The sinner, having received and been changed by the gift, responds by exercising faith in God and God's testimony as to the way of salvation.

God sent Christ to the cross to propitiate (fully satisfy) God for the judicial debt due the crime of man's sins, 1 John 2:2; Romans 3:25. Propitiation: the satisfaction Christ made to God for sin by dying on the cross. Christ's propitiation fully satisfied God's holiness and justice for the crime of sin. Christ's propitiation was of infinite merit, because his Person is of infinite worth, thereby being sufficient for all the sins of the all the world.

God himself specifically applies the infinite merit of Christ's propitiation according to his decree of election, Ephesians 1:4, through his gift of grace-faith-salvation, Ephesians 2:8. Election: The choice of a sovereign God, 1) to give the gift of grace-faith-salvation to effect the salvation of some sinners, and 2) to take no action, positive or negative, to either effect or deny salvation to other sinners. The decree of election includes all means necessary to effectuate salvation in those elected.

The sum of these things is the unlimited merit of Christ's propitiation, and the limited redemption that merit is used to accomplish. Put in terms of an ongoing controversy, Christ did not die only for the elect, he died to propitiate God for all sins. Not to redeem all sinners, but to propitiate God for all sins. In familiar terms this is known as Unlimited Atonement and Limited Redemption.

The unlimited merit of Christ's propitiation is not universal salvation. That misguided belief confuses propitiation with redemption. Propitiation is God acting toward God to satisfy God for the crime of sin. Redemption is God acting toward man to effect the forgiveness of a person's judicial debt for his or her sins.

Some Reformed theologians, from the time of the Synod of Dort (1619) have taken a shortcut through doctrine to say since the merit of the propitiation is applied only to the elect, then Christ died only for the elect. (The technical term is a metonymy (a substitution) of the effect for the cause.) But that shortcut undermines the truthfulness of the gospel call to every sinner (discussed below), and denies the clear statement of 1 John 2:2, not for our sins only but also for all the world. The careless distort doctrine and thereby create error.

The merit of propitiation (the older term is atonement) must be applied to effect redemption. Every Old Testament example of forgiveness of sin through sacrifice teaches the merit of the shed blood, the atonement, must be applied by faith to effect forgiveness of sins to accomplish redemption.

The redemption Christ's propitiation accomplishes is limited and particular, because applied according to a specific purpose, through a specific means, to specific individuals. That specific purpose is God's choice to save some not others: the decree of election, Ephesians 1:4. That specific means is God's gift of grace-faith-salvation, Ephesians 2:8, given only to the elect. The specific individuals are those whom God has chosen to give his gift of grace-faith-salvation according to his decree of election.

God's decree of election does not prevent any from coming and believing; thus the legitimacy of a gospel call to all sinners. In the forty-eight uses of the Greek words for choice, none of those uses ever says anything negative about the ones not chosen. Those words are *eklégō* (Strong's 1586); *eklektós* (Strong's 1588); *eklektós* (Strong's 1589). Do the word study, see for yourself.

The gospel call to believe and be saved is directed toward "whoever desires," Revelation 22:17; whoever believes on him, John 3:16; Romans 10:11; 1 John 5:1; whoever calls on the name of the Lord, Acts 2:21; Romans 10:13. How do we find those people? Go and proclaim the gospel call to all. If, as some propose, Christ died only for the elect, then God is a liar when he states in the gospel that "whoever desires, whoever believes, whoever calls" on the name of the Lord will be saved.

That offer to "whoever" is why propitiation is not redemption, and why election does not prevent any from coming and believing. The infinite merit of Christ's propitiation is available for any who "desire, believe, call upon" to be saved. The decree of election takes no action, positive or negative, to either effect or deny salvation to other sinners. The call to believe is a genuine offer to all, the moral responsibility to believe is genuine requirement for all, salvation is genuinely available to any "whoever" who might "desire, believe, call upon" the Lord to be saved.

Why, then, are only the elect saved? Because the unsaved sinner is unable to overcome his or her desire to remain a sinner. The evil attribute sin in human nature influences every other attribute with the inclination to sin, and in that sense sin can be said to dominate the will. The sinner freely chooses sinning because his will is of itself always inclined to choose sinning, and as being rebellious and disobedient toward God never desires to change its inclination to choose sinning to rebel against God, disobey his commandments, and seek a path in life apart from God.

Thus the necessity of God's gift of grace-faith-salvation. The propitiation (atonement) is sufficient for all, but is efficient to redeem only the elect, because only the elect receive God's gift of grace-faith-salvation. The sinner is unable to initiate saving faith because his will is of itself always inclined to choose sinning, and as being rebellious and disobedient toward God never desires to change its inclination to choose sinning.

The problem some in Reformed theology have is basic ignorance of the doctrines they profess to believe. Thus the unbiblical statement, Christ died only for the elect. No, Christ died for the purpose of fully satisfying—propitiating—God's holiness and justice for the crime of sin. That is why the propitiation was, "not for our sins only, but also for all the world," 1 John 2:2. And having been satisfied for all sins, God could act in justice and holiness to genuinely offer salvation to all, and act according to his sovereign will to apply that merit in truthfulness, justice, and holiness to those whom he has chosen to be his legacy out of the world (Ephesians 1:11).

Moreover, Christ's propitiation served more than a redemptive purpose. Because his justice has been satisfied, God may interact with the world other than in wrath, but in goodness, kindness, love, and mercy. God acts in mercy to relive distress caused by sin in the world, and in mercy to delay the just punishment of the sinner, giving the sinner time to respond to the gospel call.

None are prevented from "desiring, believing, coming," because the gospel call is legitimately made to all. But the fact of sin is that only those whom God has given his gift will desire, believe, and come.

Therefore do not confuse atonement (propitiation) with redemption. The atonement (Christ's propitiation) was directed toward God only, in order to satisfy God's justice and holiness for the judicial debt of the crime of sin. Redemption is directed toward man by God through election, Eph 1:4, to redeem sinners through the applied merit of Christ's propitiation, via the gift of grace-faith-salvation, Eph 2:8.

The definitive statement on biblical salvation was accomplished by the Synod of Dort, 1618–1619. Here are the portions applicable to this discussion, from the Canons of the Synod of Dort.

> SECOND HEAD OF DOCTRINE, Of the Death of Christ and the Redemption of Men Thereby, Article 3, "The death of the Son of God is the only and most perfect sacrifice and satisfaction for sin, and is of infinite worth and value, abundantly sufficient to expiate the sins of the whole world." In familiar terms Unlimited Atonement/Propitiation.

> FIRST HEAD OF DOCTRINE, Of Divine Predestination, Article 6, "That some receive the gift of faith from God and others do not receive it proceeds from God's eternal decree, for 'known unto God are all His works from the beginning of the world' (Acts 15:18). 'Who worketh all things after the counsel of His own will' (Eph. 1:11). According to which decree, He graciously softens the hearts of the elect, however obstinate, and inclines them to believe, while He leaves the non-elect in His just judgment to their own wickedness and obduracy."

> Article 7, "Election is the unchangeable purpose of God, whereby, before the foundation of the world, He hath out of mere grace, according to the sovereign good pleasure of His own will, chosen, from the whole human race, which had fallen through their own fault from their primitive state of rectitude into sin and destruction, a certain number of persons to redemption in Christ."

> SECOND HEAD OF DOCTRINE, Of the Death of Christ and the Redemption of Men Thereby, Article 8, "For this was the sovereign counsel, and most gracious will and purpose of God the Father, that the quickening and saving efficacy of the most precious death of His Son should extend to all the elect, for bestowing upon them alone the gift of justifying faith, thereby to bring them infallibly to salvation"

Or, as the summary states: "While the death of Christ is abundantly sufficient to expiate the sins of the whole world, its saving efficacy is limited to the elect." Unlimited Propitiation, Limited Redemption.

Christ died on the cross to propitiate God for all sin, so God could act in justice, holiness and righteousness to save sinners. Salvation: The application of Christ's infinite merit to overcome the demerit of sin and save a soul, specifically applied through God's gift of grace-faith-salvation, according to God's sovereign decree of election, then personally applied by each sinner through saving faith in Christ, in response to receiving God's gift of grace-faith-salvation.

The Universal Call of the Gospel

Someone said, "The general tone of the presentation of the gospel is its unequivocal universal call." Of course. Through the gospel God makes a universal call to all sinners for several reasons.

> One, to establish moral responsibility. All sinners, elect and non-elect are responsible to respond with faith.

> Two, to call those who are elect. The gospel is the means God has ordained to call sinners.

> Three, Christ's propitiation made a full satisfaction to God's justice for the crime of sin, see the Canons of the Synod of Dort, Second Head of Doctrine, Article 3.

Because a full satisfaction was made, God can justly act savingly toward any, elect or non-elect, who comes to him by faith in God's testimony as to the way of salvation.

From my book *Dictionary of Doctrinal Words*, (a quote that originated in my book, *God's Choices, the Doctrines of Foreordination, Election, and Predestination*, which I recommend to you).

> Election (1). The choice of a sovereign God, 1) to give the gift of grace-faith-salvation to effect the salvation of some sinners, and 2) to take no action, positive or negative, to either effect or deny salvation to other sinners. The decree of election includes all means necessary to effectuate salvation in those elected.

> Election (2). A comprehensive discussion of election is not within the scope of this dictionary. In brief, the decree of a sovereign God to redeem sinners must include all the means necessary to effect their salvation. Knowing all options (the entire human race), God in eternity past chose who he would save. God never tells us the basis on which one was elected and another was not, other than God acts according to his sovereign will. The number of the elect is not revealed, nor are the identities of the elect revealed. Election does not substitute for grace, which God extends to every person he has chosen to salvation. Election means those chosen will be saved from their sins.

> God takes no action, positive or negative, toward those not chosen which would prevent their seeking him in Christ for

salvation. God's choice of salvation for some and not for others does not hinder any sinner from seeking God in Christ for salvation. God would, in fact, act savingly toward them if they did choose to seek him and come to him for salvation.

Election (3). God never reveals the basis on which one was elected and another was not, other than God acts according to his sovereign will. A person's choices are not the reason for election. If God is reacting to man then God is arranging his plan of redemption to suit man's response to his offer of salvation. Foreknowledge of faith is not the ground of election because faith is the very blessing to which sinners are elected. God's pre-knowing a believer is not based on what they will do or believe, but is based on his decree concerning their redemption. The number of the elect is not revealed. Election is not fate; the decree of election requires the exercise of individual faith, without which none can be saved. Election requires the means, evangelism, necessary to bring sinners to salvation: evangelism, personal testimony, a godly witness in the believer's manner of living, the promulgation of God's word in written and oral form. Election does not substitute for grace: unmerited blessing is required as one of the means God uses to effect salvation. Election is not predestination, which is a decree affecting believers to conform them to be like Christ. Election to salvation does not mean a corresponding election to reprobation (eternity in the Lake of Fire); election speaks only of those chosen and says nothing of those not chosen.

Election (4). Illustration. The river of sinful humankind is justly racing toward the waterfall of death emptying into the lake of eternal fire; God reaches into the river and saves many; he prevents no one from swimming to the safety of the heavenly shore; he puts his saved people on the shore encouraging all to believe on Christ and be saved; he saves all that come to him by faith in his testimony of salvation.

Election (5). Reprobation is a Calvinistic/Reformed doctrine which teaches some sinners are elected to eternal separation from God resulting in eternal death and punishment in the lake of fire. In contrast, the scriptures teach election (Greek: *eklégō*) never indicates the reprobation of those not chosen. God chooses to save, but that choice does not directly deny salvation to the ones not chosen. The biblical doctrine is that sinners are reprobate because of their freely made choices throughout their lifetime to reject Jesus as their Savior and continue in sin.

Prior to the decree of election God viewed all human beings as sinners. God chose (elected) to save some of those sinners. In electing some God passed by the rest, taking no action to effect or deny their salvation. The doctrine of reprobation, however, requires positive action by God toward the non-elect sinner to disqualify him/her from heaven and subject him/her to judgment and eternal punishment. There is no divine decree of reprobation that would directly deny salvation to the non-elect. See: Election (1), (2), (3).

The non-elect problem is they have no desire to come and believe and be saved. (Again, from my *Dictionary.*)

> Sin, dominion of. Sin is an attribute of fallen human nature, a principle or attribute of evil that motivates human beings to rebel against God, disobey his commandments, and seek a path in life apart from God. Sin has authority (dominion, rule) over the sinner, not as some invincible overlord, but as an innate part of human nature constructively working with all the other attributes of human nature to persuasively incline the will to choose an act of sinning. The evil attribute sin influences every other attribute with the inclination to sin, and in that sense sin can be said to dominate the will. The sinner freely chooses sinning because his will is of itself always inclined to choose sinning, and as being rebellious and disobedient toward God never desires to change its inclination to choose sinning to rebel against God, disobey his commandments, and seek a path in life apart from God."

Thus, the boundaries of unsaved human nature are formed by the sin attribute, which the sinner is unable to overcome by him or herself. God gives his gift of grace-faith-salvation (Ephesians 2:8) which enlivens the soul's faculty of spiritual perception, thereby changing the boundaries of human nature, so the sinner is now able to understand the spiritual issues of sin, the Savior, and salvation, and act of his or her spiritual need for salvation by exercising faith, in response to God' gift. God is the origin and source of salvation, according to his electing choices, through his gift of grace-faith-salvation.

Salvation in the World Before Christ

Recently I was asked how people who lived before Christ, living in other parts of the world than the Middle East, were saved. The person asking the question said, "Those people did not have the written Scriptures, or a verbal witness based on the written Scriptures, so how could they be saved?" The answer requires us to consider more than one doctrine, and use a little rational reasoning, and therefore it is a little long. Read with patience and tenacity.

To begin, we must ask another question: How were the OT people saved prior to Jesus' death and resurrection? We do not find in the Old Testament any mention a coming redeemer. A coming king, yes, 2 Samuel 7:13, 16; Psalm 2, but not a coming redeemer (although that is the intent of Daniel 9:26).

You may point to Isaiah 53 (written ca. 700 BC), but you know that is about a coming Messiah-Christ-Redeemer because the New Testament told you that, Acts 8:35. But the Old Testament peoples did not know it was about Christ, Acts 8:32–34. You may point to Genesis 3:15, but that verse doesn't mention a coming redeemer, a Messiah-Christ, and is never associated with the coming Messiah-Christ-Redeemer in any OT or NT scripture. If Genesis 3:15 is never explained in Scripture as about a coming Messiah-Christ-Redeemer and is never mentioned in any kind of context as about a coming Messiah-Christ-Redeemer, then why or how would anyone in the OT think or believe it was about a coming Messiah-Christ-Redeemer? Answer: They did not.

Let's look at two people who lived before Moses wrote Genesis through Deuteronomy. How was Abraham saved? Genesis 15:6 says Abraham believed God and God counted his faith as righteousness (ESV: "And he believed the Lord, and he counted it to him as righteousness.") What did Abraham believe? God said, Genesis 15:4 (ESV), "your very own son shall be your heir." When we carefully examine these two verses, we discover: 1) Abraham believed God; 2) Abraham believed God's testimony, "your very own son shall be your heir." Abraham believed God and the testimony God revealed to him and was saved.

Let's look at Noah. Genesis 6:9 says, Noah was a righteous man. How do we know Noah was righteous? He had faith in God and God's testimony.

> Genesis 6:13–14 (ESV), And God said to Noah, "I have determined to make an end of all flesh, for the earth is filled

with violence through them. Behold, I will destroy them with the earth. Make yourself an ark of gopher wood."

Genesis 6:17–18 (ESV), "For behold, I will bring a flood of waters upon the earth to destroy all flesh in which is the breath of life under heaven. Everything that is on the earth shall die. But I will establish my covenant with you, and you shall come into the ark, you, your sons, your wife, and your sons' wives with you."

Noah believed God and God's testimony, and thereby Noah was saved from God's judgment.

Let's look at Moses and the nation Israel. Obviously Moses believed God. What was God's testimony?

Lev 4:1–2 (ESV), And the Lord spoke to Moses, saying, "Speak to the people of Israel, saying, 'If anyone sins unintentionally in any of the Lord's commandments about things not to be done, and does any one of them,'

Leviticus 4:4 (ESV), "He shall bring the bull to the entrance of the tent of meeting before the Lord and lay his hand on the head of the bull and kill the bull before the Lord."

What saved Moses and others under the Law? Not mechanically bringing a sacrifice but God's grace and the sinner's faith. The sinner making the offering by faith was accepted by God's grace (salvation is always by God's grace through the sinner's faith, Ephesians 2:8). The sinner brought the proper offering, with confession and repentance of sin, offered in the proper way. How did the sinner know the proper offering: faith in God and God's testimony. How did the sinner know to confess and repent (lay his hands on the sacrificial animal): faith in God and God's testimony. The proper sacrifice brought with faith in God and God's testimony, when accepted by God's grace, resulted in the forgiveness of sin.

Regardless of time or location in the history of the world, to be saved a sinner must always believe in the one true God and God's testimony as to the way of salvation.

Since Christ's resurrection, salvation occurs when a sinner repents of his or her sins and believes on Christ as their Savior, Acts 2:38; 3:19–20; 11:18; Romans 3:22–26; 10:9–10, 13; Galatians 3:22; 1 Peter 1:21; 1 John 3:23.

From this Old Testament and New Testament information, we can develop a principle. The sinner is always saved by God's grace through the sinner's faith in God, through God's historically current testimony as given in the progressive revelation of truth.

> The doctrine of progressive revelation is the simple observation God does not reveal all things at the same time, but over time God's revelation is completed. As God said through Isaiah 28:10 (ESV), "For it is precept upon precept, precept upon precept, line upon line, line upon line, here a little, there a little."

Salvation, from Adam into the new heaven and earth, is always by God's grace, through the merit of Christ's propitiation of God for the sinner's sin, through the sinner's faith in God as Savior and God's historically current testimony as given by God in the progressive revelation of truth. (Propitiation: the satisfaction Christ made to God for sin by dying on the cross.)

The basis for salvation at any time in the history of the world is always Christ's propitiation of God for sin. The object of saving faith is always God. The content of saving faith is always God's historically current testimony.

That "historically current testimony" is known as the content of faith: what the sinner must believe in order to be saved. Today that content of faith is Christ crucified and resurrected as the payment to God for your sin. But in the past that content of faith changed through the progressive revelation of God's testimony. The sinner is always saved by God's grace through the sinner's faith in God, through God's historically current testimony (the content of faith) as given in the progressive revelation of truth. The content of faith was not the same for Abraham as for Noah; for Moses as for Abraham; for you and me as for Moses.

Paul tells us the content of faith changed after Christ's crucifixion and resurrection.

> Acts 17:30–-31 (ESV), "God commands all people everywhere to repent, because he has fixed a day on which he will judge the world in righteousness by a man whom he has appointed; and of this he has given assurance to all by raising him from the dead."

> Acts 16:31 (ESV), "Believe in the Lord Jesus Christ, and you will be saved."

> Romans 10:9 (ESV), if you confess with your mouth that Jesus
> is Lord and believe in your heart that God raised him from the
> dead, you will be saved.

> Romans 10:13 (ESV), For "everyone who calls on the name of
> the Lord will be saved."

Paul also adds, Romans 10:14–15 (ESV), "how are they to call on
him in whom they have not believed? And how are they to believe in
him of whom they have never heard? And how are they to hear without
someone preaching? And how are they to preach unless they are
sent?" And therein lies the question, "How did other cultures that had
never heard any of the Old or New Testament Scriptures gain
salvation?"

Scripture does not give a direct answer concerning people in Old
Testament times living in other parts of the world. The Old Testament
focuses on Israel and that line of people leading to the nation Israel.
From how God treated all those people, we may develop answers to
the questions, how were they saved; how did they hear the message
of salvation?

"How were they saved?" We have seen that salvation is always by
God's grace through faith in God and God's testimony as to the means
or way of salvation, as given in the progressive revelation of truth. So
how did people in other parts of the world hear that testimony?

> Romans 1:19–20 (ESV), For what can be known about God is
> plain to them, because God has shown it to them. For his
> invisible attributes, namely, his eternal power and divine
> nature, have been clearly perceived, ever since the creation of
> the world, in the things that have been made. So they are
> without excuse.

I believe when someone living in other parts of the world
responded to God's testimony in nature, that God kept the implied
promise of Romans 10:14–15 that he would send someone to preach
salvation.

God always responds to faith, e.g., Acts 8:26–40; 10:1–48. And I
believe based on that preaching a person could be saved. But now,
since Christ, God commands all people everywhere to repent and
believe on Christ as Savior. That is the content of faith for today. And
in the New Testament we see that God scattered his saved people to
preach salvation throughout the world, Acts 8:1, an action multiplied
throughout the history of the world. How and where God sent them

cannot be known, but that God did send them is certain.

Ultimately the answer depends on answers to two additional questions. One, is God the Savior? Yes, God alone is the Savior, he saves all that come to him through faith, he saves all he intends to save. Question two, is God holy and just and love? Yes, he is all those things and more. Therefore we must have faith God acts justly and savingly toward any who will have faith in him.

"How did other cultures that had never heard any of the Old or New Testament Scriptures gain salvation?" Answer: God will respond to any who have faith in him and want to know him. He will tell them his testimony as to the way of salvation.

At What Age Salvation?

A friend posted: "Infant baptism doesn't save anyone. Infants can't choose Christ."

I absolutely agree water baptism of anyone, infant or otherwise, is not salvific. But I hesitate to limit God's salvific ability to what I think infants may or may not be able to do, based on what I am able to observe and evaluate as evidence of salvation, in those so young (or so mentally deficient at any age) as to be unable to articulate or otherwise provide those outward evidences by which we discover salvation in another.

For example, when an infant, John Baptist did not give evidence he was saved, because he could not: he was physically and mentally incapable of providing those evidences. Yet Luke 1:44 intimates he was saved in the womb. Is God's arm so short he cannot save in the womb? The God who made mind and soul is well-able to communicate with mind and soul at any stage of human development, from newly conceived to ripe old age.

I prefer to say: "Infant baptism does not save anyone, but God saves all whom he has chosen to save, without regard to age or development of mind and body." But I've always been more theologian than evangelist or apologist.

Thinking as a theologian, and I suppose as an apologist, those denying (or not understanding) God's sovereignty in salvation, must approach the issue of salvation of the unborn, infants, small children, and those older who never develop mentally, with imagination, not scripture.

In no place in the Scripture does the Holy Spirit give any exception to the means of salvation: "By God's grace though the sinner's faith in God and God's testimony." In no place does Scripture state or imply God created a special class of people who are saved by grace without faith, as would be required for the unborn, infants, small children, and those older who never develop mentally.

So some people develop a non-scriptural theology, that God has appointed a special class of people to salvation—in their mind the unborn and infants, but which must by necessity also include small children and those older who never develop mentally. These well-meaning people have developed a theology that God saves a special class of people by grace *without* faith in God and God's testimony—because those in this special class are unable to hear or mentally grasp God's testimony.

Some holding that theology will point to David and his firstborn child with Bathsheba as proof. They never ask the critical questions: was David speaking as inspired, or as a grieving father; does what David said apply to all infants, or just that one infant; how is what David said to be applied to the unborn, small children, or the mentally undeveloped? There is no demonstration in any Scripture that what David said was intended to say God has created a special class of people who are saved by grace without faith.

Others point to Christ, when he said to let the little children come to him. Of course, all Christ was saying is that little children can come to him, that they are capable of being saved. He did not create or imply a special class of people—unborn, infants, small children, the mentally undeveloped—who are saved by grace without faith.

Others will say, "these unborn, infants, etc., are innocent," and therefore not sinners. No, Scripture states, "all have sinned," and, "there is none righteous," just as clearly as it states, "there is none who understands," and "there are none who seek after God." The unborn, infants, small children, and the mentally undeveloped are, as are all human beings, guilty of not being in the image in which God created humankind. That is a sin.

All human beings have a sinful human nature, the heritage of sinful Adam's propagation, Genesis 5:3; Romans 5:12. All human beings, from the moment of conception, are judicially guilty of a crime against God, and all are culpable for, and do suffer, the penalty due that crime, spiritual and physical death. The fact the newly conceived are susceptible to death answers the question of their judicial guilt and sinful state before God: not innocent, but guilty of being a sinner.

There are other imaginative schemes that try to save the unborn, infants, small children, and the mentally undeveloped without personal faith but by divine fiat alone. All these schemes may be summarized as: "God has chosen to save all who are mentally incapable of hearing or understanding the gospel." In other words, a special class of people, saved by grace without faith in God and God's testimony. In the complete and total absence of any Scripture support for that theology, I suggest a more biblical view.

Ephesians 1:4, "God chose us in Christ before the foundation of the world." No human being, at any stage of physical and mental development, is beyond the reach of God's electing choice. All those whom God has elected will certainly be saved. As to the unborn, infants, and others similarly mentally unable to believe, if they are saved, "it cannot be on their own merits, or on the basis of their own righteousness or innocence [they have none], but must be entirely on the basis of Christ's redemptive work and regeneration by the work of the Holy Spirit within them" [Grudem, "Systematic," 500].

What I am saying is that if God has chosen any one of these mentally incompetent persons to salvation, then God will by grace give them the gift of grace-faith-salvation, and by grace they will positively respond by receiving the gift and applying it to their spiritual circumstances, thereby expressing faith, and by grace God will apply the merit of Christ to their soul, thereby causing their salvation. The manner of their positive response—how they might express saving faith—cannot be known, because they cannot tell us by word or deed. But what is certain is God who made mind and soul is capable of effectively communicating with any person's mind and soul at any stage of development.

God's electing choice is the primary condition affecting the salvation of all human beings from Adam forward: he saves whom he has chosen; he prevents no one from coming to him to be saved. Beyond this no one can go with certainty. No one can say with scriptural certainty that all, some, or none of the unborn, infants, small children, or any who never become mentally competent are saved, or not saved.

Perhaps God has elected every single person who dies in the womb, or who is born but dies before developing the mental maturity to decide for faith or no-faith. Perhaps some of these are saved and some not. Is God righteous, holy, and just only when I understand? Certainly not! For then how will God judge the world? Whatever God has decided it is holy, it is righteous, it is just.

If all the unborn, infants, small children, or otherwise mentally incompetent are saved, God is just; if only some are saved, or none are saved, God is just, God is holy. One must either accept that God is holy, righteous, and just in all his ways, including the salvation of some but not all, or one must create a means of salvation not based on Scripture. How God deals with the special cases is one of the "secret things [that] belong to the Lord our God, but those things which are revealed belong to us and to our children forever, that we may do all the words of this law" (Deuteronomy 29:29).

What has been said about the unborn, infants, small children, and those otherwise mentally incompetent cannot be applied to those who have developed the mental competence to make a decision for faith or no-faith. All mentally competent people in this age between Christ's two advents are morally required to believe on Jesus the Christ as their Savior. All Christians are required to go and preach the gospel of salvation. Therefore, let us preach the gospel to every soul with the mental competence to understand and respond to it.

What was the Purpose of Christ's Propitiation?

Beginning some years after the Synod of Dort, 1618–1619 (whose purpose was to refute the five points of Arminianism), there began and has continued an ongoing discussion of the limits of Christ's act of propitiation on the cross. The Reformed answer is "Limited Atonement," as presented in the TULIP acronym. (The Canons of the Synod of Dort were used to develop the TULIP acronym.) The discussion is, was Christ's propitiation limited in scope or unlimited in scope? Sometimes this question is framed as, "For whom did Christ die?"

Usually this discussion of propitiation is made using the Old Testament word, "atonement": "Christ," says this argument, "made a Limited Atonement," meaning he died only for the elect. The New Testament calls the atonement Christ made on the cross, "propitiation." Both the Old Testament "atonement" and New Testament "propitiation," when used in a religious context, mean a satisfaction made to God for sin.

The questions that will be asked and answered in this essay are: What was the purpose of Christ's propitiation? To whom or for whom was Christ's propitiation directed? What was the scope of Christ's propitiation? "Scope" is where the "limited or unlimited" question comes in.

Before answering the questions, let us talk for a moment about the Old Testament atonement, which forms, for us, the biblical example of forgiveness through sacrifice. Look at any Old Testament sacrifice for sin. Atonement consists of the sacrificial act that generates the merit for forgiveness and the subsequent application of that merit on the altar to effect forgiveness. The sacrifice itself does not effect forgiveness, there is no forgiveness without application. To effect forgiveness the blood of the sacrifice must be applied to the altar; only then were the sins forgiven. The sacrifice generates the merit, the application effects forgiveness: together both acts make an atonement. For example, Leviticus 14:19–20. So also Christ's propitiation.

So, let's define Christ's act of atonement, that is, his propitiation of God for sin. Propitiation is the satisfaction Christ made to God for sin by dying on the cross as the sin-bearer, 2 Corinthians 5:21; Romans 3:25; Hebrews 2:17; 1 John 2:2; 4:10, for the crime of sin committed by human beings, suffering in their place and on their behalf. Christ's propitiation fully satisfied God's holiness and justice for the crime of sin, 1 John 2:2; Romans 3:25.

The answers to the questions.

> What was the purpose of Christ's propitiation? To fully satisfy God's justice against human sin.

> To whom or for whom was Christ's propitiation directed? Christ's propitiation was directed toward God.

The purpose of Christ's propitiation was to satisfy God's justice for the crime of human sin, so God could justly act redemptively toward sinners. God's justice having been satisfied, God could act to apply the merit of Christ's propitiation to effect the redemption of sinners. (No not universal salvation. Keep reading.)

Last question. "What was the scope of Christ's propitiation?" Scripture says the propitiation was, "for the sins of the world," 1 John 2:2. No amount of linguistic acrobatics and manipulation can make "world," *kósmos*, in that verse mean anything other than the world of sinners.

So, just like the Old Testament atonement, the New Testament propitiation is both the sacrifice—Christ suffering for sin on the cross—and the application of that merit to effect redemption for the sinner. Christ's propitiation is not itself redemption, it generated the merit that effects redemption. The merit of the propitiation is applied according to the decree of election through God's gift of grace-faith-salvation. Thus, unlimited atonement, limited redemption. The unlimited merit of Christ's propitiation (atonement) for sin (1 John 2:2) is applied according to the decree of election (Ephesians 1:4) through the gift of God (Ephesians 2:8): limited redemption.

The "Limited Atonement" doctrine confuses atonement with forgiveness. "Limited Atonement" restricts the scope of Christ propitiation to the elect. But the scope of the propitiation is unlimited: infinite, all-sufficient merit for all human sin. The result of the propitiation is God's justice has been completely satisfied for all human sin. The effect of the propitiation is the limited application of its merit according to the decree of election. Unlimited Atonement, Limited Redemption.

The problem began when some of the Reformers took a theological shortcut, moving away from the Canons of Dort. Because the application of the merit of the propitiation is limited to the elect, they began to speak of the propitiation itself as though it was redemption. Because redemption is limited, they began to speak of the propitiation as limited in its scope—only for the elect. That simplistic and distorted shortcut, known as Limited Atonement, has become the standard bearer for Reformed soteriology through the TULIP. "L" = Limited Atonement.

But here is what those originally defining the doctrine of Christ's propitiation said. Canons of the Synod of Dort, 1618–1619.

> SECOND HEAD OF DOCTRINE, "Of the Death of Christ and the Redemption of Men Thereby," Article 3, "The death of the Son of God is the only and most perfect sacrifice and satisfaction for sin, and is of infinite worth and value, abundantly sufficient to expiate the sins of the whole world." (In familiar terms Unlimited Atonement/Propitiation.)

> SECOND HEAD OF DOCTRINE, "Of the Death of Christ and the Redemption of Men Thereby," Article 8, "For this was the sovereign counsel, and most gracious will and purpose of God the Father, that the quickening and saving efficacy of the most precious death of His Son should extend to all the elect, for bestowing upon them alone the gift of justifying faith, thereby to bring them infallibly to salvation."

Or, as the summary states: "While the death of Christ is abundantly sufficient to expiate the sins of the whole world, its saving efficacy is limited to the elect." In what should have been terms of the TULIP, a limited redemption out of an unlimited atonement.

Christ died on the cross to propitiate God for all sin, so God could act in justice, holiness, and righteousness to save sinners. Salvation, then, is the application of Christ's infinite merit to overcome the demerit of sin and save a soul, as specifically applied according to God's sovereign decree of election, through God's gift of grace-faith-salvation, which is then personally applied by each sinner through his/her saving faith in Christ, in response to having received God's gift of grace-faith-salvation.

But, again, the problem is some Reformers. When they hear the words "Unlimited Atonement/Propitiation" they immediately cry out "NO! That is universal Salvation," because they confuse the propitiation with redemption. But universal salvation is a strawman argument, because propitiation/atonement is not redemption. Christ's propitiation was not directed toward sinners, but toward God. The purpose of Christ's propitiation was not to redeem sinners, but to fully satisfy God's justice so God could act to redeem sinners. The application of Christ's propitiation is according to election through God's gift of grace-faith-salvation. In the TULIP, according to the Canons of the Synod of Dort, the "L" should represent "Limited Redemption."

Did Christ "empty Paradise?"

Did Christ "empty Paradise" between his physical death and resurrection? Some believe the OT saved went to a "good side" of Hades, known as "paradise" aka "Abraham's bosom," after physical death, there to await Christ's act of propitiating God for sin on the cross. Then, says this view, after Christ propitiated God, between his physical death and resurrection, Christ went to this "paradise" and then took the Old Testament saved to heaven before or after (the view varies) his resurrection. The rational for this is the OT could not go to heaven until the propitiation of God for sin through the crucifixion was accomplished.

There is no scripture stating or implying Christ went to anywhere but heaven between his physical death and resurrection. There are a few miss-interpreted in that way, but none that demonstrate the proposition. This was not the Reformed view until a century or so past, and was popularized by a few well-known "hell and fire" preachers.

There are several lines of solid proof Christ did not go to Hades, and the OT saved did go to heaven upon their physical death. One of the rules of Bible interpretation is *do not* interpret a scripture contrary to what is clearly taught.

Here are six pieces of evidence that Jesus the Christ went to heaven between his physical death and resurrection.

> 1.   Paradise is heaven, 2 Corinthians 2, 4. Because paradise is heaven there was no paradise to empty.
>
> 2. The Jews (e.g., Luke 23:43, the saved thief), understood paradise as heaven, the home of the righteous, 2 Esdras 7:36; 8:52; Apocalypse of Moses 37:4-6. The thief expected to be in heaven.
>
> 3. Paul stated, "absent from the body, present with the Lord," 2 Corinthians 5:8. What applies to every human being who is in a faith-based relationship with God must apply to the God-man, who was and is as genuinely human as he was/is genuine deity.   As a human being Christ, his human soul, was immediately present with the Lord after physical death.
>
> 4. There is no salvation without regeneration, John 3:3, so the OT saved were born-again (but not indwelt by the Holy Spirit), and therefore fully and completely saved. As fully and completely saved they went to heaven after physical death, 2

Corinthians 5:8.

5. An intermediate state between earth and heaven for the saved, (name it what you will, a "good side" of Hades, Abraham's Bosom, purgatory) is repugnant to the scriptures and the biblical view of salvation.

6. Finally, God decreed, before he created the universe, that the merit of Christ was, is, and always will be the only merit that saves, Ephesians 1:4. Everyone who was saved in the OT was fully and completely saved because Christ is the only merit for salvation, and his merit fully and completely saves.

Because Christ's propitiation for sin was decreed before the universe was created, it was and is effective for all time and eternity. Is God bound by time? No. What God decrees is certain, and God acted on that certainty to save sinners through Christ's merit, both before and after the historical crucifixion.

Here are the verses used to say Christ went to Hades. All that is necessary is to show they may be interpreted other than the assumption he went to Hades.

Ephesians 4:8–10.

8 Therefore it says, "Having ascended on high, he led captive captivity, and gave gifts to men." 9 Now that he ascended, what does it imply but that he also descended into the lower parts of the earth? 10 The One having descended, the same is also the One having ascended above all the heavens, so that he should fill all.

The exposition is taken from my book, *A Private Commentary on the Bible: Ephesians*.

In support of his main theme in this small section (4:7–16), Paul cites Psalm 68:18, using a specific phrase, *dió légō*, "therefore it says," to indicate he is making a citation. The word *dió* is properly translated "therefore," indicating this citation is the reason behind the assertion (Christ giving spiritual gifts). The word *légō* means to put forth, propound, or relate, thus a word spoken or written [Zodhiates, s. v. "3004"]. Paul doesn't give either the Hebrew nor LXX version of Psalm 68:18 in this citation; rather, he provides an interpretation of the verse in a New Testament application that conforms to its original context. Psalm 68:18 reads (NKJV):

You have ascended on high, You have led captivity captive;

You have received gifts among men, even from the rebellious, that the Lord God might dwell there.

Psalm 68:1–18 is a celebration of the victories of YHWH over his enemies, resulting in significant benefit to his people Israel. Verse 18 is the climax of the first section of the Psalm (vv. 19–35 look to the present and future), which celebrates past victories that result in God being exalted among his people and in the midst of his enemies. The event immediately in view (the occasion for the Psalm) is the movement of the Ark of the Covenant up to Jerusalem and into the tabernacle (tent) David erected (according to Moses' instructions) to house the Ark. If we will remember the history of the Ark in time of Samuel and David, it had been captured by the Philistines, 1 Samuel 4:1–11. After seven months the Philistines returned the Ark, 1 Samuel 6, and Israel took it to Kirjath Jearim, where it remained for twenty years, 1 Samuel 7:2. During that time, Samuel the prophet and judge defeated the Philistines, anointed first Saul, then David, to be king, and the history of Saul's conflict with David passes before our eyes.

Ultimately, as we know, David prevailed and became Israel's king. After ruling for seven years in Hebron, David captured Jerusalem from the Jebusites, and then drove the Philistines out of Israel into their own country, 2 Samuel 5. Afterward, David brought the Ark to Jerusalem, 2 Samuel 6. Most scholars believe Psalm 68 was written to celebrate the ascension of the Ark up to and into Jerusalem.

The Ark was a symbol of the presence of YHWH among his people, and Jerusalem sits on a mountain, thus v. 18, the ascent of the Ark is stated in terms of YHWH's exaltation: "You [YHWH] have ascended on high." God, David is saying, has ascended in triumph over his vanquished foes: the act of God, the Ark ascending on high (into Jerusalem to the tabernacle), was representative of God the victor with his long train of captives (including rebellious Israelites) following him in his triumph [Perowne, 527–528], "You [YHWH] have led captivity captive."

In his triumph YHWH has received gifts among men, i.e., as the victor he has taken tribute from men to give to his people. O'Brien connects Numbers chapters 8 and 18, Psalm 68:18, and Ephesians 4:8 [O'Brien, 293]. In this view YHWH took the Levites from among his people in order to give them back as a gift, as servants who minister to the congregation. The Levites are, then, the captives. In this view a parallel between these passages and Ephesians 4:8 makes Christians the captives in the Ephesian passage.

The final strophe could be better translated as "Yes, with the rebellious (also) shall YHWH Elohim [Lord God] abide" [Perowne, 528]. God dwells in the midst of his people and has compelled his enemies to submission. The scene is of the blessings and unity created by God the victor.

In this Psalm YHWH is symbolically exalted by the literal ascension of the Ark to Jerusalem, and YHWH is enthroned, symbolically, when the Ark is put in its rightful place in the tabernacle. In this scene Paul rightly finds a typological representation of the triumph, ascension, and exaltation of Jesus the Christ. Paul's interpretation is found in Ephesians 4:9–10. The "he" of vv. 8–10 must refer to Christ from v. 7, compare the same reference in v. 11 and the reference to Christ's incarnation-resurrection-ascension in v. 10. We will return to v. 8, "and gave gifts to men," in a moment.

First, 4:9, Paul, focusing on Christ, states, "Now this, 'he ascended' implying that Christ must first descend before he could ascend (note the parallel with John 3:13). The "lower parts of the earth" is not specifically a reference to the grave, nor to a supposed descent of Christ into hell. This view was erroneously promulgated by the Western text of the "Apostles Creed" and later defended on the basis of Ephesians 4:8–9; Acts 2:27; Romans 10:6–7; 1 Peter 3:18–20; 4:6. Out of twelve extant versions of the creed the phrase first appears in the sixth (AD 390) and then reappears five versions, 260 years, later (AD 650), and then again one hundred years later in the final version (AD 750) [Schaff, *Creeds*, 54]. The Bible never says that Christ descended into hell. Why would he? There is no second chance for the unsaved, and the saved, like the thief on the cross, were (Old Testament saints) and are (New Testament saints), in paradise (heaven) with the Lord.

The phrase "lower parts of the earth" is in parallel with, and the opposite of, "above all the heavens." When Christ ascended, Acts 1:9, he ascended above the material heavens, above the spirit second heaven, and into the third spirit heaven where God manifests his throne (Revelation 4).

There is reason to doubt the translation by others of *huperánō* as "far above." The word is used in the New Testament at Ephesians 1:21; 4:10; and Hebrews 9:5. In the Hebrews verse it simply means the cherubim were over the Ark. In Ephesians 1:21 it refers to Christ's supreme authority over all other authorities. In the LXX of Jonah 4:6 the translation "far" above would be inappropriate in referring to the gourd as over Jonah's head for shade. There is no doubt that Christ's preeminence and authority are far above all others, but that understanding comes from the word "all," *pás*. On the whole, *huperánō* should probably be translated "above" not "far above." Christ ascended above all the heavens, Acts 1:9, after having first descended to the earth, Luke 2:7. The use of *huperánō* indicates the material and spirit domains.

The exalted Christ assumed his rightful place on the throne of God, Hebrews 1:3, 13; Philippians 2:9; Ephesians 1:20. He ascended above all so that (*hína*) he might fill all. To "fill all" indicates his exaltation to fulfill his sovereign relationship toward the world as Redeemer-Messiah-King. To "fill all" in relation to the spirit domain of existence is not a redemptive view (fallen angels are not redeemed), but is his sovereign reign over all spiritual authorities as the exalted Son of God, 1:21. In relation to the present context: Christ, who is filled with God's fullness, fills the church with that fullness, as being in union with the church, and sovereignly fills the church with his spiritual gifts (1:22–23). In his office as the Redeemer, Christ gained the right to bestow gifts to the church by defeating the enemies of himself and his people.

Christ, who ascended into heaven, first descended out of heaven to the earth. The phrase "the lower parts" indicates his condescension to assume humanity to himself, and his subjection to mortality. In the parallel Scripture, Romans 10:6–7, the term "abyss" is a reference to Christ's death, as Paul explains, thus referring to Christ being subject to mortality. The sinner desiring salvation does not have to ascend into heaven to receive salvation, because Christ has descended to him; nor does he have to descend into death to gain salvation, because Christ died, was resurrected, and ascended in exaltation. One need simply believe on the Christ who descended from heaven to earth, resurrected out of death, and ascended into heaven from earth.

Just as the word "ascended" indicates his exaltation, the opposing "descended" indicates his coming to earth. Just as "ascended" incorporates all the eternal results of his exaltation, "descended" looks to his entire earthly life: his incarnation-death-resurrection-ascension. Christ came to earth, and when he had completed his mission, and had triumphed over his enemies, he ascended in exaltation leading captivity captive.

In 4:8, there is a difference of opinion among the commentators concerning the identity of the "captivity" (a collective noun for captive enemies). The discussion of "captivity" reduces to two main opinions. One, "captivity" refers to that which led others captive, which is sin, death, hell, and all evil powers. Thus, Christ triumphed over all that made men captive to eternal judgment. The other opinion is that "captivity" refers to sinners taken captive in salvation. In this view, Christ leads a triumphant procession of those whom he has "conquered" by salvation and has thereby made them his captives.

Both views have merit, and both are true. The Psalm definitely has the enemies of God in view, as the triumphant YHWH enters his city and ascends to his throne, leading (metaphorically) a procession of his defeated enemies (Philistines, Jebusites, etc.). This view also fits the historical circumstances of many nations who had just such a triumphant parade for the military victor. We can view sin, death, hell, and all evil powers as having been conquered and led in triumph as prisoners of the great Redeemer-King, never again to afflict God's people.

Or, in relation to Christ's redemptive mission, we can view sinners as having been conquered by salvation and now part of the triumph of the Messiah. As noted, both views are doctrinally correct.

The second issue is the change from "received gifts among men," in the Psalm to "gave gifts to men." The Old Testament *lāqah*, translated "received," means "to take" and never means "to give" [Harris et al., s. v. "1124"]. However, one may make a reasonable assumption that the intent of the victorious YHWH in taking (receiving) tribute from his conquered enemies was to give gifts to his people. I have noted that Paul views v. 18 of the Psalm as a typological view of Christ triumphant over sin, death, hell, and evil powers and ascended into heaven. Thus, Paul views the end result of Christ's triumph, which is to give the fruits of his victory to his people.

We need not draw an exact parallel between all the details of the Psalm and Paul's use; if for no other reason, what tribute could Christ take from sin, death, hell, and evil powers that he could give to his people? At the most, we might view these enemies as under Christ's authority and therefore unable to retain any person in their power without his permission. A somewhat similar view is found in Revelation 1:18, where Christ has the keys of hades and death. A key is a symbol of authority. Hades is the jail the unsaved go into at their physical death; spiritual death is the prison the unsaved are confined to for eternity (the lake of fire). Death is under the control of the one who has the keys. Christ will never let his people come under the control of hades and death.

However, the view that sin, death, hell, and evil powers are under Christ's authority is neither Paul's view (in this passage) nor his application. Paul interprets Psalm 68:18 in accordance with his typological understanding, and uses his interpretation to make an application of that typological truth to the present Ephesian context. Paul's point is not some tribute one might imagine Christ's taking from his conquered foes, but the triumphant king distributing the fruits of his victory to his saved people. Christ triumphed over his enemies in his condescension and humiliation, and then ascended to his exalted throne of authority over all things and all personal beings. It is in his position as the triumphant king that he gives gifts to his people. Therefore, the source of the gifts Christ gives is Christ himself.

Some view the gifts as though Christ in his human nature and through his work on earth had taken gifts from men and upon his ascension gives these gifts to men. Another view is that the Christ received gifts from the Father and then gave these gifts to men. A third view is that Paul is referring to the descent of the Holy Spirit at Pentecost as Christ figuratively descending (by or through the Spirit) to give gifts to men (an idea not found in Acts). None of these ideas are in the Ephesian passage. The point is that Christ came to earth, triumphed over his enemies, ascended in victory to heaven, and in his exaltation gives spiritual gifts to men, gifts that promote, build, and maintain the unity of his people. Indeed, because he is the king who has triumphed over all the causes of disunity (sin, death, hell, and evil powers), the unity of his people in their union with him is assured.

The other verse used to say Christ descended into Hades is 1 Peter 3:18c–20. From my book, *A Private Commentary on the Bible: 1 Peter.*

> *18c but having been made alive in spirit, 19 in which also having gone to the spirits in prison, he preached, 20 once upon a time having disbelieved, when once the longsuffering of God waited in days of Noah, ark being prepared, in which few, that is, eight souls, were saved through water.*

3: 18C, "having indeed been put to death in flesh, but having been made alive in spirit." This part of v. 18 is the subject of great discussion and varying interpretation. However, the context of suffering and blessing indicate that just as suffering did not destroy Christ, so too suffering will not destroy the believer. Christ died, but he was resurrected out from among the dead. Even so the believer may suffer death, but he will be resurrected out from among the dead. This is the application of the phrase.

The point of controversy is whether the word *pneúma*, "spirit," refers to the Holy Spirit or Christ's human soul. Before continuing, I should say I believe man is a bipartite being, composed of body and soul (see appendix one). Scripture sometimes uses the word "spirit" to refer to the soul. Although there are a few verses, most in the New Testament, that might be interpreted to mean man is body, soul, and spirit, the Scripture overwhelmingly uses "soul" to refer to the person, and "spirit" to refer to how a person acts or feels, especially how he or she interacts with God. The use of "spirit" here, however, does not refer to life, but to a sphere of activity.

The Greek text of v. 18 does not have the definite article before "flesh" or "spirit." In the Greek language the definite article was used to point out specific identity [Dana and Mantey, 124–157]. For example, in Matthew 14:3, the Greek text is "Herodias, the wife of Philip," indicating that one specific person who was Philip's wife. When the definite article is not used the stress is on quality, character, or sphere of activity. For example, the article is not present in the Greek text of 1 Timothy 3:2. The proper translation is "a one-wife sort of husband," meaning a husband whose quality is fidelity toward his wife.

Another example is, 1 Thessalonians 4:15, which some versions translate "by the word of the Lord," but there is no definite article in the text associated with "word." The proper translation is "by word of the Lord." The meaning of the anarthrous (no definite article) text is "a word whose quality or character is that it comes from one who is Lord." If the definite article had been present the meaning would have been a specific Scripture. Without the definite article the divine authority of the teaching is being stressed.

In reference to 1 Peter 3:18, the meaning is that Christ was made dead in respect to the sphere of activity of flesh, but made alive in respect to the sphere of activity of spirit. Put another way, he was dead in the material domain but alive in the spirit domain. The HCSB version gives an expanded translation to indicate this is the meaning, "being put to death in the fleshly realm but made alive in the spiritual realm."

Believers are quite used to Paul's meaning of "flesh" as the activity of the sin nature in mind and body. This use cannot be applied to Jesus, and therefore Peter has something else in mind. Peter refers to the Son incarnate in human flesh and human nature: God incarnate in a natural human body with a rational human soul.

The term "spirit" is in parallel with "flesh" and therefore must have a meaning that corresponds with "flesh," but in the proper sphere of activity. Christ "in flesh" means the Son incarnate in the world, living a life subject to the conditions of mortality, so that in the material domain—in flesh—he died. Christ "in spirit" refers to Christ in the spirit domain—which does not exclude Christ as a whole person, body and soul, reunited at his resurrection. In the spirit domain he lives.

If, as is the case, "having been put to death in flesh" means physical death in relation to the material domain of human existence, then "having been made alive in spirit" must contrast with his physical death. How was Jesus made alive in spirit? Obviously Jesus' soul was not made alive after his experience at the cross, because human life begins at conception, when a rudimentary soul is conceived at the same time as the rudimentary physical form, and then continues without cessation; the human soul is immortal. This raises the question, What is death? Whether physical or spiritual, death is separation. Physical death is when the immaterial soul leaves the material body. The body is "dead" because the animating principle, the soul, is no longer in the body. Spiritual death is when the soul is separated from God because of sin.

Jesus suffered physical death. However, Peter does not say Jesus died, but Christ died. Peter uses the words "Jesus Christ" eleven times in 1 Peter and nine times in 2 Peter. But when he used the word "Christ" without the qualifying "Jesus" he was speaking of the Christ's work on the cross: 1 Peter 1:11, 19; 2:21; 3:16, 18; 4:1, 14; 5:1. What is in view in v. 18 is the propitiation, the work of Jesus the Christ in his office of Redeemer. In the sphere of flesh he died and propitiated God for man's sin. But in the sphere of spirit he applies the benefits of his propitiation to those who believe on him as Savior. Put another way, "put to death in flesh" and "made alive in spirit" are explanatory of "that he might bring us to God."

There are other views of the verse. In one view, Christ was made alive with respect to the regenerate mode of existence because "in spirit" is "the mode of existence of the regenerate or those pleasing to God" [Davids, 136, 137]. If this is correct, the parallel must be that Christ died with respect to the unregenerate mode of existence because the flesh "in the New Testament is the mode of existence of unregenerate humanity" [Davids, 136, 137]. The logic of this view must suppose Christ was unregenerate because he was in the flesh, and through his own sacrifice he was made regenerate, i.e., became born-again. This view does not agree with the sinless nature of Christ the God-man.

Another view is that "made alive in spirit" was the activity of the Holy Spirit rejoining his human soul to his body, i.e., resurrection: "Now what does his being quickened in the spirit mean if not this, that the same flesh in which alone he had experienced death rose from the dead by the quickening spirit?" Augustine, Letter CLXIV, 4:18. This view depends on "spirit" being the Holy Spirit. One cannot say his human spirit caused his resurrection, seeing as the Bible says Jesus' resurrection was an act of deity, the joint work of Father, Son, and Holy Spirit. Therefore the "quickening spirit" in this view must be the Holy Spirit. But the text does not have the definite article which would have indicated the Person who is the Holy Spirit.

Yet another view, which looks to interpret v. 19, is that Christ's human spirit went into Hades during the three days he was in the tomb. However, Jesus told the thief on the cross that "this day" he would be in paradise with Jesus. There is no Scripture that makes "paradise" to be other than heaven: all uses, Luke 23:43; 2 Corinthians 12:4; Revelation 2:7. Like all righteous souls, Jesus' soul went to heaven immediately following his death. (His comment "I have not yet ascended" is after his resurrection, referring to the ascension of his physical body.)

The end of the discussion is that "in flesh" refers to life in the material domain and "in spirit" refers to life in the spirit domain. Jesus suffered physical death in relation to the material domain of human existence. But he was always alive in the spirit domain. Here one must understand the contrast between life and death. Just as death is always some form of separation—soul from body; sinner from God—even so life is always some form of union—the believer with God in Christ; the soul with the body. In spirit Christ was always with God. Because he had made a complete propitiation for sin he was able to be resurrected and exalted. Because he had made a complete propitiation for sin he is able to bring the sinner to God, i.e., to make the sinner alive. In the spirit domain he lives and the believer has eternal life.

19 in which also having gone to the spirits in prison, he preached,
20 once upon a time having disbelieved, when once the longsuffering of God waited in days of Noah, ark being prepared, in which few, that is, eight souls, were saved through water.

I have given these two scriptures a more literal translation so the difficulty in interpretation may be seen. The first issue is the referent of "in which." The interpretation "in spirit" in v. 18 as the sphere of spiritual activity, avoids many interpretive errors in vv. 19–20. Jesus did not preach to the "spirits in prison" face-to-face in his own Person.

However, to speak for a moment on behalf of other views, it is logical and reasonable that a human soul should have some sort of defined presence in the spirit domain when physical death has separated the person from his or her physical body. The soul is immaterial, not physical, but it is finite, and therefore not everywhere-at-once, but will have a defined presence in the spirit domain. For ease of reference we will call that defined presence a "body," recognizing it is not a material body, but some sort of defined presence suited for life in the spirit domain.

Using this definition, when Jesus physically died his soul had some sort of "body" in the spirit domain, in which and by which he could have preached to the spirits in prison. Preaching "to the spirits in prison" was some sort of activity in the spirit domain. To determine the nature of that activity, one must determine the identity of the spirits in prison.

The word translated "once upon a time," is *poté* [Zodhiates, s. v. "4210"], when, whenever. In Peter's context, which refers to "days of Noah," *poté* means once upon a time in the past. Therefore, the spirits in prison are those who disbelieved in the days of Noah. The word translated "disbelieved" is *apeithéō* [Zodhiates, s. v. "544"], to be disobedient, to disbelieve. Either translation works here. The ones who perished in Noah's day disbelieved and disobeyed when told salvation was in the ark.

Peter says Christ preached to those persons who died in the Flood. But did he do it before or after the flood? Did he do it in person or through Noah? If before the flood, there is no supporting Old Testament testimony that the pre-incarnate Christ, as the Angel of the Lord, preached to sinners in Noah's time. If after the flood, what would be the reason to speak to sinners after their death in the flood? Physical death seals the soul in its spiritual state at the time of death. Not saved at physical death means not saved for eternity. Those who died in the flood are in *hádēs* waiting their final judgment at Revelation 20:11–15. So Christ somehow preached to persons before they died in the flood, but how?

"How" is the important question, because the how answers the when and why questions. The Son sent the Holy Spirit to preach through Noah the message of salvation from coming judgment. This should not be surprising, because it is the way salvation has been preached by the church. Christ sent the Holy Spirit to the church, John 14:15–16; 15:26–27; 16:7–11, so believers could preach the message of salvation.

Building the ark took many years. Noah was five hundred years old when he had children, Genesis 5:32, the oldest of whom was ninety-eight when the flood began, 11:10, and Noah was six hundred years old when the flood began, 7:6. It is reasonable to assume that a very large boat taking shape in Noah's backyard would generate some curiosity from the neighbors. It is just as reasonable to assume that as his sons grew old enough to work with him to build the ark Noah spent time away from the work to warn sinners of the judgment to come. This agrees with the testimony of the whole Bible: God gives warning before judgment. The person who knew judgment was coming was Noah; therefore Noah preached the judgment to come and salvation in the ark. Christ—the Holy Spirit—preached judgment and salvation through God's witness for the times: Noah. The activity in the spirit domain was the Son and Holy Spirit working through Noah to preach judgment and salvation.

The abrupt structure regarding God's longsuffering requires careful interpretation. The literal word order is, "in days of Noah being prepared ark." The subject is not the ark, but God's longsuffering, which indicates the passage of time: "longsuffering" means to endure patiently with someone for a long time. To put the Greek into good English, God's longsuffering took place "in [the] days of Noah [while the] ark [was] being prepared.

Putting it all together: during the long time it took Noah to build the ark (one hundred twenty years, Genesis 6:6:3?), Christ sent the Holy Spirit to preach salvation through Noah; and probably through his sons as they came to maturity. All but Noah, his wife, his three sons, and their wives, eight souls, died. Peter speaks of those dead persons as in prison because in his time, they were. Those who were drowned in the Noahic Flood went to the place all unsaved souls go upon physical death: *hádēs*, hell.

The correct interpretation is the one proposed above: human beings living in the time of Noah but, in reference to Peter's time, are physically dead and their souls are in Hades. Four other interpretations have been proposed:

> The souls of those humans who died in Noah's flood, in *hádēs*, preached to by Christ during his three days in the tomb.

> The Old Testament saints waiting in *hádēs* to go to heaven.

> Fallen angels.

> The offspring of fallen angels and human women, identified in this particular interpretation as demons.

Some common sense must prevail. Regarding item one, unsaved souls are in *hádēs* waiting for the Great White Throne judgment at the end of the ages, Revelation 20:11–15. Neither preaching the gospel, nor berating them for their sins, would make any difference to their eternally unsaved state. Having spoken to them in love (offering salvation) during their physical life, God will next speak to them in judgment at the Great White Throne. There is never any indication in Scripture that God speaks to the unsaved dead in *hádēs*.

Regarding item two, the Old Testament saints were never in *hádēs*. The Old Testament saints experienced a full salvation, because God by his grace accepted their faith in the content of faith he had given them as the way of salvation. This is easier to explain by way of illustration, and since Peter mentions Noah, we will use Noah's time. Noah did not see Christ, because Christ did not appear and God did not preach Christ to him, read Genesis 6–8. Noah was required to believe God would judge the entire world through a flood, and that inside the ark was the only means of salvation. He believed and was saved, God counting his faith as righteous, cf. Abraham at Genesis 15:6. That Noah's soul was saved by what Christ did at the cross is certain. Ephesians 1:4 states that from eternity-past Christ was decreed as the only way of salvation. But Christ was not revealed until the fullness of the time, Galatians 3:4. Faith in the content of faith—in Noah's case, believe in coming judgment, build an ark, get in the ark to escape judgment—was counted as righteousness. Eight souls were saved by that faith, based on what Christ would do on the cross to propitiate God for the crime of sin. I mentioned this at 1:10, "the basis of salvation in every age is the death [propitiation] made by Christ; the requirement for salvation in every age is faith; the object of faith in every age is God; the content of faith changes in the various dispensations" [Ryrie, *Dispensationalism*, 115].

Therefore, the Old Testament saints were as saved as New Testament saints. They weren't waiting in *hádēs* for Christ to taken them to heaven, but were waiting in heaven to celebrate his exaltation when he ascended to heaven after his redemptive work.

The fourth item is fallen angels. Some persons believe Christ preached to the fallen angels between his death and resurrection. What could he have said, if he did speak to them as this view proposes. There is no redemption for the fallen angels. Jesus said the lake of fire was prepared for the devil and his angels, Matthew 25:41, a statement which supposes their doom was unalterable from the moment of their sin. Unsaved human beings go to the lake of fire (Revelation 20:15) because their unbelief has placed them in the same unredeemed category as the fallen angels. However, the Bible never describes or offers a way of salvation for the fallen angels; they are unredeemable.

The final alternate view is that between his death and resurrection Christ preached to the dead offspring of fallen angels and human beings. The first problem with this view is the same identified with item one: neither preaching the gospel, nor berating them for their sins, would make any difference to the unsaved. Second, angels and human beings cannot have sexual intercourse, and if they did it could not result in conception. I have dealt with this issue in a lengthy discussion in my *Private Commentary* on Jude. Here I will only state the results. There are many reasons Genesis 6:1–2, 4 cannot refer to angel-human sex.

> The term "sons of" when used figuratively, is a non-gender-specific term which means a person possesses the characteristics of who or what he or she is a "son of." "Sons of God" identifies a person (angel or human) who is in a faith-based relationship with God: God's character is reproduced in that person.

> No evil angel is ever characterized as a son of God. No unsaved human being is ever characterized as a son of God (all uses: Genesis 6:2, 4; Job 1:6; 2:1; 38:7; Matthew 5:9; Luke 20:36; Romans 8:14, 19; Galatians 3:26.)

> The term "daughters of men" is a figurative term that means the person possesses the characteristics of mankind, which in the context—after Adam's sin—must mean sinful man.

> The term "daughters of men" occurs only in Genesis 6:2, 4. It occurs there because biological reproduction and religious

infidelity was occurring between men and women. The sense is not that only males are sons of God and only women are daughters of men, but that those who were in a faith-based relationship with God married those who were not in a faith-based relationship with God. More simply, believers were marrying unbelievers. The result was that wickedness was great on the earth because men and women had compromised their faith.

God's law of biological reproduction prevents human beings from conceiving if angel-human sex was possible: each kind reproduces according to its kind. Genesis 1:11–12, 21–22, 24–25, 28; 5:3. Angels and humans are different kinds in God's biological economy.

Human beings are immaterial soul and material body; angels are immaterial, spirit beings without a material body. Humans reproduce sexually. The kind of physical contact required for sexual intercourse is not possible between immaterial and material beings. (While some angels have appeared in a human-like form, no angel ever demonstrated he was a material being, contrast Luke 24:40–43).

Angels do not have a sexual gender similar in kind to man's sexual genders, Mark 12:25 (men marry, women are given in marriage, the angels do neither). The implication of "angels do not marry" is that angels do not reproduce.

Believers, the sons of God, married unbelievers, the daughters of men, vv. 1–2.

Genesis 6:4 does not follow v. 2 and does not begin with a conjunction. Because it does not begin with a conjunction it is not trying to show the result of vv. 1-2.

Genesis 6:4, there were "giants" *before* believers married unbelievers, and there were "giants" after believers married unbelievers. Therefore, marriage between the sons of God and the daughters of men was not the cause for the "giants."

The word translated "giants" is *nᵉpîlîm*. This word is used only here and Numbers 13:33. The derivation and thus the meaning of the word is obscure. The most likely meaning is "heroes" or "fierce warriors." It could refer to a race or nation. The translation "giants" came from the LXX.

In v. 4 "the mighty men who were of old, men of renown" probably refers to the children born to the sons of God and daughters of men. The word translated "mighty men" means "the heroes or champions among the armed forces." The word translated "renown" has the meaning of "reputation."

Jude 6 and 2 Peter 2:4 do not mention Genesis 6:2, 4 as the cause of, or related to, the angels' sin. To find Genesis 6:2, 4 in Jude 6 (or 2 Peter) one must bring it to the verse.

The Genesis 6 passage does not require angels.

Based on these arguments from Scripture, one can confidently conclude that Genesis 6:1–2, 4 is not about angel-human sex. There was no angelic involvement in Genesis 6. The true interpretation of Jude 6 and 2 Peter 2:4 is that certain fallen angels committed crimes, such as habitation of human beings, for which they have been imprisoned. Peter, at 1 Peter 2:19, cannot have been thinking of the offspring of angel-human sex.

The most reasonable interpretation of 1 Peter 3:19–20 is the one proposed: during the long time it took Noah to build the ark, Christ sent the Holy Spirit to preach salvation through Noah. That Noah did preach a message of salvation from judgment is clear: Peter calls Noah a "preacher of righteousness" in his second epistle. That the Holy Spirit was present in the time of Noah is also clear, "My Spirit shall not strive with man forever."

I began this discussion in 2:18 by noting that the context is suffering and blessing. Just as suffering did not destroy Christ, so, too, suffering will not destroy the believer. The interpretation in context is this: like Noah, do not be afraid of suffering in a good cause for righteousness sake. You do not stand alone. Christ stands with you as he did with Noah, one righteous man against an entirely unrighteous world. You may suffer for your stand, but suffering for righteousness results in victory because the message and the messenger are righteous. Noah was a righteous man. The suffering of Noah for righteousness is assumed by Peter because Noah stood against the world. Even if his suffering was no more than isolation from his friends and ridicule from his peers he suffered for the sake of that righteousness which would save him and his family, and could have saved the world. The people received a message of deliverance from judgment which they did not believe; and therefore their judgment was assured. Follow Jesus, says Peter, through suffering to victory, even if you stand alone with the truth against the whole world. Stand alone, even if your suffering results in your being put to death in the flesh, because you will be made alive by the Spirit.

Nisbet offers this application. "Here is the seventh argument, pressing upon Christians constant obedience to the Gospel, notwithstanding of hardest sufferings. The sum whereof is that since there are many souls of men and women to whom Christ did once by his Spirit, in the ministry of Noah and others of his servants, make plain the way to life and salvation, who are now imprisoned in Hell for evermore, because of their slighting so much patience and pains as the Lord did exercise toward them, especially during the time of Noah's preparing the Ark, wherein a few only escaped destruction by the flood; therefore it concerns those who have the Gospel more clearly preached to them to give obedience thereunto, whatever they may suffer for it within time" [Nisbet, *1 & 2 Peter*, 145].

The scriptures used to try and teach Christ descended into Hades/Abraham's bosom to take the Old Testament saved to heaven have a different interpretation, one that is more consistent with the Scriptures concerning salvation and heaven.

The Efficiency of the Propitiation

Proposition: Christ's propitiation, accomplished at a specific moment in time, was and is efficient to completely and fully and comprehensively save any sinner at any time since the creation of the world, according to God's eternal decree.

Counter-proposition: No Old Testament sinner was completely saved until Christ accomplished his propitiation at a specific moment in time, but every Old Testament sinner was provisionally saved until that propitiation was accomplished.

I believe most reading this essay would agree the counter-proposition is not biblically sound. Yet, there is a doctrine, a doctrine many of you firmly believe and teach, that teaches exactly what the counter-proposal teaches. That doctrine is known as the "Two-Compartment Sheol" doctrine. I will explain. First, let's define some terms [from my book, *Dictionary of Doctrinal Words.*]

> Propitiation. The satisfaction Christ made to God for sin by dying on the cross as the sin-bearer, 2 Corinthians 5:21; Romans 3:25; Hebrews 2:17; 1 John 2:2; 4:10, for the crime of sin committed by human beings, suffering in their place and on their behalf. Christ's propitiation fully satisfied God's holiness and justice for the crime of sin.
>
> Eternity (1). A term used to identify the reality that is God himself, to identify the timeless and eternal existence of the increate God as separate from the time-bound existence of all things he has created, Genesis 1:1, or will create, Revelation 21:1.
>
> Eternity-past. The timeless state of reality when the increate God alone existed, before he created anything that was created. God himself is the one genuine, timeless, eternal reality within which the created time-bound reality that is our universe has its existence.

The doctrine of a two-compartment Sheol, teaches when an Old Testament saved person died, he/she went to a kind of limbo (more familiarly known as "Abraham's Bosom" or paradise) to wait until Christ competed his propitiation. As one proponent of this theory has stated it, "While Yeshua [Jesus] was in Sheol, He proclaimed to those who were with Him in paradise that the atonement had been made, and to those on the other side, His presence guaranteed their final judgment."

Now, Paul teaches that the condition of salvation affecting the believer at physical death is "absent from the body, present with the Lord," 2 Corinthians 5:8. Did that condition apply to the OT believer? Yes, it did, but to verify that positive answer we have to approach the issue from the point of view of eternity.

In the eternity past before God created the universe, he decreed the propitiation to be made by his Son would provide the only merit to save sinners, Ephesians 1:4. There is a simple biblical principle: What was decreed in eternity is effective for all time. Romans 4:17, God gives life to the dead and calls those things which do not exist as though they did exist.

Was what God decreed in eternity past—that only Christ's propitiation had the merit to save the soul—efficient to fully and completely save the believing sinner during the time before Christ made his propitiation of God for sin?

Let us ask that question another way. Is God limited by time? Time is a mechanism God created to manage the universe he created. God is never limited by his creation. Deity is not limited by time. But Deity chose to create time and create creatures limited by time. Therefore Deity has chosen to work within the temporal limits of his creatures. The universe was created in a moment of time, the incarnation was a moment in time, the propitiation, death, and resurrection were moments in time.

But the decree of salvation, which was made *before* time was created, is not bound by time, but applies to all sinners to save them (by grace through faith) at any moment in their particular time. As noted above, God calls those things which do not exist as though they did exist. When God decreed Christ's propitiation was the only merit for salvation, that act was set for a particular moment in time. But having been decreed before time, it was efficient to completely save throughout all time. I am not teaching something new, this is the doctrine of all biblically based soteriology (doctrine of salvation). Go read the theologians.

So how does Deity work to accomplish salvation within the temporal limits of his creatures, Old Testament and New Testament, Adam to you and me and yet-future? At every moment in time God worked the same way he worked to save you: God's gift of grace-faith-salvation (Ephesians 2:8); God's testimony of saving faith; the Holy

Spirit giving conviction: the sinner saved by grace through faith by the application of Christ's limitless merit (propitiation), which was decreed in eternity past so as to be efficient throughout time to completely save each and every sinner who believes.

The Two-compartment Sheol doctrine (the OT saved went to Sheol, Abraham's Bosom, paradise) teaches God is limited by time. That interpretation contradicts an essential doctrine concerning the very person of God as eternal in every aspect of his being. God himself is eternity. His essence, which is his person, is the definition of eternity, the very thing, the only thing, by which we limited, created beings have some dim comprehension of eternity.

If God's eternal decree of a full and completed salvation for those who believe is limited by time, then God is limited by time, because every decree of God is an expression of God's eternal values, which are necessarily of his essence; all that is in God is God. God did not decree salvation after he created the universe, but before he created the universe. Ephesians 1:4, "even as he [God] chose us [the believer] in him [Christ] before the beginning of the universe." Time is part of the created universe. So God decreed salvation and the only means to salvation in eternity past before he created time.

Therefore, Christ's propitiation, accomplished at a specific moment in time, was and is efficient to completely and fully and comprehensively save any sinner at any time since the creation of the world, according to God's eternal decree.

I believe the Bible teaches a person cannot be a little bit saved. The doctrine of a two-compartment Sheol teaches the OT saved were only sort of saved, a little bit saved, only provisionally saved, did not possess a completed salvation, until that historical moment Christ's propitiation was completed. That doctrine has been taught, and it has been denied, since the beginning of the early church. From the church fathers (you can find them at ccel.org; the abbreviation "ANF" means Ante-Nicene Fathers; "NPNF" means Nicene Post-Nicene Fathers.)

Justin Martyr (AD 100–165). "Their [believers'] souls, when they die, are taken to heaven." [Roberts and Donaldson, ANF, 1:239, Dialogue with Trypho, 80.]

Cyril of Alexandria (AD 378–444). "He [Cyril] presupposes the immediate entry of the souls of the righteous into heaven and the immediate chastisement of those of the wicked."[J.N.D. Kelly, *Early Christian Doctrines*, 482.]

Gregory Nazianzen (AD 329–390). "I believe the words of the wise that every fair and God-beloved soul, when, set free from the bonds of the body . . . goes rejoicing to meet its Lord . . .. Then, a little later, it receives its kindred flesh [resurrection]" [Schaff, NPNF, 7:236 (Panegyric on His Brother S. Caesarius, 21).] Gregory also believed "Abraham's Bosom" was the same as heaven. [Same reference.]

In more recent history, The Westminster Confession of Faith (1646). Chapter 32.1. "The bodies of men, after death, return to dust, and see corruption: but their souls, which neither die nor sleep, having an immortal subsistence, immediately return to God who gave them: the souls of the righteous, being then made perfect in holiness, are received into the highest heavens, where they behold the face of God, in light and glory, waiting for the full redemption of their bodies. And the souls of the wicked are cast into hell, where they remain in torments and utter darkness, reserved to the judgment of the great day. Beside these two places, for souls separated from their bodies, the Scripture acknowledges none."

Where did the Two-Compartment Sheol theory originate? It originated in early Christianity as a consequence of martyrdom: seeking a special reward for the martyrs upon their death; which must by necessity exclude those not martyred.

Tertullian (AD 160–220) [Roberts and Donaldson, ANF, 3:576 (On the Resurrection of the Flesh, 43).]

> For no one, on becoming absent from the body, is at once a dweller in the presence of the Lord, except by the prerogative of martyrdom, he gains a lodging in Paradise, not in the lower regions.

Notice that "Paradise" is a compartment but not part of "the lower regions" in Tertullian's doctrine, thus a two-compartment Sheol.

Let us look at three generations of Reformed theologians who taught Christ did not descend into Sheol.

C. Hodge, *Systematic Theology*, 2:619, 621.

First Peter 3:18, 19 . . . afford no ground for the doctrine that Christ after death went into hell.

The Romanists teach that the department of Hades to which Christ descended, was not the abode of evil spirits, but that in which dwelt the souls of believers who died before the advent of the Redeemer, and that the object of his descent was . . . to deliver the pious dead from the intermediate state in which they were and introduce them into heaven. (Hodge is opposed to the "Romish doctrine.")

Louis Berkhof, *Systematic Theology*, 342.

> [Addressing the Apostolic Creed] The Catholic Church takes it to mean that, after death, Christ went into the *Limbus Patrum*, where the Old Testament saints were awaiting the revelation and application is his redemption, preached the gospel to them, and brought them out to heaven . . .. Calvin [*Institutes*, 2.16.8] interprets the phrase metaphorically, as referring to the penal sufferings of Christ on the cross, where he really suffered the pangs of hell . . .. Scripture certainly does not teach a literal descent of Christ into hell.

Wayne Grudem, *Systematic Theology*, 281, 586, 590.

> "Not many Scripture references talk about the state of the Old Testament believers after they had died, but those that give us any indication of their state all point in the direction of immediate conscious enjoyment in the presence of God, not of a time of waiting away from God's presence."

> "An examination of the biblical evidence indicates Christ did not descend into hell."

> "Scripture gives us no clear evidence to make us think that full access to the blessings of being in God's presence in heaven were withheld from Old Testament believers when they died—indeed, several passages suggest that believers who died before Christ's death did enter into the presence of God at once because their sins were forgiven by trusting in the Messiah who was to come (Genesis 5:24; 2 Samuel 12:23; Psalm 16:11; 17:15; 23:6; Ecclesiastes 12:7; Matthew 22:31–32; Luke 16:22; Romans 4:1–8; Hebrews 11:5).

W.G.T. Shedd (1820–1894), *The Doctrine of Endless Punishment*, 59–60, summarizes the Reformed doctrine up to his times.

> The substance of the Reformed view, then, is, that the intermediate [between death and resurrection] state for the saved is Heaven without the body, and the final state for the saved is Heaven with the body; that the intermediate state for the lost is Hell [hádēs] without the body, and the final state for the lost is Hell [géenna] with the body.

When the Literal hermeneutic is consistently used, when all the doctrines concerning Christ's propitiation are consulted, when the essence of God is understood, the concept of a Two-Compartment Sheol is seen to be inconsistent with Scripture and the history of interpretation.

I believe I have demonstrated the proposition at the beginning of this essay is biblically true. "Proposition: Christ's propitiation, accomplished at a specific moment in time, was and is efficient to completely and fully and comprehensively save any sinner at any time since the creation of the world, according to God's eternal decree."

This essay is a brief presentation. For more in depth discussion (e.g., the Jewish Apocrypha on the subject) see my book *Life, Death, Eternity*, specifically the chapter, "The Doctrine of She'ôl," a verse by verse examination showing She'ôl is always the grave; and Appendix One: Two Compartment Theory of She'ôl.

Did Jesus Cease to Exist when Dead?

Annihilationism is the view that whoever and whatever cannot be redeemed by God is ultimately put out of existence. The unsaved do not suffer endless punishment, as the Scripture teaches, but God causes them to cease to exist, as if they never existed.

In recent times this doctrine has reached its logical conclusion: the soul ceases to exist after physical death, until brought back into existence at the resurrection. And the inevitable corollary: Jesus the Christ ceased to exist between his physical death and resurrection.

One response to this latest theory in annihilationism is various scriptures. One may point to Luke 16:23 and Revelation 6:9–10; 7:9–10 for the conscious torment or bliss (respectively) of the physically dead human being. Paul's "absent from the body, present with the Lord," 2 Corinthians 5:8, also has bearing on the subject.

In relation to Jesus the Christ, one might use the argument Christ went to Sheol to rescue the unsaved OT dead and take them to heaven. That argument would go a long way to proving Jesus did not cease to exist between physical death and resurrection. That particular argument does not appeal to me, for reasons biblical, rational, and historical (i.e., the history of interpretation). Some use it, and we will not pass judgment on their understanding of Scripture.

There is a more biblical path. One of the serious mistakes many make in trying to understand Scripture is the insistence on an explicit verse for every doctrine. This is especially the error of new believers as well as the error of the heretic and apostate. But as one has wisely said, the Scripture teaches through both explicit verses and "the doctrines that emerge as a necessary consequence of what the Bible as a whole teaches" [Dolezal, *All That is in God*, 37].

What does the Bible teach about the soul in general and Jesus' soul in particular?

Search the scriptures, and you will never find any word, phrase, or verse stating the dissolution of the soul. The body dies, the soul continues. What is death? Death in the Bible is always some kind of separation. Physical death is the separation of the soul from the body. Genesis 2:7 states Adam's body was non-living dirt until God breathed a soul into that inert form, and then "man became a living being." On the cross, Jesus said, " 'It is finished. Father, into your hands I commit my spirit.' And having bowed his head, he breathed his last, he yielded up his spirit" (Matt, Luke, John combined).

The body dies because the soul is separated from the body: a simple, yet profound, spiritual truth. The body lives again when the soul is rejoined to the body: resurrection. There is no scripture or teaching of Scripture that the soul ever ceases to exist. The biblical testimony—which is to say, the complete absence of opposing testimony—is the human soul continues endlessly in existence and consciousness after it comes into existence.

Now, that simple biblical truth answers the question concerning Jesus. Whether his soul went to heaven, my view (he was a believer, so 2 Corinthians 5:8), or went to Sheol to rescue the OT saved (why were they there?), his soul continued in existence throughout the physical death of his body.

So far we have been applying the rule, "what the Bible as a whole teaches." The Bible as a whole does not teach the dissolution of the soul, as it does the body—and there is no explicit verse to the contrary. But there is another way to apply that rule to Jesus Christ: what the Bible as a whole teaches about the nature of deity and the incarnation of deity.

The how of the incarnation is a mystery, but not the who or the what. We know God the Son joined himself to a genuine human body and a genuine human soul. Now the human soul may be viewed as a container filled with the animating principle "life," and that particular essence that makes the person human (as opposed to the essence that would make an angel), and with that complex of attributes we define as human nature. In the normally conceived human being the synergy of these elements create the human personality. So we may define the human soul as, "an immaterial substance that gives life and governs behavior in all living things. The soul is composed of the animating principle life and that complex of attributes which synergistically determine the nature and personality of living beings."

Now to the incarnation. When God the Son joined himself to the newly conceived human being Jesus of Nazareth, at the very instant of conception, he joined himself not just to the human body (the one cell zygote), but also to the newly conceived human soul. That newly conceived human soul had all the elements of a soul: life, essence, attributes. But that newly conceived soul did not have a personality. God the Son provided the personality, his personality, which upon joining with human nature became informed by both the deity nature and the human nature.

God the Son was one person with two natures, deity and human, with one personality informed by both natures. We see the Scripture teaches one personality, because the Scripture never (never!) speaks of his works as being done by one nature or the other. Scripture always speaks of Jesus acting as one person, not two personalities. So whether he omnipotently raised the dead, or he was tired and slept in the boat, he did all as one person, Jesus the Christ, the Son of God, the God-man.

So, let us relate those facts of the incarnation to the annihilation doctrine that Jesus ceased to exist as a soul, as a person, between physical death and resurrection.

The issue is simple: the deity person God the Son not only cannot die, he cannot cease to exist: he is increate, he has life in himself, so he is eternal. The human body into which he had incarnated died when the soul left the body ("Father, into your hands I commit my spirit"). That human soul was, continues to be, and also continued throughout the death of the body to be irreversibly, inseparably, and endlessly joined with God the Son, who has life in himself, John 5:26. Because God is the origin and source of all life, God the Son endlessly gives life to that soul into which he incarnated. Throughout physical death, the person Jesus the Christ was a living, conscious soul.

Two things are clear:

> The person Jesus Christ viewed as the God-man could not die in his deity and humanity and cease to exist as the God-man. That would be a division in the Trinity.

> The person Jesus Christ viewed in his humanity could not have died and ceased in his human consciousness while his deity remained intact. That would be a division of the God-man and violate the hypostatic union.

> [From a friend, Pastor Brannon Poore, summarizing the essay.]

In my view, there is no need to resort to an "iffy" journey into Sheol (a doctrine opposed since the days of the early church) to prove Jesus remained a living, conscious soul during the time his body was dead. The God of life gave endless life to the human soul of his incarnation, sustaining that human soul throughout the death of its human body into the endless physical life of the resurrection.

The Social Genius of Christianity

In the ancient world family took care of family and only family. Family meant those of the same womb, those who had been legally adopted, or those who entered the family through marriage.

There were no charitable institutions or rescue missions or government programs to care for the poor, widowed, or orphans—those were created by Christians.

If you were outside the family, you were a stranger to the family. If you did not have a family, you were on your own. You must steal, beg, become a slave or prostitute, or die. Family only helped family.

Christ created a new social order. Mark 3:33–35, "And he, answering them, said, "Who are my mother and my brothers?" And looking around him on those sitting in a circle around him, he said, "See my mother and my brothers. For whoever should do the will of God, he is my brother, and sister, and mother."

In Christianity, people from different nations, ethnicities, social strata, skin color, cultures, families, peoples, tribes, and tongues become one family with Christ through salvation in Christ. The saved become "of the same womb" through their mutual salvation, adopted by God as a son or daughter. They become brothers and sisters of one another.

That is why Paul, a Hebrew and Jew, could call the gentile Christians, "beloved bothers." So also you and me. If Christ is your Savior, welcome to my family, my brother and my sister.

A Polygamous Mormon Got Saved

I to get the odd question from time to time, asking for advice and a biblical opinion.

The Question.

A Mormon husband just discovered the true Jesus and is now convicted of his sin. He has four wives, only one legal wife of the four. The first of the four he was married to but divorced her to marry and adopt his fourth wife's children from her previous marriage. The first wife he is now divorced from but still claims her as his wife. The second and third wives he is not married to but claims them as his wives. He has children from all four wives. Legally he is only now married to his fourth wife.

Since now becoming a Christ follower, how should he now handle his marital lifestyle and caring for his family? Does he go on just as he has before sleeping with every wife, pretending like he is legally married to all or should he remain married and devoted only to his fourth wife while supporting all of his children from every marriage?

The Answer.

I will assume this is a real life circumstance and not a journey into hypothetical land, because that journey resolves nothing in the real world.

Complex family situations caused by acts of sinning are always difficult to resolve, regardless of the sin(s) committed. The Scripture teaches monogamous marriage, but recognizes, in both past and present times, people have sinned and continue to sin against God's moral value for monogamous heterosexual marriage.

Now he is saved and should conform his life to God's moral value for marriage. You spoke of one legal wife, so he is not living in a country where polygyny is legal.

My counsel is the man should remain married to one woman only, his legal wife. He must certainly immediately cease all sexual activities with the others. He must help the others find a place to live other than his home with his legal wife, while continuing to provide food and shelter until such places may be bought or rented.

He is not married to the other women, so no divorce is necessary. He should continue to provide for any children from those illegal unions (on the principle in 1 Timothy 5:8) until those women are remarried. No solution will seem fair to all, but what I have suggested is just because it aligns with God's moral values.

Why Doesn't Satan Have Empathy"

I was asked, not too long ago, two interesting questions. One was, "Why doesn't Satan have empathy for mankind whom he tempts?" The other was like it, "Why doesn't God force empathy on Satan?"

To answer both, we must understand the created nature of the angels. God created two self-aware races, human beings and angels. God doesn't tell us anything about how he created the angels. But he does tell us about creating human beings, and I believe we can reason about the nature of angels from what Scripture says about the nature of human beings. For example, we see humans serving God and opposing God, and we see angels who serve God and angels who oppose God. In fact, most attributes we find in human beings we may are also find in angels, holy and fallen, as we see them at work in the Scriptures.

Just as God created human beings in his image and likeness, I believe God created angels in his image and likeness. Here are the qualities and attributes of human beings as created in God's moral, intellectual, and spiritual image and likeness:

> Moral: Holiness; Sanctification; Righteousness; Justice; Mercy; Faithfulness

> Intellectual: Personality; Will; Volition; Veracity; Knowledge; Wisdom

> Spiritual: Love; Compassion; Goodness; Kindness; Longsuffering; Mercy

> (Mercy is listed as moral and spiritual, because mercy acts in two ways: a) to relieve misery; b) to delay deserved justice.)

Even so, we find these same or similar attributes in the angels. In humans and angels as first created, all the attributes of their nature were prioritized to serve God. But some angels sinned and Adam and Eve sinned, thereby changing their nature. The attribute "rebellion against God" was added to human nature and fallen angel nature. The Bible names this principle or attribute of rebellion, "sin," the principle of evil. The perfect angel nature of those who rebelled was corrupted with the attribute sin.

One of the effects of sin is to re-prioritize sinners to serve self, not God. The essence of sin is "I, I, I; Me, Me, Me." The sinner says, "I am the most important person. I will satisfy my desires, my dreams, my wants, my lusts, no matter what it costs others, because I am the most important person in my world." The sin attribute affects every aspect of the nature of humans and fallen angels, to turn away from God and others, in order to focus on self. As the Puritan Thomas Manton said (commentary, James 1:11), "Man fallen is but the anagram of man in innocency. He has the same affections and delights, only they are transposed and misplaced."

Now, we see in the world that not every human being is as bad as he or she might be. That is because God gives a measure of grace to human beings and exerts his omnipotence to limit the expression of sin in human beings. And God's saved people exert an influence on the world as the salt that preserves morality and the light that reveals the truth.

But God does not give any grace to the fallen angels. There is no positive influence in their life. They are as bad as they might be, as bad as they can be. They will not and cannot be saved, the Lake of Fire was created for the Devil and his angels, Matthew 25:41.

God's omnipotence limits the full expression of their evil in the world. (We see this in the story of Job. Satan must ask permission to act, and may act only so far as he has permission.) The entire life of a fallen angel is focused on the satisfaction of his desires to rebel against God. They express that rebellion by acting against God and God's creation, especially against God's saved people.

In their rebellion against God is the answer to the first question. Sin unrelieved by grace does not have sympathy or empathy for any person. The fallen angels do not even have sympathy or empathy for one another. The essence of sin is to serve self, no matter what the cost to others. We see there are some human beings who are as bad as they might be; we call them psychopaths. In human terms, every fallen angel is a psychopath: incapable of empathy for other beings. This is the distortion of the attribute "justice," the corruption of the attribute "mercy," and the absence of the attribute love. They have no mercy and no love so they know no empathy.

The second question was, "Why doesn't God force empathy on Satan?" The answer is free will. God created humans and angels with the moral authority to decide their path in life: free will. Free will is not the license to do anything I want. All freely made choices are limited. The limits of choice are the physical, moral, and spiritual boundaries of human or angel nature.

Again, let us reason from what we know about human nature. I will give an example using the physical aspect of human nature. This will seem silly, but please bear with me. You might freely choose to flap your arms and fly to the store. However, the physical limits of your human nature will allow you to decide to flap your arms, but you cannot choose to fly by flapping your arms. The physical limits of human nature sets a boundary to your freely made choices.

Even so, sinful human and angel nature creates limits to moral and spiritual choices. In an illustration, I put my five year old grandson in my fenced-in back yard. He can do anything he chooses to do within the boundaries of the fence. But he cannot choose to do anything outside the fence because it is impossible for him to climb the fence. Sin is like the fence: it sets boundaries, it limits choices.

Scripture speaks of the choices the fence of sin prevents. For example, 1 Corinthians 2:14 (ESV), "The natural person [the unsaved sinner] does not accept the things of the Spirit of God, for they are folly to him, and he is not able to understand them because they are spiritually discerned." The unsaved sinner is "dead in trespasses and sins," spiritually dead, so while he may understand some facts of Scripture, he/she cannot understand the spiritual things, nor how those thing apply to him. The unsaved sinner might decide to worship God, but because he doesn't understand God, he/she creates an idol, or false religion, which Paul describes very well in Romans 1:20–23. The unsaved sinner cannot work his or her way to salvation, Ephesians 2:8–9. God must give his gift, Ephesians 2:8, to change the boundary of human nature to understand the spiritual the issues of sin, the Savior, and salvation.

We look around the world and see our fellow human beings—we even see in ourselves—we see people making wrong moral choices. Why doesn't God stop everyone from making the wrong choices? Because he has respect for what he created, the moral authority to make choices. God is a faithful God: he warns against the wrong choices, he rewards the right choices, and he does and will punish the wrong choices.

God allows the moral authority he designed into human nature to function as he created it to function: to make choices. Sinful human beings tend to make wrong choices, but as mentioned above, God gives grace and exerts his omnipotence to prevent everyone from being as bad as he or she might be. And so there is a measure of goodness and kindness and morality in the world, even though unrestrained human nature would never act in kindness or goodness or morality.

And that is the answer to the second question. God doesn't force empathy on Satan, because God created the angels with the moral authority to make choices, and God has respect for what he created. Their moral authority is distorted by sin in the fallen angels, but it still functions. Fallen angels consistently make wrong choices in rebellion against God. But whatever a fallen angel might choose to do, God omnipotently decides what will actually be done (as we see in the Book of Job), for the good of humankind.

But, a person might say, of both the fallen angels and unsaved human beings, why doesn't God prevent all wrong choices. Well let's begin with you, reader. Let's prevent all your wrong choices. But now your authority to make decisions has been taken away. You are no longer a thinking self-aware being. You are now an animal operating only on instinct.

That is not how God created human beings or angels. He gave the both the moral authority to make choices and the responsibility to make right choices. That responsibility makes angels and humans accountable and liable for their choices. God rightly rewards, or punishes, for our choices. Those humans who choose to deny Christ will be punished for their choices, even as the fallen angels are to be punished for their choices: The lake of fire was created for the devil and his angels, and became the eternal prison for fallen angels and unsaved human beings. Both unsaved humans and the fallen angels will live in endless punishment, Revelation 20:10–15, because of their choices.

Question: "Why doesn't Satan have empathy for mankind whom he tempts?" Answer: He sinned, and sin focuses on self, not others. Satan is incapable of empathy, and God never gives grace to the fallen angels. God omnipotently limits the choices of the fallen angels to prevent them from acting in the worst way possible toward what God has created, including toward human beings. The reality of sin is unsaved human beings do not require help from the fallen angels to rebel against God, harm themselves, and harm one another.

Question: "Why doesn't God force empathy on Satan?" Answer: God designed the angels with the moral authority to make choices. What God created he allows to function, even though wrong choices may be made. The fallen angels are responsible to make right choices, and are held accountable and liable for their wrong choices. They will be endlessly punished in the lake of fire. So also unsaved human beings.

The Silence of God

Why does God not take action—why is God silent—when the wicked practice their wickedness and swallow the righteous? The wickedness of the wicked seems to swallow up the righteous—to completely devastate and destroy the righteous—without any just response from God.

In Old Testament times, in ancient Israel, God was silent as the righteous suffered because he had already spoken concerning the wicked. God had told his covenant people Israel what would happen if they violated the covenant, committed injustice, and acted like the pagan nations surrounding them. We need only turn to Deuteronomy 28:15–68, ca. 1405 BC, to hear God's wrath against the unrighteous in Israel.

God is also silent because in longsuffering he gave his covenant people Israel many opportunities to repent and return to him. Every prophet prior to Habakkuk, during whose time Jerusalem was razed by the Babylonians, and every prophet after, was a patriot to Israel, calling the nation to return to the covenant, worship only YHWH, live moral lies, and do justice.

God is silent today, in this New Testament church age, "because he has spoken his last word of mercy and love, and judgment must await the 'day of judgment'—there can be no place for it in this 'day of grace'" [Anderson, 165].

Today, this New Testament church age, is a day for salvation, which if ignored will bring judgment to those who reject saving faith in Jesus Christ. But every day of silence by God, every day he does not act in just judgment, is a day some one or another will be saved.

Finally, what is God's purpose toward his saved people when they suffer by the evil hands of the unrighteous? The most basic answers are: to glorify God; to be purged from indwelling sin and love of the world; to be purged of independence from God; to testify of the grace and salvation of God.

The Ancient World Is Still With Us.

In the ancient Greco-Roman religious world in which Paul and his fellow missionaries traveled, the many schools of philosophy had left the campus and taken to the streets. Philosophers became, "hucksters, salesmen marketing the ideas and beliefs of their respective schools. Addressing crowds on street corners and in the marketplace, they offered advice on how to live one's life and deal with personal problems. Appealing less to reason and logic, philosophers appeared as traveling evangelists, directing their hearers to the wonderous accomplishments of the founder of the school, its venerable tradition, or the high regard in which many people viewed it." [Wilken, 74.]

Of course, the "traveling evangelists" of the philosophical schools took money to support their work. Some schools even consisted of itinerant beggars, such as the "begging priests of Cybele" [Wilken, 96]. The Greek religious traditions of wandering gods and men seeking transformation of existence from the social conventions of worldly disorder [Martin, 23], seemed similar to the Christians wandering the world seeking to transform their hearers with the gospel of Christ. In this historical-cultural context, we see Paul defending Christianity against charges it was just another school of philosophers, e.g., 1 Thessalonians 2:1–12.

Today, television and radio have taken the place of the market square. The philosophers of the modern world have "talk shows" to spread their philosophy, and have become the high priest or priestess for the celebrity sinners' pilgrimage to publicly confess their faults. The hucksters are also still with us, making money off a feel-good, positive-thinking gospel from thousands of shallow followers. Those promising transformation are here too, in the prosperity gospel sweeping the religious world. But, like Paul, the gospel must be presented in word and the power and conviction of the Holy Spirit; not of error, nor of impurity, nor deceit; through preachers proven as messengers of God as through conflict and persecution entrusted with the gospel of salvation.

As you "preach the Word," never forget the worldlings are competing with you, preaching the world's philosophies for life-transformation, greedy riches, and immoral lifestyles. Make your preaching different; make it of Christ.

Are We in the Last Hour of the Last Days?

A rather well-known Christian posted on Twitter, "Biblically, according to all signs around us we are in the last hour of the last days."

Are we?

It is possible we are in the ending days of the "last time/hour," which is the New Testament term, 1 John 2:18; 1 Peter 1:5; Jude 18, for the New Testament church age from Pentecost to Rapture.

The popular term "last days" occurs six times in Scripture. It is not an eschatological synonym for the rapture or Tribulation.

> At Genesis 49:1 it refers to national ethnic Israel after Jacob' death, part of the typical death-bed blessing and division of inheritance to his sons, relevant to the promises of the Abrahamic covenant.

> At Acts 2:17 Peter uses the term to describe what is happening at Pentecost. The Old Testament prophet Joel, whom Peter is quoting, used "last days" to refer to the Second Advent of the Messiah.

> At 2 Timothy 3:1 ff. it refers to conditions during this present New Testament church age, as is apparent to anyone who understands the events of New Testament church history from AD 33 to the present.

> Hebrews 1:2 refers to the First Advent and the New Testament church age. Christ spoke in these last days.

> At James 5:3, James is speaking to his historical contemporaries, men and women living during this New Testament church age, and by application to you and me.

> At 2 Peter 3:3 the term speaks to conditions during this present New Testament church age, as the term "scoffers," 3:3, and the subject of their scoffing, 3:4, which is Christ's Second Advent, clearly indicates.

So, of course we see signs of the "last days," because the New Testament church has been living in the last days since AD 33, and will continue to do so until the rapture of the New Testament church.

I and many other believers thought we were "in the last hour of the last days" in 1975. I had been a believer for about 1 year, so my ignorance of eschatology was deep and unwavering. We were so certain we were mentally packing our bags.

Martin Luther thought we were, "in the last hour of the last days," in AD 1532 when he wrote and published, "*The Signs of Christ's Coming and the Last Days*." But in the predominant eschatology of his times, Luther thought of the last days as, "Antichrist is present among us and Christ is soon to return and conduct the final judgment," based on his Roman Catholic Amillennial eschatological learning.

Many Christians throughout the New Testament church age, wherever and *whenever* they have lived throughout the world, have thought at one time or another, we are "in the last hour of the last days," as they watched events in the church and in the world.

The biblical fact is Christ said, six (6) times, "You Cannot Know When," the last time being at his Ascension. Prognosticating a "when" or a "season" based on the observation of church and world events is not only historically and biblically ignorant, but worse, such a prediction completely denies Christ's declaration in Acts 1:7 (which restates Matt. 24:36), and his five declarations in Matthew 24:36; 42, 44, 50; 25:13, that No One Can Know.

No apostle in any New Testament letter gave any kind of sign to tell us when or if, "we are in the last hour of the last days." They believed Christ. If Peter, and Paul, and Jude, and Luke, and James, and John, and the unknown Hebrews Writer did not give any kind of sign to tell us when or if "we are in the last hour of the last days," then Why Do Some Not Believe Christ?

If Christ said we cannot know when, then those persons who believe the signs in Matthew 24:3–35 supposedly tell us "we are in the last hour of the last days," are calling Christ a liar, because five times following that discourse he said, No One Can Know, Matthew 24:36; 42, 44, 50; 25:13.

The fact is Matthew 24:3–35 are signs for national ethnic Israel during the Tribulation. That is the importance of 24:33.

If Christ said we cannot know, then believing Paul's advice to Timothy, e.g., 1 Timothy 3:1–9 is supposed to tell us "we are in the last hour of the last days," is calling Christ, and Paul, a liar.

Here is the sign for Christians. "We certainly know that when he [Jesus Christ] is made visible we will be like him, because we will see him as he is, " 1 John 3:2. John says to his readers (you and me), I don't know when Christ will appear, but when he does appear, this is what will happen, "we will see him as he is." Sounds like Paul at 1 Corinthians 15:51–53.

Then John told us what to do until "when" takes place. "Now every person having this hope continually in him [Jesus Christ] is constantly purifying himself, just as he is pure," 1 John 3:3. The "hope," which is to say, the assurance of Christ's return for his church, is to sustain the believer, not signs.

Stop looking for signs. There are none. Jesus said so. Believe him. Simply remain prepared for the at-any-moment, unknown time-day-season of his return by living like him in this world.

Thoughts and Advice on Prayer

The apostle Paul gives a great description of prayer in Philippians 4:6. "Be anxious about not even one thing or person, but in everything by prayer and petition on behalf of yourself and others, with thanksgiving, make your requests known to God" (my translation).

Paul says the believer is not to be anxious—not to have mental distress or uneasiness or fear or be greatly worried about anything, but rather pray about everything. The believer is to pray to God, and to petition (ask, supplication) God, and give thanks to God. Give thanks to God whether his answer to your prayer is yes or no.

The believer is not to be anxious. Paul says anxiety may happen as one encounters the circumstances of the world, but the believer is to overcome anxiety through being satisfied and compliant with the Lord's will, whatever the outward circumstances might be, and however the Lord might choose to answer.

We tend to think of prayer as asking. But Paul says, "by prayer and asking." He separates "prayer" from "asking" because the first thing prayer is, the most important thing about prayer, is that prayer is an act of worship. Through prayer I recognize God is in charge, not me. In prayer we say to God, "I am dependent on you and I submit to your will for my requests." We come to God through prayer and say to him, "Not my will be done, but your will be done."

That is because prayer is not a blank check made out to the believer. A check begins with a line saying who is being paid, and another line saying the amount that is being paid. When God answers prayer he makes the check to himself and Jesus Christ, and the amount is always the same, "To glorify God and his Son Jesus Christ." On every check there is a little memo line. That is where your name goes. Memo: "For my faithful believer's request." God only and always answers our requests when they will, "glorify God and his Son Jesus Christ."

Jesus says, Matthew 7:7–8 (ESV), Ask, and it will be given to you; seek, and you will find; knock, and it will be opened to you. For everyone who asks receives, and the one who seeks finds, and to the one who knocks it will be opened." But we tend to ignore the next thing Jesus said. God knows how to give good things to those who ask him, 7:11. If it isn't good for us, God says "No." And all that is good for us is always and only what "will glorify God and his Son Jesus Christ."

God answers prayer in five ways because he is a wise and loving heavenly Father:

> "No, I love you too much," meaning we have asked for something that is inappropriate or harmful to our welfare. In this instance one should cease to pray that prayer.

> "Yes, if you insist, so you will learn to trust me in the future."

> "No, not yet," because the request is good, but the timing is "not yet." In this instance prayer should continue.

> "Yes, but what took you so long to ask," meaning God's timing in giving was waiting for the means by which it was to be given: our prayer.

> "Yes, and here is more," as God not only grants the request but adds to it as he knows is needful for our welfare, or for the person for whom we are interceding.

Ask in faith for the things God has promised. Receive by faith whatever God gives. Receive a Yes or No with equal praise and thankfulness.

Let us look more closely at Matthew 7:7–8. The verbs in those verses are in the Greek present tense, which indicates continuing action. Ask and keep on asking; seek and keep on seeking, knock and keep on knocking. Persistence in prayer reveals our dependence on God and our submission to his will. Keep on asking, keep on seeking, and keep on knocking until an answer is received, and then accept that answer, whether a Yes or No, with praise and thankfulness. In one way or another, according to his perfect timing, God will let us know if his answer is a Yes or a No.

What if your heart says don't stop praying?" Of course, my first bit of advice is what I have said above about persistence in prayer. Keep on asking, seeking, and knocking until you get an answer. God will give you an answer in his own timing and in his own way. Watch for that answer. I know in my life God often gives me a "No," by removing the object of my prayer, or by moving me in some way, either physically so the prayer cannot be answered yes, or emotionally so I no longer want the things I am asking for.

As to the feeling in your heart, I cannot help but think of the prophet Jeremiah 17:9 (ESV), "The heart is deceitful above all things, and desperately sick; who can understand it?" The mature believer puts his or her trust in God's moral values and rules of living. Scripture first, then conform feelings to Scripture.

A personal experience in prayer. In response to something I wanted very much I had asked, "God give this to me or I will die." I felt strongly about receiving the object of my prayer. God gave it to me. And after I had it for a little while, I realized how wrong it was for me, and then God in mercy took it away. I never asked for that again, nor have I again asked in that way.

From that experience, I developed a few guidelines about seeking God's will and finding solutions to life's problems.

> Don't role-play the solution. God doesn't need your help. He waits for your cooperation.

> Don't Do It Yourself and afterward ask God to bless your solution. He probably won't. God blesses works that conform to his Word.

> Don't go around an immovable obstacle. It is there for a reason. If God wants it removed only prayer will remove it.

> Don't try to resolve a problem by yourself. Believers are a community. Every believer needs a counselor. Every counselor needs counselors.

> When a door is closed, don't force it open. The right doors open with reasonable effort. The wrong doors open just enough to tempt you to sin.

> Do what the Word says. God's will is found on the path. Problems tend to fix themselves when one is on the path.

> Ask in faith for the things God has promised. Receive by faith whatever God gives. Receive a Yes or No with equal praise and thankfulness.

Listen for God's response. Wait for it. Beware of deciding a course of action without an answer to your prayer. Some decisions take the believer down a path he should never have taken, deliver him to a place he should never have come to, prevent him from returning to his starting point to begin anew, requiring him to live with the consequences of his actions.

Ask yourself these questions:

Does what you want agree with God's values?

Will your life continue if you do not receive what you desire? (I am pretty sure it will.)

Is God arranging circumstances in your life that do not agree with your desire?

What is more important, what you want, or what God wants for you?

Stay on the path. Problems tend to fix themselves when one is on the path. Keep on praying and be willing to watch, wait, look, and listen for the answer.

Range of Interpretation

An interpretation of a biblical text is not simply a matter of deciding "this one, not that one." Every biblical text is susceptible to more than one interpretation—hence the origin of heresies, false doctrine, schisms, cults—and many texts allow for more than one credible interpretation. There is also the ever constant danger of substituting an application of a text for an interpretation of the text.

The interpretation available for every biblical text ranges from what is possible, to what is plausible, to what is probable, to what is certain.

A simple example using Samson, Judges 13:25–14:1. What is the interpretation of Samson moving in a direction other than that direction in which the Holy Spirit was moving him? There are two plausible interpretations. One, the Spirit changed Samson's direction (without telling the reader) and moved him into confrontation with the Philistines. Two, Samson was not being obedient to the leading of the Holy Spirit, but God used his disobedience to accomplish God's purpose for Samson. In analyzing the text for an interpretation, one must ask, "Why was the Holy Spirit moving Samson between two cities in Dan?" And one must ask, "How does Samson's action here fit into his entire history?" The answer to those questions will decide if one of those plausible interpretations is more probable than the other. However, in the absence of a definite statement from God, no answer rises to the level of "certain."

Discovering the interpretation of a biblical text begins with a careful analysis of the contexts followed by the progressive determination of what interpretation(s) is possible, or plausible, or probable, or certain.

The process begins by analyzing every historical-cultural, contextual, lexical-syntactical, literary, theological, and doctrinal context applicable to the text or available in the text.

Here are the contexts:

> Historical-Cultural analysis: considers the historical-cultural milieu in which the author wrote. The facts of the historical-cultural background involve the task of reconstructing or comprehending the historical and cultural features of the specific passage. This requires an understanding of:
>
> > The situation of the writer, especially anything that helps explain why he or she wrote the passage.

The situation of the people involved in the text and/or the recipients of the book that can help explain why the writer penned this material to them.

The relationship between the writer and audience or the people involved in the text.

The cultural or historical features mentioned in the text.

Contextual analysis: considers the relationship of a given passage to the whole body of an author's writing. Three aspects of the contextual context are especially important.

How did the author construct his argument, sentence by sentence, word by word?

How does what the author said in the text under consideration fit into what the author has said in a related nearby text(s)?

What was the author's intent in the specific text and how does that intent fit into the overall argument, declaration, or exhortation?

Lexical-Syntactical analysis: develops an understanding of the definitions of words (lexicology) and their relationships to one another (syntax).

A word study of how the author uses a key words in similar contexts may be necessary and will always be useful. The word study may need to be expanded to discover how the Old Testament and/or New Testament defines a key word through consistent use in similar contexts.

Literary (Genre) analysis: identifies the literary form or method used in a given passage: historical narrative, letters, doctrinal exposition, poetry, wisdom, prophetic.

A study of how the author uses figures of speech in similar contexts may be necessary and will always be useful. The study may need to be expanded to discover how the Old Testament and/or New Testament defines a figure of speech through consistent use in similar contexts.

The five unbreakable rules for figures of speech must be observed.

A figure of speech is a comparison (by example or analogy) of one thing with another that clarifies some aspect of the thing being illustrated by the figure of speech.

A figure of speech does not teach doctrine. A figure of speech clarifies what is being taught for the purpose of helping the understanding.

(Exception, the Parable. A parable is an illustration told in a word story in order to teach a single point.)

A figure of speech clarifies one aspect, not all aspects, of the thing being illustrated.

A figure of speech is based in something literal and is intended to teach something literal.

A figure of speech does not teach the literal thing on which it is based.

Theological analysis: studies the level of theological understanding at the time the revelation was given in order to ascertain the meaning of the text for its original readers. It takes into account related Scriptures, whether given before or after the passage being studied.

Doctrinal analysis: the harmonization of doctrine in a specific passage with the full teaching of Scripture on that doctrine.

After the analyses of the various contexts are concluded, the interpreter will find it helpful to make a comparison his or her work with the work of other interpreters who also use the literal hermeneutic.

Here is the process

Seeking what is possible is the discovery of every available interpretation of the text whether likely or unlikely, good or bad, acceptable or unacceptable, true or false, etc.

Seeking what is plausible is the determination which, if any, among the possible interpretations is credible in relation to the various contexts.

Seeking what is probable is the determination which, if any, of the plausible interpretations has more evidence for than against when the various contexts are carefully considered.

Seeking what is certain is deciding which of the probable interpretations, if any, is free from all doubt, having been established as conforming to every context.

The best answer is the one(s) that is the most credible because satisfying as many of the several contexts as is possible. This means some texts may not rise above what is possible, or what is plausible, or what is probable, or attain to the level of what is certain.

The interpreter continues the analysis until he/she an interpretation or range of interpretations that best fits the biblical text.

After an interpretation is decided—what is possible, plausible, probable, or what is certain—the interpreter will find it helpful to make a comparison of his or her conclusions with the conclusions of other interpreters who also use the literal hermeneutic. In this way common errors and heresies may be avoided.

The Bible teacher, whether in a local church setting or in a higher education institution, must explain the credible interpretations, how these were derived, which interpretation is in his or her opinion the most likely/credible, and encourage his listeners to embrace that view on rational biblical grounds.

Interpretation and Authorial Intent

Authorial intent: the author's truth-intention; what the author meant to say when he wrote.

Authorial intent provides the only genuinely discriminating norm for ascertaining valid or true interpretations from invalid and false ones.

Authorial intent. The first objective of interpretation is to make clear the text's verbal meaning: what the author intended. The Scripture says what it means and means what it says.

Authorial Intent. "The primary meaning of any Bible passage is found in that passage" [Michael J. Vlach, Dispensationalism (Los Angeles: Theological Studies Press, 2017), 31]. That is authorial intent.

The consequence of authorial intent is also well-stated by Vlach [same reference]. "The New Testament does not reinterpret or transcend the Old Testament passages in a way that overrides or cancels the original authorial intent of the Old Testament writers."

The Old Testament, as written by the original author, and as read by the original audience, had a specific meaning for that author and that audience within their particular historical and cultural circumstances.

To change that specific meaning using later revelation obscures or eliminates the original author's intent, thereby deleting God's intent in inspiring that Old Testament revelation for that particular author and people.

Beware of the way Reformed theology interprets the Old Testament scriptures. The interpretive rule of Reformed theology is, "Christ in every Scripture." To accomplish that goal, Reformed interpretation must use the New Testament revelation to override or cancel the original authorial intent of the Old Testament authors.

The Old Testament people could know only what had been revealed to them in the existing Scripture already given by God up to the time God gave them new revelation (the doctrine of progressive revelation).

Abraham could not know what David knew; David could not know what Isaiah knew; Isaiah could not know what Daniel knew; Mary, having only the Old Testament revelation, could not know all that Matthew, Mark, Luke, and John knew about the Christ when they wrote their gospels. To say these and others knew what had not been revealed is to inject either New Testament revelation, or extra-biblical (not in the Bible) revelation, into authorial intent.

The Scripture says what it means and means what it says, only when you follow the rule of authorial intent.

Miracles

Do miracles happen today? Depends on your definition of a miracle.

If a miracle is an effect that has God as the only cause, then "No," there are no observable miracles today.

More formally and technically: "A miracle is an exceptional activity of God in the material realm, not explainable by man's understanding of the physical laws governing the universe, brought about by the immediate efficiency or simple volition of God."

If a miracle is defined more loosely (and inaccurately) as God using natural (existing) means to accomplish something awe-inspiring, then yes, we can multiply miracles to our heart's content. Example: God using the body's natural immune system to rid the body of a disease. God using the natural mechanics of a storm to deflect a tornado from a believer's person or property. God using natural means is providence, grace, blessing, but not a miracle.

For example, Naaman the leper was told by Elisha (2 Kings 5) to wash in the Jordan River seven times and he would be cleansed of his leprosy. Do we really believe submerging seven times in river water accomplished that healing? Or was the act of immersion the means of expressing faith, and God responded to faith with a miracle: something only he could do?

In the NT we sometimes see Jesus using natural means. For example, Jesus made a blind man see by making mud with dirt and his spit, putting the mud on the man's eyes, and having the man wash in a certain pool of water (John 9). Do we really believe Jesus' spit mixed with dirt then washed off with water accomplished that healing? Or were those things a means to an end: facilitating the man's faith through a tangible act expressing that faith?

Was the woman cleansed healed a flow of blood (Mark 5) healed by clothing Jesus was wearing, 5:28–29, or because power and authority came from Jesus, 5:30? Touching the clothing her faith expressing itself.

When Jesus used means—means that could not possibly accomplish a healing, such as clothing, or spit and dirt—it was to give faith a tangible object to grab hold of, whereby faith could exercise itself. In the OT, the death of lambs and bulls and goats had zero power to forgive sins, Hebrews 10:4. What those sacrifices did was give a tangible medium through which faith in God's testimony (bring the proper sacrifice in faith, confession, and repentance) could express itself.

The OT (and the gospels are OT historical narrative) treated the believer as a child who must have a tangible experience to express the intangible thing that is faith. In this NT age, God treats the believer as an adult, although many continue to act as children (e.g., is lighting a candle really prayer; will God listen better because of the candle?)

On the whole, I prefer defining a miracle as God being the sole cause of the effect, natural means not needed or used. There are no observable miracles today.

Definition

A miracle is an exceptional activity of God in the material realm, not explainable by man's understanding of the physical laws governing the universe, brought about by the immediate efficiency or simple volition of God, designed to arouse awe and wonder as a witness of God.

More simply, an effect in the natural world of which God is the sole cause.

Sometimes what are called miracles are "special providences: events brought to pass obviously by God, indeed, but through the medium of second causes" [Warfield, "The Question of Miracles," *Selected Shorter Writings*, vol. 2]. A miracle is when God alone is the cause of the effect.

If the cause of an effect in the natural world is natural causes or God using natural causes, that effect is not a miracle.

A miracle is not the suspension or counteracting of natural laws. A miracle does not interact with natural laws, because God, not the natural law, is the cause of the effect.

A miracle is an effect caused by something other than natural laws, which continue without interruption. To wit, God himself as the sole cause creating an effect in the natural world, an effect not producible by any means of the natural world as cause, whether as primary or secondary cause, which once produced by God as sole cause is subject to natural laws.

E.g., no natural law was violated when Lazarus was healed of his physical death. The body was dead because the soul was not in the body, a natural law. God did what only God could do, he rejoined the soul with the body, an act to which no natural law is opposed, to which effect the natural law responded by the soul enlivening the body, cf. Genesis 2:7. Had God also rendered Lazarus' body endlessly incorruptible and his soul endlessly sinless (one type of resurrection) that effect would also have been caused by God alone, to which natural law would have responded with the continuation of physical life.

The New Testament Church

The New Testament church is a body of believers called out from the world by Christ to worship and serve God Father-Son-Spirit. The New Testament church needs no tent or building or place for worship. These are conveniences to aid in worship, but are not essential to worship. Each believer is a temple of God, 1 Corinthians 6:19; 2 Corinthians 6:16, and therefore he or she may worship God in spirit and truth at any time in any place. The New Testament church corporately is the body of Christ, 1 Corinthians 12:27, a holy temple to the Lord, Ephesians 2:21, and therefore believers come together in local assemblies to worship God in spirit and truth, at any time in any place. The New Testament believer is able to worship privately at any time and place, and is able to gather in any suitable time and place with other believers for corporate worship.

The local church began as the congregation of believers living in one location, and through the expansion of the number of believers (and it must be said, of denominations) most towns and cities have more than one local church. However, no building was (or is) needed, a fact more apparent in less developed regions and countries. But from the earliest days Christians took advantage of the security and comfort of a building, meeting first in individual houses, Acts 2:46; Romans 16:5; Colossians 4:15. But during those times when Christianity has been made illegal or is being persecuted, believers have used open spaces, or abandoned buildings, or some other enclosed space (e.g., the underground catacombs in ancient Rome) as suitable for congregational worship. Only after Christianity was declared a legal religion in the Roman Empire (Edict of Milan, AD 313), did the early Christians begin to regularly meet in buildings.

That the synagogue was used as a pattern or model for the church is obvious, but the differences are essential. We see something of the order of synagogue worship in the gospels and through historical documents. The rulers of the synagogue were administrators and also performed some judicial functions in the local community. The members of the congregation, as selected by the "ruler of the synagogue," conducted the worship. In a typical Sabbath service, one person read prayers. Others read from the Mosaic Law. Another read a passage from the prophets. Another translated for those who did not understand the Hebrew language. Another interpreted the passages from the Law and prophets, thereby functioning as a preacher, by reading the traditional interpretations made by Rabbis from the past.

"The two elements of the ancient service were, speaking broadly, worship and instruction, the latter originally predominating" [Burton, *The Ancient Synagogue Service.*] There was no song service.

The New Testament believers—initially established and trained by former Jews—adapted the synagogue order of service to its needs. In the synagogue women were physically kept separate from men. In a New Testament church everyone worships together. There was a reader for those who could not read. Literacy was high in the ancient world, but as today not 100 percent. The Old Testament Scriptures were read, and any letter from an apostle, e.g., 1 Thessalonians 5:27, Colossians 4:16. An elder or elders interpreted the Scriptures and gave the gospel—he/they preached. Songs may have been sung, Ephesians 5:19; Colossians 3:16, and probably were, because songs were sung in the temple, and each local church is a temple of Christianity.

But whatever use the New Testament church made of Jewish synagogue practices, we must understand the New Testament church was not pagan or Jewish nor some combination of both. The church is in the Father and Jesus Christ, something neither Judaism nor paganism can claim. The wall of the Mosaic Law that kept Jews and Gentiles separated had been eliminated by Christ, Ephesians 2:14–15, who through the cross reconciled believers out of Judaism and paganism into one body, the New Testament church, with one Savior, one Father, and one Holy Spirit. They congregated together as Christians, not as Jews or Gentiles.

Governor Pliny's letter to Emperor Trajan, AD 112, mentions some Christian meeting practices in Pliny's province of Bithynia (modern day Turkey).

> That they were wont, on a stated day, to meet together before it was light, and to sing a hymn to Christ, as to a god, alternately; and to oblige themselves by a sacrament [or oath], not to do anything that was ill: but that they would commit no theft, or pilfering, or adultery; that they would not break their promises, or deny what was deposited with them, when it was required back again; after which it was their custom to depart, and to meet again at a common but innocent meal. [1 Corinthians 11:20?]

We know from other historical accounts that food and clothing were distributed to the poor and widows at these meetings. Paul, in 1 Corinthians 11:23 ff. speaks of the practice of the Lord's supper during congregational meetings.

The New Testament church had and has two biblical offices, those of elder (*epískopos, poimḗn, presbúteros*) and deacon. The elders are identified by three Greek words. They were elders of the church, *presbúteros* [Zodhiates, s. v. "4245"]. They were shepherds of the church, *poimḗn* [Zodhiates, s. v. "4166"]. They were overseers of the church, *epískopos* [Zodhiates, s. v. "1985"]. Not every elder performed all three duties, as often happens in the modern church. The deacons were servants of the church, *diákonos* [Zodhiates, s. v. "1249"].

Governor Pliny mentions "deaconesses," who probably served the same function among the women as that of the male deacons among the congregation in general.

Such was the local New Testament church the apostles established. A few definitions of a local church.

> A local church is a company or community of persons who strive to please God in celebrating his worship. [Owen, *Biblical Theology*, 144.]

> A local New Testament church is an organism composed of individuals joined together so that each can make vital contributions to the work and welfare of the whole body.

> A local church is a body of baptized New Testament believers, joined together upon a credible profession of saved by grace through faith in Christ the only Savior, regularly meeting together under the leadership of elders and deacons, participating together in a common purpose to worship God, to propagate the gospel locally and worldwide, to make disciples, to observe the ordinances of baptism and the Lord's supper, to present a common witness of faith and doctrine centered on the word of God, and to encourage one another in the daily practice of the principles, precepts, and values of God as expressed in his Word.

The word "church" is from the Greek *ekklēsía*, whose basic meaning is "called out." Believers are called out from assembling with the world to assemble together in Christ. This is how the New Testament uses *ekklēsía*, "assembly."

> An assembly of citizens, Acts 19:30–32

> The assembly of national ethnic Israel, Acts 7:38

> The body of Christ, Acts 15:14

The body of living New Testament believers, Galatians 1:13

A group of local New Testament churches in one area or region, Galatians 1:2

The complete body of Christ from Pentecost to the Rapture, Ephesians 5:25

A local New Testament church, so used 92 times in the New Testament, 1 Thessalonians 1:1; 1 Corinthians 1:2, et al.

The local New Testament church is the primary organization of Christianity.

A Dispensational Interpretation of Matthew 24

Originally published in James D. Quiggle, *A Private Commentary on the Bible: Matthew's Gospel* (Amazon/KDP, 2016), 345–367. Lightly edited to the present purpose.

Translation Matthew 24:1–3

1 And Jesus having gone out was going away from the temple, and his disciples came near to point out to him the buildings of the temple. 2 Now he answering said to them, "Do you not see all these? Truly I say to you, there will be none left here, stone upon stone, which will not be thrown down." 3 Now as he was sitting upon the Mount of Olives, the disciples came near to him privately, saying, "Tell us, when these things will be; and what is the sign of your coming; and the completion of the age?" [Unless otherwise noted, all Scripture translations are from James D. Quiggle, *Translations of Select Bible Books.* (2018, Revised, Amazon/KDP, 2020).]

Exposition

True to his word in 23:39, Jesus leaves the temple area. He crosses the Kidron Valley to the Mount of Olives. As he is leaving the temple, his disciples direct his attention to the magnificent buildings. This particular version of the temple, known as Herod's temple to historians, had been in progress for forty-six years (John 2:20), and construction would continue for another thirty-six years. Josephus stated that Herod began the temple in the eighteenth year of his reign, which Josephus related to the visit of Augustus to Syria in spring or summer 20 BC; thus the reconstruction of the temple began in late 20 or early 19 BC. The sanctuary and inner courts were completed late 18 or early 17 BC, but the outer courts were not completed until AD 62. The temple mount was, by all accounts, a beautiful complex.

Jesus said it would be destroyed, and it was, at the conclusion of the AD 70 war with Rome. All that was left was part of one retaining wall supporting the temple mount. Today it is known as the western wall or the Wailing Wall, a name given to it by Gentiles. For many years after the Jewish wars with Rome, Jews were forbidden to enter Palestine, except one time a year, to visit the ruins of Jerusalem. Gentiles hearing the Jews weeping at the wall gave it its name.

What follows in Matthew 24 and 25 are several prophetic announcements and explanations. The disciples didn't understand then (cf. Acts 1:6) and many do not understand now.

The very nature of any prophetic message does not require a complete understanding by the recipient. For example, in Psalm 22, David wrote what Christians now understand to be a hymn about the suffering of messiah. However, from David's point of view, his psalm was a hymn about his own suffering, using poetic imagery. The eunuch's comment (Acts 8:32–34) about Isaiah 53 (the same subject as Psalm 22), reflects the Jews' misunderstanding of these passages. Neither Isaiah, nor his immediate audience, nor readers in generations to come, fully understood the language, signs, and symbols of the prophecy. Jesus was the embodiment of messianic prophecies studied for centuries, yet even those who came to accept him as the promised messiah did not, at the time, grasp the necessity of his death and resurrection. A full and complete understanding of any prophecy waits for those who will experience the prophecy.

This is not to say some degree of understanding must wait until all the prophesied events are in progress or fulfilled. By comparing Scripture with Scripture one will find a suitable understanding of any prophecy, guided as always by the divine illumination and sovereign will of the Holy Spirit. We need not restrict the explanation of these prophecies in Matthew 24 and 25 to what the disciples and first century believers may have understood. Jesus gave these prophecies for his saints in every generation until his return.

Those parts that continue to remain unknown or uncertain will be understood by those living in the moment of fulfillment, as was Psalm 22 and Isaiah 53. However, every reader may understand enough for their faith and faithful living. Prophecy contains sufficient information to allow the interpreter to find an objective meaning and the significance of the text. In relation to these particular prophecies in Matthew 24, 25 more than enough can be understood to form an interpretation of the events leading up to and following the second advent of Christ, and an application for every believer from the first advent to the second.

My understanding of eschatology conforms to Dispensational theology. God has separate eschatological programs for different people groups: the fallen angels; the peoples from Adam to Moses, national ethnic Israel, the New Testament church, unsaved Gentiles, Tribulation believers, and people living during the Davidic-Messianic kingdom of Christ on the earth. The prophecies in Matthew 24, 25 find their fulfillment in national ethnic Israel and the unsaved world during the Tribulation period and second advent. (The Tribulation is a period of about seven years during which Antichrist rules the world, God brings judgments upon the peoples of the world for their rejection of Christ, but many believe on Christ and are saved. The Tribulation period ends at Christ's second advent.)

Returning to the gospels, Mark and Luke more clearly indicate the disciples are admiring the buildings. I can imagine a different vocal emphasis from Jesus than from the disciples. The disciples said, "Do you *see* these things?" Jesus said, "Do *you* see these things?" In direct response to their admiration of the temple he predicts its complete destruction.

One might draw one or more moral lessons here, but the plainest lesson takes into account the Jews' rejection and murder of Jesus. What seems magnificent to men is worthless to God without faith and obedience toward God. The temple God looks for is his active presence in the souls of his people.

The disciples were undoubtedly astonished. However, what Jesus said may have led them to believe the messianic reign would soon begin. Ezekiel 40 ff. describes a new city and temple built for Messiah's reign. If the current temple was to be destroyed, does that mean Jesus is about to bring about the end of the age and inaugurate his reign? Their questions are thus prophetically connected. When they reached the Mount of Olives, which was across the Kidron Valley opposite the city and temple, they asked Jesus to explain. Jesus sat down, the position of a teacher.

I believe the disciples thought they had asked one question with two intimately connected parts. They had, in their thoughts and theology, connected Jesus' statement about the temple with the messianic reign. They believed he was the Christ. Jesus had repeatedly told them he would be killed, a statement they had accepted but not understood because it did not fit into their messianic theology. He had repeatedly told them he would be raised the third day, a statement they did not comprehend—they believed in one general resurrection (e.g. Daniel 12:2; cf. John 11:23–24) prior to Messiah's Davidic Kingdom. Jesus had entered Jerusalem according to messianic prophecy. Now he was telling them the temple would be destroyed.

They knew from Zechariah 14 and other Old Testament passages that the world would worship the Lord in Jerusalem in the new age. From Ezekiel 40ff they knew that a new temple would be built for the messianic reign. How can all these things, some of them seemingly contradictory, be true? What is the prophetic order in which these things will come to pass? The disciples are more focused on Messiah's Davidic Kingdom than ever before. So, they are asking, "Tell us when all these things will come to pass; what will be the sign that this age has ended and your reign begins."

Many commentators acknowledge two questions by the disciples, but I find they have asked three questions:

> When will these things be?
>
> What will be the sign of your coming?
>
> What will be the sign of the end of the age?

To understand Jesus' answers to these questions, we must understand the context in which they were asked and answered. The immediate subject was the temple, the essential component of Judaism, which would be present during Messiah's Davidic Kingdom, Ezekiel 40–48. Who was Jesus? The Messiah. What was the occasion? A prediction that Judaism would be destroyed. Who were the questioners? Jewish men looking for the Jewish' Messiah's Davidic Kingdom and believing Jesus was the Messiah of that Kingdom. What were the men expecting? Jesus the Messiah to judge his enemies, cleanse Israel, make the people ready, and bring the Davidic Messianic Kingdom into existence—soon.

The answers Jesus gave are not about the New Testament church. These Israeli men were concerned with Israel. Israeli men were asking the Israeli Messiah about the Israeli Kingdom. Jesus answered them as Israelis concerned with Israel. Every sign in Jesus' end-times discourse in Matthew (and Mark and Luke) concerns Israel, and every sign (except Luke 21:20–24, a prophecy of the AD 70 destruction of Jerusalem and Israel) concerns the Tribulation period.

The "end of the age" in the disciple's theology, and that of Jesus' also, see v. 14, was the end of "the times of the Gentiles" followed by the reign of David's son, the Messiah/Christ, on the earth. The "times of the Gentiles" is the rule of the Gentiles over the earth in general and over Israel in particular, see Luke 21:24. The times of the Gentiles began with the captivity of Israel by the Babylonian empire, and ends at Christ's second advent.

Jesus' answers to their questions arcs over the New Testament church age to the Israel of the future as Messiah's advent approaches. Many commentators believe the answers to the disciples' questions are interwoven throughout the discourse, so that it is not possible to clearly distinguish which answers belong to which questions. This is view is understandable because some of the characteristics that define the New Testament church age are similar to the characteristics of the times at the end of the church age. However, in the eschatological discourses in the Synoptic gospels (Matthew 24, 25; Mark 13; Luke 21) Jesus gives prophecy about national ethnic Israel, not the New Testament church.

Jesus does not directly address the New Testament church anywhere in the synoptic Gospels prior to his resurrection. This includes passages such as the Sermon on the Mount. In that sermon things such as the ethics of the kingdom and the reign of the King over his kingdom are applicable to the church, because the New Testament church will be part of the messianic kingdom with national ethnic Israel. Many other parts of the Synoptics are likewise applicable. However, the New Testament church is the mystery form of the kingdom, which is not revealed, except in parables (Matthew 13), until after the resurrection, and does not begin until the day of Pentecost, Acts 2.

In the Synoptic gospels Jesus addresses 1) the Jewish people for whom he is the messianic king, 2) the nation of Israel which is his messianic kingdom, and 3) in this eschatological discourse the relationship that nation and people bear to the Tribulation period and the second advent. This discourse is about Israel, not the church.

Where does Christ address the New Testament church? In the gospel of John, Jesus addresses the characteristics of the New Testament church age and his coming to remove the church from the world at the end of this present age. In John's Gospel Jesus speaks of tribulation the church will endure during the present age. In the Synoptics Jesus speaks about national ethnic Israel during the Tribulation period. Verses such as Matthew 24:4–14 (and their parallels in Mark and Luke) have an historical application to the New Testament church age, but these verses primarily concern Israel during the Tribulation. The events in Matthew 24:15–51 begin after the New Testament church has been removed from the world (the rapture).

The Olivet discourse may be divided into four parts.

> Vv. 4–14, the character of Tribulation

> Vv. 15–28, the great Tribulation period

> Vv. 29–31, the signs of Messiah's second advent.

> Vv. 32–51, the signs and character of the end of the age.

The AD 70 destruction of the temple is revealed in Luke 21:20–24, but not in Matthew. Historically, when Christians saw the Roman armies began to mass against Jerusalem in AD 70, they took it as the sign the abomination had come, Matthew 24:15 (cf. Daniel 9:27), and fled Jerusalem. However, that event was not the abomination of desolation.

Translation Matthew 24:4–14

4 And answering Jesus said to them, "Beware lest anyone misleads you. 5 For many will come in my name, saying, 'I am the Christ,' and they will mislead many. 6 Now you will hear of wars and rumors of wars. See that you are not alarmed, for it is necessary to take place; but not yet is the end. 7 For nation will rise against nation, and kingdom against kingdom. And there will be famines and pestilences and earthquakes in various places. 8 But all these are the beginning of sorrows. 9 Then they will deliver you to tribulation, and will kill you, and you will be hated by all the nations, on account of my name. 10 And then many will take offense, and they will betray one another, and will hate one another; 11 and many false prophets will arise, and will mislead many. 12 And because lawlessness is to be multiplied, the love of many will grow cold. 13 But the one having endured to the end, he will be saved. 14 And this good news of the kingdom will be proclaimed in all the world for a testimony to all the nations; and then the end will come.

Translation Note

In v. 7 the words "and pestilences" are not in some manuscripts, and are considered by some as imported from Luke 21:11.

Exposition

There is no denying that the things described in vv. 4–14— wars and famines and pestilences and earthquakes—have been seen in the world repeatedly since Jesus gave this discourse, and will continue throughout the New Testament church dispensation, from the present to the rapture of the church. However, a similarity between an historical event and a prophecy is not necessarily the fulfillment of the prophecy. Though wars and natural events have occurred for the past (almost) 2,000 years, other, related, prophesied events have not occurred. Until those other events occur, the world will continue to experience wars and famines and pestilences and earthquakes, and it will not, yet, be time for the Tribulation.

Jesus' eschatological prophecies in the Synoptic Gospels may easily be applied to the character of the present age, the New Testament church age, because there have been, and will continue to be, wars and famines and pestilences and earthquakes. But as I have discussed extensively in other publications, the New Testament church age is the last time before the end times. [Other publications: *Dispensational Eschatology, An Explanation and Defense of the Doctrine*; *Antichrist, His Genealogy, Kingdom, and Religion*; *A Private commentary on the Bible: Daniel*; *A Private commentary on the Bible: John's Epistles*; *The Epistle of Jesus to the Church: A Commentary on the Revelation.*]

The "end times" (a phrase not used in Scripture) are the Day of the Lord prophesied in the Old Testament. The end times begin with the rise of Antichrist to power through a covenant he makes, and there will be wars and famines and pestilences and earthquakes, Revelation 6:1–7, unlike any preceding period of time in the world, "such as has not been from the beginning of the world until now, no, nor may be" (Matthew 24:21). But until the Antichrist comes to power (Daniel 7:8, 20; 9:27, the time is not the end times, but the last time, i.e., the New Testament church age.

The end times are the Tribulation and second advent. The last time, identified by that term in 1 John 2:18; 1 Peter 1:5, 20; Jude 18, is the present church age. The second advent of Christ has been imminent from the ascension, Acts 1:11, and the so-called "signs of the times" (wars and famines and pestilences and earthquakes) have been in evidence since the ascension.

From the time of Christ's ascension the world has seen, and the church has suffered, wars, and famines, and diseases, and earthquakes, and persecution, and tribulation. The world has persecuted Christians. Christian has betrayed Christian. False prophets have claimed to be Christ, or that the end is near, or here. False prophets have proclaimed false gospels and created false religions and have mislead many. Lawlessness has multiplied.

Because of these things many have abandoned their faith, and the love of many toward Christ has grown cold, i.e., they have followed the values and ways of the world. These are the things that have characterized the world and the church in church age. Nor is today different from the past. Martin Luther in AD 1532 thought Christ's advent was near when he wrote, *The Signs of Christ's Coming and the Last Days*. In 1843 people left jobs and houses and lands and friends to gather in fields and on hills for the return of Christ (the Millerites), and were disappointed. Today many continue to look for signs.

Why do cultural-political-social-generational-national-regional-tribal unrest and violence continue if it is not time for the end times? Because Satan does not know when the Tribulation begins; he does not know when Christ will return. Satan keeps the world in readiness with wars and rumors of wars, nation rising against nation, kingdom against kingdom, people against people, and famines, and pestilences in various places because he does not know the time of the end, but he wants to be ready. He sends his many antichrists to claim they will bring peace, so when the time of the end does come he and the world are prepared for his peacemaker, the Antichrist, who does bring peace, for a little while. These things—wars and rumors of wars, nation rising against nation, kingdom against kingdom, people against people, and famines, and pestilences, and antichrists—must come to pass during the New Testament church age, but the time of the end, i.e., the Tribulation, the Antichrist, and Christ's return, is not yet. Only God—not the world, not Satan, not the church—only God knows when it is time for the end times, Acts 1:7.

The religious, historical and cultural context of Matthew 24 requires we see the apostles not as leaders of the New Testament church, but as Israelis looking for the Davidic Kingdom in Jesus the messiah, and interpret Matthew 24 relevant to national ethnic Israel and Messiah's Kingdom. At this point in their history the apostles were looking for the kingdom, not the church, and Jesus answers them accordingly.

Let us now look at Matthew 24:4–14 in outline, so we can see how the prophecies here coordinate with the Revelation. Before beginning, I want to again emphasize that these prophecies of the end times refer to national ethnic Israel, not the New Testament church.

The events of 24:4–13 describe the beginning of the Tribulation period, specifically Revelation 6:1–8. There Antichrist initiates his kingdom (Daniel 2:40–43; 7:7–8, 20, Daniel 9:27 describe this time period) and God begins to bring judgment to the unsaved.

Matthew 24:13, "But the one having endured to the end, he will be saved," is not a conditional statement but a statement of fact. The believer's salvation—whether the New Testament Christian or the Tribulation believer—is secured by the merit of Christ, not the believer's works. In the prophetic Tribulation context "the end" is the second advent. The "end" Jesus prophesies is not the end of the New

Testament church age that precedes the Tribulation. It is not the Tribulation period that immediately precedes the second advent. "The end" is when the kingdom is realized on the earth, therefore "the end" is the return of the king to destroy his enemies and inaugurate his kingdom rule on the earth, Revelation 19:11–20:6.

The consummating purpose of the second advent is for God to take up his great power and reign, Revelation 11:17. The reign of God is the Messianic Kingdom of Jesus the Christ visible and active on earth. Therefore, to "endure to the end" in the context of "this gospel of the kingdom" means the Tribulation believers are to endure even unto death, for most, or to the second advent and into the Kingdom, for some. "This gospel of the kingdom," Revelation 11:17, is the king returning to take up his great power and reign.

Matthew 24:14 reflects two passages in Revelation: the good news of the coming kingdom and the eternal good news (the good news of salvation).

> Revelation 11:17, We thank You, Lord God, the Almighty, who is and who was, because You have taken Your great power and have begun to reign. (HCSB)

> Revelation 14:6–7, Then I saw another angel flying in midheaven, having the eternal gospel to announce to the inhabitants of the earth—to every nation, tribe, language, and people. He spoke with a loud voice: "Fear God and give Him glory, because the hour of His judgment has come. Worship the Maker of heaven and earth, the sea and springs of water." (HCSB)

The prophecy of Matthew 24:14, "this good news of the kingdom will be proclaimed in all the world for a testimony to all the nations," is not fulfilled by the New Testament church. The church has, over the centuries, proclaimed the gospel of Salvation worldwide. But the prophetic fulfillment is in the verses above, Revelation 14:6–7, when there are so few believers left alive (after persecution and martyrdom) to preach the word, that God in mercy sends an angel to proclaim the simplest form of the good news of salvation, during the last half of the Tribulation. Then the end will come, i.e., then it will be time for Christ's return, Armageddon, and the Messianic Kingdom.

Revelation 14:6–7 is a particular form of the good news of salvation designed for the Tribulation believers. The means of salvation is the same: faith in God; the propitiation made by Christ.

The content of faith has been simplified: "Fear God and give him glory, because the hour of his judgment has come. Worship the Maker of heaven and earth, the sea and springs of water." This is the good news that will be preached "in all the world as a witness to all the nations before the end comes."

As the moment of the second advent draws near, God in his mercy has simplified the message of salvation to its most basic component: I am coming to judge you earth dwellers; turn from idolatry and worship me. Thus, the timing of the message within the chronology of the Tribulation is of importance. The beast has secured his authority over mankind. He is making war against the saints and overcoming them (Revelation 13:7); the living remnant of believers is diminishing. The voice of God's witness through human believers is being silenced. Millions are turning in fear to the beast. Then, from an earth-dweller's point of reference, the very heavens cry out with an eternal message of salvation: "Fear God and give glory to him."

To fear God requires self-humiliation and self-surrender to him. To give God the glory is an idiom of repentance. The means of this proclamation is the work of angels, a voice that cannot be silenced (the first and only time angels preach the good news). The subject is salvation. The timing is the coming return of the Lord Jesus and the judgments that accompany and immediately follow his return (Revelation 19:11–20; Matthew 25:31–46; Ezekiel 20:33–38). The recipients are those who dwell on the earth, i.e., those being led, duped, or coerced into worshiping the beast. The purpose is the mercy of God in saving souls.

In viewing this simple message of salvation, one should look to the larger picture. During the Great Tribulation God has many witnesses of his grace and mercy: the 144,000 (Revelation 71–8); those saved by the ministry of the 144,000 (Revelation 7:9–17; the two witnesses (Revelation 11:1–14); the angelic preaching (Revelation 14:6–7). The Tribulation may be the greatest period of evangelism and salvation in human history, Revelation 7:9. Surely God is merciful!

The content of the gospel may change, but the message is always the same, "fear God and give him the glory," compare Zechariah 14:16; Isaiah 2:2, 3; Micah 4:1, 2. One should not suppose a contradiction between the gospel that Paul, or Peter, or James preached, and this eternal gospel. The first duty of the creature has always been to "fear [reverence and awe] God and give the glory to him." The outward presentation of that duty is the message of salvation, because to accomplish the duty one must turn from sin to God in faith. As previously discussed above, the content of the "good news" message has varied according to the several economies of God's grace toward mankind from Adam to Christ. In this New Testament age of grace and church, the content is Jesus Christ crucified, buried, and resurrected. In the Tribulation period I have no doubt that the 144,000 will be preaching Jesus crucified, resurrected, ascended, and shortly arriving at his second advent; and souls will be saved.

I realize most readers have been taught to relate Matthew 24:14 solely to the New Testament church. However, this verse does not define the commission or mission of the church. The church's commission and mission are defined in Matthew 29:18–20; Mark 16:16–15; Luke 24:44–49; John 20:31; 21:22; Acts 1:8. The character of the New Testament church age reflects the coming events of the end times because during these last times the world is being kept in readiness for the end times.

Translation Matthew 24:15–22

15 "Therefore when you shall see the 'abomination of desolation' spoken of by Daniel the prophet, standing in the holy place,' the one reading let him understand. 16 Then those in Judea let them flee to the mountains. 17 The one on the housetop, let him not come down to take anything out of his house. 18 And the one in the field, let him not return back to take his garment. 19 But woe to those pregnant, and to those nursing infants, in those days! 20 Now, pray that your flight might not be in winter, or on a Sabbath. 21 For then there will be great tribulation, such as has not been from the beginning of the world until now, no, nor may be. 22 And if those days had not been shortened, there would not have been anybody saved, but because of the elect, those days will be shortened."

Translation Note

In v. 22 the English past tense, "if those days had not been shortened" and "there would not have been anybody saved," is a result of translating the Greek aorist tense into English. The aorist presents an event as a whole, complete (but not necessarily completed) event without regard to time. In God's plan for these yet-future days, the days have been shortened so some believers survive to enter the kingdom.

Exposition

Beginning in v. 15 Jesus transitions from describing the character of the Tribulation period to describing actual events occurring during the Tribulation. The "abomination of desolation" is the first of these events, a prophecy given at Daniel 9:27.

The abomination of desolation is an event that occurs at the mid-point of the Tribulation period, at which the Antichrist of the first half of the Tribulation becomes the beast of the last half of the Tribulation: same person, different name and character. Neither Jesus nor the Revelation nor other New Testament writings say much about the rise of Antichrist to world dominance during the first half of the Tribulation. I have previously listed the most relevant of these verses: Daniel 2:41–43; 7:8, 20; 9:27; Revelation 6:1–2. To this list may be added Revelation 13:1–2; 17:1–12.

Beginning at 24:15 Jesus talks about that time of the Tribulation known as the Great Tribulation, which is the last half of the Tribulation, after the Antichrist becomes the beast, 2 Thessalonians 2:3–4, Revelation 13:3–4. The abomination of desolation is described at Daniel 9:27.

> He will prevail in a covenant with many for one seven, but in half a seven sacrifice and offering will cease and on a corner [of the temple] will be the detestable idol which makes desolate, until the full end determined be poured out on the desolator. (JQT)

I have explained this prophecy in depth in my commentary on Daniel and my book Antichrist. Without going into the explanation, a "seven" in this prophecy is 2,520 days, "half a seven" is 1,260 days. The 2,520 days is the length of the Tribulation period (nominally seven years), which is divided into two periods of 1,260 days each. The abomination of desolation occurs at the end of the first 1,260 days.

The person "he" in Daniel 9:27 is "the coming prince" in Daniel 9:26, who is the Antichrist in 1 John 2:18, the man of sin, son of perdition, and lawless one in 2 Thessalonians 2:3, 8, and the "beast" in Revelation 11, 13–17; 19–20. The Antichrist's act of desolation, Daniel 9:27, or as Jesus calls it, abomination of desolation, is explained at 2 Thessalonians 2:4,

> He [the man of sin, son of perdition, lawless one] opposes and exalts himself above every so-called god or object of worship, so that he sits in God's sanctuary, publicizing that he himself is God. (HCSB)

Which is why Jesus says the abomination of desolation will be standing in the holy place (in the temple), the place where "sacrifice and offering" take place Daniel 9:27. The Antichrist's act of abomination will take place at the "half a seven," i.e., the mid-point of the Tribulation, 1,260 days after the covenant that begins the Tribulation.

The abomination of desolation is both the man and his act in the temple. He goes to a rebuilt temple, pretends to be God, and demands everyone in the world worship him. The word "antichrist" describes his character. He is opposed to Christ and supplants Christ in the view of the world. After his pseudo-resurrection, Revelation 13:3, he commits his abominable act, 2 Thessalonians 2:4, and becomes the "beast" who rules the world and persecutes believers. The title "beast" names the man and describes the violence and brutality of his kingdom. In the fullness of his apostasy the unholy trinity of the beast, the false prophet, and the dragon (Satan), lead mankind into abominable idolatry.

Jesus describes those days in the most intense manner. He is prophetically addressing those persons, national ethnic Israel, who will be living during the Tribulation, who will be in Jerusalem when the event occurs. Jesus tells them, no matter where you might be when the act takes place, run away. Don't stop or return to grab anything. Take your life and flee. Pray that certain conditions do not prevail which would make your flight more difficult. The flight spoken of in vv. 16–20 most likely corresponds to Revelation 12:13–17. (See my commentary on the Revelation, The Epistle of Jesus to the Church).

We know the time is the Tribulation period because Jesus says the troubles will be greater than any that have ever occurred and an event of that magnitude will never occur again. That is also how we know the Tribulation has not occurred to this date. The terrible events that have occurred thus far in the history of the world have not been of the magnitude Jesus describes. Moreover, the events that have occurred in the history of the world have repeatedly occurred. The Tribulation has not yet taken place.

The coming days of the Tribulation are so terrible, that if God's plan had not shortened those yet-future days, no one would survive. The fact the duration has already been shortened in the plan of God is expressed in the aorist tense, indicating a complete act: the days have already been shortened. This is possible because the Tribulation is an event already planned and prepared on God's prophetic calendar, waiting for the proper day and time to begin. God has shortened the days so some believers survive to enter into Messiah's Kingdom.

Translation Matthew 24:23–28

23 "Then if anyone says to you, 'Look, here is the Christ,' or 'Here,' don't believe. 24 For false christs will rise and false prophets, and will give great signs, and wonders, so as to mislead, if possible, even the elect. 25 Look, I have foretold it to you. 26 If therefore they say to you, 'Look, he is in the wilderness,' do not go; 'Look, he is in the inner rooms,' do not believe. 27 For just as the lightning comes from the east and shines as far as the west, so will be the coming of the son of man. 28 For wherever the carcass might be, there the vultures will be gathered."

Exposition

No one living today, or tomorrow, or at any time in the future until after the Tribulation begins, can know the date—year or month or week or day—when Christ will return. If they say they know, "Don't believe." Believers during the Tribulation are to look for the sign of Christ's return appearing in the sky (Revelation 11:15–19; 19:11–16). The sign is caused by Christ's return. So when the sign is seen, and not before, then there will be no doubt as to when Christ is returning to reign over the earth. Therefore all who read or hear Christ's words during this New Testament church age cannot know. And all those enduring the trials of the great Tribulation should not be deceived by those claiming to be the messiah, for when the time for his appearing has come, the signs in the sky will make that appearing unmistakable.

Now, a word needs to be said about the duration of the Tribulation relevant to Christ's coming. According to Daniel 9:27 (coordinate with Revelation 6:2; Daniel 7:8, 20), the Tribulation begins with a covenant that is supposed to last one seven, which is 2,520 days. Because the context of the prophecy is Daniel's people, national ethnic Israel (9:24), one assumes it is a covenant that brings peace to the Middle East. So, someone knowledgeable could understand from the date the covenant is made that Christ is returning in 2,520 sunset-to-sunset days.

Again according to Daniel 9:27, with Revelation 13:3, and 2 Thessalonians 2:4, that covenant will be broken when the man of sin stands in the temple declaring himself to be God. Because Daniel 9:27 states the covenant is broken in the middle of the seven, then a knowledgeable person could count 1,260 sunset-to-sunset days to

Christ's return from the date the Antichrist declares himself to be God.

These facts are all the more reason for believers not to be deceived by false Christs and seemingly miraculous signs and wonders. Even for these knowledgeable persons, what confirms the arrival of the second advent are the signs Christ's advent causes when it occurs.

So let me state again, no person today, during this New Testament church age, can know when Christ is returning. The three events that foretell when Christ is returning are Daniel 9:27a, the covenant that begins the Tribulation, Daniel 9:27b, the broken covenant in the middle of the Tribulation, and Revelation 11:15–19; 19:11–16 the sign in the sky caused by Christ returning.

Verses 23–28 are the Antichrist-beast and false prophet deceiving the world. Verse 24 refers to the Antichrist and the false prophet, Revelation 13. Verse 27 looks to Revelation 11:15–19; 16:17. Verse 28 corresponds to Revelation 14:17–20. In v. 28 the Greek word translated "vultures" means either eagles or vultures, because both are carrion eaters; the former as an act of opportunity, the latter as a career. The saying is proverbial in nature. When the messiah returns he will gather all his enemies into one place for destruction, Revelation 19:17–18.

Translation Matthew 24:29–31

29 "Now immediately during the tribulation of those days, the sun will be darkened, and the moon will not give its light, and the stars will fall from the sky, and the powers of the heavens will be shaken. 30 And then will appear the sign of the son of man in the heaven, and then all the tribes of the earth will mourn, and they will see the son of man coming on the clouds of heaven with power and great glory. 31 And he will send his angels with a great trumpet call, and they will gather his elect from the four winds, from the ends of the heavens to the ends of them."

Translation Note

In v. 29 the word I have translated "during" is meta, which is translated "after" by other versions. The word means "mid, amid, in the midst, with, among, implying accompaniment." When used with the accusative case ("tribulation" is in the accusative case) it "strictly implies motion toward the middle or into the midst of something." The idea is one thing accompanies another thing, thus, the things happening to the sun, moon, etc., accompany—are part of—the Tribulation. Other translations view meta as indicating succession in time (thus, "after") because of the preceding "immediately."

Exposition

Verses 29–30 correspond to the sixth seal and the seventh bowl, Revelation 6:12–17; 16:18–21. Verse 30 corresponds to Revelation 14:14–16, 17–20; 16:17–21; 19:11–21. Verse 31 relates to several Old Testament prophecies of the gathering of the Jews to the land of Israel for the Davidic Messianic kingdom, e.g., Zechariah 8:7–8; Ezekiel 20:33–38.

This is how Jesus answered the disciples' questions:

> Question One: "When will these things be?"
> Answer: "When you see these events happening, that is when these things will be."
>
> Question Two: "What will be the sign of your coming?"
> Answer: "My coming will be as unmistakable as the lightening."
>
> Question Three: "What will be the sign of the end of the age?"
> Answer: "When my sign appears in heaven it marks the end of the age."

Obviously Jesus did not give sufficient information—no information at all—to justify the continual date-setting and constant watching for signs-of-the-times which some members of the New Testament church have engaged in for almost 2,000 years.

Translation Matthew 24:32–35

32 "Now learn the parable from the fig tree: when its branch is already become tender and it puts forth the leaves, you know that the summer is near. 33 And so you, when you see all these things, know that it is near, at the doors. 34 Truly I say to you, that this generation may by no means have passed away until all these things may have taken place. 35 The heaven and the earth will pass away, but my words by no means may pass away."

Exposition

Verses 32–33 are plain enough: believers during the Tribulation are to look for the coming of the messiah. They are to gauge the timing of his coming by events in the world, the events Jesus has just described. Jesus is again answering the questions in general terms:

when you see these things happening—events occurring during the tribulation—then my coming and the end of the age is near.

Though some would apply this to the church, there are no signs for the coming of Christ to take his New Testament church out of the world; there are no signs for the rapture. That coming is imminent: occurring at any time without any preceding signs. All the signs Jesus has revealed come after the church has been taken out of the world.

The New Testament church age believer is to wait in constant expectation for Jesus to deliver the church from the wrath to come, 1 Thessalonians 1:10; Revelation 3:10. These signs in Matthew indicate the wrath of God has arrived, so believers living during that period of wrath, the Tribulation, are to look for Jesus who is coming to bring God's wrath to its conclusion, Revelation 14:17–19; 19:11–21.

"This generation," v. 34, refers to the generation alive when "all these things take place." Obviously the generation of the people of the disciples he is speaking to died before Christ returned. The same is true in modern times; many generations have passed away. Some believe "this generation" refers to the Israel that became a nation in 1948. These people have to keep extending the duration of a generation, because sixty-eight years have passed, to date. The beginning of the generation Christ speaks of is the generation alive when all those things he is speaking of begin, which is the Tribulation period. Verse 35 is Jesus' confirmation that these things he has prophesied are truth and will come to pass. Jesus himself is the confirmation of every word of God.

Translation Matthew 24:36–39

36 "But about that day and hour no one knows, not even the angels of the heavens, nor the son, except Father only. 37 For as were the days of Noah, so will be the coming of the son of man. 38 For as they were in those days, before the flood, eating and drinking, marrying and giving in marriage, until that day Noah entered into the ark, 39 and they knew not until the flood came and took all away; and so will the coming of the son of man."

Translation Note

In v. 36, the phrase "nor the son," is not in the majority of the witnesses of Matthew, including the later Byzantine text [KJV/NKJV text]. On the other hand, the best representatives of the Alexandrian and the Western types of texts [NIV, NASB, HCSB] contain the phrase.

The probability of omission due to doctrinal considerations is more likely than the addition of the phrase by importing it from Mark 13:32.

Exposition

No one can know when the tribulation begins or when Christ will return, until the Tribulation begins. Not even the son of God knew at the time the prophecy was given. During his earthly ministry the God the Son incarnate limited his divine omniscience to those things revealed to him by the Holy Spirit, whether it was the thoughts of men, or the end-times calendar, because he chose to live his life as a Holy Spirit-filled man. If these things were not revealed to the Son when he was incarnate on the earth, why do some people think the Holy Spirit will reveal it to them?

At vv. 37–39 Jesus said no one can know. He was referring to the Noahic Flood. Someone may say there were signs of impending judgment because Noah was building the Ark. The Ark was not a sign of judgment but of salvation. In these verses Jesus plainly states life continued as normal until the day Noah entered the ark. We don't know how long after the Ark was completed until God commanded Noah to enter; and after he entered seven days passed before the flood began. Noah didn't know when the flood would begin. The people who would die in the flood "did not know until the flood came." So also will be the coming of the son of man. If we view Noah entering the Ark as analogous to the rapture, then Noah didn't know when to leave the earth—enter the Ark—until God called him up into the Ark. No one, not Noah, not anyone, except God, knew if the flood was near or when the flood would begin. So too the rapture and the Tribulation.

The fact that God the Son in his incarnation did not know during his time on earth when the Tribulation and the second advent would occur is not a limitation of his deity, but a function of the Christ in his prophetic office during his first advent. Pragmatically, if Jesus had known the day and hour, but did not tell us, then the New Testament church would have launched itself on an endless search to discover knowledge of that day and hour somewhere in all the words Jesus spoke during his first advent. As it is, even though Jesus said no one except the Father knew, compare Acts 1:7, men have still tried to assign a day and hour to these events. Naturally Jesus after his ascension knows, because the self-imposed limitations of his earthly ministry are removed.

In vv. 37–39 Jesus says life will be unassumingly normal before these events begin. The world at large will not be looking for or expecting in any sense a messiah, let alone the messiah, Jesus the

Christ. When God begins his judgments, and allows the Antichrist to rise to power, then in the ensuing wars, famines, disease, and lawlessness men will begin to look for a savior, and accept the Antichrist as filling that position. In the interim, few will know and fewer will care that Christ is returning to reign. Judgment will overtake all those who do not enter the ark of redemption which is faith in Jesus the Christ.

Translation Matthew 24:40–44

40 "Then two will be in the field: one is taken and one is left; 41 two grinding at the mill: one is taken and one is left. 42 Therefore keep watch, because you do not know on what day your Lord is coming. 43 But know this, that if the householder had known in what watch of the night the thief comes, he would have watched, and not have allowed his house to be broken into. 44 And on account of this, you be ready, for the son of man comes in that hour you do not expect."

Exposition

This is a simple description of the suddenness of judgment, and a warning to be prepared by having faith in Jesus the coming Messiah, because the unsaved do not know when Jesus is coming. In vv. 40–41 the one taken is taken in judgment, not salvation. The context of vv. 42–44 is the example set by the unbelievers in Noah's day: they did not know until judgment came. How do we know one is taken in judgment? Because the other is left. What comes after the Lord's return? The Davidic Messianic kingdom. The one left is left for the kingdom. Notice also that vv. 42–44 come on the heels of the judgment stated in vv. 40–41.

Translation Matthew 24:45–51

45 "Who then is the faithful servant, and wise, whom the master has set over his household, to give to them food in season? 46 Blessed that servant, whom the master having come, will find doing thus. 47 Truly I say to you, that he will set him over all his possessions. 48 But if that evil servant should say in his heart, 'My master delays,' 49 and should begin to beat his fellow servants, and to eat and drink with the drunkards, 50 the master of that servant will come in a day in which he does not expect, and in an hour which he is not aware, 51 and will scourge him and will appoint him a place with the hypocrites; there shall be the weeping and the gnashing of teeth."

Translation Note

In v. 51 the word I have translated "scourge" is dichotoméō, literally, "to cut in two or asunder." A metaphorical meaning is required, because after the unfaithful servant has been dichotoméō, he/she is appointed a place with the hypocrites. The figurative meaning of the word is "scourging." The unfaithful servant will be judged and punished. The punishment is eternity in the place of weeping and gnashing teeth: ultimately the lake of fire.

Exposition

Let us not be confused by the sound of words. Believers are used to hearing the word "servant" in the context of a Christians serving Jesus. But let us remember Jesus is prophetically addressing national ethnic Israel during the Tribulation. The "servant" is a representation of the people of the nation. The faithful servant is the saved servant who obeys the Lord through worship, service, obedience, and fellowship, always prepared for whenever Christ should appear. The unfaithful servant reveals by his actions that he is the unsaved person. The exhortation is for all to become faithful servants. The person who is unfaithful will be taken in eternal judgment. There is an application for believers in any time: be a faithful servant; and for unbelievers: believe and be saved.

The Apostle Paul as Mother and Father

An extract from my book, *A Private Commentary on the Bible: Thessalonians*, published 2021.

In his first letter to the Thessalonians, Paul uses two metaphors to describe his feelings and actions toward the Thessalonian believers. Through these metaphors we learn something about being a Christian leader. (My translation.)

> 2:7–8, We were gentle in your midst, as a nursing mother might cherish her own children. So, being affectionate toward you, we were pleased to have imparted to you not only the gospel of God, but also our own lives, because you have become beloved to us.

> 2:11–12, As a father his own children, encouraging you and comforting and solemnly charging you to live lives worthy of God.

The "nursing mother" image is easy for us to understand, though the world has sought to portray a mother nursing (breast-feeding) her child as a burden detracting from her femininity and her life apart from her family roles. In using this metaphor Paul is saying, "I did not take from you, but rather I gave to you."

Paul had said (2:6), "I could have been a burden, requiring housing and to be fed," because that was his right as one of Christ's apostles (cf. 1 Corinthians 9:1–6). But instead, he uses the image of a mother giving to her children. The image is very emotional, very tender, and speaks of him giving of his own self, as a nursing mother gives of herself to nourish her child with her breast milk. He took nothing from them, he gave his all to them. They received his love and he theirs.

The second metaphor is "as a father to his own children." The world, especially the world of entertainment, shows the family father as gruff, unable to communicate emotionally, unwilling to show kindness, lacking empathy, usually lacking sympathy, and too unaware to teach his children anything. This is not true, it is a gross distortion of the relative differences between men and women. The world exaggerates the mother's emotional roles in the family so as to diminish the father's, in an effort to destroy biblical family roles and values.

The Bible has a different view of the family. The mother in the ancient world was responsible to care for her children when they were young. The father was responsible for the child's education. In the Old Testament, YHWH is like a mother and a father to his people.

> Isaiah 66:10 (NKJV), As one whom his mother comforts, So I will comfort you.

> Psalm 103:13 (NKJV), As a father pities his children, So the Lord pities those who fear Him.

> Proverbs 3:12 (NKJV), For whom the Lord loves He corrects, Just as a father the son in whom he delights.

Even so, Paul toward those whom Christ had given into his care. "Pastor" Paul took the time to personally interact with each believer by teaching, guiding, and exhorting as might be necessary. He loved them as a mother who loves her children. He taught them as a father who loves his children.

Paul uses three additional words to communicate his actions (the first three words he used were holily, righteously, blamelessly, 2:10). Paul's goal was to teach the Thessalonian believers "to live lives worthy of God." God has called his saved people into his kingdom and glory; his saved people are to live worthy of that call.

The first word is "encouraging you." The word "encouraging" is the Greek *parakaléō*, "to aid, help, comfort, encourage" [Zodhiates, s. v. "3870"]. This word is used over 100 times in the New Testament, about one-half of those occurrences are in Paul's writings. *Parakaléō* is used eight times in 1 Thessalonians, three times in 2 Thessalonians. In 1 Thessalonians the word is best translated "encourage" in 2:12, 3:2; 4:18; 5:11.

> 2:12, encouraging you . . . to live lives worthy of God who calls you into his kingdom and glory.

> 3:2, and we sent Timothy, our brother and fellow worker of God in the gospel of Christ, to strengthen and to encourage you to benefit your faith.

> 4:18, Therefore, encourage one another with these words.

> 5:18, Therefore encourage one another, and build up one another, just as also you are doing.

The point is not encouragement to resist or overcome depression, or evil, or persecution but encouragement to continue living a life well-pleasing to God, in every circumstance of life. It is like the "pat on the back" that says, "You are doing a good job, don't stop." It is like saying, "I am with you, you can do this, we can do this together."

The next word is "comforting," the Greek word *paramuthéomai*, "to speak kindly, to comfort" [Zodhiates, s. v. "3888"]. This word is used four times in the New Testament, John 11:9; 11:31; 1 Thessalonians 2:12; 5:14. In the other three uses it means to speak kind words to those who are in distress. This is also a father's work. When the Thessalonians suffered persecution for their faith, Paul spoke kindly to them, giving them comfort in their distress. In emotional terms, the (relatively) stronger and experienced father lent his strength to the (relatively) weaker and less experienced children. The mature person helped the less mature person learn how to cope with their problems.

"Solemnly charging" is my translation of *martúromai*, "to witness, attest, affirm" [Zodhiates, s. v. "3143"]. This word is used four times in the New Testament, Acts 20:26; Galatians 5:3; Ephesians 4:17; 1 Thessalonians 2:12. In every occurrence the idea is "testify." In 1 Thessalonians 2:12 it means to testify as an exhortation. The thought is an exhortation based on personal experience—a testimony of, "I met the challenges of the Christian faith, you can too."

Paul says he teaches the Thessalonians (as a father) about living the Christian life because they are to "live lives worthy of God who calls you into his kingdom and glory." The kingdom in view is the Spiritual Kingdom. (There are four kingdoms relevant to Christ and the New Testament church, a post for another time.)

The Spiritual Kingdom is the faith-community of all the saved from Pentecost to the rapture. The Thessalonians had become members through their salvation. The Spiritual kingdom is within, but is very different from, the Mystery Kingdom, which is the New Testament church the world sees, composed of saved and unsaved. (The Mystery and Spiritual forms of the kingdom are described in Matthew 13.) Every local church is a manifestation of both the Spiritual and Mystery kingdoms. Only as the believer brings glory to God by living a Christ-like life is the Spiritual Kingdom able to be discerned within the worldly Mystery Kingdom. Not all will be able to understand, but they will see the difference.

Paul, like a mother and like a father, loved and taught his spiritual children.

The Order of Bible Study

Bible study has a certain order. It is an inflexible order, which if varied or violated will yield inaccurate results.

Step One. Ask the Holy Spirit to teach you. Bear in mind the Holy Spirit expects you to apply what he has taught.

Step Two. What is the context of the passage? Before interpreting discover the literary context: what has been said before and after. Then seek the historical and cultural contexts.

Step Three. What does it say? What is the plain and normal meaning of the words? What is the meaning of the key word(s), the phrase(s), the sentence, paragraph?

Step Four. What does it mean? How do all the parts fit together? What is the sense or meaning of the bit under study. (Example. What is the difference in meaning between "run to the store" and "run the store"?) How does the bit under study fit into the whole? How does it fit into what the Bible as a whole says?

Step Five. How does it apply to my life? Personal application must always be the last step. Otherwise application is substituted for meaning (step one) and interpretation (step two). The Scripture order is always teaching, then application.

Each of the steps is of equal value and each of equal necessity. The only priority is the order in which one performs the steps of Bible study. This is the order: What does it say? What does it mean? How does it apply?

A Conversation on Sin and Sinning

He said: "Brother, I am becoming lazy in spiritual things."

Me: "Happens to us all. Don't let it continue. Refocus on Christ, prayer, reading, study—all the things you know you are supposed to be doing. Remember to make personal application of what you are reading-studying. If you do the things you are supposed to be doing, God will help you. If you do not, God will help you in a different way. The first way is better.

"But, really, probably not laziness. Probably more like more complacency in what you know, which is to say, taking the things of Christ for granted. Work on putting these core values at work in your life.

> I will enter God's presence and have intimate fellowship with him through a life filled with worship, praise, prayer, thanksgiving, service, and obedience.
>
> I will daily ask God for grace, power, guidance, and help for myself and others to live according to His values and His rules for living.
>
> I will actively seek to know God and understand His Word.
>
> I will live out my faith without wavering and without fear, for God is my strength.
>
> I will tell others about Christ the Savior, and extend God's offer of salvation to them.
>
> I will assemble with believers of like faith to worship, fellowship, and serve.
>
> I will encourage others and myself to practice acts of godly love and good works.
>
> I will practice forgiveness, longsuffering, and mercy toward others.
>
> I will practice humility, which is valuing myself as God values me and esteeming others as better than myself.
>
> I will strive to live a life filled with righteous acts in order to be holy as God is holy.

I will pay attention to and care for the spiritual and physical well-being of others.

I will remember Christ promised to return, and he is faithful.

I will continue active in my faith until Christ takes me home to heaven.

"Doing is often a path to becoming. But make sure the doing is for Christ's sake first, yourself second, others third. Christ first, because he is the focus of life. Yourself next, because unless you are spiritually healthy you cannot give to others, Others last, because you have prepared yourself to serve others through Christ."

He said: "At times I struggle with sinful thoughts like lust." He said: "How can I get over a constant struggle and desire for sin?"

Me: "Dude, we all, men and women, struggle with lust, whether it is sexual lust, lust for material things, for honor, recognition, reward, praise. The focus of sin is "Me," the desire of sin is "I want." Focus on Christ, focus on what is right, Philippians 4:8. And when you sin, repent, confess, ask for forgiveness, forgive yourself, and begin again where you left off.

"Getting over the desire for sin. We begin to get over the desire for sin when we understand the cost of the Christian life. The Christian life is the product of God's grace, but a lot of personal effort must be expended as well.

"God chooses to work his will through us, with us. He chose not to make you sinless until after physical death (or rapture). He chose to empower you to overcome your sins in this mortal life, and also choose for you to do the actual work of overcoming, by receiving and using the power he gives you. I have absolute confidence the Holy Spirit has told you what to do, in his Word, because I read the same Word of God.

"He gave you a new, born-again, nature that is naturally inclined to godliness and righteousness and holiness, and definitely disinclined to sin and sinning. John said, 1 John 3:6, the one abiding in Christ does not sin, and at 1 John 3:9, God's seed is in the believer, and the believer cannot sin, because he/she has been born of God. That seed, which is God's eternal life given at salvation, cannot sin, and the believer abiding does not sin.

"As Augustine said, 'In so far as the believer abides in Christ, in so far he does not sin.' Whoever is abiding does not sin, whoever is not abiding does sin. Therefore an occasion of sinning is inversely related to the habit of abiding.

"The motivating desire of the Christian life is to please God, not self. You have the spiritual power to say "No" to temptation and enforce that decision. The believer may occasionally choose to sin, but will habitually choose righteousness.

"Here is the cost of Christian living. Here is how we learn to say "No." We must choose to give up the things of the world and choose replace them with the things of Christ. We must choose to practice living rightly. The more one practices, the more the practice becomes habit. There is no magic solution, just the hard works of living for and like Christ through submission to and dependence upon God."

———————————————

He said: "Sometimes it seems to me that I am a disobedient man. So I feel ashamed. Because I am not faithful to what I genuinely understood."

Me: "It is good you feel ashamed. The unsaved do not. Turn that shame into repentance and confession, and resolve to live according to God's values. Practice those values. Repeat until the habit of life. Be aware sin ALWAYS is tempting. Practice saying "No," and replacing the world and the flesh with godly values. No one but God Father-Son-Holy Spirit can help you in this. You have to live your life, no one can live your life for you."

He asked: "You pray daily?"

Me: "Daily? More often than that. There are so many things to pray for. As we are communicating, even as I am typing, I am praying for you. Persevere in the faith by means of faith!"

(Although the above is based on an actual conversation, it has been appropriately edited. If you don't tell them it was you, they will think it was them.)

Piercings and Tattoos

Every now and then I am stunned by what people claiming to be Christian think of Christ. I am dismayed by what they add to the gospel of salvation.

Here was someone who thought a tattoo will keep a person from salvation. How poorly they understand Christ! How little they think of God's mercy and love in salvation!

Jesus Christ propitiated (fully and completely satisfied) God for every sin. Every sin, no matter how heinous it seems to us, is like a tear drop in the ocean of Christ's infinite merit dying and resurrected for our salvation.

Look at Acts 16:31. The Philippian jailor, who was a Roman soldier, had a tattoo. Roman soldiers were tattooed with the mark "SPQR," for *Senatus Populusque Romanus* ("the senate and people of Rome"). Another tattoo was used to identify membership in a military unit.

Paul DID NOT say, "you cannot be saved because you have a tattoo." He said, "Believe on the Lord Jesus Christ!" and you will be saved.

Leviticus 19:28 does not say (updating the language a bit) "you cannot pierce your skin and you cannot have a tattoo." Leviticus 19:28 says, in context, do not pierce your skin or get a tattoo as a means of mourning the dead or as a memorial for someone who has died. But if you insist on following this verse, be sure to follow every other regulation in that chapter, for you have just placed yourself under the Mosaic Law.

A tattoo or piercing does not prevent a sinner from being saved. What genuine Christianity does prohibit is a piercing or a tattoo to say or do something immoral, or foolish, or conforming to the worldly anti-Christ culture around you.

Daniel 9:24–27, A Very Brief Explanation

My translation of Daniel 9:24–27.

24 Seventy sevens are determined upon your people and upon your holy city: to finish the transgression and to make an end of sin; to make reconciliation for iniquity and to bring in everlasting righteousness; to seal up the vision and prophecy and to anoint the most Holy.

25 Know and understand, from the issue of the word to restore and rebuild Jerusalem until Messiah the Prince, there shall be seven sevens and sixty-two sevens; the market place will be built again, and the wall, even in times of distress.

26 After sixty-two sevens Messiah will be cut off and have nothing for himself. The people of the coming prince will destroy the city and the sanctuary. The end will come with a flood, until the end will be war; desolations are decreed.

27 He will prevail in a covenant with many for one seven, but in half a seven sacrifice and offering will cease and on a corner [of the temple] will be the detestable idol which makes desolate, until the full end determined be poured out on the desolator.

A reader familiar with this passage may have noticed I translated "seventy sevens" not "seventy weeks." That is because the Hebrew word translated "weeks" does not mean "week" but "seven." Yes, a certain order of seven days, Sunday through Saturday, is a week. But not in Old Testament times in Israel. The Hebrew word means "a period of seven."

The context decides the duration of a period of seven—seven days, seven months, seven years, etc. To translate the Hebrew word as "weeks" is the translator's way of accommodating to a modern point of view. The Hebrew in Daniel 9:24 is "seventy sevens," meaning seventy groups of seven periods each. A much longer discussion (see my commentary on Daniel) is needed to show that each group of seven periods is in years, not weeks. If one is going to translate "weeks" then it must be translated "seventy weeks of years," to indicate each seven is seven years.

The seventy sevens are divided into three groups. The first group is seven sevens, which corresponds to 9:24, "to finish the transgression and to make an end of sin." The transgression and sin in view are the sins that led to the destruction of Jerusalem and the 70 years of Babylonian Captivity for the Jews, 609–539 BC. The captivity will come to an end and, 9:25, "the market place will be built again, and the wall, even in times of distress."

This means Jerusalem will be rebuilt, within a time period of, nominally, 49 years (each year of a "seven" is actually 360 days. See my commentary on Daniel or my book "Antichrist" for an extensive proof.) The 49 years began Nisan 1, 444 BC, Nehemiah 2:1–10. (The Jews began to return in 538 BC, but neither the wall nor the city, Daniel 9:25, was rebuilt until 444 to 395 BC. Between 538–444 BC, they built an altar for sacrifices and a few homes and lived among the ruins of the city, see Ezra 3, 4.)

The second group is sixty-two sevens, which corresponds to 9:24, "to make reconciliation for iniquity and to bring in everlasting righteousness." The crucifixion and resurrection of Jesus the Christ is in view, 9:25, "from the issue of the word to restore and rebuild Jerusalem until Messiah the Prince, there shall be seven sevens [first group] and sixty-two sevens [second group]" (a total of 173,880 sunset to sunset days or 476.03 years from 444 BC to AD 33) and 9:26, "After sixty-two sevens [second group] Messiah will be cut off and have nothing for himself." (Nothing for himself: the literal kingdom promised to David, 2 Samuel 7:13, 16; through the Messiah, Psalm 2, did not happen.)

The next part of 9:25 occurs after the sixty-two sevens, but is not part of the seventieth seven (9:27), but is what happened to Israel after the sixty-two sevens are completed, after "Messiah is cut off." The passage is, "The people of the coming prince will destroy the city and the sanctuary. The end will come with a flood, until the end will be war; desolations are decreed." This looks to the Jewish wars with Rome, from AD 66 to AD 135.

Then in 9:27, the seventy sevens of 9:24 are brought to a close with the seventieth seven. This corresponds with 9:24, "to seal up the vision and prophecy and to anoint the most Holy." To understand this last part, we must go to Daniel 9:24, "Seventy sevens are determined upon your people and upon your holy city." All the prophecy of the seventy sevens is all about the future of Israel—Daniel's people, the Jews, and Daniel's city, Jerusalem. The seventieth seven is part of the prophecy set out in 9:24, which was to answer Daniel's prayer in 9:1–19, which sums to "what will happen to my people Israel?" compare 9:20, 23.

Therefore, prophecy of the seventy sevens ignores the many years between the end of the sixty-two sevens and the fulfillment of the seventieth seven, because the prophecy is about national ethnic Israel, and Israel ceases to exist as a nation after the sixty-two sevens.

Let us apply a little logic and a little secular history. We know from 9:26 and secular history the Jerusalem temple was destroyed AD 70, and Israel as a nation ceased to exist from AD 135 to AD 1948. So nothing in 9:27 could be accomplished, because the prophecy is all about Israel as a nation, and there was no nation of Israel. Obviously, there is an interval of time (so far almost 1900 years) between the end of the sixty-two sevens and the beginning of the seventieth seven.

Nor did the seventieth seven begin in 1948. The seventieth seven is described in 9:27. The "he" of 9:27 is the prince of the people who would come and destroy Jerusalem in AD 70 (as history shows, "the people" were the Romans). The people came, but that prince has not yet come, and no covenant of one seven ("he will prevail in a covenant with many for one seven") has been made concerning national ethnic Israel, and obviously a non-existent covenant has not been broken in the middle of the seven.

Nor has the temple, which ceased to exist in AD 70, been rebuilt, so the, "sacrifice and offering will cease and on a corner [of the temple] will be the detestable idol which makes desolate" has not yet occurred. Jesus said this event had not occurred up to his time, Matthew 24:15. The temple was destroyed less than 40 years later, and the "abomination of desolation" both Daniel and Jesus spoke of had not occurred. I believe the seventieth seven is the Tribulation period, and the "he" is the person identified as the "antichrist" and "beast" who will make the abomination of desolation, 2 Thessalonians 2:4, Revelation 13:4.

Regardless, the seventy sevens is divided into three groups, as per Daniel 9:24.

> Seven sevens, to rebuild Jerusalem after the Babylonian Captivity.

> After the seven sevens, then sixty-two sevens until Messiah is cut-off.

> (A gap of time between Messiah cut off and the seventieth seven.)

> Then one seven that ends the seventy sevens, which I believe

is the Tribulation.

Resources for further study on these verses include, James D. Quiggle, *A Private Commentary on the Bible: Daniel*; Sir Robert Anderson, *The Coming Prince*; John F. Walvoord, *Daniel, the Key to Prophetic Revelation*; J. Dwight Pentecost, *Things to Come*; James D. Quiggle, *Antichrist, His Genealogy, Kingdom, And Religion*.

For those who see the New Testament church as Israel in this prophecy, the (above) work by Pentecost is recommended, as well as my book, *Dispensational Eschatology, An Explanation and Defense of the Doctrine*. Also recommended is Michael J. Vlach, *Has the Church Replaced Israel?*; and my work *Understanding Dispensational Theology*.

KJV Translators View of their Translation

What did the KJV translators think of the Bible translations that came before their work?

They did not see their work as the one and only inspired translation.

> [W]e affirm and avow, that the very meanest [poorest] translation of the Bible in English, set forth by men of our profession, containeth the word of God, nay, is the word of God.

They used prior translations in their work. For example, the majority of KJV readings in both Old Testament (76%) and New Testament (83%) reproduce the AD 1526 Tyndale Bible.

> Truly (good Christian Reader) we never thought from the beginning, that we should need to make a new Translation, nor yet to make of a bad one a good one, but to make a good one better, or out of many good ones, one principal good one, not justly to be excepted against; that hath been our endeavor, that our mark.

They believed other translations were the Word of God, and used them to create an English version.

> Neither did we think much to consult the Translators or Commentators, Chaldee, Hebrew, Syrian, Greek or Latin, no nor the Spanish, French, Italian, or Dutch; neither did we disdain to revise that which we had done, and to bring back to the anvil that which we had hammered: but having and using as great helps as were needful, and fearing no reproach for slowness, nor coveting praise for expedition, we have at the length, through the good hand of the Lord upon us, brought the work to that pass that you see.

The 1611 edition gave alternate readings in the margins. They did not believe their translation was inspired.

> Some peradventure would have no variety of senses to be set in the margin, lest the authority of the Scriptures for deciding of controversies by that show of uncertainty, should somewhat be shaken. But we hold their judgment not to be so sound in this point.

They did not know how to properly translate some Hebrew or Greek words.

> There be many words in the Scriptures, which be never found there but once, (having neither brother nor neighbor, as the Hebrews speak) so that we cannot be holpen by conference of places.

They believed other translations are useful.

> Therefore as S. Augustine saith, that variety of Translations is profitable for the finding out of the sense of the Scriptures: so diversity of signification and sense in the margin [their alternate translations written in the margin], where the text is no so clear, must needs do good, yea, is necessary, as we are persuaded.

They believed other translations are useful.

> They that are wise, had rather have their judgments at liberty in differences of readings, than to be captivated to one, when it may be the other.

They translated a Hebrew or a Greek word using many different words, "for there be some words that be not of the same sense everywhere."

> For is the kingdom of God become words or syllables? why should we be in bondage to them if we may be free, use one precisely when we may use another no less fit, as commodiously?

Source: 1611 KJV Bible, "The Translators to the Reader."

Did The Apostles Know Jesus Was God Incarnate?

Introduction

The question this article asks and will answer is this. Did the apostles know, from the day they met Jesus, up to the day they met with Jesus after his resurrection, did they know Jesus was God incarnate? The purpose of this article is to show from Scripture they did not know—that no one believed Jesus of Nazareth was God incarnate during the time of his earthly ministry, whether or not they believed him to be the Messiah.

The reason most believers today do believe the apostles believed Jesus the Christ was God the Son incarnate, is due to the traditions of Reformed theology, particularly preaching traditions based on English translations. Traditions are wonderful servants but terrible masters. They become terrible masters when "God's word is made of no effect on account of your tradition," Matthew 15:6. [Unless otherwise noted, Scripture translations are from James D. Quiggle, *Translations of Select Bible Books* (Amazon/KDP, 2018, rev. 2020).]

Let me pause for a moment and assure the reader I believe Jesus the Christ was and is God the Son incarnate in Jesus of Nazareth. At the moment the human being Jesus was conceived in Mary's womb, God the Son joined himself to that newly conceived and still rudimentary human body and human soul. From that moment both the human being and the deity were inseparably the God-man. [See my book, *God Became Incarnate*.]

The hermeneutic used by Reformed theology is to blame for the belief the apostles and other disciples supposedly knew (during the time of his earthly ministry) Jesus was God incarnate. The basis for the Reformed hermeneutic is interpreting the Old Testament revelation by the New Testament revelation. In this hermeneutic the Old Testament revelation is not allowed to speak for itself; original authorial intent is made subordinate to New Testament revelation. But as Vlach has said,

> The primary meaning of any Bible passage is found in that passage. The New Testament does not reinterpret or transcend Old Testament passages in a way that overrides or cancels the original authorial intent of the Old Testament writers. [Vlach, *Dispensationalism*, 31.]

The issue, then, is Dispensational: the proper use and application of the Literal hermeneutic. Too many Dispensationalists follow

Reformed traditions. This article is part of an ongoing effort to correct that error.

To close this introduction, there are many side paths we might take during this discussion—for example, the Old Testament difference between Messiah as King and Messiah as Redeemer. To keep this article to a manageable length, I will avoid as many of those "rabbit trails" as possible.

Old Testament Revelation

Let us, then, begin with what the Hebrews of Jesus' time knew about the Messiah. The first necessary action is to set aside all we know about the deity of Jesus Christ from the New Testament revelation. That revelation was not available when Jesus walked the earth. The New Testament revelation can play only a limited part in answering the question, "Did the apostles know Jesus was God incarnate?" We can only look at the Old Testament revelation, and examine what is recorded as spoken by angels, Jesus, the apostles and other disciples, and the enemies of Jesus, in the four gospels.

The Hebrew word *māshîah*, transliterated in the English "messiah," means "anointed" to an office or function. (The equivalent Greek word is *christós*.) The word *māshîah* occurs thirty-nine times in the Old Testament. However, only three times in those thirty-nine occurrences does *māshîah* refer to the person who would be Jesus the Messiah. Those three times are Psalm 2:2, Daniel 9:25, 26.

We may immediately dismiss Daniel 9:25, 26 from this discussion. Only in the light of New Testament revelation is the advent of the Messiah, and Messiah "cut off," understandable. Those scriptures are never directly referenced in the gospels. The Jews did not connect 9:25 to the Triumphal Entry (to which it almost certainly refers, Luke 19:42), and the apostles did not connect 9:26, "Messiah cut off," to Jesus' several declarations of his impending crucifixion. No one in gospel times connected Jesus with Daniel 9:25–26. [Beale and Carson, *Commentary*, index.]

Psalm 2

The key Old Testament scripture for understanding how the Hebrews understood the person and office of Messiah is Psalm 2. I have highlighted the key words. In the ESV:

> 1 Why do the nations rage and the peoples plot in vain? 2 The
> kings of the earth set themselves, and the rulers take counsel

together, against the Lord and against his *anointed*, saying,

3 "Let us burst their bonds apart and cast away their cords from us." 4 He who sits in the heavens laughs; the Lord holds them in derision. 5 Then he will speak to them in his wrath, and terrify them in his fury, saying, 6 "As for me, I have set my King on Zion, my holy hill."

7 I will tell of the decree: The Lord said to me, "*You are my Son; today I have begotten you.*

8 Ask of me, and I will make the nations your heritage, and the ends of the earth your possession. 9 You shall break them with a rod of iron and dash them in pieces like a potter's vessel." 10 Now therefore, O kings, be wise; be warned, O rulers of the earth. 11 Serve the Lord with fear, and rejoice with trembling. 12 Kiss the Son, lest he be angry, and you perish in the way, for his wrath is quickly kindled. Blessed are all who take refuge in him.

This is the psalm of Messiah the King, not Messiah the Redeemer of souls from sin. YHWH would anoint a man to conquer and rule the gentiles. Without the New Testament revelation, that is what the Psalm says. A man would be anointed, 2:2, by YHWH to hold the offices or functions of king, 2:6, God's son, 2:7, conquer the rulers of the earth, 2:9, and rule as God's representative, 2:10–12.

Every Bible-believing Hebrew believed he or she was a son of YHWH, Hosea 11:1. Every believer is a "son of God," Genesis 6:2, Job 1:6; 38:7; Romans 8:14; Gal 3:26.

The biblical "sons of" is a description of character. The biblical terms "seed of," "offspring of" "sons of," or "daughters of," are, when speaking metaphorically, those persons whose characteristics are like the person of whom they are a "seed of," "offspring of," "son of," or "daughter of."

When used symbolically neither "sons of" nor "daughters of" is a gender specific term. The term "sons of" means a person possesses the characteristics of the person or thing he or she is a "son of." The "sons of rebellion," at 2 Samuel 23:6 were the rebellious. The "sons of the prophets," 2 Kings 2:3, were those men who were faithful to God and preached his Word. The sons of fools, and the sons of vile men, Job 30:8, were fools and vile.

The term "sons of God" (Hebrew: *benê 'ĕlōhîm;* Greek: *huiós theós*) is used in Genesis 6:2, 4; Job 1:6; 2:1; 38:7; Matthew 5:9; Luke 20:36; Romans 8:14, 19; Galatians 3:26. In every use it refers to persons who are like God because they are in a faith-based relationship with God. No fallen angel and no unsaved human being are ever characterized as a son of God. [Quiggle, *Dictionary,* s. v. "Sons of."]

The Hebrews hearing Jesus had no issue with being identified as "sons of God." For example, no Hebrew objected to this saying by Jesus, "Blessed the peacemakers, because they will be called sons of God," Matthew 5:9. Compare Matthew 5:45, "So that you may be sons of your father in the heavens." Those in the resurrection—which every devout Hebrew expected to achieve—were "sons of God," Luke 20:36.

Do not be misled by translations. Every Bible version capitalizes "son" when referring to Jesus the Christ. In the mouth of Jesus such capitalization is appropriate, he knew who he was. In the mouth of his enemies it is highly inappropriate. In the mouth of disciples and apostles it is an assumption not born of Scripture.

In the absence of New Testament revelation, Psalm 2 meant to its Hebrew readers that the Messiah would be a devout Hebrew (devout because he would be the son of God), anointed by YHWH to conquer the gentiles and rule over them. In the absence of New Testament revelation, Psalm 2:7 does not teach an incarnation of God in human flesh, but a consequence of God anointing a human being to be king and God's son.

Nor could the Hebrews imagine or accept God becoming incarnate. The idea was repulsive, being too similar to the pagan concept of demigod: a human being as the offspring of one of the gods and a human female, such as Hercules (1264 BC) or Perseus (700 BC). (Psalm 2 was written ca. 1000 BC.) No right thinking Hebrew would commit such blasphemy. Every time Jesus declared himself to be God he was accused of blasphemy.

Isaiah 9:6

Someone will say, "Surely Isaiah 9:6 taught the Hebrews the Messiah was God incarnate?" And so it would seem, "his name will be . . . mighty God . . . everlasting father." The first thing to note is the word *māshîah* occurs only once in Isaiah, at 45:1, where it refers to the Persian king Cyrus. There is a reference made to King David at 9:7. The child to be born will sit on David's throne, "even forever."

What did this mean to Isaiah and subsequent Hebrew readers? One thing it mean is a child to be born would be the Messianic king (as the *Targum Isaiah* states [Beale and Carson, *Commentary*, 19]), thereby confirming 2 Samuel 7:13, 16 and Psalm 2. Second, this would be a human child, again confirming both 2 Samuel and Psalm 2. At this point it is difficult to see how any Hebrew would believe this child would be God-in-the-flesh, God incarnate. That was a pagan belief.

Again, we cannot allow ourselves to be misled by a translation. The only word in 9:6 that needs to be capitalized is *'êl*, the most basic Hebrew word for God or god. For certain, this verse does not teach the Messiah will be YHWH incarnate. However, in a later chapter, Isaiah uses the same words, mighty God (*'êl*) to refer to YHWH. So Isaiah 9:6, in conjunction with other scriptures, does teach the Messianic King is God; the child to be born must in some way be God—a way not yet disclosed; Isaiah 7:14 had no obvious connection with Psalm 2:2, 7. (The angel Gabriel did not make that connection of Isaiah 7:14 with 9:6 or Psalm 2, see Matthew 1:23–23; Luke 1:31–33.)

What use did the people in gospel times make of Isaiah 9:6? Nothing. Not an angel, not Jesus, not his mother or Joseph, not his disciples or apostles, not his enemies. Nothing. Isaiah 9:6 is not quoted, not referred to, not alluded to in the four gospels. No one, except perhaps Isaiah, learned from this verse that the Messianic King would be God incarnate. But let us remember Isaiah has said he is quoting God, 8:11, writing direct revelation word for word, "YHWH spoke thus to me." So Isaiah might not have understood; there is no indication one way or the other. What is certain is no one during Jesus' time on earth applied Isaiah 9:6 to messianic prophecy or to Jesus. With the application of New Testament revelation we can see it; but without that New Testament revelation no Hebrew understood it.

New Testament Revelation in the Four Gospels

What do the four gospels say about the beliefs of the Hebrew people concerning Jesus? What were they told, what did they understand, what did they believe? Space limitations permit examination of only a few scriptures.

Matthew's Gospel

Let us begin in Matthew.

Matthew 1:23, Behold, the virgin shall be with child, and bear a son, and they shall call his name Immanuel, which is translated, "God with us."

The Hebrew words *immānū ʻēl* occur at Isaiah 7:14; 8:8, 10. The Greek equivalent, *emmanouēl*, occurs at Matthew 1:23.

The angel makes sure Joseph knew what the Greek word *emmanouēl* meant: God with us. The angel quotes from Isaiah 7:14 (ESV), "Therefore the Lord himself will give you a sign. Behold, the virgin shall conceive and bear a son, and shall call his name Immanuel [*immānū ʻēl*]."

Again, subtracting all subsequent New Testament revelation from our interpretation, we must look only at the uses Joseph knew. Did *emmanouēl* indicate to Joseph that this child born of a (the Hebrew word) ʻ*almâ* (a young unmarried girl—thus, a virgin) would be God-in-the-flesh?

No. As New Testament believers, having the benefit of all the New Testament revelation, we interpret "God with us" as "God incarnate." But all *immānū ʻēl / emmanouēl* really means is God would be with Israel, without specifying how God would be with Israel.

A plain example is Isaiah 8:10 (ESV), "Take counsel together, but it will come to nothing; speak a word, but it will not stand, for God [*ēl*] is with us [*immānū*]." God is with us to help us. No more can be known from the name, *emmanouēl*, in Matthew 1:23, within the historical context and the scriptures given up to that time.

Earlier prophecies might have shown Isaiah this "Immanuel" will be of the Davidic line, thus heir to the Davidic-Messianic throne (2 Samuel 7:13, 16; Psalm 2). Isaiah 8:8 refers to "your land, Immanuel." Isaiah and others probably made the connection between Immanuel and the coming Messiah who was to be the heir of David. But, again, this is not the understanding of an incarnation. Nothing in the promise of an heir to David, as interpreted without adding in the New Testament revelation, indicates any one of those many heirs of David will be God incarnate.

That last statement unavoidably requires us to take small side path away from the main discussion. At 2 Samuel 7:13, 16, the prophet says Davids' rule (his "throne) will be established "forever." How does the Bible use the term "forever?" A small excursus.

Excursus: Forever, Everlasting, Perpetual

Words such as forever (or "for ever," depending on the Bible version), everlasting, and perpetual are similar to the word "all" in that the meaning is determined by context. Sometimes "all" means "everything without exclusion," but more often the content of "all" is circumscribed (limited) by the context.

For example, Genesis 6:12 (NKJV), "So God looked upon the earth, and indeed it was corrupt; for all flesh had corrupted their way on the earth." But if "all" in 6:12 means every person without exclusion, then the verse contradicts 6:8, "But Noah found grace in the Lord," and 6:9, "Noah was a just man, perfect in his generations" (NKJV). In 6:12 the word "all" means everyone except those who, like Noah, were righteous before the Lord.

So also the words forever, everlasting, and perpetual. For example, at Exodus 29:26–28, certain portions of meat from the offerings were to be for "Aaron and his sons by a statute forever." Here "forever" means as long as the levitical priesthood and the sacrifices and offerings of the Mosaic Law are in effect.

Another example is Genesis 13:15 (NKJV), "for all the land which you [Abraham] see I give to you and your descendants forever." How long is this forever? At the least until this present earth is destroyed and a new earth created, 2 Peter 3:10; Revelation 20:11; 21:1, and perhaps longer, Revelation 21:12. On the other hand, Exodus 15:18, "YHWH shall reign forever," means YHWH will reign without end, because YHWH is eternal, and Scripture reveals nothing that will change the essence of God. Revelation 20:10 means the fallen angels, the Antichrist, and the false prophet will suffer in the Lake of Fire without end, because Scripture does not reveal a change or end to their sinful condition or to the Lake of Fire.

The mountains are "everlasting" and the hills are "perpetual," Habakkuk 3:6 until God scatters the mountains and bows the hills, same verse, compare Revelation 16:18, 20. The "everlasting" covenant of the rainbow endures until this present earth is replaced, because it was declared to be a sign this present earth would not ever again be destroyed with a flood, Genesis 9:11.

YHWH is the "everlasting God," Genesis 21:33, meaning his existence is without beginning and without end. God made with David an "everlasting," covenant, 2 Samuel 23:5, a reference to the "forever" son and throne of 2 Samuel 7:13, 16, which we know from New Testament revelation is a reference to David's greater heir Christ. Christ will reign as King of kings and Lord of lords in his Davidic-Messianic-Millennial Kingdom commencing at his second advent, Revelation 20:4, and then without end in the new heaven and earth, Revelation 21:1, 22–23.

The person who savingly believes in Christ will have everlasting life, John 3:16, which is not merely immortality of body and soul, but a significant quality of life. Compare John 5:24. Because everlasting life comes from God, and God himself is everlasting, the everlasting life God gives his saved people is without end.

The word perpetual is to be treated the same, i.e., understood in context. Jeremiah 5:22 says God has "placed the sand as the bound of the sea, by a perpetual decree, that it cannot pass beyond it?" (NKJV). This perpetual decree will endure until the new heavens and earth, Revelation 21:1, which has no sea.

To sum up. Words relating to God's essential being are understood to mean without beginning and without end. Words relating to the promise of life to those whom God has saved are understood to mean life without end. Words relating to the punishment of the unsaved are understood to mean punishment without end. Words relating to conditions that do change, such as the Levitical priesthood, or the present earth, are "forever, everlasting, perpetual" until the condition upon which those things were predicated changes, such as the perpetual decree of the sea, or the forever covenant of the rainbow. [Quiggle, *Life, Death, Eternity*, 37–38.]

Returning to the discussion, within the Old Testament context, without adding in New Testament revelation, what the Davidic covenant meant to David and his fellow Hebrews, was as long as there is a kingdom of Israel, so there will be a descendant of David on the throne. With the New Testament revelation added in, it is a prophecy of the Davidic-Messianic Kingdom, which as Dispensationalists we believe exists for a millennium. So even in the Dispensational point of view, the "forever" Davidic-Messianic Kingdom has an end, which is the end of this present earth, 2 Peter 3:10; Revelation 20:11; 21:1.

Luke 1:32, 41; 2:11

Although there are more verses to consider in Matthew's Gospel, the angel Gabriel's conversation with Joseph calls to mind his months earlier (about three months earlier) conversation with Mary of Nazareth. The pertinent verse is Luke 1:32 (ESV), "He will be great and will be called the son of the Most High. And the Lord God will give to him the throne of his father David." I have changed the ESV in one place, making "Son" to be the more proper "son." Neither Mary then, nor Luke later, could hear a capital letter in the angel's voice. ("Most High" and "Lord God" were recognized titles of YHWH.) Mary would not have thought of a capital "Son" of the Most High, because a human being as God was blasphemous.

Everything in the angel's announcement conforms to 2 Samuel 7:13, 16; Psalm 2:2, 7. Indeed, it conforms to Isaiah 7:14, although Mary was not told of that connection, as Joseph was later. Nor in any recorded words of Mary throughout the four gospels do we see her making a connection with Isaiah 7:14. Nothing Mary says in the four gospels indicates she thought of her son Jesus as God. Nothing in Mary's song to Elizabeth infers or implies or alludes to an incarnation. No recorded word of Mary in the four gospels infers or implies or alludes to an incarnation.

Nor is an incarnation to be found Elizabeth's comment. Through the Holy Spirit Elizabeth recognized Mary as the mother of the Messianic King, not of God incarnate. Because that is what Elizabeth knew—that her son would be Messiah's herald, Luke 1:17. Nor did the shepherds know their Messiah was God incarnate. The angel told them the *māshîah* prophesied in Micah 5:2 had come to Bethlehem just as prophesied (and to their barn, as prophesied, Micah 4:8).

Matthew 4, the Temptation of Jesus

Did the fallen angels know Jesus the Christ was God incarnate? If they did, then those human beings they influenced against Jesus might know the same from them. But the fallen angels did not know.

One proof they did not know is the actions of their leader, Satan. In his third temptation Satan said to Jesus, Matthew 4:9, "These things [the kingdoms of the world and their glory], to you I will give all, if falling down you will worship me." If Satan had understood Jesus Christ was God the Son incarnate, he would not have made the offer. Satan knew God is "Holy, Holy, Holy," Isaiah 6:3, or as the later revelation of James 1:13 states, "God cannot be tempted by evil." God who created will never worship one of his creation.

Why, then, did Satan say, Matthew 4:3, "If you are the son of God," as though assuming Jesus' deity? I will show this statement by Satan did not refer to Jesus' deity. Satan was demanding Jesus prove God was right when God had said, "This is my son," at Jesus' baptism. We will see this by examining two issues. First, what does the "if" mean? Then, what does the term "son of God" mean?

The "if" in the phrase, "if you are the son of God," performs a certain grammatical function (in the Koine Greek dialect in which the New Testament was written) known as a condition of the first class. This is a "simple conditional assumption with emphasis on the reality of the assumption (not of what is being assumed); the condition is considered a real case" [Morris, *Matthew*, 73, n. 11]. Satan is stating a condition that was presented as reality (God had said, "This is my son"), but Satan is questioning whether the condition is factual by demanding Jesus furnish proof that God was right. Satan could be viewed as saying, "I assume as true that you are the son of God, so prove it by commanding these stones to become bread." Or, he could be viewed as saying, "In view of the fact that you are the son of God, command these stones to become bread." Satan's "if" meant, "Prove what God said about you is true. Prove you are a son of God."

(Side issue: why did Satan ask Jesus to "command" the stones to become bread, if he did not believe Jesus was God? Because Satan doesn't know much more than anyone else. Because Satan also reads commentaries and listens to preachers and Bible teachers. The Rabbis taught that the Messiah, as a prophet like Moses, Deuteronomy 18:15, would give them bread like Moses—their belief, John 6:31.)

Satan said, "if you are the son of God." The term "son of" in Scripture, when not used of literal physical descent, indicates a person has the characteristics of the person or thing of which he (or she) is a "son of." Sons of men are sinners, Psalm 4:2; 58:1–2. Sons of the sorceress are offspring of the adulterer and the harlot, Isaiah 57:3. The sons of the prophets (1 and 2 Kings) were preachers and keepers of God's Word, like the prophets. Adam was a son of God, Luke 3:38, a human being in a faith-based relationship with God. The phrase "sons of God" in the Old Testament identified human beings (Genesis 6:2, 4; Job 1:6; 2:1) and holy angels (Job 38:7). The completed revelation of scripture (Matthew 5:9; Luke 20:36; Romans 8:14, 19; Galatians 3:26) supports the earlier revelation. The "sons of God" are holy angels and human believers who are in a faith-based relationship with God. No fallen angel and no human sinner is ever identified as one of the sons of God. The sons of God possess the moral character of God, obey God's commandments, and glorify God in their words and deeds.

Satan tried to accomplish with Jesus what he did with Eve: he used God's words to suggest rebellion against God. Could this "son of God" prove he was a son of God? Jesus did, but not the way Satan proposed. Satan's temptations provided Jesus son of God the opportunity to act independent of God's will. Adam son of God self-originated sin when tempted to act independent of God's will (Genesis 2:17; 3:6). Will Jesus seek his own way, like Adam, or will he honor God?

Put another way, the claim Jesus was a "son of" God was to be tested. Because Satan did not understand Jesus was God the Son incarnate, he presented temptations that would test the faith of a human son of God. Jesus chose to endure the trial through the natural limitations of his humanity, because as a genuine human being the designation, "This is my son," defined the character of his humanity, not his deity.

Satan did understand Jesus was the Christ. This was part of his motive for tempting Jesus. He had heard this Jesus would be given "the throne of his father David," Luke 1:32, and had heard this Jesus was "Christ the Lord," Luke 2:11. (The fallen angels are one-third, Revelation 12:4a, of an innumerable host, Revelation 5:11—thus present in sufficient numbers to know what is happening on the earth in both spirit and material domains.) Satan's understanding of the Christ was the same as the religious leaders: the Christ would be a human being, much like themselves, who had been specifically anointed (*māshîah*), Psalm 2:2, to be king, 2:6, be God's son, 2:7, to conquer the rulers of the earth, 2:9, and rule as God's representative, 2:10–12.

We must, therefore, wash away our presuppositions and interpretive traditions to place ourselves within the progressive revelation of biblical knowledge at that time, which was Genesis through Malachi. At this time in history, Satan did not use the term "son of God" to identify Jesus as the God-man (no one did). To Satan, Jesus was a human being in a faith-based relationship with God who had been *māshîah*, anointed, Psalm 2:2, by God, to fulfill the coming king and kingdom prophecy of Psalm 2. To Satan, Jesus of Nazareth was just another human being in a long-line of "sons of God" that he would defile, just as he had defiled the first son of God, Adam.

Like their leader, the fallen angels knew Jesus was the Christ, but did not know Jesus was God the Son incarnate.

> The divinity of Christ, or his identity with a divine person, does not seem to have been known to the spirit [Mark 1:24], but only that the man whom he addressed was one, to use his own expressions, whom the Father had sanctified and sent into the world (John 10:36), i.e., chosen and commissioned for an extraordinary service. [Alexander, *Mark*, 22.]

Why then did the fallen angels call Jesus, "the holy one of God"; "son of the Most High God"; "son of God"? These titles came from what they had heard: the angel Gabriel's announcement to Mary that this Jesus was "son of the Highest," Luke 1:32, the "holy one" and "son of God," Luke 1:35.

Conclusion. The fallen angels believed Jesus of Nazareth was the Christ, but none of them understood Jesus the Christ was God the Son incarnate.

Mark 1:23–25 is Jesus' first encounter with an angel inhabiting a human being.

> 23 "And shortly [after he had begun teaching] there came into their synagogue a man with an unclean spirit. And he cried out,

24 saying, "What do you have to do with us, Jesus of Nazareth? Are you come to destroy us? I know who you are, the holy one of God."

The confrontation Mark reports here was the first such confrontation in Jesus' ministry, and it was the only time such a confrontation was initiated by a fallen angel. The angel who was cast out was undoubtedly surprised God had delegated this authority to a human being. The others, being warned by their comrade's experience, avoided Jesus as much as possible. In other such confrontations recorded in the New Testament, the fallen angels had not sought out Jesus but met him due to varied circumstances. See Mark 5:2, 8; 7:25, 30; 9:18, 25; Matthew 9:32–33; 12:22. The same is true during Jesus' preaching and healing tours, e.g., Luke 6:18. After this first encounter they knew he would cast them out.

The fallen angel asked, "Are you come to destroy us?" Various translations give, "Did you come to destroy us? (NKJV), or "Have you come to destroy us?" (HCSB, NIV, ESV). The angel wasn't questioning Jesus' origin, but purpose.

If my analysis, above, is correct, then this purpose question must be seen in the light of the prophesied duties or works of the Messiah-Christ. One of those duties is expressed at Isaiah 61:1, "to proclaim liberty to the captives, and the opening of the prison to those who are bound." Jesus had quoted this verse at Nazareth a month or two earlier, Luke 4:18, "To proclaim liberty to the captives . . . to set at liberty those who are oppressed" (NKJV, ESV).

The fallen angel's question was about himself and others like himself who were inhabiting human souls. Did "to destroy us" fit into the mission Isaiah had prophesied, and which Jesus had announced at Nazareth? Yes. Casting out demons wasn't all that prophecy meant, but casting them out was included.

The word translated "destroy" is *apóllumi*, to destroy, perish, deprive. Understanding *apóllumi* depends on how one views the fallen angels' understanding of Jesus.

If one believes the fallen angel in Mark 1:23–25 understood Jesus was God the Son incarnate, then *apóllumi* refers to eternal imprisonment in the lake of fire, Matthew 25:41, which verse was not yet spoken, but the demons knew from the beginning (of their original sin) that the "everlasting fire was prepared for the devil and his angels." The fallen angels are intelligent but have no grace for understanding scripture. First Corinthians 2:14, the natural person does not understand spiritual matters, applies to them as it does to any unsaved soul. They did not understand two advents, so they could have wondered—if they understood Jesus was God incarnate—whether the time had come for their eternal imprisonment.

If one believes, as I and others do, that the fallen angels did not understand Jesus was God the Son incarnate, then *apóllumi* refers to some other kind of loss. The most reasonable interpretation is fear of imprisonment in the abyss for the crime of habitation of a human being, Luke 8:31 (LEB), "And they began imploring him that he would not order them to depart into the abyss."

The fallen angel, Mark 1:23–25, came on behalf of his comrades (the plural "us" in his questions) to find out who this Jesus was, and what this Jesus, "Christ," would do. He found out. Jesus cast into the abyss all fallen angels he came into contact with inhabiting a human being, thereby fulfilling (at least toward these particular angels) the messianic prophecy of Isaiah 61:1; Luke 4:18. Because Jesus did cast out every angel he met inhabiting a human soul, we may assume a law against habitation, and the punishment imprisonment in the abyss, there to join the large number of fallen angels already imprisoned, Jude 6, 2 Peter 2:4; Revelation 9:1–3. I believe every fallen angel Jesus cast out of a human being went into the abyss, per Luke 8:31. They knew the power to cast them into the abyss was from God. They may or may not have known, until that first confrontation, the Old Testament revelation gave the Messiah the authority to cast them out. They did not know Jesus of Nazareth was God-in-the-flesh.

Matthew 11:3, The Baptist Doubts

Did John the Baptist know his relative Jesus of Nazareth was God incarnate? Some think so from failure to consider all of John's testimony. When Jesus came to be baptized, on seeing him, the Baptist said, Matthew 3:14, "I have need to be baptized by you, and you come to me?" It would seem he knew. But the Baptist also testified, John 1:31, "I knew him not." He knew his relative Jesus. They had known each other for almost 35 years (from their births, ca. 5 BC, to Jesus baptism in late AD 29). They had seen each other every year at the three mandatory feasts, and probably at other times also, as the families visited one another over the years. The Baptist knew Jesus to be a righteous man. The Baptist was preaching Messiah was coming, but he did not know who the Messiah would be, until he saw, "the Spirit descending and abiding on him," John 1:33. No testimony of the Baptist states or implies he knew the Messiah would also be God incarnate.

If John Baptist knew Jesus was God incarnate, then why did he doubt he had baptized the right man? If you know the Messiah is God incarnate, then there is no doubt. John was informed by Old Testament revelation, neither more nor less. He knew the Messiah was coming to be king. He had not seen that expectation fulfilled. He did not understand Messiah as Redeemer of men from their sins. Jesus, 11:5 gave him the signs of Messiah the Redeemer, Isaiah 35:5–6; 61:1, which the Baptist knew. Jesus told him to have faith, 11:6.

Matthew 14:33

At Matthew 14:22–33, we have the incident when Jesus and Peter walk on water. When Peter and Jesus got into the boat, those in the boat, "bowed to him, saying, "Truly you are God's son." The issue here is not the Greek text, but the English translation. The common English translation says, they "worshiped him." Naturally, the reader assumes those in the boat believed Jesus the Christ was God incarnate. But the word English versions translate "worship" is *proskunéō,* to "do obeisance, show respect, fall or prostrate before, literally to throw a kiss in token of respect of homage" [Zodhiates, "4352"]. To translate *proskunéō* as worship assumes what is not evident: that the apostles/disciples believed the man who had just walked on water was God-in-the-flesh.

Let us think clearly. If the twelve believed God was literally in their presence in the person of Jesus of Nazareth, then they would not have been able to function as his companions. They would have fallen flat on their faces and remained prostrate before him in reverent awe. They would have feared for their lives, because God had said to Moses, "No person shall see my face and live," Exodus 33:20 (NKJV). They were in awe of him, but not the worshiping, "you are God," kind of awe. No prophet had ever done what Jesus had just done. So they had continued to ask themselves, "Who is this man?" Here they come to a conclusion.

What, then, did they mean when they said, "Truly you are God's son"? Three meanings are available.

> One, they understood he was God incarnate in Jesus of Nazareth. This is unlikely. They were completely discouraged following the crucifixion, e.g., Luke 24:21, "we were hoping that it was he who was going to redeem Israel." They didn't understand he would resurrect, and didn't believe when they

were told he had resurrected. The Holy Spirit withheld spiritual perception of Jesus as deity incarnate until after the ascension, compare Matthew 28:17 with Acts 3:33.

Two, they could have been declaring him a true son of God. The Hebrews believed they were sons of God. If this was the disciples' meaning, then they were giving respect to a prophet who had shown that he truly was a son of God, i.e., one to whom God had given great authority and power.

Three, they bowed to him and called him, "God's son" in the sense of Psalm 2:7, "I will declare the decree: YHWH has said to me, 'You are my son.' " If this was the case, it was a moment when they began to believe Jesus was the messiah—not merely a prophet in the Old Testament mold, but the deliverer and king promised by the prophets.

My view is that they saw him through the lens of options two and three.

Matthew 16:16, Peter Confesses Jesus is the Christ

Peter states Jesus, "is the Christ (of God, Luke 9:20), the son of the living God." Jesus says this understanding, that Jesus of Nazareth was the Christ of God, was given Peter by, "my Father who is in heaven." How did Peter know about the Christ of God? From schooling at the village synagogue, which every boy attended in his home village. From a lifetime of hearing about the Messiah when he attended the synagogue on Sabbath. What Peter knew about the Christ of God was what the Scriptures said and what the Rabbis taught. Everything Peter confessed fits into Psalm 2.

Peter: You are the Christ of God.
Psalm 2:2, YHWH and his *māshîah.*

Peter: son of the living God.
Psalm 2:7, You are my son, today I have begotten you.

Peter did not think of the Messiah as God incarnate. If he had he would have confessed, "You are God the Christ." If we doubt, and some will, let us look to the sequel, 16:22. Peter rebuked the Christ for revealing the Christ must die. If you believe the person in front of you is God incarnate, you do not correct him. You worship. You politely ask for an explanation of the thing you do not understand.

The Bible scholars did not believe the Messiah was God incarnate.

"And the high priest said to him, "I adjure you by the living God, that you tell us if you are the Christ, the son of God." Jesus says to him, "You have said. Moreover, I say to you, from now you will see the son of man sitting at the right hand of the Power, and coming in the clouds of heaven."

Caiaphas needed legal justification in order to sentence Jesus to death and present the case to Pilate for Jesus to be executed. We see in 26:63 that Caiaphas obviously knew Jesus had performed miracles and that many people believed him to be the Christ. The question Caiaphas asks understands the terms "Christ" and "son of God" as indicating a relationship with God. But it is doubtful that Caiaphas used these terms in the same sense that Christians understand them today.

The question Caiaphas asks, although not in these words, is whether or not Jesus will testify under oath that he himself is the Christ, the son of God. Jesus answers the question because 1) Caiaphas has asked in his official capacity as high priest, 2) the question is about Jesus' messianic claims, and 3) Caiaphas has called on Jesus to tell the truth with God as his witness.

Jesus' reply, "You have said," is an idiom meaning "You have stated the fact." This reply, in itself, was not sufficient to condemn Jesus to death. And Jesus knew this. The Christ was perceived by all as a man anointed by God to be king of Israel. We see this was the way the Sanhedrin understood the Christ by their accusation before Pilate—the accusation that caused Pilate to condemn Jesus.

John 19:12, but Jews cried out, saying, "If this man you release, you are not a Friend of Caesar. Anyone making himself a king speaks against Caesar."

The accusation that made Pilate condemn Jesus was the claim he was a king. They had previously tried to get Jesus condemned for blasphemy, but that failed,

John 19:7, The Jews answered Pilate, "We have a law, and according to the law he ought to die, because he made himself Son of God."

How had Jesus made himself, "Son of God." Not when Jesus had agreed with the high priest, Matthew 26:63–64a, that he was, as the high priest had stated, "the Christ, the son of God." No one got excited over that claim. Claiming Psalm 2 applied to you was not blasphemy.

The blasphemy was the next thing Jesus said. "I say to you, from now you will see the son of man sitting at the right hand of the Power, and coming in the clouds of heaven." To sit on the throne of God ("at the right hand of the Power") is to be equal with God. To come on the clouds of heaven is to command the angelic armies of heaven, which is authority possessed only by deity.

> 65 Then the high priest tears his clothes, saying, "He has blasphemed! Why have we any more need of witnesses? Look, now you have heard the blasphemy! 66 What do you think?" Now answering they said, "He is deserving of death." 67 Then they spit in his face, and struck him. Others slapped him, 68 saying, "Prophesy to us, Christ, who is he having hit you?"

Obviously, they did not believe his claim to deity. No knowledgeable Hebrew believed a man could also be God. That was blasphemy.

After the Crucifixion and Resurrection

Did the apostles/disciples grasp Jesus was God incarnate after the crucifixion? Not until Jesus appeared to them. In the days between the crucifixion and resurrection the apostles and disciples went into hiding, not expecting Jesus would resurrect. John 20:19. What about when the empty tomb was reported by the women? No, their words seemed like idle tales, Luke 24:11. How about when Peter and John saw the empty tomb. No, Peter was amazed at what happened, Luke 24:12, and John believed a miracle had happened, but "they did not yet understand the Scripture, that Jesus must rise out from the dead," John 20:9.

Late on the resurrection day, about 8:00 p.m. [Westcott, *John*, 288], Jesus appeared to ten apostles, and others, Thomas being absent, John 20:19. Did they then believe? They "rejoiced, having seen the Lord," but there is no positive indication they believed he was God incarnate. Eight days later Jesus again appeared to his apostles, and this time Thomas was present, John 20:26. Thomas sees Jesus and declares him to be, "My Lord and my God." All the events of the preceding three years suddenly added up for him to faith in Jesus as his God. Did the other apostles came to this same belief then, or perhaps eight days earlier? There is no positive indication they did, no indication they did not.

The same is true in John 21, when Jesus appeared to some of them at the lake in Galilee. Thomas was there, and Peter, John and James, and two who are not identified, so we know there was at least one, Thomas, who believed Jesus was God incarnate. Many days later Jesus appeared to the eleven in Galilee, at "the mountain which Jesus directed them. And having seen him, they worshiped; but some doubted," Matthew 28:16–17. Believing the man in front of you is deity is a difficult thing to grasp, even if he has resurrected from the dead.

At Matthew 28:19, prior to the ascension, Jesus gives the Trinitarian statement, but we do not have any comments about or from those who were present. Nor do we see any comments about or from the apostles and disciples at the ascension, as recorded in Mark 16:15–20, Luke 24:47–43. [For the order of events during the forty days between the resurrection and the ascension, see my book, *The Passion and Resurrection of Jesus the Christ.*]

At the Ascension, and on the Day of Pentecost

Did the apostles believe Jesus was deity at the ascension? Matthew's statement at 28:17 probably still applies, "they worshiped, but some doubted." They asked the Messiah about the kingdom, Acts 1:6, which supports the view some believed he was the Messiah, and some doubted he was God incarnate. But on the day of Pentecost, they were given understanding. Acts 2:33, "Therefore [the Christ] being exalted to the right hand of God." Acts 2:34, "God has made this Jesus, whom, you crucified, both Lord and Christ." Peter makes the same claim Jesus did at his trial, "you will see the son of man sitting at the right hand of the Power," Matthew 26:64. The Holy Spirit had come in power and given them understanding.

Jesus the Christ is the God-man

I have addressed selected scriptures to show that during Jesus' earthly ministry, the apostles did not understand this man, Jesus of Nazareth, whom they came to believe was the Christ, was also God incarnate. I have shown that the fallen angels did not realize Jesus the Christ was also God the Son incarnate. Nor his family, nor his enemies.

We must be clear their disbelief was not because Jesus was reluctant or hesitant to reveal his deity (see below). But why did they not believe? There were those who naturally lacked the spiritual perception, 1 Corinthians 2:14, to comprehend God could and did become incarnate, because they lacked faith in Jesus as the Messiah.

In those who did have faith Jesus was the Messiah, the Holy Spirit withheld their understanding of Jesus as the God-man.

I believe the Holy Spirit withheld understanding so Jesus the Christ could interact with his apostles and disciples as a normal human being. There is a holy fear when you believe God is standing in front of you, e.g., John 21:12. Although Jesus the Christ is clearly the God-man, and gave clear and sufficient evidence he was the God-man, it is just as clear he lived his life in complete dependence upon and submission to God. His life set the pattern for every believer. Believers are not to ask, "What would Jesus do?" because no believer has the same mission, nor the spiritual empowerment (every spiritual gift) that Jesus was given, to do what Jesus did. The believer is to walk with Jesus daily, in that same attitude of submission to and dependence upon God that characterized Jesus' life on the earth.

Jesus did reveal his deity. In every miracle Jesus revealed his deity; but they believed God had given great power and authority to a prophet, who might be (and some came to believe) was the Messiah.

In John 5, Jesus reveals his deity.

> John 5:17, My Father is working up to the present moment, and I am working.

The Hebrew scholars had asked themselves, "If God keeps the universe running on the Sabbath, is God violating the Sabbath day by working on the Sabbath?" No. The Jews rationalized their law by recognizing the entire universe as God's domain. Therefore, in working on the Sabbath God did not break their Sabbath rules; but for anyone else work on the Sabbath was a religious and civil violation. Thus the enormity of Jesus' declaration: if Jesus had the authority to work when the Father worked, then Jesus was equal to the Father. But the Hebrews rejected Jesus' claim, "because he not only was breaking the Sabbath, but also he called God his own father, making himself equal with God."

Jesus claimed to be increate. John 5:26, "For as the Father has life in himself, so also to the Son he gave life, to have in himself." Only God is eternal (without beginning or ending), and only God has life-in-himself (self-existent, Exodus 3:14, "I exist because I exist"). The Father has granted the Son to have life-in-himself. Does this mean there was a time when the Son did not have life-in-himself, but now the Father has given him life-in-himself? Or, perhaps Jesus meant that his incarnate self was granted life-in-himself by the Father. No. John clearly states that God the Son always had life-in-himself, 1:4, "in him was life." When Jesus the Christ made this claim he was claiming deity.

Jesus claimed, John 10:30, "I and my Father are one." The word translated "one" is the neuter *hen* not the masculine *heis*. Jesus and his Father are not one person, as the masculine would imply (else Jesus could not pray to the Father, or act in obedience to the Father, or be able to say, "I and my Father."). What is asserted is not identity but unity. Because of their essential deity unity they are one in the action of preserving the sheep. The neuter *hen* might lead some to believe the Father and Son are only one in purpose and action, a union of persons, not a unity of persons. But the Jews understood Jesus to be saying he and the Father were a unity of essence, 10:33, "You, being a man, make yourself God." They didn't believe him, but they understood his claim.

Application of this Doctrine

The views expressed in this article honor the scriptures as the accurate, authentic, and therefore credible record of all that was said and done—in a word, inspiration. One applies the inspiration of the Scripture by understanding the words in the plain and normal sense of their meaning—the Literal hermeneutic. Using the analyses methods of the Literal hermeneutic one arrives at an accurate interpretation—the historical-cultural, contextual, lexical-syntactical, theological, literary, and doctrinal analysis of the Scripture.

By properly using the Literal hermeneutic, performing all the required analysis, the interpreter avoids two errors. The first is the one mentioned at the beginning of this article: preaching Reformed traditions. The Reformed traditional interpretations that "discover" (meaning insert) Christ into every Old Testament Scripture bleeds over into the New Testament interpretation that "discovers" the apostles and disciples knew the Christ was God incarnate. The conflict that view sets up is unbearable. If, as proposed, the apostles knew Jesus was God incarnate, then why did Peter rebuke the God-man for announcing his death? Why did Judas betray the God-man? Why did all but John abandon the God-man at the crucifixion? Why did the eleven hide in fear after the crucifixion? Why did "some doubt," after the resurrection, Matthew 27:17? We come away believing the apostles were faithless men, not true to their convictions, and justify our own lack of faith.

Better is the view expressed in this article. When we see the apostles as men of faith beset with the weaknesses that trouble every believer, our faith is encouraged and strengthened. They persevered.

So too every believer is able to persevere.

The second error is even more pernicious: adding to the gospel of salvation. The gospel of salvation is simple volitional faith in God's testimony concerning ourselves as sinners and the risen Christ as Savior. Nothing else is required. But some want to add to the gospel, by making belief in Christ as deity necessary to saving faith. The apostles were saved without understanding Christ was deity.

We see their salvation in the spiritual perception given to them by the Holy Spirit. One sample should suffice, John 6:68–69, spoken by Peter after the feeding of the 5,000. Jesus had forced a crisis of faith. He had accused those who sought him after that event of seeking not him, but what he could give him—prizing the gift more than the giver. Some of those following Christ responded to this crisis negatively, they "turned back and no longer walked with him." Jesus asked the twelve, "Do you also desire to go away?" Peter gave the response of a saved man, "Master, to whom will we go? You have the words of eternal life. And we have believed and have known that you are the holy one of God." Not, "you are the holy God," but, "you are the holy one of God," exactly as the Scripture testifies: the *māshîah*, the *christós*, is the son of the living God.

Conclusion

During the time of Jesus' earthly ministry, the apostles did not understand Jesus was God incarnate. Their daily interactions with him argue against that understanding. A simple example. In the last few months of their third year with him (between January–March, AD 32), Jesus will go to the tomb of Lazarus. Philip says to his fellow disciples, "Let us also go, that we might die with him." Even after three years, after watching all the miracles, hearing all the discourses, they still did not believe Jesus was God incarnate. That would be blasphemy, and the thought was never entertained. The Holy Spirit withheld their understanding, as suitable to the mission of the Christ.

The apostles interacted with Jesus as a man, not as the almighty God YHWH. The man born blind and healed by Jesus expresses the understanding of all who believed Jesus was the Christ. John 9:33 (highlighting added), "If this *man* were not *from* God, he would not be able to do anything." In their understanding Jesus was a man sent from God, not a man who was God. [Some of the comments in this article are from my commentaries on Matthew's Gospel and John's Gospel.]

Stand and Withstand

Want to lead the kind of Christian life that stands in the storms of life? Practice the basics, strengthen the basics.

The four basics practices of the Christian life never change:

Worship of God in Christ

Fellowship with God and with one another

Obedience to the principles and moral values found in God's Word

Acts of service for Christ's sake toward one's fellow believers and the world

The means by which the four basics are strengthened also never change.

Prayer privately and with other believers

Praise and devotion privately and with other believers

Bible study privately and with other believers

Assimilation (application) of what one has learned from the Word into the manner of living

Saying "No" to temptation

Confession and repentance when an act of sinning has occurred

Personal, daily encouragement toward one another to persevere in the faith by means of faith

Not deserting the assembling together with one another, but thereby being encouraging.

If the above are the diligently practice of your Christian life, you will stand and withstand life's tribulations.

Identifying the Relevant and the Incidental in Prophecy

The careful Bible student should recognize that some details and facts of any prophecy are not relevant to an interpretation. There is a danger in interpreting every detail of a prophecy. Some parts of a prophecy are just there to carry the message, not to be interpreted as part of the message. Examples.

In Daniel 7, the Median-Persian Empire is represented as a bear. While we might, with caution, take some of the essential and prominent attributes of a bear as characteristic of the Medo-Persian Empire, should we also apply, for example, the fact a bear hibernates, or is omnivorous, or protects her cubs with a murderous ferocity? No. The main point of the symbol (and the other animal representations in Dan. 7) is a contrast with the statue representation. The statue presents mans' empires as man see them: noble and magnificent. God sees mans' empires as ravening wild beasts.

The statue Nebuchadnezzar saw in Dan. 2 is the statue of a man because the empires represented are man's empires. The two arms and two legs are incidental, because they are a natural part of a man. Every human being naturally has two arms, two legs; so too a statue of a man. To seal their fate as incidental they are not specifically called out as part of Daniel's interpretation, and are therefore not essential to the prophecy.

A further indication the two legs are incidental, not relevant to the prophecy, is they are the same length. If the legs were prophetic of the divided Roman Empire (as some believe) one leg would be much shorter than the other. The Western Empire collapsed AD 476. The eastern Empire ended AD 1453.

Understanding context helps the interpreter understand when something is incidental and when it is relevant. The seven spirits of Revelation 1:4 are sometimes identified as angels, based on seven angels at 8:2. But in this case the number seven is incidental to an identification of the spirits. It is true that angels are spirit beings, and it is true that there are seven angels before the throne in Revelation 8:2. But there are seven angels because God has seven trumpets. If there had been six or eight trumpets, the number of angels would have been six or eight. Therefore, the number of angels in 8:2 is not relevant to an interpretation of the seven spirits in 1:4. Both at 1:4 and at 8:2 "seven" as a literal number is incidental to the interpretation. When we add the other facts, using the seven angels of 8:2 to interpret the "seven spirits" falls apart:

The paragraph (1:4ff) speaks of the Father and Son, therefore the most natural interpretation for the seven spirits is that this symbol represents the Holy Spirit.

The Holy Spirit is always represented symbolically in the Revelation; angels are always seen in distinct angelic form.

The "seven spirits" in 1:4, are bracketed by the Father and the Son. Angels cannot be part of that divine company.

Peace and grace do not come from angels but from God. To suggest the seven spirits are angels also suggests worship of angels, contra Revelation 19:10; 22:9.

The angels in Revelation 8:2 are referred to as *ággelos*, angel, not *pneúma*, spirit. The consistent identification of Spirit in Revelation is *pneúma*, the consistent identification used for angel in Revelation is *ággelos*.

Note the several analytical tools used in making this determination: theological analysis, angels are not to be worshiped; linguistic analysis, *ággelos* versus *pneúma*; literary analysis, the passage speaks to Father and Son, thus the other party mentioned is most reasonably the Holy Spirit. I also compared Scripture with Scripture. The *ággelos* are messengers. A reference to angels as the givers of peace and blessing, or as in some way causing the events of the coming conflict, would be inconsistent with all other Scripture explaining their role in God's government. Their role in the Revelation is always that of messenger, never investigator, jury, judge, or executioner; they do not cause the (trumpet, bowl) judgments, they simply deliver them.

Moreover, to infer that the angels are judges of mankind "would be an intrusion of created beings into the Holy Trinity" [Thomas, 67]. The interpreter must use all the tools in his exegetical toolbox if he is to derive the right interpretation of a passage.

The right tool for the "seven spirits before the throne" in Rev. 1:4 is to see the number in its context. Revelation 1:4–5 forms a representation of the Trinity: "him who is and who was and who is to come"; the seven spirits; and Jesus Christ.

In this context the "seven spirits" represent the Holy Spirit. The meaning is not dependent on the plural "spirits." The plural is incidental: it is grammatically required by the number 7; more than one requires a plural. The number seven is not used literally but as some sort of symbol representing the activity of the Holy Spirit.

A word study of symbolic uses of "seven" indicates the number represents completeness. Zechariah 4:1–10 (ESV) provides an example. The number seven in that passage represents the Holy Spirit's perfect (complete) omnipotence, omniscience, and omnipresence.

In the New Testament we have a view of the Holy Spirit's activities in the world and in the church, and it is in this context the number seven becomes relevant. The Holy Spirit is the administrator of the church, guiding and empowering. The Holy Spirit acts governmentally from heaven on earth to accomplish the purpose, plans, and processes of God. "By '*the seven spirits*' we must understand, not indeed the sevenfold operations of the Holy Spirit, but the Holy Spirit sevenfold in his operations" [Trench, 9].

The number seven represents the fullness of the Spirit's operations. In the church he is teaching, illuminating, guiding, and empowering. The Spirit is holiness, truth, life and glory. He is the Spirit of wisdom and understanding, counsel and might, knowledge and fear of the Lord. His ministries in the church are sanctifying, regenerating, indwelling, empowering, fructifying, illuminating (teaching, preaching, meditation, devotion), and in "carrying" the believer's prayer, praises and worship.

The many offices and ministries of the Spirit are summed up in Revelation 1:4 in this one symbolic representation of completeness, "seven spirits." As related to the grace and peace extended to the believer by the godhead, these will be as "mighty and efficacious as the manifold influences of the omnipotent Spirit" [Ramsey, 46].

Adam And His Sin

Introduction

Two questions always pop up in any discussion about Adam and Eve. Question one: Were Adam and Eve created sinless? Question two: If Adam and Eve were created sinless, how could they sin? The purpose of this essay is to answer those questions. A third question is seldom asked, but must also be answered: Why did God give Adam a test of faith?

Were Adam And Eve Created Sinless?

The answer is, "Adam and Eve were created without sin in their human nature. Let us explore that answer.

Sin is not a nature. Most theologians and pastors refer to sin as a nature, but the Bible does not. Human beings were created with a human nature. Human nature consists of several principles of life, known as attributes. Some of the attributes of human nature are love, fear, sex, survival, self-sacrifice, and the more negative attributes that are the result of sin, such as greed, selfishness, deceit, etc. The attributes act synergistically to form the nature and personality. The attributes act together to make the decisions required for living.

Sin is a principle of rebellion, an attribute added to human nature by Adam's act of rebellion against God. The action of sin toward God is to reject God and disobey his commandments. The action of sin in human beings is constant temptation to rebel against God by disobeying his commandments and determining one's path in life apart from God. Humankind was created to serve God, be in submission to him, and be dependent upon him. The attribute sin has reprioritized the other attributes of human nature to serve self not God, to act autonomously, and do everything without God.

Adam was created with a sinless human nature, and the Woman formed from Adam, body and soul, was sinless because Adam was sinless. Adam was not created innocent. Creation in a state of innocence would mean Adam knew neither right nor wrong, implying that he was indifferent to one or the other [Shedd, 2:96–97]. He was not indifferent but was inclined to righteousness. The condition of his probation (Genesis 2:16, 17) required that he understood right-ness, or righteousness, as conformity to God's will.

Adam was created in positive holiness. Holiness was the grace God added to Adam's human nature so he could maintain himself in a state of righteousness. Adam knew that it was right to obey God, and was created with the desire to obey (inclination) and the moral ability (disposition) to live righteously within the moral boundaries of God's authority.

Adam was created morally pure. His moral purity inclined him to live under God's authority by conforming his thoughts and actions to God's will (expressed in his commandments). Every part of Adam's complex humanity was disposed to glorify God and experience fellowship with God. He had every moral, spiritual, and intellectual equipage to be holy as God is holy. To Adam, God's commandments were not a restraint, nor a taskmaster, but were in perfect harmony with his own nature. "The positive holiness, then, with which man was endowed, consisted in an understanding enlightened in the spiritual knowledge of God and divine things, and a will wholly inclined to them" [Shedd, 2:99].

Adam possessed the spiritual perception necessary to fully comprehend God's will as it applied to him and the Woman (and so did she). To submit and obey was what he desired. He was given grace and had every spiritual, moral, and intellectual aspect of personality and character he needed to fulfill his desire. Since Adam's will was inclined to glorify God and participate in fellowship with God as the ultimate goal of his life, the only motives that influenced his choices were spiritual in nature. There was no defect in Adam's humanity.

The image and likeness of God in which man was created was designed by his Creator to empower his creature to live in perfect harmony with God, as being voluntarily obedient to his commandments, taking pleasure in worship and intimate fellowship, and actively serving God as his vice-regent over the material creation. There was no defect in the human essence that required Adam to sin, no power to the contrary that impelled him to self-originate sin. Adam's nature was designed and built to fulfill God's purpose in creating humankind.

Adam was given stewardship over the earth. He was to manage the earth and all its creatures in accordance with God's values and under God's authority. One thing only, the tree of knowledge good and evil, was withheld from him, to test his willingness to be in submission to God and dependent upon God. Adam (as did the Woman) chose to act autonomously—apart from God's authority. That decision, to rebel against God, added the principle of rebellion, the sin attribute, to Adam's sinless human nature. The sin attribute reprioritized all the attributes of human nature to serve self, not God.

The addition of the sin attribute was permanent. God confirmed Adam in his choice. God did not abandon his relationship with Adam, God restored Adam and the Woman to fellowship, and gave them moral values and conditions that would help them manage the sin attribute in their lives, by being in submission to and dependent upon God, through faith.

Sinful Adam and the Woman, now named Eve, procreated, and their descendants, me and you included, inherited their sinful human nature, e.g., Genesis 5:3; Romans 5:12. All human beings are conceived with a sinful human nature.

Why Did God Give Adam A Test Of Faith?

In the garden God put two special trees among the others: the tree of life, and the tree of knowledge good and evil. They were located "in the midst" of the garden, which does not necessarily mean in the exact middle, but means among the other trees of the garden. The same word, *tāwek*, is used in 3:8 when Adam and his wife "hid themselves . . . among (*tāwek*) the trees of the garden."

The literal fruit of these two trees was not special. The one fruit was not life-giving, the other not poisonous. Both kinds of fruit were visually appealing. The fruit was the tangible aspect of the spiritual trial God would use to test Adam's faith. The spiritual trial was this: did Adam's faith rest in God's authority? The hinge on which the great door of faith opened or shut was God's command, "Do not eat."

We must understand the setting. Adam had been given dominion over the earth and all living things. He had been given as food "every tree whose fruit yields seed." The fruit of the tree of life was included, 2:16. Adam was, however, denied authority over the tree of knowledge good and evil. His dominion was limited by God's command, without explanation, but simply a statement of the consequences for disobedience.

If an explanation must be found it is "Obey because I said so." Would Adam respect God's authority by obeying this one limitation to his authority? Adam's authority was a delegated and therefore limited authority. For example, he had dominion, but he must exercise his dominion responsibly, caring for the animals, cultivating and keeping the plants. His wife had come out of his body, and in keeping with his dominion over all living things he had named her (*Ishsha:* woman, wife), but she was his equal and must be treated with respect and loved.

God had given him authority over all living things, and had given him the fruit of every tree—except one. God had placed a limit on Adam's dominion to test whether or not Adam was willing to live under God's authority: as a created being Adam must submit to the authority of his Creator. Put another way, his submission was a condition of the continuation of his "very good" relationship with God.

The question the tree represents, then, is who will be the source of moral authority in the world? God's authority is innate, absolute, sovereign; Adam's authority is derived, limited, and dependent. Could Adam accept that his own authority, so seemingly unlimited in its scope, was in fact limited by God's authority; that his authority depended on God's authority for its origin and effective power to do good? Put differently, would Adam decide to be his own boss? Would he deny God's authority by exercising his own authority? Did God or Adam know what was best for Adam's life? Would Adam live dependent on God, or would Adam be self-governing?

This one tree was denied to Adam as a test of his faith. The spiritual object of this test was moral authority: was Adam dependent or autonomous? God's command was the sharpened point to prod Adam to depend on God, not himself. The fruit was the efficient means by which the outcome of the test would be made known.

God tests faith to demonstrate its reality, assess its quality, and cause it to mature. These things are for man's sake, not God's. Trials exercise faith; by its exercise faith becomes stronger, more resilient, more practiced at meeting and overcoming trials. In a trial one discovers if personal faith exists. In a trial one discovers the strengths and weaknesses of his or her faith. By trials faith becomes mature as it overcomes the trial, bruised perhaps, but intact and matured. Through trials a person discovers if their faith depends on God or on one's self for solutions to trying circumstances. As James says, 1:3–4, "the testing of your faith produces patience. But let patience have its perfect work, that you may be perfect and complete, lacking nothing." God's intent was that Adam's faith be confirmed. God wanted Adam to decide he would depend on God to direct his life, and in so doing discover the greatest measure of freedom possible to man, freedom from the possibility of sin.

Reasons For The Test

There are two reasons God allowed Adam to suffer this test of his faith. The first is that God, having created a sentient creature, desired his creature to make a choice to worship God freely and not by necessity. All other material creatures worship God by instinct. Where there is no sentience there is no choice. Non-sentient creatures do worship, e.g., Revelation 5:13, every creature in heaven, on the earth, under the earth, and in the sea, praise and worship the Lord. When, Psalm 148, the sun, moon, and stars; waters above the heavens; great sea creatures and all the depths; fire and hail, snow and clouds; stormy wind, mountains and all hills; fruitful trees and all cedars; beasts and all cattle; creeping things and flying fowl—when these praise and worship the name of YHWH, the inanimate things do so by displaying God's works, the animate non-sentient creatures by instinct. Man, however, being a sentient being, was (and is) given a choice.

The second reason is that God created Adam with the possibility of change (mutability) and allowed the possibility of sin. The possibility of change was for Adam's good, so he could grow in understanding and wisdom. The possibility of sin was so he could exercise his choice to worship and thereby confirm his humanity in the image and likeness in which he had been created. The possibility of sin must not be confused with the tendency to sin. The possibility of sin means one possesses the moral power of self-determination, but has not exercised it to originate sin *ex nihilo* (from nothing). The tendency to sin means the moral power of self-determination has previously been exercised to originate sin.

If Adam And Eve Were Created Sinless, How Could They Sin?

Adam had the moral power of self-determination. In relation to the command, "Do not eat," his moral responsibility was to choose to obey; his moral power was sufficient to fulfill his responsibility. However, his mutability gave him the possibility to use his self-determination to make a decision contrary to his responsibility.

Since Adam was created without defect, he possessed the tendency to maintain his human essence as created, and exercise his mutability to improve his knowledge and appreciation of God through obedience to his moral responsibility. Since he was created mutable, he had the authority to exercise his self-determination to maintain or change the attributes of his humanity.

His probation, a time of testing or trial designed to reveal the character of his faith, was intended to serve a threefold purpose. One, he was to exercise his sentient choice to worship God. Two, he was to exercise his moral authority to live according to God's will. Three, should he choose these things his mutability would have been permanently prevented from the possibility of sin.

However, should he turn away from worship, should he choose to self-determine apart from God's will (thereby self-originating the principle/attribute of rebellion (sin) within his human nature *ex nihilo*), then the possibility of sin would become the tendency to sin. The outcome God desired is clear. "God did not place Adam in a state of probation from mere curiosity to see if he would fall; or from malevolence to cause him to fall; but from a benevolent desire that Adam, in the exercise of the ample power with which he was endowed, might merit and obtain, as the recompense of his fidelity, a final and everlasting deliverance from the possibility of sinning" [Shedd, 2:151].

Adam had the authority and the power to choose God or self as the source of his moral authority. Once the choice was made God would confirm Adam's soul in his choice. If Adam's choice had been to maintain himself in God's will, then God would have confirmed that choice and given Adam the grace of indefectibility, and thereby preserved his soul from the possibility of sin. The goal of Adam's probation was to confirm him in that perfection of body and soul in which he had been created. Sinning was a possible outcome. The commandment was the means whereby his power of choice would be exercised. Would he depend on God's authority and make the choice to continue in worship, fellowship, service, and obedience? Or would he self-determine and make a choice contrary to God's will?

Satan can persuade but he cannot compel anyone to sin. Satan did not compel the Woman to eat the fruit. He never suggests that she eat the fruit, he only suggests that she might gain something desirable by eating. Satan can make sin look harmless, desirable, needed; but he cannot make a person sin.

Adam, the Woman, and every human being make a decision to commit an act of sinning; a decision to keep on sinning; and then sinning becomes a habit. In Adam and the Woman an act of sin was contrary to their sinless nature. However, the mutability of their nature allowed them to self-originate an evil inclination. In so doing they changed their humanity. Their descendants inherited that corrupted humanity, which continuously inclines them to commit acts of sinning as a habit of life.

In Adam and the Woman an act of sinning was contrary to their sinless nature. However, the moral authority they were given allowed to make a decision, and the mutability of their nature allowed them make a wrong decision: to self-originate an evil inclination. In so doing they changed their humanity. Their descendants inherited that corrupted humanity, which continuously inclines them to commit acts of sin as a habit of life.

God had given both Adam and the Woman the authority to decide their path in life in relation to his commandment, and had given them holiness to influence a choice for obedience. The mutability in their human essence allowed for disobedience, but did not require them to exercise a choice contrary to their holy, righteous nature. They could decide to continue in obedience. Each, for different reasons, came to a point where they decided it was right for them to reject what God had said. In so reasoning their human nature self-originated an evil inclination to disobey, in order to achieve a goal forbidden to them by God. The woman anticipated wisdom; the man anticipated autonomy. What they gained was an experiential knowledge of evil and a sense of (judicial) guilt.

Conclusion

Adam and the Woman self-originated an act of sinning through the misuse of their moral authority to determine their path in life. That choice was contrary to their sinless human nature. But the mutability God had designed into their nature—given so they could grow in knowledge and understanding of their responsibilities, and in their relationship with God—allowed a choice contrary to their sinless human nature. As a result, their human nature was permanently changed by the addition of the sin attribute

There are few books that focus on Adam's creation and his fall into sin. One helpful resource is, *Adam and Eve, A Biography and Theology*, by James D. Quiggle, see chapters, "Their Nature" and "Their Crime." The other book referenced in this essay is W.G.T. Shedd, *Dogmatic Theology*, which discusses some of these issues in volume two.

What is the Gospel of salvation?

The gospel is sin, salvation, and the Savior. The gospel consists of the accusation of sin with the proclamation of the risen Jesus Christ the only Savior. We may example the gospel of salvation in five statements.

"You are a sinner before God; you need to be saved from the penalty due your sin; the risen Jesus Christ is the only Savior."

"I am a sinner and the risen Christ is the only Savior for me."

"I am a sinner; my sins have completely separated me from God, so that I am without hope in the world; Jesus Christ satisfied God for my sins; through faith in the risen Jesus Christ God will forgive my sins and bring me into a relationship with himself in Christ."

Come to the risen Jesus Christ as a hopeless and helpless sinner, seeking pardon from the Redeemer, so that your rebellion against God may be ended and you are given peace with God through Christ.

At once submit to God by placing your trust in the only person whom God has appointed to be Savior, the Lord Jesus Christ. Agree with God, from within your innermost being, that God sent Jesus to die for your sin, and then God raised him from the dead, because the judicial debt for your sin had been paid.

These statements are not intended to say all that may be said. If they spark further interest in the sinner, then you know the Holy Spirit is at work. If there is no interest, then there is nothing more to be said at that time. Let the Holy Spirit work as he wills.

In whatever way and by whatever means the good news of salvation in the risen Christ may be presented, the two essential elements, the accusation of sin with the proclamation of the risen Jesus Christ the only Savior, must always be present.

Do You Really Want To Understand The Scripture?

Today I'm giving away the secret for free. But it will cost you.

Step 1, Ask the Holy Spirit to teach you. Bear in mind the Holy Spirit expects you to apply what he teaches.

Step 2, Select a Bible book to study. If a beginner start small. Study from the first word in the first verse to the last word in the last verse.

Step 3, Study that Bible book as best as you are able. (No one is good at the beginning; skills take time and practice.) The use of language helps and reference books (Bible atlas, dictionary, etc.) are allowed. Study a verse (sentence, passage) yourself before comparing your results with a commentary. Adjust your results as may be necessary.

Step 4, Write down what you discover. Keep a notebook (manual or computer), "What I found when I explored the Bible Book of __________." Put down a key word(s), make a note(s), write an outline, use sentences and paragraphs if you are able. You are not writing a book (although you could), but a discovery journal.

Step 5, When you are finished with that Bible book, select another Bible book and repeat steps 1-4 until you have studied all 66 Bible books. After you have studied all 66 books, and if you are still mentally competent (you will be older) begin again.

In addition to studying an individual book, maintain your Bible reading schedule.

That's all there is to it. Simple.

Reading theologies and commentaries is okay and can be very helpful, but 1) you have to understand the source in order to properly evaluate the works of others, and 2) over years (yes, years) you will learn more from independent Bible study than from other sources, who, BTW, studied the Bible to produce what you are reading.

So, don't take that easy shortcut all the time, spend time in the Word for yourself. Your Christianity is a lifetime journey. Why not use and understand the only "travel guide" provided for that journey?

(BTW, reading, "How to live your Christian life," kind of books is mostly (not always) a waste of your time. Just sayin'. It's all in the

Bible. Biographies of Christian men and women of the past are more useful.)

You will know you have begun to understand the Scripture when you can do what the Holy Spirit does: compare Scripture with Scripture and get it to add up to understanding.

Since 2007, I have completed the study of eight Old Testament and sixteen New Testament books (number seventeen in progress), so it can be done. That independent study of twenty-four Bible books has generated another twenty-one books about the Bible, on a wide variety of subjects.

What Is The Manner Of The Christian Life?

Any discussion must begin with the quality of that life. Christians are given "eternal life," John 10:28. That eternal life is both the duration and the quality of life.

> Eternal life of the believer. The duration and quality of life experienced by the believer. The duration is everlasting. The quality of eternal life is God sharing his communicable attributes in the fullest measure possible for a saved finite soul to receive, thus effecting intimate fellowship and communion between God and the believer. The believer has eternal life as a present possession, and experiences it in part during his or her mortal life (as he or she is being made conformed by the Holy Spirit to the likeness of Christ), but the fullness of eternal life begins following physical death. [Quiggle, *Dictionary.*]

In 1 Timothy 6:1–19 Paul describes the negatives and positives of eternal life.

> Negatively, flee the things listed in 6:3–10 (ESV): wrong doctrine, unsound words, conceit, controversy, quarrels, envy, dissension, slander, evil suspicions, constant friction, depraved mind, the desire to be rich, the love of money.

> Positively, pursue the things listed in 6:11–19 (ESV): righteousness, godliness, faith, love, steadfastness [perseverance], gentleness, keep God's commandments, be rich in good works, be generous and ready to share.

Most of these words are known, but godliness may be unfamiliar. In the simplest term, godliness is "God living and active in humanity, humanity acting and living according to God's values." In more detail.

> Godliness is when the believer's thought, will, and action conform the believer's manner of life to the moral, holy, and righteous standard set by God's own character. In simpler terms, to be Christ-like. Godliness arises out of the new nature birthed by the Holy Spirit. God takes delight in those whose character and actions reflect his character and actions. God's character defines the worth of the actions performed by all beings: they are godly or ungodly. [Quiggle, *Dictionary.*]

Godliness is not naturally generated by the believing soul, but depends on the work of the Holy Spirit through the grace he gives to all believers to live a godly life pleasing to God. While it is true a life of faith is the product of God's grace, it is also true that a lot of personal effort must be expended in order to live a godly and righteous life. There is a cost to living a life of faith: denying the temptations of sin in the mind and flesh; alienation from the world and worldly practices; separation from sinning and sinners engaged in sin; caution in one's relationships with sinners. [Quiggle, *Dictionary.*]

The way in which a believer is to live out his or her Christian life is in harmony with that eternal life he/she was given at salvation.

The Dual Presence of Jesus Christ

Do you believe Jesus Christ is God the Son incarnate in the human being Jesus of Nazareth? Do you believe God the Son joined himself to the rudimentary human body and rudimentary human soul of the newly conceived Jesus of Nazareth in Mary's womb? Is that what you believe? Yes? Good. That is the incarnation. That is the biblical doctrine. God the Son became permanently incarnate ca. 7–5 BC (I believe late August/early September 5 BC.)

The names-titles, "Son of God, Christ, Jesus Christ, Jesus the Christ, Christ Jesus, Lord Jesus, Lord Jesus Christ, Jesus Christ our Lord," are the biblical terms referring to the incarnate person and only to the incarnate person; they appear only in the New Testament. (A profitable study is to examine the 980 occurrences of "Jesus" in the New Testament.) Knowing these terms refer only to the incarnate person—not to Jesus of Nazareth, not to God the Son, but only to the incarnate person—is critical to understanding both Old Testament and New Testament Scripture.

The person Jesus Christ is fully God and fully human: the God-man. Scripture never divides the acts of the incarnate person into those performed by the deity or those performed by the humanity. The person Jesus Christ slept, ate, peed, pooped, wept, was thirsty—all the human functions all humans do. The person Jesus Christ healed the sick, stilled the storm, raised the dead, knew what was in the heart of men—all the things only deity does. The two natures acted together in perfect harmony. Human nature was created in the image and likeness of God. God the Son incarnated in that human nature.

Jesus Christ was and is one person with one personality, that of God the Son, a personality that is informed by both the deity nature and the human nature. A nature is not a personality. Jesus Christ did not have a deity personality plus a human personality. Jesus Christ is one person with one personality, that of God the Son. Jesus Christ has two natures, deity and human, and he has two wills, deity and human. Jesus Christ is one person with one personality, two natures, two wills.

The two natures are distinct, they do not merge, they do not combine. The relation of Jesus Christ's humanity to his deity is threefold. His humanity was so interpenetrated by his deity that his humanity was perfected (not exalted), and thus attained the divine ideal for human nature: perfect worship, perfect intimate fellowship, perfect obedience, and perfect service toward God. The result was perfect harmony between his human and deity natures, so that the

God-man always acted in perfect unity with the Father. His humanity was empowered by the indwelling Holy Spirit such that he was given more than sufficient authority and power to accomplish his mission. As being perfectly filled with the Spirit, his human nature cooperated perfectly with the Spirit.

Jesus Christ had two wills, human and deity. The will is the decision-making faculty of the soul. The will is a function of human nature, not a function of personality (personality is the behavior patterns resulting from the nature expressing itself in the will; a nature is an effect of the animating principle (life) with the synergistic action of the attributes). Jesus Christ had two wills. One will was the function of the deity nature and one will was the function of the human nature. How did these two wills interact in the one person?

"The single person of the incarnate Christ retained the total complex of divine attributes and possessed all the complex of human attributes essential to a perfect human being . . .. It seems to me that every single decision stemmed from either the 'will' of His divine nature or the 'will' of His human nature or a blending of both, making it proper to think of two 'wills'" [Ryrie, "Basic Theology," 287–289.] The blending (agreement, cooperation) of the two wills in every act seems to me the proper view.

Now we are biblically prepared to address the topic of this essay: the dual presence of Jesus Christ in the universe. The one person Jesus Christ was always omnipresent and localized at one and the same time. The deity nature remained deity, and therefore was omnipresent, an attribute of the person God the Son. The human nature remained human, and therefore was in one place in space and time, an attribute of human nature.

> The person Jesus Christ is both eternal (his deity) and immortal (his soul and body).
>
> The person Jesus Christ is both omniscient (his deity) and limited in knowledge and understanding (his humanity).
>
> The person Jesus Christ is both omnipotent (his deity) and limited in ability (his humanity).

This raises some interesting observations. Jesus had a beginning: in Mary's womb. The incarnate person, Jesus Christ, both had no beginning (was increate) and had a beginning (was human). Jesus did not create the universe. God the Son created the universe before the incarnation, before Jesus existed, because Jesus did not exist until conceived in Mary's womb. Jesus Christ, the God-man is said, once, Colossians 2:16–17, to have created the universe, because he is one person, and Scripture attributes all the acts of either nature to the one person.

Here are other observations, usually unwelcome. The "Christ" did not exist before the incarnation. The Christ is an office of the incarnate person, Psalm 2:2, 7. Therefore Jesus Christ did not appear in the Old Testament (as Reformed theology insists). There was no "Christ," in the Old Testament because there was no "Jesus Christ" prior to the incarnation. The name-title "Jesus Christ" always refers to the incarnate person (search the scriptures). There was no incarnation until the conception of Jesus in Mary's womb. God the Son appears in the Old Testament, usually as the Angel of YHWH, but no one in the Old Testament knew of or was aware of the as yet non-existent incarnate person Jesus Christ. Nor did any human being or fallen angel believe Jesus the Christ was God incarnate between his birth and resurrection (again, search the scriptures, see them in their context, understand the Greek words not the translations). See the essay in this book, "Did the Apostles Know Jesus Was God Incarnate?"

Summary:

One of the jobs of the Christian is to maintain the genuine humanity of the God-man as passionately as he/she maintains the genuine deity of the God-man.

The person Jesus Christ experienced both deity and human attributes at the same time as a result of the union of his deity and human natures. That is how he functioned on earth, that is how he functions in heaven, and that is always how he will always function. As William Ames (1576–1633) explained.

> There were in Christ two kinds of understanding: a divine understanding whereby he knew all things, John 21:17, and a human whereby he did not yet know some things, Mark 13:32. So there were two wills, one divine, Luke 5:13, and the other human, with a natural appetite, Matthew 26:39. So Christ has a double presence, but the human presence cannot be everywhere or in many places at once. [*Marrow of Theology*, 131.]

Is the dual presence of Jesus Christ beyond our comprehension? Yes, but it is the reasonable outcome of the incarnation of deity with humanity.

Balance

One of the ways to understand Scripture is recognizing what I call "balance."

All aspects of Christianity, whether doctrine or practice—but especially practice—have balance.

In the practical aspects of Christianity, the balance is between what is negative (e.g., "admonish the disorderly") and what is positive (e.g., "encourage the fainthearted, support the weak, be long-suffering toward all"). (1 Thess. 5:14.)

In doctrine the balance is between that which is God's responsibility and that which is the sinner's or the believer's responsibility. For example, Ephesians 2:8-10. Salvation is by God's grace and by the sinner's faith. Good works are what God has prepared beforehand, in which the believer is to conduct his or her life.

Recognizing the balance in Scripture gives the believer a better understanding of his/her responsibility in both faith and practice. In fact, practice is the balance to faith.

Resisting the New Social Order

In the days of the early New Testament church, there wasn't prejudice or bigotry based on skin color. But there was prejudice and bigotry. Everyone belonged to this or that social class. There were slave, freedman, and free born. Male and female had their rigid roles to play. The rich and the poor and the one's in between—but not a middle class, which was a teeny-tiny number of people in those days.

You were family or not family, and if not family you did not matter to family. If you were a child you produced nothing and therefore had almost no social worth. If you were unborn or newly born you were not yet a person and therefore had no worth. And the usual politicians, businessmen, farmers, sailors, soldiers, artisans, and nobodies. Each thought the other inferior; except the nobodies and the slaves and the poor, who knew they were on the bottom of the social order.

Many of those things of worldly worth have endured and are with us today.

The social genius of Christianity was to make every saved person the brother and sister of one another, because all were in the same family, the family of God in Christ. Within the church prejudice should not exist. As Paul said so very clearly: neither slave nor free, neither male or female, neither civilized (Greek) or trailer-park-trash (barbarian). And certainly not skin color, wealth, social status, or any other worldly category by which the worth of a human being is falsely created.

Today's Woke World seeks to restore the old prejudices, albeit by inverting the social order, deciding who will be on top and who will be on the bottom of society's social-worth ladder. The professing church will cooperate, thinking to gain power with men—but they will be consumed by their new friends.

The genuine New Testament church cannot let itself become part of this new Woke order, even as it did not let itself become part of the old order. There will be great pressure to conform, and for the best of reasons: evangelism, a safe place to worship, ministry opportunities in the world, money to support those ministers and ministries. Resist— not alone, but together.

Consistency in Theology

Young Bible students. As you continue to study doctrines and Bible books throughout the early years and into the middle years of your Christian life, you must take care to develop a theology that has external and internal consistency.

> Externally, your theology must be developed from the whole counsel of God, so your theology, in the whole and in the parts, is in agreement with the Scripture in the whole and in the parts.

> Internally, the various parts of your theology must agree with one another, as well as agree with the whole of your theology, which must in turn agree with the parts.

The manner in which you express your theology—the way you put words together to express and explain ideas—must be consistent not only with the whole of your theology, but all the individual explanations must be internally consistent with one another, while at the same time faithfully expressing the ideas and concepts and words of the Scripture.

A simple example to illustrate. Your theology states salvation cannot be lost. What, then, to do with the scriptures that exhort the believer to a righteous life, especially those that imply salvation might be lost through unrighteous actions?

Your theology must not only defend the concept of endlessly saved, but also give a defense of the scriptures that seem to put that concept in doubt, by explaining those scriptures in such a way that each individual explanation harmonizes with the Scripture as a whole, with the main proposition, and with all individual parts of the explanation.

The task is not as easy as it sounds, for it is the long process of years of learning. With every doctrine in your theology, you must develop an externally and internally consistent theology from those doctrines.

The same is true for the interpretation of one individual Bible book with the whole of the Bible.

A lack of that needful external and internal consistency in theology is how false teaching and heresies are born.

In the Twinkling of an Eye

At 1 Corinthians 15:52, Paul says the rapture will take place in the twinkling of an eye. How fast is the twinkling of an eye?

Some define a "twinkling" as an eye blink. An eye blinks lasts approximately 300 to 400 milliseconds (a millisecond is 1/1000 of a second).

Others define "twinkling" as the time it takes for light reflected from the eye of one person to reach the eye of another person watching the first person. Because of the speed of light (186,000 miles per second), the time for reflected light to pass from one person to another person is, to our perception, instantaneous.

Let us see what the Bible says. 1 Corinthians 15:52 reads, "in a *átomos*, in the *rhipé* of an eye."

The word *átomos* is the word from which we get our English word "atom." The Greek word means "indivisible," because the Greeks thought of an atom as the smallest particle of matter in the universe. (Today we know atoms are composed of smaller, subatomic, particles.) As applies to time, *átomos* means an indivisible moment in time. Technically, a moment in time so small it cannot be divided into smaller units of time. In relation to human perception, *átomos* means in a moment, in an instant.

The word *rhipé* means a quick moment, a moment in time, a blink, a wink, a twinkling.

Putting these two words together, as Paul does, the rapture of the New Testament church will take place rapidly. The event will occur so quickly as to appear instantaneous to an observer. If someone were looking at a believer when he or she was raptured, the person watching could not perceive the transition from present to not present. One moment present. The next moment not present.

The rapture of the New Testament church will occur so quickly as to appear instantaneous to an observer, who would not be able to perceive the transition from present to not present.

The Principles of Charity

Charity, or giving to aid the poor, is a fixed value in God's economy, both Old Testament and New Testament. One way that value is taught is in the Old Testament law of gleaning. The book of Ruth presents the example.

Under the law of gleaning, the poor, the homeless, the jobless could glean a field—pass through a harvested field picking up stalks of grain—when the reapers had completed reaping the grain. Gleaners were allowed to pick up whatever grain stalks the reapers dropped or missed. They were also allowed to harvest the corners of the field, which the farmer was not to harvest, but to leave for the gleaners.

The lessons of the law of gleaning.

Principle one: The self-respect of work. Everyone needs the dignity of working for their necessities. Although some did beg for money in Israeli society (those physically unable to work, as happens in every society), God's welfare program was to work. Those who could not find work for money were able to work for their food by gleaning. Picking up the grain stalks was only half the work. The grain must also be removed from the stalks. It was hard work for the gleaner. The greedy and faithless farmers despised and prevented gleaning. Farmers with faith allowed and aided the gleaners.

Principle Two: Working to help others. Ruth not only gleaned for herself, but also for her mother-in-law, Naomi, who was too old to glean in the fields. Ruth worked to "attend to her own," 1 Thessalonians 4:11. Ruth understood the principle, "if anyone is not willing to work, neither let him eat," 2 Thessalonians 3:10. (Did you think Paul invented those principles?) Therefore Ruth gleaned for herself and "her own," i.e., her mother-in law.

Principle Three: Giving is by faith. The amount to give was according to the giver's faith. YHWH told the farmer to leave the corners of his field un-harvested. How big was a corner? The size was up to the individual farmer. Could the farmer trust God would provide enough for himself if he provided for others by taking from what God had given him? Centuries later the religious leaders defined the size of a corner, but that was not God's plan. Moreover, the farmer could let the gleaners follow more closely to the reapers. And he could have the reapers leave more in the reaped field for the gleaners to glean. Boaz told his reapers to, "Let Ruth gather even among the sheaves; do not rebuke her. And also draw out from the bundles and leave them that she may gather them up, and do not rebuke her," Ruth 2:15–16. Faith trusts God to provide in a sufficient amount for oneself and enough also to help others.

Principle Four: A society without the poor is against God's design. This may be the most difficult lesson from gleaning. "For you always have the poor with you," said Jesus, "and whenever you want you are able to do them good," Mark 14:7. He was referring to Deuteronomy 15:11, YHWH's statement that the poor will never cease from the land. God has providentially designed human society with the rich and the poor, that we human beings may learn to act godly. Helping the poor is not the only act of moral worth, because there are other needs which must be satisfied and other persons to be helped, such as family, self, the church, Christian Brethren, and gospel ministries. But helping the poor is a required moral value, and the poor will always be present.

The first welfare system in the USA began in 1935. In response to the economic depression, President Roosevelt created federal work programs for those who could not find work. Whether he knew it or not, he followed the biblical rule: the self-respect of working for one's necessities. In time, the economy recovered and the federal welfare programs were not needed.

In the 1960s federal welfare was revived, but not as before. The poor are always present, but social conditions had created a subclass of workers with inadequate employment and education. President Johnson's "Great Society" legislation (passed in a Democratic congress) gave money without work; it gave more money to single parents than it did to two-parent families. These programs abandoned all four principles of God's law of gleaning. We can look back on sixty years of federal welfare programs and see they have created chaos within American society.

Times have changed since the days of Ruth. In some countries Christians may not be able to follow God's precepts (specific laws) regarding gleaning. But we all, as Christians, have a continuing obligation to follow God's principles and moral values in all aspects of life. That includes having the faith to trust God will provide in a sufficient amount for our self and our family, and enough also to help others.

Are Human Beings God's Victims?

Recently I read this statement on social media: "Romans 9 clearly teaches that God does with people as He wishes, and we have no say in the matter." That simple statement simplistically ignores the most basic aspect of free will, which is the God-given authority to make a choice.

The writer's first example to attempt to prove his premise demonstrates the flaw in his thinking. Romans 9:9, "For God had promised, 'I will return about this time next year, and Sarah will have a son.'" Were Abraham and Sarah victims of God's divine fiat? Or did they choose to cooperate with God to fulfill God's promise?

Common sense, supported by Scripture, tells us Abraham and Sarah made a choice to cooperate with God by choosing to do that most basic activity required to have a child: they had sexual intercourse with one another. They might have said to themselves, "What can we do? God has made this choice for us. We have no free will, we will wait for God to create a child in Sarah's womb." No. Their freely made choice to have sexual intercourse was an expression of their faith in God's promise that, "from one man, and him good as dead," one could be born by the power of God giving life, Hebrews 11:12.

How do we know they had sexual intercourse? Only one person in Scripture is said to have been conceived in the womb by the power of God, Luke 1:35. Sarah did not have less faith than her husband. "By faith Sarah received strength to conceive," Hebrews 11:12. Whose faith? Sarah's faith. And how was Sarah's faith expressed? She chose to have sexual intercourse with her husband, knowing by faith God would give her a son, just as God had promised, through their cooperation by faith to do what was required to have a son.

What is obvious in Scripture—and so obvious in Hebrews 11 as to be blindingly bright—is God has chosen to work mediately, not by divine fiat. He works through the choices of others to always accomplish his will. Whether those choices are by faith or by sin, God's will is always accomplished.

Free will *is not* that you can make choices and decisions free of any internal and external determining factors. That view is willfully blind to the obvious. Free will in the creature is never the license to do whatever a person might want to do, for there are known boundaries to choice, which everyday experience confirms. All choices made within those known boundaries are freely made.

The free will to choose free of any external determining factors is native only to the sovereign God. God's creatures are always subject to external and internal factors that influence their choice.

A human being's free will is corrupted by sin in the unsaved, influenced by sin in the saved. That is the spiritual boundary: "Free will is the moral authority to make choices within the physical, moral, and spiritual boundaries of human nature,"

A few simple examples. I put my 5 year old grandson in the fenced-in back yard. The fence is too tall and too strong for him to climb over or break through. The gate in the fence is securely locked. Does the five year old have free will? Yes, he has the same free will he had before I placed him in the back yard. He may make any decision he wants within the physical boundaries of his environment and his own physical, moral, and spiritual limitations.

Can you decide to flap your arms up and down and fly? You can choose to flap your arms, but you cannot choose to fly by that method. Do you have no free will because you cannot choose to fly by flapping your arms? Obviously, you made the choice to try, and ran into the physical boundary of your nature.

A person in a jail cell continues to have free will, but is now subject to a physical boundary he did not have before, the bars of his physical prison. The unsaved person chooses to reject God because the spiritual boundary of sin is a prison he cannot leave on his own, an insurmountable fence he cannot scale.

Believers have been wrongly taught by Reformed theology through the use of analogy with a physically dead body that the sinner is unable to choose to respond to God. That analogy is false. The unsaved sinner definitely chooses to respond to God: he rebels, he disobeys, he rejects. The sinner spiritually dead means he/she always chooses to spiritually rebel against God.

Only God can open the prison door, only God can open the gate in the fence, through giving the unsaved sinner God's gift of grace-faith-salvation, Ephesians 2:8. Then the sinner will make the choice to believe God's testimony of salvation through faith in Christ the Savior.

What the author of the post I referred to in the beginning envisions is a universe without responsibility. And if no responsibility then no accountability and no liability. Responsibility, accountability, and liability are the consequences of a God-given free will. If we deny free will, then we have denied those consequences.

What the author of that post proposes is a world without those consequences. A world of anarchy (Judges 21:25) or a world where human beings are non-sentient animals driven by instinct and limited reasoning capacity. What underlies that post's thesis is the desire to be sovereign, the desire to make the rules, the desire to be God. Such is the essence of sin.

Scripture is not a dictionary, nor a theological treatise. But Scripture does present a comprehensive and well-organized theology. Scripture does explain what it means and does define words, through careful observation of what Scripture does say, and interpretation of the plain and normal meaning of the words and language Scripture uses.

As defined by the Scripture, free will is the moral authority to make choices within the physical, moral, and spiritual boundaries of human nature, as further influenced by internal and external motivations and consequences.

Whether by faith or by sin, human beings have free will.

A Slave to Sin?

Let us reason together. Popular sermons and Bible expositions speak of the unsaved sinner as a "slave to sin." But if the unsaved sinner actually was a "slave to sin," he/she has no choice but to commit acts of sinning. If that were truly the case, then the unsaved sinner would have no responsibility for his/her acts of sinning, and therefore could not be justly punished for their acts of sinning. If there is no responsibility there is no accountability, and therefore no liability. A slave is accountable only to his master, his only responsibility is to obey. He/she is neither punished nor rewarded for obedience.

The Scripture does not say the unsaved sinner is a *doúlos*, "slave, servant," to sin. What the Scripture does say is the believer is no longer under the dominion of sin, implying he/she was at one time under sin's dominion. Therefore the unsaved sinner is under sin's dominion. But if we press "dominion" too literally, we run into the same problem we have with "a slave to sin." There is no liability for actions a sinner had no responsibility for committing.

The Scripture does say the believer is a *doúlos*, "slave, servant," to Christ, but if *doúlos*, is understood as "slave" there is the same problem, a lack of responsibility, accountability, and liability, and therefore the believer cannot be chastised for his sins nor rewarded for his good works, for neither are his responsibility.

Nor does Christ say the believer is a slave. John 15:15, " I no longer call you *doúlos*, because the *doúlos* knows not what his master is doing. But you I have called friends [*philéō*], because all things that I heard from my Father I have declared to you." The slave obeys without thinking, without love for the master, without friendship from the master. The Christian serves the Master he/she loves as friends and servants loved by the Master, John 15:14, "You are my friends [*philéō*, not *doúlos*], if you do what I command you."

While there may be an individual verse here or there in the NT where "slave" is a more appropriate translation, on the whole the Christian is a servant, not a slave.

Returning to the unsaved, the better analogy is to view the sinner as having sold him or herself to sin, and therefore is the willing servant of sin. That is, in fact, how the Scripture uses *doúlos*, "slave, servant," of the believer: not as a slave to Christ without choice, but as the servant of Christ—the willing, voluntary servant.

Understanding the sinner under sin's dominion requires an understanding of sin and free will. Free will is the God-given moral authority to make choices within the physical, moral, and spiritual boundaries of human nature, as further influenced by internal and external motivations and consequences. Sin creates a spiritual boundary in the unsaved sinner, whereby he/she naturally chooses sin over God.

Sin is an attribute of fallen human nature, a principle or attribute of evil that motivates human beings to rebel against God, disobey his commandments, and seek a path in life apart from God.

Sin has authority (dominion, rule) over the sinner, not as some invincible overlord, but as an innate part of human nature constructively working with all the other attributes of human nature to persuasively incline the will to choose an act of sinning.

The evil attribute sin influences every other attribute with the inclination to sin, and in that sense sin can be said to dominate the will. The sinner freely chooses sinning because his will is of itself always inclined to choose sinning, and as being rebellious and disobedient toward God never desires to change its inclination to choose sinning to rebel against God, disobey his commandments, and seek a path in life apart from God.

The unsaved sinner willing serves sin, is a willing "slave" to sin, always choosing sin over God. Therefore he/she is responsible for the choice to sin, and thus accountable and liable for the acts of sinning committed.

The believer is no longer a servant of sin. Romans 6:14 states sin no longer has dominion over the believer. The saved person freely chooses righteousness because the saved person's will is of itself always inclined to choose righteousness, and as being in salvific relationship with God, doesn't desire to change its inclination to choose righteousness.

The choice to live righteously is freely made, because the person's disposition is inclined to holiness and righteousness toward God. (Sometimes the saved act on temptation, because the sin attribute remains as part of human nature, but the saved will habitually act righteously, sinning occasionally and confessing their sins when committed, out of love for Christ and a desire to please him.)

Sometimes Romans 9:14–23 is used to argue the sinner is not culpable. Someone asks,

> Isn't your argument the same one that Paul argues against in Romans 9?

> You will say to me, therefore, "Why then does he still find

> fault? For who resists his will?" On the contrary, who are you, a human being, to talk back to God? Will what is formed say to the one who formed it, "Why did you make me like this?" Or has the potter no right over the clay, to make from the same lump one piece of pottery for honor and another for dishonor? (Romans 9:19-21)

Doesn't Paul argue that the sinner is still culpable for their sin even though they cannot do otherwise? How do you reconcile this?

We always need take care we are not confused by the sound of words (an interpretive principle from A. W. Pink). Are the words "formed" and "make" used in the context of the creation of human beings. No, because God formed and made humanity sinless, therefore only for honor not dishonor. Paul cannot mean God created humankind to be sinners.

The context for these words is in 9:17. God placed the Pharaoh in a position of authority. The Pharaoh acted out of his sinful nature—he could have submitted to God's authority, God did not make him sin. God formed and made him in that place of authority because the Pharaoh's choices would declare God's name.

The sinner chooses sinning because that is his/her nature, but the sinner is not compelled to choose sinning. Other attributes e.g., self-interest, persuade the sinner to make a different choice should the temptation lead to unwanted consequences. That is why we must see the sin attribute as one among many, each making an input into the decision of the will, but the sin attribute is the most powerful of the attributes. The sin attribute has reprioritized all the attributes to serve self, not God. So that even when an act that might be categorized as "good" is performed, the reason was not to please or glorify or obey God, but for some perceived self-interest.

I have before used the illustration of my 5 year old grandson in the fenced-in back yard. The grandson cannot choose to leave the yard because of the fence. But the grandson can make any possible choice within the yard. So, too, the sinner, who can freely make any choice his or her attributes allow, except the choice to self-originate saving faith. Only the gift of God (Ephesians 2:8) can change the boundaries of the sinner's nature to allow a choice for saving faith. Thus the sinner is culpable for every choice. Only the sin attribute prevents the choice for faith.

My argument responds to two principles. One is God gave

humankind the moral authority to make choices, and those choices are always made—cannot otherwise be made—within the physical, moral, and spiritual boundaries of the human nature. In the unsaved the sin attribute is one of those boundaries. The other principle is that accountability and liability require responsibility. Responsibility and freely made choices walk hand in hand, so the sinner is culpable for his or her choices.

1 Thessalonians 4:15

An extract from my book, *A Private Commentary on the Bible: Thessalonians*, published 2021.

As I work my way through 1 Thessalonians 4:13–17, I see new (new to me) things in the passage. For example, 4:15, "For this we declare to you by the word of the Lord, that we the living remaining unto the coming of the Lord, shall never no never precede those having fallen asleep" (my translation).

The first thing to notice is, this explanation of the rapture of the New Testament church is, "by the word of the Lord." Paul gives to the Thessalonians (and to you and me), the revelation he received from Jesus concerning the rapture of the New Testament church, which revelation extends to 4:17.

Now we should take care we do not disparage all else Paul has said just because he did not preface it with, "this we declare to you by the word of the Lord." All that Paul has written, in all of his letters, and all he said that is recorded in the Acts, was inspired by the Holy Spirit.

The practical meaning of "inspiration" is the accuracy, credibility, and authenticity of what is recorded in the Scripture. Paul gives this preface, "this we declare to you by the word of the Lord," for the same reason he said at, Galatians 1:12, I neither received the gospel from man, nor was I taught the gospel, but the gospel I preach is by revelation from Jesus Christ.

Much of what the apostles taught may be traced to the Old Testament revelation given to God's people group, national ethnic Israel. Most of what is not from the Old Testament may be traced to what Jesus said in the gospels, e.g., Colossians 2:9.

In other words, much of what the apostles taught it is not new revelation, but preexisting revelation repeated and applied to a new people group, the New Testament church. Many of Paul's exhortations concerning the believer's behavior have their source in God's revelation through the Old Testament prophets, or Jesus in the gospels.

But there are doctrines, such as the rapture of the New Testament church, that originate through the apostolic witness as received by direct revelation from God. Therefore, there are times when it is crucial we be reminded of the source of biblical revelation, because those with doubts will distort the doctrine to fit their assumptions. Some deny this doctrine of the rapture of the New Testament church. Paul says it cannot be denied, because it is by revelation from Jesus Christ.

Verse 15 continues, "that we the living remaining unto the coming of the Lord, shall never no never precede those having fallen asleep."

Whenever Christ will return for his New Testament church, there will be living believers to greet him. This, of course, is to be expected. Jesus said, "I will build my church, and the gates of hades will not prevail against it," Matthew 16:18. The city gates were used as a metaphor for strength, for the gates closed and barred refused entry to the enemy. Thus, they were a symbol of permanence, because as long as the gates stood the city was secure.

There will always be a New Testament church. "Father, those you have given me, I desire that where I am they also might be with me," John 17:24. "And so always with the Lord we will be," 1 Thessalonians 4:17. Here we discover that when Christ returns for his church, there will be physically living believers, however long the time until Christ returns for his church. Those who have predicted, or bewailed, the demise of the New Testament church are in error.

The double negative, "never no never" reflects the Greek text. The Greek language used a double negative to emphasize the impossibility of a thing. There will be a living New Testament church at the rapture, because both physically dead believers and living believers will be transformed and glorified at the same event. As Paul will explain in 4:16, the bodies of the physically dead believers will be resurrected and reanimated in a glorified state before the living believers are transformed and glorified. Thus the living do not precede the dead in glorification.

Both Paul and the Thessalonians believed they personally would be transformed and glorified as living believers and taken to heaven by Jesus Christ. The hope of Christ's return—the rapture—was actively anticipated by the apostolic church. They daily lived in that assurance of a removal from the earth by Christ as living believers. The rapture of the New Testament church is not a new doctrine.

But that belief—to be taken to heaven without passing through physical death—raised a question. If Christ was returning for the living New Testament church, what about those believers who had died before he returned? (Notice this indicates some believers had already died in Thessalonica. From persecution?) Paul explains in the next verse.

God In a Box?

A person told me "Dispensationalism has God in a box." I will admit I was incensed at his ignorance.

So I asked him: What box? (He never replied.)

You mean the box of understanding every Scripture equally in the plain and normal meaning of the words and languages? Unlike Reformed and other theologies that interpret some scriptures by allegory or mysticism.

Do you mean the box that applies grammatical-historical, contextual, lexical-syntactical, theological, literary-genre, and doctrinal analysis equally to every scripture to arrive at authorial intent? Unlike Reformed and other theologies that interpret some scriptures by allegory or mysticism and deny authorial intent.

Do you mean the box that understands how God works in history through different economies? Unlike Reformed and other theologies that imagine covenants not described in Scripture.

Do you mean the box that, because Dispensationalism understands Scripture in the plain and normal meaning of the words and languages, it recognizes the name Israel in Scripture always means national ethnic Israel and the church is always New Testament believers? Unlike Reformed and other theologies that because they interpret some scriptures by allegory or mysticism confuse the distinction between Israel and the New Testament church.

Do you mean the box that understands God will literally fulfill every covenant promise to national ethnic Israel? Unlike Reformed and other theologies that believe God lied to the Old Testament saved because he has abandoned Israel and transferred all the promises to the New Testament church, to be fulfilled less than literally, or not at all?

If you mean those "boxes," then I am glad the Holy Spirit taught me to be a Dispensationalist.

Friends, if you oppose dispensational theology, at least be knowledgeable of what you oppose. I recommend you read these basic works: the Bible, any translation; Ryrie, *Dispensationalism*; Vlach, *Dispensationalism*; Quiggle, *Understanding Dispensational Theology*; Virkler, *Hermeneutics*; Pentecost, *Things to Come*.

Clarence Larkin, "Dispensational Truth"

Every now and then I see Clarence Larkin's book, *Dispensational Truth* posted or even recommended. The believer should use this book with great caution. The book is in many ways a caricature of Dispensationalism. Many of Larkin's explanations have been further developed and better stated in the years since 1918.

Great caution and discernment are also required because of doctrinal errors in the book. Here is short list, pages 1–50.

> Larkin's view of divine inspiration. Larking promotes the mechanical dictation theory of divine inspiration. The New Testament church has never held to this view of inspiration.

> Larkin's view of Christ's Second Coming: "the time of the Second Coming of Christ is the key that unlocks all 'Dispensational Truth.' The Second and Premillennial Coming of Christ is the key to the Scripture." No. The "key" to Dispensationalism and Scripture is the consistent application of the grammatical-historical hermeneutic.

> Larkin misuses a verse about Tribulation judgment, Luke 17:34–36, to explain the rapture of the New Testament church.

> Larkin views both rapture and second coming as imminent. Only the rapture is imminent. The timing of the second advent is known, being 1,260 days after the abomination of desolation.

> Larkin subscribed to the "day-age" theory of human history and eschatology. The day-age theory is the seven days of creation are supposed to symbolize seven, one thousand-year periods in human history. This theory originated with the Jewish Rabbis. Larkin accommodates it to his dispensational scheme.

> Larkin (in a hyper-dispensational manner) compartmentalizes certain parts of the Scripture, even to specific verses, as applicable to only the Jew, or only to the church. For example: Romans 8 is for the New Testament Church; Romans 11 is for the Jew; Hebrews 6:4–6 and 10:26 are for the "apostate Jewish professors of Christianity." While there is a kernel of truth here (although some bad exegesis) Larkin gives lip service to the truth that "ALL Scripture is profitable," by denying some Scripture to all believers.

> Larkin's dispensational divisions extend even to dividing the

ministry of Christ as prophet, priest and king, stating he held/will hold each office successively, from creation to the eternal age. The Scripture reveals Christ was, is, and will always be prophet, priest and king: the spirit of Christ is the spirit of prophecy; the lamb slain from the foundation of the world; his kingdom is forever.

Larkin uses Hebrews 1:1 as justification to "distinguish between the class of people God has spoken to, as to the Jews, Gentiles, or the Church." Larkin's interpretation is not what Hebrews 1:1 means. The contrast between "various times and various ways . . . by the prophets," and "in these last days . . . by his Son," indicates God began his message in or through the prophets and has completed his message by and through the person of Jesus Christ.

Larkin believed in an original creation damaged by a Luciferian rebellion, followed by a recreated earth. Much of his creation "history" depends on this interpretation. There is no Scripture support for this theory.

In the chart titled "The Relation of Jew, gentile and Church to Each Other," Larkin shows "The Church" on both sides of the crucifixion, which not only contradicts earlier assertions but is contrary to Scripture and to Dispensational beliefs.

Larkin defines a dispensation as a "moral" or "probationary" period in the world's history. This is an early attempt to define a dispensation. Ryrie's definition is better: a dispensation is "a distinguishable economy in the outworking of God's purpose."

Larkin states "God did not create the light, the word for create is not used." This fits into his pre-Adamite-creation-destroyed-by-Lucifer doctrine. As I understand Scripture, "By faith we understand that the worlds were framed by the word of God, so that the things which are seen were not made of things which are visible." Therefore, when God by divine fiat commanded "let there be light" God did more than cause light to be created ex nihilo, he caused the entire spiritual-material universe to come into existence. Then, God formed and shaped his creation as to be consistent his purpose and plans. The statement "Let there be light" is a statement of ex nihilo creation.

Larkin denies the sinless creation of Adam and the Woman, by creating a qualitative difference between innocence and righteousness. He also confuses righteousness with holiness. Adam and the Woman were in fact not innocent but knew right from wrong. They were created sinless and given righteousness and holiness to maintain their sinless state.

Larkin divides history into two "ages." He defines the "present age" as extending "from the [end of the] flood to the second stage of Christ's Second Coming, called the Revelation" by which he means Christ's return to the earth. This is contrary to every dispensational scheme of history.

Larkin names the Dispensation of Grace, the "Evil Age, as seen in the character of its civilization. After nearly 1900 years of gospel preaching the world is in a worse state, in proportion to its light, that it was in the days of Christ, and seems headed toward some greater crises. The spirit of lawlessness is in the air, and despite all efforts to quench it, it is strangely becoming unmanageable and perverse and determined to break away from all authority and law."

Larkin states, the New Testament church during the millennium "will reign during the millennium from the heavens over the earth, as Satan and his hosts do now." Larkin's point of view was that Satan is roaming around in heaven at this very moment. There is no Scripture to validate that view.

The above is a sampling of Larkin's errors in the first 50 pages of his book.

Larkin's also uses the Great Pyramid of Egypt to explain Dispensationalism. In this he greatly errs (chapter, "The Dispensational Teaching of the Great Pyramid.")

I studied this book as a seminary class. If you will accept my advice, don't buy it, read it, use it, or try to learn from it. There are better materials available.

Christian Progressivism

Copied from Brent Tysinger, as it appeared on "The Wesleyan Resistance" FB page.

"I would define Christian Progressivism as a theologically liberal movement in and around Christianity which embraces secular humanistic philosophy and rejects or redefines those portions of Christian Scripture and dogma which are seen as incompatible with the current state of, or trends in, culture.

"It has a view of God which selectively appropriates and rejects His divine attributes, focusing only on the ones it sees as positive (His grace, mercy, love, etc.), while ignoring His attributes it sees as negative (God's holiness, justice, wrath, etc.).

"Along the same lines, it is marked by a selective reading of the Bible which does not embrace those portions of holy writ which might be understood as harsh, judgmental, or morally prescriptive—unless the moral prescribed is one that fits the Christian progressivist narrative.

"As to the church, it largely abandons Christian evangelistic efforts (i. e. attempts to convert the lost), and replaces them with social justice efforts and charity, as defined by a Christian progressivist worldview. In many Christian progressivist churches, good works do not flow from salvation, they are the means to salvation.

"In Christian progressivism, the depth of Christian doctrinal tradition is largely dispensed of in favor of the newest, most esoteric, "discoveries" in theology, and biblical scholarship.

"It is further marked by a rejection of traditional, biblical, gender roles, seeking to erase any and all of the distinctive of the created male-female binary, the God-designed family unit of father, mother, and children, and the normal order of male-female sexuality. Homosexuality, transgenderism, heterosexual sexual promiscuity, and other forms of sexual deviancy and gender confusion are first tolerated, then defended, then enthusiastically embraced.

"Christian progressivism sees the sanctity of life as an issue to be marginalized because of its political implications. Christian progressivists will seek to undermine efforts of the anti-abortion/pro-life community by attempting to point out their hypocrisy if they do not have an equal passion for all other social ills which might arise. They use the phrase "pro-life vs. pro-birth" to diminish the importance of the issue. In its middle stage on the issue, Christian progressivism sees the killing of the unborn as a moral wrong, but a legal right. In its final stage, it encourages and celebrates the killing of the unborn.

"Christian progressivism also embraces Critical Theory, whereby the defining characteristic of a person is the group or groups to which they belong. People are not judged on their individual merits and moral character, but rather on their sex, race, socioeconomic position, sexuality, religion, and nation of origin. The world is viewed in terms of an oppressor / oppressed paradigm, and the biblical prohibitions against partiality are dropped in favor of classification biases. The ultimate goal is cultural revolution, where the "haves" and the "have nots" switch places.

"Finally, and maybe most strangely, Christian progressivism has a creeping hatred for all things masculine. When a woman—so long as she is progressive—becomes accomplished and powerful, strong and successful, this is noble and good. When a man exemplifies the same traits, it is toxic. In Christian progressivism, the effeminate man is the model male. He is to be passive, retiring, and in many ways, neutered and neutralized. Masculinity is not a force to be harnessed for God and for good. It is a pathogen to be excised or suppressed."

I believe it is essential Christians should understand the details of Christian progressivism. Progressive "Christianity" is to this generation what "Modernism" was to a previous generation. The major response of that generation was to produce and publish "The Fundamentals." This generation may require something similar. Certainly Christian Progressivism is an insidious infection in the Body of Christ.

Missions Philosophy

What kind of missions model is appropriate for the New Testament church? The most often used model is meeting physical needs in order to predispose people to hear the gospel. The most often met needs are food and medical. Full bellies and sound bodies are today considered essential to preaching the Word of salvation.

The "needs first, gospel second" missional philosophy began in the 1800s as a good faith attempt to emulate Jesus. But the scripture model for New Testament evangelism is Paul. Jesus met certain physical needs in response to Old Testament prophecy concerning the identification of the genuine messiah to the Hebrew people. No such prophecy or need was or is necessary to evangelize during the New Testament church age. Paul worked to support himself, not to meet the physical needs of others and then incidentally preach the gospel.

Hindsight gives perspective. The misguided "needs first, gospel second" model has slowly deteriorated over the preceding century into the current social justice movement that ignores the gospel of salvation from sin.

Paul's advice to succeeding generations was, "preach the Word," 1 Corinthians 1:17; 2 Timothy 4:2, "to preach the gospel, in the regions beyond," 2 Corinthians 10:16. Not once did Paul say heal the sick or feed the hungry, then preach the gospel. He lived and labored among the unsaved as a man of Christ who preached the Word of salvation.

We never see Paul telling Luke the physician, "Go heal someone so I can preach Christ." We never find Paul advising the local church to feed people and then preach Christ. We have forgotten the state of the body is not essential to saving faith. The thief on the cross was saved in the most awful physical state. The conflict in the sinner is in his or her soul. Meeting physical needs simply distracts and postpones meeting the spiritual need. There are no preconditions to be met in order to preach the gospel.

Don't make sinners pay for your help by making them listen to a gospel presentation. Freely give. Separate physical aid from spiritual aid. Separate the chapel from the clinic and the dining room. Help all who come and invite all to the chapel. There preach the gospel to those who come, trusting the Holy Spirit to bring to the chapel those whom he wants to hear the Word of salvation. Trust the Spirit. You are but the ambassador, he is the Savior.

Perhaps historical perspective will develop into wisdom, resulting in restoration of the Pauline missional model, both home and abroad.

Five Point Calvinism

I am a Dispensational Calvinist. Every now and then I am asked if I am a "5-point Calvinist," or a "4-point Calvinist," or "Just what kind of Calvinist are you?!?"

Those questions reflect a misapprehension about Calvinism, even among Calvinists. The misapprehension is that Calvinism is a neither more nor less than a system of soteriology (doctrine of salvation). That, of course, is not true.

Calvinism was a revival of Augustinianism (Augustine of Hippo, d. AD 430). You are affirming the Calvinistic system of doctrine if you believe in the inspiration of the Scriptures, saved by grace through faith, the sovereignty of God, the three offices of the Christ (prophet, priest, king), the deity of Jesus Christ, and the deity, personality, and ministries of the Holy Spirit (conviction, salvation, teacher, administrator of the New Testament church, etc.). Calvin is, in fact, the person who defined for the New Testament church the person and work of the Holy Spirit as we understand that doctrine today.

But I digress.

Unfortunately, the entire Calvinistic system of theology has become defined by an acronym, the TULIP (explained below), developed from the Canons of the Synod of Dort, after the Canons were published, by some who did not wholly agree with the Canons, to express a particular view of soteriology.

The Synod of Dort was a year-long examination of the soteriology of Jacobus Arminius. Both Arminius (1560–1609) and Calvin (1509–1564) were dead by the time of the Synod (1618–1619), so the theological conflict was debated by the followers of both systems of theology using the Bible and their respective writings. The decision of the Synod was published in a document known as the Canons of the Synod of Dort (available at many web sites). The Arminian view of soteriology was declared false, the biblical arguments of Calvinism were declared the true understanding of biblical soteriology.

But the TULIP does not accurately reflect Calvinistic soteriology as defined by the Canons of the Synod of Dort. Let us first examine the TULIP, albeit briefly. These may not be the definitions you have heard or read.

> T — Total Depravity. This means every aspect of human nature—physical, moral, spiritual—is negatively affected by the sin attribute in human nature, with the result an unsaved human being is always in rebellion against God. The effect of

the sin attribute on the spiritual aspect of human nature is to make the soul's faculty of spiritual perception grossly dulled, to the extent the sinner is unable to comprehend spiritual matters, but instead rejects them, and as a result is unable to initiate saving faith.

U — Unconditional Election. This means God chose (election, Ephesians 1:4; 2 Thessalonians 2:13; 1 Peter 1:2), for reasons not stated and therefore unknown, to give some human beings his gift of grace-faith-salvation (Ephesians 2:8), in order to redeem them from their sinful state of existence. And it means God chose to take no action, positive or negative, toward human beings he had not elected. God's choices were not based on any intrinsic or foreseen merit in those whom he chose to elect to salvation, for when the decree of election was given, God saw all human beings as sinners, all completely undeserving of redemption.

L — I will explain this below.

I — Irresistible Grace. This means the grace God gives to an individual sinner through his gift of grace-faith-salvation (Ephesians 2:8) will enliven the sinner's faculty of spiritual perception, so that the sinner who has received God's gift will comprehend the spiritual issues of sin, the Savior, and salvation, with the result the sinner willingly chooses to exercise saving faith in God's testimony as to the way/means of salvation. God's gift of grace and faith always results in salvation.

P — Perseverance of the Saved. This means the saved person will continue in the faith by faith all the way through life and death, when (after death) he/she will receive the grace of indefectibility. Perseverance is often mischaracterized by another acronym, OSAS, Once Saved Always Saved, resulting in silly hypothetical questions from skeptics. Perseverance is not OSAS. Perseverance is both the continuance of faith and the continued practice of the faith. God gives the grace of perseverance to the believer, and the believer uses the grace of perseverance to mold his/her life of faith to continue in the faith by means of faith all the way through life and death.

Looking now to the 5-point/4-point issue. The "L" in the TULIP represents "Limited Atonement." This is where the TULIP strays from the Canons of Dort. Limited atonement refers to Christ's act of propitiation on the cross and his subsequent resurrection. It will be helpful to define Christ's atonement-propitiation.

Propitiation. The satisfaction Christ made to God for sin by dying on the cross as the sin-bearer, 2 Corinthians 5:21; Romans 3:25; Hebrews 2:17; 1 John 2:2; 4:10, for the crime of sin committed by human beings, suffering in their place and on their behalf. Christ's propitiation fully satisfied God's holiness and justice for the crime of sin. Christ's propitiation was of infinite merit, because his Person is of infinite worth. Christ accomplished the propitiation of God for sin by enduring spiritual and physical death on the cross. Christ endured spiritual death when he was separated from fellowship with God ("My God, my God, why have you forsaken me?"), and physical death when he separated his soul from his body ("[B]owing his head, he gave up his spirit.")

The point I want to emphasize here is this: The propitiation fully satisfied God's holiness and justice for the crime of sin.

In the TULIP acronym, Christ's propitiation, the "L," has different meaning: Christ's death on the cross fully satisfied God's holiness and justice for the crimes of the elect. This is often stated in the question, "For whom, did Christ die?" The TULIP answer is, only for the elect. But that is a significant departure from the Canons of Dort on which the TULIP is based.

The divines of the Synod of Dort were of two camps on the issue of Christ's propitiation. Some believed in limited efficacy (only the elect are redeemed) and some believed in unlimited sufficiency (all the sins of the whole world are paid for). The Synod resolved this issue, as they did with all the issues, biblically. Both sides recognized the Scripture teaches both views. The Synod therefore taught both the universal sufficiency of the propitiation (atonement) and the limited effectiveness of the propitiation to save only the elect.

The Synod stated, Second Head of Doctrine, Article 3, "The death of the Son of God is the only and most perfect sacrifice and satisfaction for sin, and is of infinite worth and value, abundantly sufficient to expiate the sins of the whole world." Thus, the gospel is offered "to all persons promiscuously [indiscriminately] and without distinction." Thus, an unlimited atonement.

Article 5. That many die unsaved is not due to "any defect or insufficiency in the sacrifice offered by Christ upon the cross, but is wholly to be imputed to themselves." Thus, an unlimited atonement.

The Synod then stated, Second Head of Doctrine, Article 8, "For this was the sovereign counsel, and most gracious will and purpose of God the Father, that the quickening and saving efficacy of the most precious death of His Son should extend to all the elect, for bestowing upon them alone the gift of justifying faith, thereby to bring them infallibly to salvation: that is, it was the will of God, that Christ by the blood of the cross, whereby He confirmed the new covenant, should effectually redeem out of every people, tribe, nation, and language, all those, and those only, who were from eternity chosen to salvation and given to Him by the Father; that He should confer upon them faith, which together with all the other saving gifts of the Holy Spirit, He purchased for them by His death; should purge them from all sin, both original and actual, whether committed before or after believing; and having faithfully preserved them even to the end, should at last bring them free from every spot and blemish to the enjoyment of glory in His own presence forever." Thus, a Limited Redemption, sometimes known as Particular Redemption.

The "L" in the TULIP should have been "Limited Redemption," not "Limited Atonement. Why did those who created the TULIP (not the divines of Dort) distort the teachings of the Synod? Because of a peculiar habit of the Puritans, perpetuated by Reformed Theology.

The Puritans had a bad habit of replacing the cause with the effect. The difference between election and predestination gives an example. The Puritans, and Reformed theology, always name election as predestination. But these are different decrees of God with different effects. Definitions.

> Election. The choice of a sovereign God (Ephesians 1:4), 1) to give the gift of grace-faith-salvation to effect the salvation of some sinners (Ephesians 2:8), and 2) to take no action, positive or negative, to either effect or deny salvation to other sinners (Romans 10:13; Revelation 22:17). The decree of election includes all means necessary to effectuate salvation in those elected.

> Predestination. God's decree to conform the believer to be like Christ according to certain aspects of Christ's spiritual character and physical form (Romans 8:29–30; 1 John 3:2), and to place the believer in the legal position of God's son and heir (Ephesians 1:5, 11), so that the believer has an inheritance from God and is God's heritage.

More simply, election is a decree concerning sinners, predestination is a decree concerning the saved. Election is the cause, predestination the effect. Election-salvation is the cause of the effect predestination: to be like Christ. But the Reformed theology goes straight to the effect and names election as predestination.

So too Christ's propitiation and the sinner's redemption. Christ's propitiation completely satisfied God's justice for the crime of human sin. Then, God's justice having been satisfied, the infinite merit of the propitiation is applied by God according to his decree of election via his gift of grace-faith-salvation. Propitiation is the cause, redemption the effect. But the Reformed theology goes straight to the effect and names Christ's propitiation/atonement as redemption. Thus the confusion caused by the TULIP, and Reformed soteriology.

When the Canons of Dort are faithfully expressed, then one's soteriology must acknowledge unlimited atonement/propitiation and limited redemption. But because Reformed theology distorts the atonement/propitiation to be redemption, they reject unlimited atonement, calling it universal salvation.

Unlimited Atonement (propitiation), is not universal salvation, because the direct purpose of the atonement was not redemption but judicial satisfaction toward God for the crime of sin. More than redemption was accomplished by Christ's propitiation. Because God's justice has been satisfied, God can act otherwise than in wrath toward the world.

For an atonement (propitiation) to be redemptive it must be applied by faith to the sinner's demerit (his or her sin). That is clear from every Old Testament sacrifice for sin. On the first Passover in Egypt, the merit of the lamb's blood was sufficient for every household, but must be applied to each household to be effective for that particular household, Exodus 12:13. The blood of the sin offering, collected at the moment the animal was killed, was sufficient to atone for sin, but must be applied, Leviticus 5:5–7, to be efficient for forgiveness. The blood on the day of atonement was sufficient for all, but must be applied to the Ark of the Covenant to be efficient to forgive sins.

The direct purpose of Christ's atonement-propitiation was toward God. The merit of Christ's propitiation of God for the sins of the whole world, 1 John 2:2, is sufficient for all, so that the call of the gospel and the duty to believe may be legitimately offered to all and required of all.

The effect or result of the propitiation is the application of its merit toward sinners. That merit is specifically applied via God's gift of grace-faith-salvation (the salvation principle, "saved by grace through faith") as determined by God's decree of election, in order to effect the redemption (salvation) of those whom God has chosen to salvation. Without application there is no redemption.

The unlimited merit of Christ's propitiation could be applied to save any non-elect person: "whoever believes," as the Scripture states. God takes no action, pro or con, toward the non-elect, but leaves them in their sinful state. The non-elect are unable to initiate saving faith because unable without God's gift to overcome the rebellion and disobedience engendered by the sin attribute in human nature. If they could believe, God would act savingly toward them, but they won't believe because they always choose to disbelieve: that is the nature of the sinner.

Unlimited Atonement (Propitiation), Synod of Dort, Canon 2, Article 3, does not teach universal salvation: the merit of the propitiation must be individually applied through faith. Canon 2, Article 8, Limited Redemption, does not teach Christ died only for a particular group, but that the merit of his propitiation is applied only to the elect.

Thus: Unlimited Atonement/Propitiation, Limited/Particular Redemption.

Returning now to the original question, "What is a 5-point Calvinist?" To be a five point Calvinist one must affirm all five points of the T, U, L, I, P. A four point Calvinist is someone who does not agree with Limited Atonement/Propitiation. A 4-pointer affirms T, U, I, P.

But, and it is a BIG objection, the 5-pointer, as discussed above, rejects the statement of the Canons of Dort concerning the unlimited sufficiency of the atonement, focusing only on the redemptive effect of the propitiation, not the limitless merit of the propitiation. This is, in part, due to Reformed theology's definition of the purpose of God in the world: to redeem sinners. If God's purpose in the world is redemption, then one must devise a theology that accounts for so many sinners not being redeemed. The Reformed theology solution is to limit the sufficiency of Christ's propitiation to the redemption of the elect alone.

The 5-point Calvinist is a distortion of Scripture, and the creation of the 4-point Calvinist is a straw-man designed to support the untenable 5-point position. The dual perspective of Christ's propitiation as "sufficient for all, efficient for the elect" is the true Calvinist soteriology. This is the perspective of the Scripture. The dual perspective accounts for the universal call to believe, Romans 10:13, "whoever calls upon the name of the Lord will be saved," and "Revelation 22:17, "Whoever desires let him take of the water of life freely." The dual perspective accounts for the limited redemption effected by God's choice. Ephesians 1:4, "God chose us in Christ before the creation of the universe," and 2 Thessalonians 2:13, "God from the beginning chose you for salvation," and 1 Peter 1:2, "elect according to the foreknowledge of God the Father."

The "L" in the TULIP is too entrenched by centuries of false teaching to be changed. But if I could change it, that "L" would represent "Limited Redemption," in agreement with the Canons of the Synod of Dort.

Slavery, Exodus 21:20–21

Not too long ago, I was asked a question about Exodus 21:20–21, "Why does God allow beating a slave, as long as the slave does not die from the beating?" Let us begin with the verses. I am using the ESV.

> When a man strikes his slave, male or female, with a rod and the slave dies under his hand, he shall be avenged. But if the slave survives a day or two, he is not to be avenged, for the slave is his money.

Let me first address some translation issues. You may have noticed the ESV reads at the end of 21:21, "the slave is his money," while other versions read "he is his property." The Hebrew word the ESV translates "money" is *kesep*, "silver" [Harris, word number. "1015a," Strong's word number "3701"]. Because silver was one form of money in Old Testament times, the translation "money" is reasonable.

The translation of *kesep* as "property," is not so much a translation as an interpretation. A slave is the property of another. The slave represents a monetary investment of considerable worth, and therefore some versions thought "property" captured the meaning of the verse. However, I believe it is important to stick with the Hebrew: "he is his silver." I will explain why, below.

The words translated "male" and "female" in 21:20 are specific Hebrew words meaning a male slave and a female slave. You can see the Hebrew text (with translation) here:

https://biblehub.com/interlinear/exodus/21-20.htm. (Remember, Hebrew reads right to left.)

A more appropriate translation is,

> And if a man beats his male slave or his female slave with a rod, so that he dies by his hand, surely he shall be punished. Nevertheless, if he remains alive a day or two, he shall not be punished, for he is his silver.

Let us now look at what these verses teach. To understand we must talk about slavery in ancient times. When God gave this instruction as recorded in Exodus, slavery was already a centuries-old institution in the ancient world. The gentile world had well defined legislation on slavery. A slave was considered a piece of property, like a rake or shovel, an extension of the master's hand. Some argued a slave might not have a soul. Others argued some people were born to be slaves and others born to be masters. None of this is the biblical view.

Slavery in ancient times in the gentile world was not based on skin color, ethnicity, national origin, or any other similar reason. People captured in war could be made slaves. Some were slaves because their parents were slaves—they were born into slavery. Others sold themselves into slavery in order to pay debts. (Sadly, some sold their children into slavery for the same reason.)

Slaves were divided into two main groups: domestics and field workers. The domestics worked in the home, and field workers on farms and in the mines. A domestic could be uneducated: someone who did the laundry, cooking, cleaning, child care, etc. Some domestics were highly educated, serving as teachers, doctors, financial managers, property managers, etc.

Most nations had legislation allowing a slave to buy his or her freedom, with the master's approval. Most slaves were paid a small wage so they had spending money, which they could save to buy their freedom (again, only if the master approved). Slaves captured in war could be bought by friends and relatives out of slavery, if the master was willing to sell the slave. A master could free a slave. He could even adopt a slave as his or her adult child if he so desired. Most ancient societies consisted of three social groups: born free, freed slaves, and slaves.

Most societies also had laws regulating how a slave should be treated. Most societies disapproved if a master injured a slave or caused the death of a slave (but there was no punishment). Very few slaves were seriously injured or killed by their master because a slave was a significant money investment. During the times of Jesus and Paul, a domestic slave cost about 1500 denarii, in a day when a day's wage was a little less than a denari. (A denari was sixteen assárion. A typical day's wage was 10–12 assárion. Even a Roman Centurion only earned about 300 denari a month, a very high wage.)

When God gave the Law in Exodus, the Hebrews knew about slavery and owned slaves. God did what he usually does: he worked within the culture of the times, taking people where they are at and bringing them to where he wanted them to be. He does the same thing today. When a person is saved, the Holy Spirit knows that newly saved person has a worldview and moral values that do not agree with a Christian worldview and God's values. The Spirit does not demand instant and immediate conformance to God's values. The Spirit works to teach the new believer God's values, and slowly convicts him or her that the old values are wrong, and gives the believer time and grace to replace old values with new values. Over time we learn and grow, a step at a time, and begin to conform our Christian life to be like Christ.

Isn't the believer the servant of God? Isn't the believer's attitude to be the same as a slave? "Speak Lord, for your servant listens to hear your voice and will obey your commands." Neither in the Old Testament or the New Testament did God set out to change the world, but to change individuals, one saved person at a time. Through his saved people God influences the world.

So God did not eliminate slavery, he made slavery conform to his values. God's laws set different rules regarding the treatment of slaves. God made a slave to be a person, not property (this is why the translation "property" is wrong), with certain rights. For example, a person could be held as a slave for six years, and then must be set free, Exodus 21:2. He or she could decide to remain a slave, but that was his/her decision, not the master's. There were other rules regarding slaves. For example, Leviticus 25:39–55; Deuteronomy 5:13–15.

Slavery was a social institution that would not go away—slavery continues to exist in these present times. God acted to change the rules and make a slave a person with human rights. The point of Exodus 21:20–21, and other applicable scriptures, was to control the treatment of slaves. The slave was as "silver" to his master, meaning the slave had great value both as a person and as an investment.

That point of view served to control any possible physical abuse. But, if a slave was abused due to an evil intent by the master, and the slave died, the master had committed murder and would be justly punished—murderers were executed under the Law, see 21:12–19, 22–25. If the slave was severely injured the slave was set free, see 21:26–27. Abuse was not tolerated because a slave was not property, as in the gentile world, but was a person with human rights.

"Why does God allow beating a slave, as long as the slave does not die from the beating?" Answer: God does not set out to change all the world, but to change his people—those people with whom he has a relationship. God gave Israel laws that changed a slave from property to a person with rights (compare Ephesians 5:9). The master's treatment of his slaves must be humane and respect their human rights. If the master abused his position by failing to treat his slaves humanely, the slave was set free. If a master murdered his slave, the master was executed. No slave in Israel could be kept a slave except by his own choice, but must be set free after six years. Slavery in Israel was not the slavery of the gentile world, and was not the slavery we think of today.

An Exercise In Interpretation

A few necessary rules of interpretation.

Analogy of Scripture: the amount of revelation given prior to any particular Scripture.

Example: David (ca. 1000-970 BC) did not know what Isaiah (ca. 740-680 BC) knew, but Isaiah knew what David knew. Example: Mary and Joseph knew the revelation given in Genesis through Malachi, but did not know the revelation given in Matthew through Revelation, except for specific pieces of revelation revealed by the angel Gabriel, Matthew 1:23–23, Luke 1:30–37.

Analogy of faith: the entire revelation from Genesis through Revelation. This is what everyone could know from the second century AD forward.

Authorial intent: the primary meaning of any passage of Scripture is found in that passage of Scripture, not in earlier or later passages of Scripture.

What conclusions may we draw from the Analogy of Scripture, the Analogy of Faith, and Authorial intent?

You should not interpret any Bible passage with the knowledge gained from later revelation.

You should not reinterpret any Bible passage with the knowledge gained from later revelation.

You should not override, change, or cancel original authorial intent by using later revelation.

Any application made from any Bible passage should agree with the meaning of that particular Bible passage as interpreted or clarified by later revelation. (For example, Mathew 1:23 interprets Isaiah 7:14 to apply to Jesus of Nazareth.)

Let's put it to the test with Isaiah 7:14. "Look," said Isaiah, "this will be a sign to you, Ahaz, from YHWH. A young woman who is currently unmarried (and therefore a virgin) will marry, conceive, and bear a son, and she will name him Emmanuel."

Did Isaiah know the Holy Spirit would cause a virgin to conceive ca. 700 years after this prophecy? No. There was no previous revelation to tell him that information.

Did Isaiah know he was speaking a prophecy about a coming messiah? No. There was no previous revelation to tell him that information, and that information was not revealed in the prophecy.

Did all the people who read Isaiah from ca. 700 BC to ca. 7–5 BC know Isaiah was speaking about a coming messiah. No. There was no revelation to tell them that information, then or later.

The fact is, the Isaiah passage does not mention or refer to the coming messiah in any way, direct or implied. No one during Old Testament times applied this verse to a coming messiah-king.

What did Isaiah and others know? There are only two uses of the Hebrew "messiah" in relation to a coming messiah. Those two use are Psalm 2:2 and Daniel 9:26. All those living between Psalm 2 and Malachi knew there would be a messiah-king sometime in the future. That is what Psalm 2 teaches.

According to Psalm 2:7, this messiah-king would be a human being and live according to the Mosaic Law. In terms of the Old Testament revelation, not only in Isaiah's time, but at any time from Genesis to Malachi, the statement, Psalm 2:7, "you are my son, today I have begotten you," simply indicated a man of faith in YHWH living according to the Law." Later New Testament revelation does not expand much on that phrase. A son of God is a person (angel or human) in a faith-based relationship with God. (Genesis 6:2, 4; Job 1:6; 2:1; 38:7; Matthew 5:9; Luke 20:36; Romans 8:14, 19; Galatians 3:26.) Every Israelite who followed the Law considered him or herself a son of God. Today we know every Christian is a son of God.

Daniel 9:26 said this messiah would die. No one understood. No one accepted this verse. As Peter told Jesus, you cannot die, you are the messiah.

There are no other Old Testament scriptures that use the word "messiah" in connection with the coming messiah. In the passage of time, some Hebrews attached certain scriptures to the messiah-king prophecy. Isaiah 7:14 was not one of those Scriptures. Neither was Isaiah 53, the messiah-redeemer prophecy. For a comment on how the Hebrews *did not* understand Isaiah 53, see Acts 8:34.

In relation to the Isaiah 7:14 passage, the analogy of Scripture means Isaiah wasn't speaking of a coming messiah, because that Scripture should be interpreted according to what Isaiah and his audience knew about a coming messiah, which was not a virgin birth and not deity incarnate. They did know there would be a messiah-king, Psalm 2, a human being anointed by God to conquer the gentiles and rule the earth. But Isaiah 7:14 says nothing about the coming messiah-king. To find it there is to import it into the passage.

But in the light of the analogy of faith, which does include later revelation, we, the recipients of that later, New Testament, revelation, know from Matthew and Luke that the Holy Spirit intended the Isaiah Scripture to be applied to the messiah's birth. But not that he was deity incarnate. That is later revelation, about 30 years later, spoken by Christ himself, and learned by us from the New Testament documents written 20–30 years after the ascension.

So you and I, having received the entire revelation concerning the messiah, we can say he was God the Son incarnate in the human being Jesus of Nazareth, who (Jesus of Nazareth) was miraculously conceived by the Holy Spirit in the womb of the virgin Mary, per Isaiah 7:14.

Isaiah didn't know the messiah would be conceived in a virgin; Joseph (Matthew 1:20-23) and Mary (Luke 1:32) knew the one conceived in her virgin womb would be the messiah-king who would save his people from the gentiles, Psalm 2. They did not know Mary's son was God the Son incarnate, because no Old Testament revelation stated the coming messiah-king would be God incarnate. (Psalm 2:7 says that *only* if you reinterpret the verse with New Testament revelation.)

If we violate the rules of interpretation, then we can reinterpret some Old Testament passages to reveal a God incarnate redeemer-king born of a virgin. But if we follow the rules, we must interpret the Old Testament passages according to authorial intent and the analogy of Scripture. The Old Testament revelation said the Messiah would be a coming king, born of a woman by ordinary means, a man of faith in the Law, a man anointed by God to conquer the gentiles and rule the world.

Only those who have received the completed revelation (the analogy of faith) are able to put it all together, and say Jesus the Christ (Psalm 2:2) was the son of God (Psalm 2:7) conceived in and born of a virgin (Isaiah 7:14), to inherit the throne of his ancestor David (Luke 1:32) as the Messiah-King (Psalm 2:6–12) and Messiah-Redeemer (Isaiah 53; Daniel 9:26) and was/is God the Son incarnate, (e.g., Colossians 2:9), being the God-man.

We may make an application: no one knew Jesus of Nazareth was

God incarnate prior to his crucifixion. That revelation had not yet been given.

A hand goes up. What about 1 Peter 1:10–12?

> Concerning which salvation prophets earnestly sought to understand and searched very diligently, who prophesied concerning the grace coming to you: searching into what or what sort of season the Spirit of Christ in each was continually revealing, declaring beforehand the sufferings of Christ and the glory after these things. To whom it was revealed that not to themselves, but to us ministered these same things which have been declared unto you through the ones who preached the gospel to you by the holy Spirit sent out from heaven; toward which things angels desire to look into more closely.

The questioner says, "I think it's important to note this passage in conjunction with what you said. I think the prophets knew more than you attribute in your thesis, at least that many of their prophecies were in regard to the future. Also I think it important to note that a passage did not necessarily have to mention the term Messiah to have clear implications that the Jews were able to interpret. For example with the wise men in Matthew 2 who cite the following verse in Micah 5:2."

> But you, Bethlehem, in the land of Judah, are by no means least among the rulers of Judah; for out of you will come a ruler who will shepherd my people Israel.

(The questioner continues) "The religious leaders and scribes quoted this verse in direct relation to the Messiah also known as the King of the Jews. I think it important not to presume that simply because the passage did not directly say Messiah that the Jews were unable to notice that it was prophesying to a later time. I'm not saying they put it all together and they certainly had a wrong perception of what the Messiah would be and what He was actually coming to do. Of course the external religious oral system in that day did not help matters. But we do see here them putting some things together in Matthew 2."

My response. I am in essential agreement with you. I believe that in many instances the prophets were led by the Holy Spirit to understand their prophecies had some kind of application to an unknown future regarding the messiah. But we cannot demonstrate that understanding, because Scripture does not say.

Our belief that they understood more than they said may only rise to the level of conjecture, else we are supporting extra-biblical revelation, a dangerous proposition. We have no supporting information for that belief except the 1 Peter passage, and that is a very general statement.

For example, whatever Isaiah may or may not have understood about his chapter 53, Israel in the time of Christ did not understand, see Acts 8:34, and therefore we cannot demonstrate what Isaiah may have understood.

Moreover, Peter speaks only of the prophets, not those who read their prophecies. I have read there were some in Old Testament times (not prophets, but like you and me, students of the Bible) who conjectured a suffering messiah; but they were in a distinct minority. We cannot, we dare not, try to demonstrate more than what the scripture passage reveals, nor assume more understanding by the prophets and those who read the prophets, than what the Scripture (re: analogy of Scripture) reveals.

So while we cannot dismiss the possibility Micah understood both 5:2 and 4:8 had a yet-future messianic application, we cannot go beyond a cautious conjecture. A more immediate future is in view in 5:2, deliverance from the Assyrians by an heir of David (see, e.g., Waltke, 279).

Looking to the yet-future, The Scripture testifies the Jews knew Messiah would be born in Bethlehem, because, and only because, the Scripture names the town, Micah 5:2, as the place the ruler of Israel—in other words, the Messiah-King—would be born.

I believe both the shepherds and Jesus' parents were by the Holy Spirit given understanding, in the moment, that Micah 4:8 applied to the birth of Jesus. The parents demonstrated their understanding by going to the Tower of the flock when there was no room in Bethlehem. The shepherds demonstrated their understanding by running to find the object of the angel's announcement, to the Tower of the Flock, the cave under the Tower being the barn for the shepherds.

My point was, as interpreters using the Literal hermeneutic, we should always look for an interpretation that is within the Old Testament passage before we use our knowledge of the completed revelation to make an application, especially a messianic application.

As a simple example, Reformed soteriology will try to convince us, based on a few versus in Galatians, that Abraham hearing the promise of a son from his own body, believed on Jesus Christ, and was thereby saved by that belief. Reformed soteriology would have us believe

Abraham received extra-biblical revelation of a coming messiah (a person not yet mentioned in the progress of revelation), and some Reformed will say Abraham believed specifically in Jesus Christ. Yet, the Old Testament passage specifically says the basis of Abraham's faith was in what God revealed to him, not an extra-biblical understanding.

The Christocentric interpretive methodology of Reformed theology has distorted many a scripture. Hence, Vlach (31), "The primary meaning of any Bible passage is found in that passage. The New Testament does not reinterpret or transcend Old Testament passages in a way that overrides or cancels the original authorial intent of the Old Testament writers."

Another hand goes up. What about John 8:56?

> Abraham your father rejoiced in that he should see my day, and he saw and rejoiced.

Some read this as "Abraham saw me." No, "Abraham saw my day." He understood there would come a day in which the promises YHWH had given him would be completely fulfilled in a distant heir through the son promised to him, Isaac. That is faith (the point of Christ's statement), not the prescience a Christocentric hermeneutic demands. His faith, and that of others in the Old Testament, was in God and God's promises in a general sense until the specific revelation of our Lord, Jesus Christ.

Another hand springs into the air. This one is a bit more thoughtful.

> Just as Christ cannot be separated from the Godhead neither can faith in Christ be separated from the entirety of the God, which the Son manifested into the person of Jesus Christ to represent. Any "faith" which doesn't believe Christ specifically and trust in all the persons of the Trinity is not faith at all.

I respond. The first issue in the comment is the Trinity. The Trinity may be legitimately found in the Old Testament, if you are looking for the Trinity, based on the New Testament revelation of the Trinity.

The second issue with the comment is the Old Testament people were not required to have faith in Jesus Christ to be saved. We cannot speak of the content of saving faith in the Old Testament in the same way we speak of the content of saving faith in the New Testament.

Let us take the simplest example. What did Noah have to believe in order to be saved? Certainly not in Jesus Christ. Nor in a coming messiah not yet mentioned in Scripture. He was a righteous man when God called him to build an ark. His faith is exampled in his belief in the word from YHWH (summarizing, not quoting), "Judgment is coming. Build an ark to save yourself, your family, anyone who will have the same faith in me as you have, and all animals I will bring to you."

So also under the Law of Moses. Salvation was not accomplished by bringing a sacrifice. That was sufficient to maintain the covenant relationship, but not for salvation. Salvation during the time of the Law was accomplished by God's gift of grace through personal faith in God's testimony. That testimony was, when the proper sacrifice was brought by faith with repentance for sins the result would be forgiveness of sins. Saved by grace through faith in the content of faith given to them in their historical circumstances.

We should, we must, understand the content of saving faith according to the doctrine of progressive revelation. The Old Testament people in their generations (Adam to Noah, Noah to Abraham, etc.) responded by faith to God's current, historical testimony as to the way (means) of salvation.

Ryrie stated it best: "The basis of salvation in every age is the death [propitiation] of Christ; the requirement of salvation in every age is faith; the object of faith in every age is God; the content of faith changes in the various dispensations" (Ryrie, *Dispensationalism*, 1995, p. 115).

An Exposition of 1 Thessalonians 5:1

An extract form my book, *A Private Commentary on the Bible: Thessalonians*, published 2021.

"Now about the times and the seasons, brothers, you have no need to be written to you" (my translation).

The phrase "about the times and seasons" is literally "of the times" and "of the seasons." The phrase reflects two different Greek words about time, each with its own particular meaning. The word "times" is the Greek *chronós* [Zodhiates, *Dictionary*, "5550"], time in a quantitative sense, time as measured by the passing of successive moments. The word "seasons" is *kairós* [Zodhiates, *Dictionary*, "2540"], a fit time, a proper season. One could say it is the harvest *kairós*, but could also say the *kairós* for action is now, both uses reflecting the idea of a fit or proper time or season. Christmas a both a *kairós*, the Christmas season, and a *chronós*, from 12:01 a.m. December 25th to 11:59 p.m. December 25th.

Together these two words form an idiomatic expression indicating the character of particular circumstances of a current or yet-future event. The "times and seasons" of the rapture is just this: that particular yet-future event is always imminent—it is always the time and always the season for the at-any-moment return of Christ to the air for this church.

> The Rapture is the imminent, pretribulational, premillennial, bodily return of Christ for his church to resurrect the dead in Christ, transform the living and the resurrected to be fit for God's presence, call the transformed church up to himself in the air, and take the church to heaven, John 14:2–3; 1 Thess. 4:13–18. Christ's return for his church is not preceded by any signs but may occur at any moment, 1 John 3:2–3. [Quiggle, *Dictionary*, s. v. "Rapture".]

(Is the rapture pretribulational? See the discussion in my book, *Dispensational Eschatology*, chapter, "The Rapture of the New Testament Church.")

Paul doesn't need to remind the Thessalonians of the details of the times (*chronós*) they were experiencing nor of the quality of the times (*kairós*) they were experiencing. They understood the times they were living in because he had taught them about yet-future events, 2 Thessalonians 2:5.

Let us place this saying within the immediate context, ignoring the man-made chapter division. They understood their times were not the time of the rapture of the church that Paul had just mentioned. They understood that their times were not the time of "the day of the Lord" (the Tribulation), Their times were not the time of "unexpected destruction."

> Day of the Lord: the Tribulation period following the "last time" (the New Testament church dispensation) during which God moves in judgment and salvation. Scripture discussions of the day of the Lord usually incorporate the second advent. However, 2 Peter 3:10–13 looks to the end of the current heavens and earth, Revelation 20:11; 21:1, not the Tribulation or advent. Examples: Isaiah 2:12; 13:6, 9; Ezekiel 30:3; Joel 3:14; Obadiah 15; Zephaniah 1:7, 8, 14, 18; Malachi 4:5; Acts 2:20; 1 Thessalonians 5:2; 2 Peter 3:10. Sometimes referred to as "that day," e.g., Isaiah 19; 52:6; Ezekiel 38:19; Zechariah 14:9. Once referred to as "the time of Jacob's trouble," Jeremiah 30:7. [Quiggle, *Dispensational Eschatology*, 43.]

> Tribulation. A period of seven prophetic years (2,520 days) beginning at an unknown time after the rapture, ending at the second advent, during which the Antichrist will rule the world and demand worship, God will send terrible judgments upon the world, many will be killed, and many will be saved. [Quiggle, *Dispensational Eschatology*, 44.]

Nor should we have expected them to know the times and seasons of the rapture or the Day of the Lord.

> Acts 1:6–7 (ESV), "So when they had come together, they asked him, 'Lord, will you at this time restore the kingdom to Israel?' He said to them, 'It is not for you to know times or seasons that the Father has fixed by his own authority.'"

If, as is the case, the apostles and disciples at Christ's ascension were not told and therefore did not and could not know the times and seasons of Christ's return, then no one can know the details (*chronós*) of his return for the church or second advent, and no one can know the character (*kairós*) of his return for the church or second advent. One cannot forecast the rapture or the Tribulation by looking at the times and seasons.

But some Christians have always tried to forecast the times and seasons of the rapture and the Tribulation. Here is why they cannot.

First, the entire New Testament church age is the last time before the end times.

> 1 John 2:18, Little children, it is a last hour, and as you have heard that antichrist is coming, even now many antichrists have arisen, whereby we know that it is a last hour.

> 1 Peter 1:5, the ones [the saved] by the power of God being guarded through faith unto a salvation ready to be revealed in a last season.

> Jude 18, [the apostles] said to you, that in the last time there shall be false prophets, according to their own desires living a life of ungodliness.

In the biblical view, the last time covers the entire period of time between Christ's ascension to the Tribulation. The apostle John says "now," in his lifetime, it is a last hour.

Second, all the signs the "end times" seekers are pointing to exist throughout the "last time," which is to say, during the entire New Testament church age. False prophets? Yes, from the earliest days of the church. Earthquakes, famines, wars, rumors of wars? Check. Epidemics and pandemics? Check. Trials, persecutions, and tribulations in the world? Check. All these have been, and will continue to be, occurring during the New Testament church age until the Rapture of the church. Why?

Because Satan has no more understanding of God's timing than you or I. because the rapture could occur at any moment since Christ ascended, Satan has kept the world in constant preparedness for the Tribulation. For almost 2,000 years Satan has manipulated the religions, politics, economics, etc., of the world so that, should the rapture occur, he and the world would be ready for the Tribulation. Satan has brought man after man into a position that, should the rapture occur, he would be prepared with a would-be biblical-world-ruler—his Antichrist—for the Tribulation. Satan is doing better than many believers—to their shame!—in that he is constantly waiting, watching, and prepared for the rapture (as believers are supposed to be) so he can press forward into the Tribulation with an anti-Christian world prepared for his anti-Christian man.

What we see today is Satan prepared, as he has been prepared from the beginning of the New Testament church age. All the current events we see—that Christians have seen for almost 2,000 years, are not a "times and seasons" sign that the "end times" are upon us. They are a sign the entire New Testament church age is the last time/last hour before the latter days/Day of the Lord (Tribulation), then second advent, and Christ's millennial kingdom.

The church doesn't need, and shouldn't be looking for, someone to tell the times, signs, and seasons, because every Christian since Christ ascended has been living in the times, signs, and seasons preceding the "occurring at any moment" rapture and Tribulation.

Do I need to be more plain? The church dispensation is itself the sign that the rapture always was, is now, and always will be (until it happens), imminent; likely to occur at any moment. Every moment of the church dispensation is the sign that the church dispensation is the last times before the end-times begins, 1 Peter 1:20; 1 John 2:18; Jude 18.

Therefore, there are no specific signs to tell us when the rapture or Tribulation might be near, because every so-called sign only indicates what is already known: the rapture is imminent, the Tribulation to follow. The duty of the New Testament church is to be constantly prepared for the imminent rapture, 1 John 3:3. Live in the hope of Christ's return, not in false signs of the "end times."

Free Will

Someone asked me to give them a scripture showing free will. Out of, literally, thousands, I choose Genesis 3:6 and Mark 10:52. Both of those persons made choices. Adam chose to sin. The woman chose faith.

I continue to address this subject in every volume of *Biblical Essays* because free will is so poorly understood by the Christian community. Reformed theology has made such a mess of free will by comparing spiritually dead with physical death. The spiritual dead person absolutely does respond to spiritual things—by choosing to reject them, because he does not understand (1 Corinthians 2:14), and has no faith in God. He/she chooses to reject God, and his salvation in Jesus Christ.

Simple logic tells us every sinner has free will and exercises that free will to rebel against God. God holds every sinner responsible for his or her every act of sinning; therefore the act of sinning must arise from a choice to commit an act of sinning. Again, simple logic: without responsibility there is no accountability, and without accountability there is no liability. Without liability there can be no judgment.

Free will is not a license to think or do anything I want. Free will is the moral authority to make choices within the physical, moral, and spiritual boundaries of human nature, as further influenced by internal and external motivations and consequences.

Free will is the ability of sentient creatures to make decisions within the boundaries of the physical, mental, and spiritual aspects of their nature. These aspects are easily demonstrated.

I put my five year old grandson in the fenced in back yard. He can make any choice he is physically capable of making within the boundaries of the fence. He cannot decide to leave the yard.

You can decide to flap your arms up and down, but you cannot decide to fly by that means: a physical boundary. You can decide to tell the truth or to lie: the moral boundary permits both choices. You cannot decide to exercise saving faith because the spiritual boundary of the sin attribute prevents faith in the one you reject.

Sin is an attribute of fallen human nature, a principle or attribute of evil that motivates human beings to rebel against God, disobey his commandments, and seek a path in life apart from God. Sin has authority (dominion, rule) over the sinner, not as some invincible overlord, but as an innate part of human nature constructively working with all the other attributes of human nature to persuasively incline the will to choose an act of sinning. The evil attribute sin influences every other attribute with the inclination to sin, and in that sense sin can be said to dominate the will. The sinner freely chooses sinning because his will is of itself always inclined to choose sinning, and as being rebellious and disobedient toward God never desires to change its inclination to choose sinning to rebel against God, disobey his commandments, and seek a path in life apart from God.

The will is not neutrally suspended between good and evil, but is inclined toward one or the other by the several principles of life (the attributes of human nature) which compose the sentient nature. In the case of unsaved human beings, the will is inclined toward sin because of the principle of evil (the sin attribute) that became part of human nature following Adam's sin and propagation. Free choice or freely made choices means choices made within the context of the will as circumscribed by the nature of the sentient being (human, angelic, demonic) making the choice.

The inclination of sin is to rebel against God and disobey his commandments, thereby effectively persuading human beings to choose their path in life apart from God. In the case of the unsaved, free will means choices made within the context of the will as circumscribed by their sinful human nature. The unsaved human being is unable to overcome the influence of the sin attribute without God's gift of grace-faith-salvation.

The sinner freely chooses to sin. When we deny that free exercise of the will, we have denied God made humankind with the power to choose, the moral authority to exercise choice, the responsibility to choose rightly, and the accountability and liability for every freely made choice. When we deny the free exercise of will, we have proclaimed God made human beings soulless automatons that merely dance on the strings of some master puppeteer. We have reduced humankind to the level of instinct.

God's gift of grace-faith-salvation changes the spiritual boundaries of human nature by enlivening the soul's faculty of spiritual perception in the unsaved sinner to understand and have faith in the spiritual issues of sin, the Savior, and salvation.

Definitions.

Spiritual perception is a faculty of the soul that allows man to perceive, understand, and communicate with God. The ability of the soul to receive and understand spiritual things. A faculty of the soul through which man has communion with God. The ability of the soul to receive, understand, and appropriately apply biblical knowledge to live godly in this present world.

In the unsaved soul the sin attribute has rendered spiritual perception grossly insensitive, such that the unsaved person does not have the spiritual discernment to receive or understand the things of the Spirit of God, 1 Corinthians 2:14. In the saved soul spiritual perception has been enlivened by the work of the Holy Spirit (the soul becomes born-again).

Spiritual death means separated from a relationship with God and in the spiritual condition of active rebellion against God. Spiritual death is described as "dead in trespasses and sins," Ephesians 2:1, which is defined at 1 Corinthians 2:12–14 as a lack of the spiritual perception necessary to understand the things the Holy spirit teaches.

Salvation is the remission of sin's penalty by the application of Christ's merit by God's grace through the means of personal faith, Ephesians 1:4; 2:8; 2 Thessalonians 2:13. Salvation is obtained by grace through faith, not works, and is maintained by grace through faith, not works. In this New Testament age salvation occurs when a sinner repents of his or her sins and believes on Christ as their Savior, Acts 2:38; 3:19–20; 11:18; Romans 3:22–26; 10:9–10, 13; Galatians 3:22; 1 Peter 1:21; 1 John 3:23.

Saving faith. A sinner is not enabled to believe, he or she is convicted through the work of God the Holy Spirit of the truth of personal sin, the judicial guilt and punishment of sin, the need for salvation by faith not works, and the all-sufficiency of the propitiation made by Jesus Christ the Savior required to save his or her soul. On the basis of that conviction the sinner personally appropriates these truths to satisfy his or her spiritual need for salvation. That personal appropriation of truth to satisfy the spiritual need for salvation is the exercise of saving faith.

Simple volitional faith is the requirement for salvation. The gospel is the accusation of sin coupled with the proclamation of Christ as Savior. Saving faith does not produce a changed life. Salvation—being born-again by the Holy Spirit—produces a changed life. Let us preserve the Scripture order: saved, Ephesians 2:8, for good works, 2:10, not committed to good works, and then saved.

A Human Person

I saw a meme, and somebody—I don't know who, I can't keep track of these popular preachers (there is a "Gospel Coalition" banner in the background)—someone was saying, from a pulpit or a lectern, "We don't know what policies reduce abortion."

Preposterous. We know exactly what policy will reduce abortions: legally declare the unborn, almost born (looking at partial-birth abortions), and newly born a person. Then the 14th amendment kicks in. Then abortion legally becomes a civil rights violation; but in my view abortion would then be legally recognized as the act of pre-meditated murder that it is.

But that cure doesn't have much support, even among those naming themselves "Christians." Amazing. They will allow the unborn or newly born are alive, and human, but not a human person.

Most Christians believe God can save the soul of the unborn (thus, the unborn is a person), but don't want to take the next step required by that belief: legally declare the unborn and newly born child to be a person.

Abortionists do not believe the unborn nor the newly born are a person. Nor are these legally defined as a person—hence, the legality of abortion and infanticide (the born alive child cut apart for body parts) by the abortionist.

A person has an independent existence as an immaterial soul. A person is "a non-material substantive entity" ("substantive" means "existing independently"). In shorter terms, a person is a soul: an immaterial individualized subsistence. The soul may be envisioned as a container in which are the principle of animation which we know as "life," and the human essence that makes us a human being, and all those attributes of human nature that synergistically act to create the personality.

The soul is conceived when the body is conceived. The biblical doctrine of traducianism teaches, "that the soul, as well as the body, comes from the parents" [Harrison, *Baker's Dictionary of Theology*, s. v. "Traducianism"]. The historical doctrine of the New Testament church is the traducian view: "both the soul and the body of the individual person are propagated" [Shedd, *History of Christian Doctrine*, 2:13]. Paul's argument in Romans 5:12–14 is developed from a traducian view of human reproduction: Adam's descendants inherited his sinful human nature, cf. Genesis 5:3. The traducian view exactly corresponds to God's biological law of reproduction: each kind reproduces according to its kind. Sinful Adam and Eve reproduced their sinful kind, body and soul, in their descendants.

Exactly how a new human soul is propagated is a mystery. A solution is suggested by physical propagation. In meiosis, sperm and ovum are specialized body cells that carry one-half the normal number of human chromosomes. These cells are separate from other cells; their existence neither adds to nor subtracts from the unity of the body. At conception these halves unite to form a complete chromosomal structure, and a new human being is conceived. Since the sperm and ovum are living cells, as they merge to create a new human life the animating principle within these cells must also instill a soul, so that what is conceived is a human person, body and soul. "Life" is an element of the soul. "Life" is present in every living cell. Sperm and ovum must contain the necessary elements of a soul needed to form an individualized soul. Because the formation of an individualized soul is a process of the spirit domain it cannot be fully understood . . .. The animating principle in sperm and ovum gives the newly conceived person life, a soul. In the final analysis, however, the propagation of the soul is a process of the immaterial, spirit domain, and therefore knowable and understandable only if revealed by God. God does not tell us about the process, only the method: each kind reproduces according to its kind. Therefore each human soul reproduces a human soul. [Quiggle, *Adam and Eve, A Biography and Theology*, 43–44]. Because the soul doing the reproducing is a person, then the soul that has been produced must be a person.

The soul is conceived when the body is conceived. The soul is the person. The unborn and the newly born are persons. The developing zygote-embryo-fetus is humanity reproducing itself: the human soul, that spirit substance or essence God created when he breathed into Adam the breath of life and Adam became a living human being, Genesis 2:7. Adam and Eve propagated soul as well as body (the doctrine of traducianism). The animating principle in the gametes gives life, and therefore gives a soul (because life is in the soul) to the zygote. The soul—the person—that was propagated in Cain, Abel, Seth, and "sons and daughters," was generated from their parent's soul—it had no other source.

The human body and soul continues to be propagated by parents to their children. Therefore, no matter how rudimentary, how elementary, how incomplex, or how instinctual the human soul may be, Adam's children are personal human beings—persons—beginning at the moment of conception. The pregnant woman is not going to be a mother, she is a mother, responsible to preserve and protect the human person developing inside her body.

Without a human soul animating the body, even when the body is only one fertilized cell, the cell would not be a human person. That is an impossible condition. God's law of biological reproduction is that each kind of being reproduces the same kind of being, and no other kind. Therefore, beginning at conception, the person conceived through the propagation of two human persons is him or herself a human person, body and soul.

The soul is the person: the individual personality with its characteristics and attributes. God created the immaterial substance "humanity" in his image and likeness. Each soul is individualized humanity. The soul contains all the fundamental principles that are necessary to govern biological life, instinctual actions, and sentient behavior.

But, says the abortionist, as he or she kills the unborn and sacrifices the newly born for body parts, these blobs of tissue are not sentient, therefore not a person. The basic meaning of sentience is "self-aware." In the human person, sentience is a quality of self-perception that only God, humankind, and angels possess. The unborn and the newly born resemble a human person, but acts by instinct to stimuli, and sentience is neither observable nor provable. Are they not sentient?

Yes, both unborn and newly born are a sentient being, a person, despite not exhibiting the observable qualities of sentience that identify a living being as a human person. Let us reason from the lesser to the greater. "No one supposes reason [the intellectual faculty] to be the result of education, or the effect of circumstances, merely because its operations cannot be detected from the first moment of existence. The uniformity of its manifestation under all circumstances, is regarded as sufficient proof that it is an attribute of our nature" [C. Hodge, quoted in Noll, *Charles Hodge, The Way of Life*, 80].

Body and soul develop together, side-by-side as it were, from rudimentary to fully mature in body and soul. Thus sentience, which manifests as the human person develops, is a part of human nature from conception, as created by God in the likeness and image of his own sentience. Otherwise, we have permission to kill, as we would an animal, the unborn, the newly born, the small child, the mentally undeveloped, and the elderly with dementia.

That march of legalized death from unborn to newly born to any others not demonstrating a required measure of sentience is the logical progression from abortion. When abortion was legalized the newly developed fetus could be killed. Now the child may be killed during the birthing process, and the newly born are sacrificed—infanticide—for body parts.

No one can rationally argue the developing zygote-embryo-fetus of a human person is not sentient or human because its sentience or humanity cannot be detected from the first moment of existence. But the death cult that demands the sacrifice of humanity's children has from ancient times never been rational.

For the genuine Christian the argument from theology must be conclusive in favor of life, not murder. God is able to save any human person at any stage of existence, from the just conceived to the more developed sinner, proving the unborn and newly born are human persons. As stated above, all of Adam's descendants are human persons beginning at conception, regardless of the rudimentary state of body and soul. Without a human soul animating the body, even when the body is only one fertilized cell, the cell would not be human. That is an impossible condition because of God's law of biological reproduction, each kind reproduces its own kind.

This is the next battleground in the war against abortion and infanticide: to legally declare the unborn and newly born as persons, therefore entitled to all the protections the law applies to persons.

Counting the Years in the Ancient World.

Here is a fun subject I really enjoy. Have you ever thought about how the ancient world calculated the passing of time? The issue is ever so much more complicated than you ever thought.

In the ancient world there was no standard calendar as we think of a calendar today (our calendar began in AD 525). The issue is much more complex than I can explain here—I will give a brief outline of the facts—and I refer you to this book: David Ewing Duncan, *Calendar, Humanity's Epic Struggle to Determine a True and Accurate Year.*

Some countries in the ancient world used the solar year—the time it takes the earth to make one orbit around the sun—which is approximately 365.25 days (365.2564 days as measured against a fixed point). Most countries used a lunar year—the time it takes for twelve cycles of the moon; one cycle is one new moon to the next new moon —which is (approximately) 354 days.

To make this more complicated, the ancients using a lunar year knew it did not match the solar year, because the seasons (spring, summer, etc.) would drift against their lunar calendar, and so sometimes they were growing crops but their calendar said it was winter. So from time to time (every few years) they added a few days, weeks, sometimes a whole month, to realign their lunar calendar with the solar calendar. This is what ancient Israel did.

Years were numbered from some significant event. For example, In Egypt, years were counted from the accession of a new Pharaoh. So there would be Year One when a Pharaoh came to power, and when he died the count started over with Year One of the next Pharaoh. The Romans counted the years from the founding of the city of Rome. Jesus Christ was born between 747–749 AUC. The acronym AUC represents Anno Urbis Conditae, which means "in the year of the city" of Rome. Jesus was born about Year thirty (or so) of King Herod the Great, King of Israel.

The way of numbering years by BC (Bello Christo, Before Christ) and AD (Anno Domini, In the Year of our Lord) didn't take place until the year we think of as AD 525. When the BC/AD system was adopted, the year in which it was adopted had to be adjusted by eleven days to match the solar year. (The year had already been adjusted eighty days by Julius Caesar in 46 BC.) Our current calendar was slowly adopted by most nations over the next 1300 years (the last nation adopted the modern calendar in 1921). Today, the world's calendar and the year are counted by the atomic clock in the USA, and the time of day is known known as Coordinated Universal Time (UTC).

To complicate biblical matters, the kings in Israel counted their regnal (ruling) years by two different methods. When Israel was divided into two kingdoms, Judah and Israel-Samaria, Judah's civil year began in the Fall, Israel-Samaria's civil year began in the Spring. The Kings of Israel-Samaria began counting their years as ruler the very day they became kings: the non-accession year method. The kings of Judah began counting their years as ruler on the first day of a new civil year after they became king: the accession year method.

Quiggle & Hollingsworth, *Old and New Testament Chronology*, Appendix Fifteen, have an easy explanation of what are known as the "accession" and "non-accession" ways of counting a king's rule. For a more complete and complex explanation see, Edwin R. Thiele, *The Mysterious Numbers of the Hebrew Kings*.

Don't let anyone tell you we know the exact date some ancient event took place. Historians can get close, but no one knows exactly. For example, we know Christ died on Nisan 15, Jewish calendar. That is the only fixed date for Christ's death, because Passover was always Nisan 14. But every Jewish month began with the first sighting of the waxing crescent moon, and then the priests calculated backwards a day or two to approximate the date of the new moon, when the month actually began (a new moon cannot be seen), and this sighting was especially iffy when the weather was cloudy. So we really don't know when Nisan began in relation to the modern calendar, which means we really don't know when the 15th of Nisan corresponds with the modern calendar. Today we just mathematically calculate the new moon in the appropriate year and month and add 15 days. But what year? The year was probably 787/788 AUC. We think that corresponds to April 4, AD 33 (or maybe AD 30, 31, 32, 34). The issue is really very complicated.

The monk who developed the BC/AD system of marking time was not quite accurate—but it wasn't his fault, he just didn't have all the data. He based his calendar on the birth of Christ. He decided Jesus was born a few months before Herod died in April 754 AUC. However, centuries later it was discovered Herod died in 750 AUC, which we believe corresponds to 4 BC (a few days after the new year began in Nissan/March), so Jesus was born in 5 BC, or perhaps 6 or 7 BC. By the time historians knew Herod had died in 750, not 754, every historical event from past to present was arranged according to the monk's BC/AD calendar. Rather than change every historical date, historians adjusted the date of Christ's birth to somewhere between 7–4 BC. The most likely date, using the evidence Luke provides, is late August/early September, 5 BC (see my book, *God Became Incarnate*, chapter Two, "His Virgin Birth.")

Covenantalism and Dispensationalism.

There are five essential differences between Covenantalism (aka: Reformed) and Dispensationalism.

1. Dispensationalism consistently applies the Literal hermeneutic to all scriptures and doctrines. Covenantalism (aka Reformed) uses an allegorical hermeneutic for some scriptures and the doctrines of eschatology, ecclesiology (where it interfaces with eschatology), and soteriology.

2. Dispensationalism teaches the revelation of God to the world is progressive throughout history, as exampled by Isaiah 28:10, "here a little, there a little," culminating in the 66 books of Scripture. Covenantalism (aka Reformed) also teaches progressive revelation, except in Old Testament soteriology, where it teaches an extra-biblical (not in the Bible) revelation of Christ coming as necessary for Old Testament salvation.

3. As a result of its Literal hermeneutic, Dispensationalism teaches the content of faith necessary for salvation from Adam to the end of the ages is always saved by grace through faith in God and God's historically current testimony as given in progressive revelation of truth. As a result of its allegorical hermeneutic, Covenantalism (aka Reformed) teaches salvation pre-Adam's sin was by works, and post-Adam's sin salvation is saved by grace through faith in Christ coming (OT, extra-biblically revealed) or Christ present (NT).

4. As a result of its hermeneutic, Dispensationalism teaches the New Testament church is a separate people group from national Ethnic Israel in the purpose, plans, and processes of God in the world. The New Testament church and national ethnic Israel have separate but complementary destinies. As a result of its hermeneutic, Covenantalism (aka Reformed) has historically taught the New Testament church has replaced or superseded national ethnic Israel in the purpose, plans, and processes of God in the world, and has more recently taught the New Testament church is the continuation of national ethnic Israel in the purpose, plans, and processes of God in the world. Either teaching says the New Testament church is the new Israel.

5. Dispensationalism teaches the purpose of God in the world is his glory. Covenantalism (aka Reformed), while not ignoring God's glory, teaches the purpose of God in the world is the salvation of sinners.

See my book, *Understanding Dispensational Theology*.

The Covenantalism/Reformed positions in 2 and 3 were drawn directly from three generations of CT theologians. C. Hodge, "Systematic," 2:371–372; L. Berkhoff, "Systematic," 262, 272. 277, through 300; W. Grudem, "Systematic," 519, 539.

I am not the only person to see "extrabiblical revelation" in Covenantalism/Reformed soteriology. The allegorical hermeneutic in Covenantalism/Reformed is well known and professed by all Covenantalism/Reformed theologians.

See Waldron, *MacArthur's Millennial Manifesto*, pp. 6–7, for the current Covenantalism/Reformed definition of the New Testament church as a new Israel.

To be Covenantal/Reformed is by definition to apply an allegorical hermeneutic to some scriptures, to be Amillennial or Postmillennial, and to see God's promises to Israel taken from Israel and given to the New Testament church (even if, as some Covenantal/Reformed CT always have, and some still do, see some kind of redemptive future for Israel as a nation); and it is to group all of God's purposes in the world under the category of the covenant of grace.

Dispensationalism is not New

To believe Dispensationalism is a new doctrine developed by Darby and Scofield in the late 1800s, is inexcusable ignorance in the light of the publications demonstrating Dispensationalism has a documented history beginning with the early church fathers.

You may not agree with what Dispensationalism teaches, but don't make the mistake of thinking it is neither ancient nor biblical.

The documented history of dispensationalism begins with the early church fathers. See James C. Morris, *Ancient Dispensational Truth, Refuting the Myth Dispensationalism is New*. Summarizing from that book, here are a few of the church fathers whom Mr. Morris quotes.

> Justin Martyr (AD 100–165), Dialogue with Trypho, chapter 80, 81; The First Apology of Justin Martyr, chapter 52. (Literal hermeneutic, millennium, millennial temple)

> Clement (AD 35–88), The First Epistle of Clement, chapter 26. (Literal hermeneutic)

> Irenaeus (AD 130–ca. 202), Against Heresies, 3.10.4; 4.20.7; 5.32.1; 3.11.8.; 5.29.1; 5.30.4; chapter 35. (Literal hermeneutic, dispensations, rapture, Antichrist and Tribulation, restoration of national ethnic Israel, millennium)

> Tertullian (AD 155–220), The Five Books Against Marcion, 3.25; 4.1; 5.9; On the Resurrection of the Flesh, chapters 17, 20. (Literal hermeneutic, dispensations, millennium)

> Augustine (AD 354–430), On Christian Doctrine; To Marcellinus, CXXXVIII, 5, 7, 8; City of God, 20:229. (Literal hermeneutic, dispensations)

> Cyprian (d. AD 258), The Treatises of Cyprian, treatise XII. (Mosaic and New Testament dispensations)

> Papias (AD 60–163), in Eusebius, Ecclesiastical History, 3.39. (millennium)

> Lactantius (AD 240–330), Divine Institutes, 7.24; 7.26. (Revelation 20:1–3 literal, millennium, new heavens and earth following the millennium)

> Pseudo-Ephraim (ca. 373). On the Last Times, the Antichrist, and the End of the World, paragraph 2. (rapture, tribulation)

The writings of the early church fathers are also available at ccel.org.

About the time of Augustine, the New Testament church lost faith in the imminent return of Christ, and the basic truths of Dispensationalism began to disappear. New theologies were developed to explain why Christ had not yet appeared, and when he would appear. A dispensational view of the Bible did not agree with the new views of Christ's return. Augustine (d AD 430), developed Postmillennialism, and then Amillennialism. The premillennialism of the early church fathers was abandoned.

But as Morris abundantly proves, premillennialism was the doctrine of the early church.

See also William C. Watson, *Dispensationalism Before Darby, Seventeenth-Century and Eighteenth-Century English Apocalypticism.* That's two centuries before Darby and Scofield.

Here are a few resources proving Dispensationalism is a biblical theology.

Charles C. Ryrie, *Dispensationalism.*

Michael J. Vlach, *Dispensationalism, Essential Beliefs and Common Myths.*

James D. Quiggle, *Understanding Dispensational Theology.*

Dispensationalism is not new, and it is biblical. Don't continue in ignorance, educate yourself on the subject.

Dispensationalism is the True Reformed Theology

Today, October 31, is the day many Christians celebrate the beginning of the Reformation: Martin Luther nailed his "95 Theses" against Popery to the front door of the Wittenberg church.

Dispensationalists also celebrate this day, and that Reformation Luther began, which Calvin and others completed.

Many of the Reformed persuasion believe Dispensationalism is a heresy. In this, they are like the anti-Calvinist who condemns an entire theological system for one doctrine—the anti-Calvinist really doesn't understand Calvinism or Calvinistic soteriology, they just know it's bad.

So, too, the Reformed reaction to Dispensational Theology. Most don't understand it, they just know it's bad.

So, on this Reformation Day, let's check off the Reformed doctrines Dispensationalism believes, practices, and preaches.

The Trinity? Check.

The deity of Christ and the Holy Spirit? Check.

The personality of the Holy Spirit? Check.

Saved by grace through faith? Check.

Verbal, plenary inspiration? Check.

The depravity of human beings because of sin? Check.

Election? Check.

Predestination? Check.

Christ propitiated God for sin? Check.

Justification and sanctification through imputation of Christ's righteousness? Check.

Experiential Sanctification? Check.

An eternal heaven and an eternal hell? Check.

So, just where is Dispensationalism supposedly "heretical?"

Hermeneutics. Reformed theology uses the Literal hermeneutic— understanding Scripture through the plain and normal meaning of the words and language—on almost every scripture and almost every doctrine, but not for their eschatology and ecclesiology: the last times and the New Testament church, respectively. Dispensationalism applies the Literal hermeneutic without exception: to every Scripture and to every doctrine.

Ecclesiology. Reformed theology believes God abandoned national ethnic Israel, and his promises and covenants to that people, when Christ was crucified, and made the New Testament church the new Israel (or as newer Reformed put it, the continuation of Israel). Dispensationalism believes God did not abandon national ethnic Israel; that the New Testament church is a separate people group in God's purpose and plans; that Israel and the New Testament church have separate but intertwined destinies.

Eschatology. Reformed theology interprets eschatology using an allegorical hermeneutic—the interpreter's imagination decides what Scripture means—that denies the literal fulfillment of yet-future events: no rapture, no tribulation, no Davidic Kingdom as promised to Israel, and a general judgment for both believers and unbelievers. Dispensationalism applies the Literal hermeneutic to all eschatological scriptures: there is a yet-future rapture, Tribulation, Davidic Kingdom, and a judgment for the unsaved to punish them eternally for their no-faith and evil works. Dispensationalism believes the saved are judged at the rapture for rewards for good works, not for salvation.

Soteriology. Despite over 110 years' worth of Dispensationalists saying, "salvation is by grace through faith, is a free gift, and is wholly without works," Dispensationalists are still accused to teaching a different way of salvation. [C. I. Scofield, *Scofield Reference Bible*, 1909, note, summary of salvation, at Romans 1:16.] Ryrie, *Dispensationalism* (1966, 1995) quotes several prominent Dispensationalists that salvation is always by grace through faith.

What are the differences between how Dispensationalism views salvation and how Reformed theology views salvation.

Both Dispensationalism and Reformed Theology (post-Adam's sin), agree salvation is by God's gift of grace-faith-salvation (Ephesians 2:8). Both theologies agree the basis of salvation was, is, and always will be the propitiation made by Christ. Both agree the requirement of salvation in every age is faith. Where Reformed-Covenant soteriology and Dispensational soteriology disagree is the object of saving faith and the content of saving faith.

> Dispensational soteriology: the object of faith in every age is God.
>
> Reformed soteriology: the object of faith in every age is Christ.
>
> Dispensational soteriology: the content of faith changes in the various dispensations.

Reformed soteriology: the content of faith is always Christ, either coming (Old Testament), or arrived (New Testament).

The Reformed theologian believes the object of saving faith is always Christ coming or Christ arrived. He believes the Old Testament sinners were saved by believing in a coming Messiah; some will say because they believed in the person Jesus Christ. The reader may check this for him or herself.

Charles Hodge, *Systematic Theology*, (Grand Rapids, MI: Eerdmans Publishing, 1981) 2:371–373.

Louis Berkhoff, *Systematic Theology* (London: Banner of Truth Trust, 1959), 262–300

Wayne Grudem, *Systematic Theology*. (Grand Rapids, MI: Zondervan, 1994), 117, 519.

Hodge makes clear saving faith in the Old Testament was based on extra-biblical revelation. Quoting Romans 4:20–21 he wrote, "The Apostle [Paul] proves that the specific promise which was the object of the faith of the patriarch [Abraham] was the promise of redemption through Christ." Does this agree with Scripture? What was the promise God gave Abraham?

Promise one, "A person who will come from your own body will be your heir."

Promise Two, "Look now toward heaven, and count the stars is you are able to number them. So shall your descendants be."

How did Abraham come to believe in a coming Messiah from those promises? By means of extra-biblical (not in the Bible) revelation from the Holy Spirit.

Hodge meant was that every saved person in the Old Testament understood that certain prophecies—even those (e.g., Genesis 3:15; 15:4, 5, 18) having no stated relation to a coming Redeemer or Messiah—were understood as the promise of redemption through a coming Redeemer or Messiah. Hodge also meant that every divine illustration of the Person and work of Christ (the Old Testament types) was fully understood by those saved in the Old Testament as the promise of redemption through a coming Redeemer or Messiah.

Am I misstating Hodge's belief? "It was not mere faith or trust in God, or simple piety, which was required, but faith in the promised Redeemer, or faith in the promise of redemption through the Messiah"

[Hodge, 2:371–372].

But Hodge cannot point to an Old Testament Scripture that clearly taught the Old Testament sinner to place his or her saving faith in Jesus Christ the Redeemer. Hodge simply states as though a fact that the Old Testament sinner had to have faith in Jesus the Christ. Not "mere faith or trust in God," but faith in Jesus, "the promised Redeemer, or faith in the promise of redemption through the Messiah."

So also other Reformed theologians. Grudem, *Systematic Theology*, 519, stated, "The *condition* (or requirement) of participation in the covenant [of grace] is *faith* in the work of Christ the Redeemer (Rom. 1:17; 5:1, et al.). This requirement of faith in the redemptive work of the Messiah was also the condition of obtaining the blessings of the covenant in the Old Testament, as Paul clearly demonstrates through the examples of Abraham and David (Rom 4:1–15). They, like other Old Testament believers, were saved by looking forward to the work of the Messiah who was to come and putting their faith in him."

Grudem unequivocally states the Old Testament believers understood the redemptive work of a specific person yet-to-come and placed saving faith in him. In order for an Old Testament sinner to gain participation in the Covenant of Grace—to be saved—he or she must place their faith in Christ the Redeemer—faith in Jesus Christ, as he later makes clear. They must "look forward to the work of the Messiah," Jesus Christ.

This kind of faith in a personal Redeemer was impossible to the Old Testament sinner, unless the Holy Spirit said something to each that the Spirit did not record in the inspired written scriptures. Without that extrabiblical revelation, none of the Old Testament saints prior to Christ's appearing could have understood they were to place their "faith in the work of Christ the Redeemer."

That, is the Reformed doctrine of soteriology.

That is not the Dispensational doctrine of soteriology. Dallas Theological Seminary stated, "We believe . . . that the principle of faith was prevalent in the lives of all the Old Testament saints. However, it was impossible that they should have had as the conscious object of their faith the incarnate, crucified Son, the Lamb of God (John 1:29), and it is evident that they did not comprehend as we do that the sacrifices depicted the person and work of Christ (Dallas Seminary, Doctrinal Statement, Article V)."

The Dispensational doctrine of soteriology was succinctly stated by Ryrie [*Dispensationalism*, 1996, p. 115].

> The basis of salvation in every age is the death [i.e., propitiation] of Christ; the requirement of salvation in every age is faith; the object of faith in every age is God; the content of faith changes in the various dispensations.

The Dispensationalist hold to a doctrine first stated by the Reformers, the doctrine of progressive revelation. God did not reveal everything all at once but "here a little, there a little," as Isaiah said, 28:10, 13. Stated a little differently, Dispensationalism demands "the Old Testament be taken on its own terms rather than reinterpreted in the light of the New Testament" [Vlach, 30].

Dispensationalism responds to progressive revelation with the term "content of faith." The "content of faith" is God's historical testimony at any point in the history of salvation. A few examples.

> Enoch's content of faith was to live the manner of life prescribed by God: he believed and walked with God.

> Noah's content of faith was judgment is coming, get into the ark to be saved.

> Abraham's content of faith was the promise of the land to him and his descendants through an heir from his own body.

> The content of faith under the Mosaic Law was faith in God and his testimony that repentance of sin with confession of sin and a proper sacrifice for sin would result in forgiveness of sin.

> In these New Testament times, the content of faith is God's testimony that salvation is in Jesus Christ alone, Acts 2:38; 3:19–20; 11:18; Romans 3:22–26; 10:9–10, 13; Galatians 3:22; 1 Peter 1:21; 1 John 3:23.

In Dispensationalism, the object of saving faith is God through the content of faith he has delivered at any one point in the history of humankind. Dispensational soteriology teaches the means of salvation is the same for everyone, beginning with Adam: saved by grace through faith by the merit of Christ's propitiation. Dispensational soteriology recognizes that salvation is always accessed by faith. Dispensational soteriology believes God is the proper object for saving faith, because it is God who has given testimony in his Word as to the content of that faith. The content of faith changes in the various dispensations

With this sole exception—the content of faith concept which

accurately reflects the progress of revelation in the Scripture—Dispensational soteriology is the same as Reformed soteriology: saved by grace through faith by the merit of Christ's propitiation of God for sin. Dispensational soteriology does not depend on extrabiblical revelation, but precisely on the Literal interpretation of the inspired revelation God gave the sinner in his Word within the sinner's specific historical-cultural context.

Through the Literal hermeneutic. Dispensationalism is more true to the Scripture revelation that Reformed theology.

Bottom line: Dispensationalism is Reformed, it is the genuine biblical Reformed theology, because only Dispensationalism consistently understands all of Scripture, every Scripture, using the Literal hermeneutic.

There are many books by Dispensationalists explaining Dispensational theology as a whole (Charles Ryrie; Michael Vlach; James D. Quiggle), Dispensational eschatology (J. Dwight Pentecost; Thomas Ice; John Walvoord; James D. Quiggle), and Dispensational hermeneutics (Henry Virkler; James D. Quiggle).

There are also books showing Dispensationalism is the ancient doctrine of the New Testament church (William Watson; James Morris) Buy some.

Discover for yourself Dispensationalism is not a heresy.

Is it Possible for a Christian to Lose Salvation?

The short answer is "No." The limitless merit of Jesus Christ secures the believer's salvation for eternity. Although one might point to a verse here or there that seems to say "Yes," there are clear, unambiguous scriptures that teach genuine salvation is eternally secure. The New Testament presents five witnesses testifying salvation is eternal: 1) the foundation of eternal salvation; 2) the seal of eternal salvation; 3) the assurance of eternal salvation; 4) perseverance in eternal salvation; 5) the character of eternal salvation.

The Foundation of Eternal Salvation.

The propitiation made by Jesus Christ through his death on the cross and his subsequent resurrection is the foundation of eternal salvation. At 1 John 2:2 the apostle John wrote, Jesus "is the propitiation for our sins." John does not set any limitations. "Our sins" refers to every sin a believer has or may commit, past, present, and future. When "God chose us in Christ," Ephesians 1:4, it was "before the foundation of the world," so God had in view all sins a believer would commit. Jesus Christ propitiated (satisfied) God for our every sin.

Sin is the failure to conform fully to God's image and likeness, and sins are actions in thought, word, or deed that rebel against God through disobedience to his commandments. Jesus propitiated God for our sins. The word "propitiate" has the same meaning as the Old Testament "atone," and the English word "expiate."

A good synonym for propitiate is "satisfied." God's holiness and justice require satisfaction for the crime of sin. The penalty for the crime of sin is physical death and spiritual death (the separation of the soul from God). At 2 Corinthians 5:21, Paul tells us God made Jesus Christ "to be sin for us." God imputed the sins of the world to Jesus, 1 John 2:2, when Jesus was on the cross. Jesus suffered God's wrath for our sins.

The result was Jesus made a full satisfaction to God for the crime of sin through his death, Romans 3:23–25, making propitiation for the sins of his people, Hebrews 2:17, because God loved us and sent his Son to be the propitiation for our sins, 1 John 4:10. Through his suffering on the cross Jesus fully satisfied God for all the sins you and I have committed or might yet commit.

Propitiation, then, is the complete satisfaction of God's holiness and justice that Christ made to God by enduring spiritual and physical death on the cross for the crime of sin committed by human beings, suffering in their place and on their behalf. When by faith a sinner applies the limitless merit of Christ's propitiation to their sins, God is completely satisfied the debt for all his/her sins was paid, and forgives all those sins past, present, and future.

On the cross, in order to make the propitiation for sins, Christ endured the penalty for sin: spiritual and physical death. Christ endured spiritual death when he was separated from fellowship with God ("My God, my God, why have you forsaken me?" Matthew 27:46), and physical death when he separated his soul from his body ("Bowing his head, he gave up his spirit," John 19:30).

We can understand that Christ paid the full debt for sins in three actions.

> One, before his death he cried out, "Father, into your hands I commit my spirit," indicating he was no longer separated from God. He had paid in full the sin debt imputed to him.

> Two, when the propitiation was completed Christ cried out "It is finished," John 19:30. The particular word he used, *teléō*, was a cry of victory, in a verb tense (perfect) indicating his work of propitiation was brought to completion. No other work is needed to satisfy God for the crime of our sin.

> Three, Christ resurrected from the dead. Each member of the Trinity participated in Christ's resurrection (Romans 6:4; John 10:17; Romans 8:11), showing that Christ had made a complete satisfaction for sin. As Paul stated, 1 Corinthians 15:17, "If Christ is not risen, your faith is futile" (vain, empty).

Because the propitiation completely satisfied God for sins past, present, and future a believer's salvation is eternally secure. "There is no condemnation to those who are in Christ Jesus . . . "Who is able to bring a charge against God's elect? It is God who justifies . . . it is Christ who died . . . and is risen . . . and makes intercession for us," Romans 8:1, 33–34, compare 1 John 2:1; Hebrews 7:25.

The writer of Hebrews says Jesus established a new covenant with God, 8:6, through his death. The conditions of the covenant are that Jesus would offering one sacrifice effective for all for sins, forever, 10:12, and God would make a commitment with every person saved through faith in Christ: "their sins and their lawless deeds I will remember no more," 10:17. Jesus "offered one sacrifice for sins forever," and then "sat down at the right hand of God," because his work of propitiation was completed. Because of Jesus' sacrifice on the cross there is no more sacrifice for sin forever, Hebrews 10:12, 18. Jesus Christ propitiated God for every sin.

At John 10:27–30 Jesus said he knew who his saved people were (his "sheep"); that he gives his saved people eternal life; that his saved people will never perish (because they have eternal life); that no person and no thing can remove a genuinely saved person from Christ's hand or the Father's hand; compare Paul at 8:38–39, Peter at 1 Peter 1:5, and John at 1 John 5:11–13. His saved people will never perish forever, and they are eternally secure forever, because what Christ did on the cross fully satisfied God for the sins of every person who believes on Christ as Savior.

In an illustration, the finite demerit of the believer's sins—past, present, future—are like a teardrop in the ocean of Christ's limitless merit. Once a person is saved, he/she cannot lose their salvation, because the infinite, limitless merit of Christ secures salvation for every person who believes on him as Savior. There is no sin a believer might commit that would cause loss of salvation, because Jesus propitiated God for every sin.

The Seal of Eternal Salvation.

Sealing the believer in his/her salvation is an act of God the Holy Spirit occurring the moment a sinner believes on Christ as his/her personal savior. The apostle Paul wrote at Ephesians 1:13, "having believed, you were sealed by the Holy Spirit of promise." The "promise" is a reference to the advent and indwelling of the Holy Spirit prophesied in the Old Testament (Jeremiah 31:33; Joel 2:28–32), announced by Christ (John 14:16–18, 26; 16:7, 13–15; Acts 1:4–5, 8) and fulfilled after his ascension (Acts 2:17–18; 8:17; 10:44).

"Sealing" is an allusion to the method used to secure ancient documents. When a document was completed, it would be rolled up (a scroll), and a blob of wax was used to affix the end of the scroll to the rolled up body. A mark or image was impressed into the wax before it cooled. The purpose of the seal was to secure the document against damage or tampering. The purpose of the image impressed into the wax was to certify the authenticity of the document. In today's terms, the seal was the mark of a notary, or a witness, authenticating the document and its contents. Thus, sealing indicates a completed act and means security, authenticity, genuineness, identification, and ownership.

The sealing accomplished by the Holy Spirit is God's witness that the believer is genuinely and eternally saved. The seal of the Spirit keeps the believer secure in his or her salvation, for no one can break God's seal. The seal is impressed with God's mark—the image of Christ the Savior—indicating the believer is God's property. Sealing confirms the believer's faith from the moment of salvation forward into eternity future.

The Assurance of Eternal Salvation.

A believer can know for certain that he/she is eternally saved. The apostle John stated, "I have written to you who believe in the name of the Son of God, that you may know that you have eternal life," 1 John 5:13. Jesus said he has given his saved people eternal life and 1) they shall never perish, and 2) no person or thing is able to take the believer out of Christ's hand or the Father's hand (John 10:27–29). The apostle Paul wrote that "there was no more condemnation to those who are in Christ Jesus," Romans 8:1, and that no person and no thing "shall separate us from the love of God which is in Christ Jesus our Lord," Romans 8:31–39. Because the believer is no longer subject to condemnation, and because nothing can separate the believer from Christ, a believer in Christ as his/her Savior cannot lose their salvation.

Perseverance in Eternal Salvation.

God gives every genuine believer the grace to continue in the faith by faith, and the believer uses that grace to continue in faith, righteousness, and holiness. Jesus said, John 10:28 "I give them [his saved people] eternal life, and they shall never perish." Paul wrote, Philippians 1:6 "He [God] who has begun a good work in you will complete it until the day of Jesus Christ." Peter wrote, 1 Peter 1:5, that believers are "kept by the power of God through faith."

There are times when a Christian seems to fail, but the apostle John said that Christians have sin, 1 John 1:8, and Christians will occasionally commit acts of sinning, 1 John 1:10, but that God has made a remedy to restore the sinning Christian to fellowship with himself, 1 John 1:9. The scriptures do tell the Christian to strive to life holy and righteous lives, which some have interpreted to mean salvation can be lost if one's life is not always holy and righteous. But the verses telling the believer to strive depend on the ability to strive and succeed, which is God's grace of perseverance. God never commands what he does not also give. If the commandment is to strive, then God's mighty power works in the believer so he/she can strive and succeed, Colossians 1:29. God gives the grace of perseverance and the genuine believer uses the grace of perseverance. Because every genuine believer possesses the grace of perseverance, he/she will always overcome sin and the world by the grace of perseverance. The salvation of the believer is eternal.

The Characteristics of Eternal Salvation.

The life of the saved person demonstrates certain characteristics that an unsaved person's life does not. The saved person habitually lives a godly life. The unsaved person habitually lives a life of sinning. The saved person may sin occasionally, but the unsaved person sins habitually. The apostle John wrote, 1 John 3:6, that every person habitually abiding in Christ is not habitually sinning, and that every person habitually sinning does not know Christ. The characteristics of daily living testify a genuine believer has eternal salvation.

The saved person is like Christ: he/she is godly. Godliness, that is, a godly life, is when the believer's thoughts, decisions, and actions conform to the moral, holy, and righteous standard set by God's own character. Positively, a genuine believer loves the Father, Son, and Holy Spirit; he/she enjoys associating with and worshiping with others sharing the same faith in Christ; a believer has a hunger and thirst to learn the Word of God, to read the Word, study the Word, hear the Word preached and taught; the person who is genuinely saved loves to hear about Christ the Savior. The genuine believer recognizes the truth of Scripture, 1 John 2:21; but the unbeliever does not continue in the truth, 1 John 2:19.

Negatively, the person who is genuinely saved is bothered by sin and sinning. He/she is embarrassed by sinning because Christ has been disappointed. The believer takes no lasting pleasure in sin and sinning—there may be a moment of pleasure when an old sin habit is indulged, but in a short time the pleasure fades. The genuine believer is saddened when Christ is dishonored. The genuine believer is righteously angry when the Scripture is twisted to say what it does not mean. The genuine believer holds the world and the things of the world loosely, lightly, knowing he/she is to be in the world, but not of the world. Death is not a terror to the genuine believer, because physical death is merely the way Christ brings his saved people to heaven to be with him forever. The characteristics of a genuine salvation testify to an eternal salvation.

Conclusion.

There are times of failure in the Christian life, and times of doubt. There are some verses that seem to say salvation may be lost. But the scriptures give a clear and unambiguous witness that salvation cannot be lost. So by the testimony of five things—Christ's limitless merit; sealing by the Holy Spirit; the Scripture's word of assurance; perseverance in the faith by faith; and the characteristics of a genuine Christian—the believer has assurance that salvation is permanent.

Of these five the first is the most important: Jesus paid the full and complete debt for sins, completely satisfying God's holiness and justice, such that that no other action, work, or sacrifice is required. A genuine believer cannot lose his or her salvation; a genuine believer is permanently sealed into salvation; a genuine believer perseveres in the faith by faith; a genuine believer knows from Scripture they have eternal life and can never perish; a genuine believer practices genuine Christianity.

Example

When answering objections about the doctrine of eternal security, I answer first with the clear testimony of Christ's propitiation, and then interpret the scripture that raised the question. Below is a question I have been asked. In answering I began with the propitiation, and then provided the interpretation. Here I will give only the interpretation.

Here is the question: "Does Romans 8:13 mean if Christians live according to the flesh they lose their salvation?" Romans 8:13, "For if you live according to the flesh you will die; but if by the Spirit you put to death the deeds of the body, you will live" (NKJV).

Paul was writing to the members of the church in Rome. He greets them as saved, Romans 1:7, but Paul knows every person in a church is not saved. His many arguments against sinners in chapters 1–7 show he knows some are professing but not saved.

In 8:1–11, Paul begins by saying there is no condemnation to those persons who are in Christ, and then he says, "who do not walk [habitually live] according to the flesh, but [habitually live] according to the [Holy] Spirit." Paul is sounding a warning to his readers: those who live according to the flesh have set their minds on their flesh, are the enemies of God, and cannot please God. But those who live according to the Spirit have the Spirit in them, the Spirit gives them life, and they are the ones who are saved. Therefore, 8:12–13, those who are saved are to put to death the works of the flesh (compare

6:11–14) and live for Christ. Those who are not saved are living according to the flesh: to be carnally minded is death, 8:6.

Beginning at 8:14 to the end of the chapter, Paul addresses himself only to the saved, having given his warning in 8:1–13. Those living according to the flesh are unsaved. Those who are saved are reckoning themselves dead to sin, as he said at 6:11, and as he says at 8:14, "As many as are led by the Spirit of God, these are the sons of God." Scripture teaches the moment a person is saved God gives eternal life, John 10:28; 17:2–3; Romans 6:23b; 1 John 2:25. Eternal life is just that: eternal, unending. Genuine salvation cannot be lost.

Resurrection and Judgment

Many persons who believe in an afterlife believe in an eschatological general resurrection and judgment: that after physical death they will be resurrected with all other human beings and their works will be judged to determine where they will spend the next phase of their life. Many Christians believe in an eschatological general resurrection at the end of the age where saved and unsaved are judged at the same time, some for eternal reward, some for eternal punishment. Some christianized cults believe in some sort of eschatological punishment after death which cleanses the soul of unconfessed sin to prepare the person for an afterlife in heaven, or on a paradise-like earth.

The Bible doesn't support those views. God does not judge the righteous with the wicked, Genesis 18:23, 25; Psalm 28:2–6, so the eschatological judgment of God's saved people is a different time and place than that of the unsaved. Physical death seals the soul in its spiritual state, Luke 16:26; Hebrews 9:27, so the outcome of eschatological judgment is not salvation, for either the saved or the unsaved. There is more than one eschatological resurrection and judgment, which this essay will show.

Two dominant theologies within Christianity, covenant theology and dispensational theology, have opposing views of eschatological resurrection and judgment. Covenant theology teaches saved and unsaved are resurrected and judged simultaneously at the Great White Throne judgment. The outcomes are different for saved and unsaved, but the time and place of judgment is the same. Dispensational theology teaches several eschatological resurrections and judgments for various groups of the saved, and one eschatological resurrection and judgment for the unsaved.

The non-dispensational views of eschatological resurrection and judgment are in two camps. The first camp denies a millennial reign for Christ. Hodge (1873) wrote, [2:838] "this general resurrection [and subsequent judgment, pp. 844–845] is to take place 'at the last day,' which is "the second coming of Christ." Boettner stated [275], "The doctrine of the Judgment traditionally held by the Church and set forth in the great historic confessions of faith is that there is to be a day of Judgment immediately following the resurrection, and that all mankind will be included"; "Amillennialism teaches [Boettner, 4] . . . At the second coming of Christ the resurrection and judgment will take place, followed by the eternal order of things."

The second camp accepts a literal millennial reign, but teaches a general resurrection and judgment; Grudem [1140, 1142] wrote, "Scripture frequently affirms the fact that there will be a great final judgment of believers and unbelievers. They will stand before the judgment seat of Christ [Rev. 20:11–15] in resurrected bodies and hear his proclamation of their eternal destiny"; "The final judgment will occur after the millennium."

Dispensationalism notices that God has different eschatological resurrections and judgments for his saved people and the unsaved. The first eschatological resurrection and judgment of saved persons is at the rapture of the New Testament church. At 1 Corinthians 15:51–53; 1 Thessalonians 4:16–17; 2 Thessalonians 2:1 Paul teaches that physically dead saints will be resurrected and physically living saints will be transformed and caught up (raptured) into heaven with them. The consequence of this resurrection and rapture is that body and soul are freed from sin forever, to live sinless for eternity in God's presence.

The immediate aftermath of the resurrection-rapture is the Judgment Seat of Christ, the *béma* judgment. Salvation is not the issue. Believers are judged for the works they did after they were saved. See 2 Corinthians 5:10; 1 Corinthians 3:12–15. Then, the believers are in heaven in God's presence for eternity, to be always wherever Christ is present.

The second eschatological resurrection and judgment of saved persons is the Old Testament saints. Daniel 12:1–3 places this resurrection at the end of the Tribulation period. One may infer from Revelation 19:14 that the Old Testament saints are resurrected prior to the second advent. The Old Testament saints are in attendance at the wedding supper of the Lamb, Revelation 19:1–10.

At Revelation 19:14 Christ returns with the armies of heaven. These armies would be holy angels, the resurrected and raptured church, and would most likely include the resurrected Old Testament believers. The judgment of the Old Testament saints for reward (not for salvation) is not stated, but by analogy with the New Testament church, that judgment is immediately after their resurrection.

The third eschatological resurrection and judgment of saved persons is the resurrection of the Tribulation saints. These believers died because they maintained their testimony. See Revelation 6:9–11; 7:9–15; 14:13–16. They are resurrected, Revelation 20:4–6, in order to "live and reign with Christ" for a thousand years, and then enter into the eternal state. The judgment of the Tribulation saints for reward (not for salvation) is not stated, but by analogy with the New Testament church, that judgment is immediately after their resurrection.

There is a fourth eschatological resurrection and judgment, which is all the unsaved from Cain forward. This resurrection and judgment takes place at the Great White Throne (GWT), Revelation 20:11–15. This judgment is also not for salvation. The matter of salvation is decided in this mortal life. No person is judged after physical death as to the salvation of their soul. Only works are judged. The works of the unsaved are judged to determine the circumstances of their endless punishment.

Revelation 20:13 carefully states that all the unsaved dead and only the unsaved dead are resurrected: "the sea gave up the dead who were in it, and the death and the *hádēs* gave up the dead who were in them" (my translation). The dead in the sea looks to the cultural experiences of John and his readers. Literally the sea is a resting place of the body. Not merely for those who die at sea, but for everyone, because rains, rivers, and floods wash physical remains into the sea, where the dust and atoms of what was once living flesh rests until judgment.

The phrase "the *hádēs*," indicates unsaved souls, for only unsaved souls go to *hádēs*, there to await judgment at the GWT. The bodies (the sea) and the souls (*hádēs*) will be brought together in resurrection for judgment at the GWT. And just to make sure no one misunderstands, the ones present for judgment are "the dead." Not just any dead, but the dead ones in the *hádēs*, the ones who were physically dead and continue to be spiritually dead. The dead in v. 12, "the dead, the small and great, standing before God," are thus defined by v. 13 (cf. v. 5). as the spiritually dead, the unsaved.

While it is true the great creedal confessions of the past looked to a general eschatological resurrection and judgment, it is also true the scriptures teach believers and unbelievers are judged separately. The pattern set by salvation continues into eschatological judgment. The sins of those who are saved are judged at the cross. Their eschatological resurrection and judgment is for the works they did as believers, after which they continue in eternity with God in Christ. The sins of the unsaved are judged at their physical death. The result of that judgment is confinement in *hádēs* to await their eschatological resurrection and judgment of their works at the GWT, from which they will continue in punishment for eternity.

The Principle of Salvation

Not long ago I was asked, "What is the relationship between faith and works in the Old Testament?

When we speak about the Old Testament, we must recognize we are speaking of a very long period of time: the period of time from Adam to Christ. We may divide this long period of time into several smaller periods. From Adam to Noah, Noah to Abraham, Abraham to Moses, Moses to Christ. God interacted with humankind under different covenants during these period of times: the covenants with Adam, with Noah, with Abraham, and with Moses. Each covenant gave humankind information about God, informed their faith about God, and gave them responsibilities toward God and one another.

Looking at God's covenants with humankind, we must consider what is known as the doctrine of progressive revelation. God revealed himself, his purpose in creating the world, his plans to fulfill that purpose, and his relationship with humankind a little at a time. Isaiah 28:9–10 says something about God's method of revelation. He wrote (ESV), "To whom will he [God] teach knowledge? . . . For it is precept upon precept, precept upon precept, line upon line, line upon line, here a little, there a little." When we have finished reading the book of Exodus we understand more about God's purpose and plans than after we finished reading the book of Genesis. By the time we have read Genesis through Malachi we have learned a great deal about God and his purpose and plans. There is more to be revealed in the New Testament. That is progressive revelation.

We can, in a sense, view the world as a household run by God—the Writer of Hebrews, 3:3–6, uses that analogy. Every household is run in a particular way, which we might call an "economy." From time to time God changes his economy—the way in which he manages his interaction with humankind—as human civilization develops.

We can easily see God interacted with humankind differently after the Flood than before the Flood; differently after Christ than before Christ. A different economy was in place for Adam and his descendants than for Noah and his descendants. Some things that applied to Adam and his descendants remained the same for Noah and his descendants, some things were changed, and some things were new.

Noah and his descendants knew more about God and their responsibility toward God than did Adam and his descendants, because God revealed more about himself and his plans—the doctrine of progressive revelation. Today, we have God's completed revelation,

Genesis through Revelation, so we know more and are responsible for more.

So, when we speak of "the Old Testament context," we are really speaking of several different contexts or economies. Each of these economies had certain responsibilities toward God, and each had certain things they were required to believe, based on the amount of revelation that had been given in each economy.

We can call what they were required to believe "the content of their faith." A simple example is to compare Noah with Abraham. Noah was required to worship God only, believe judgment was coming, and build an ark. Abraham was required to worship God only, believe he would have an heir from his own body, and move to a new land.

So, there was a progressive aspect to revelation, and thereby a progression in what human beings were required to believe in order to have a relationship with God. Let me use a very clear contrast as an explanation. Noah was not required to believe on Jesus Christ as Savior. Today, we are. Noah was not told about Jesus Christ. We have been told.

The content of Noah's faith, in order to be saved, was not, "Believe on the Lord Jesus Christ, and you will be saved (Acts 16:31), because God never told Noah about Jesus Christ. Noah's content of faith was worship God only, believe judgment is coming, build an ark for your deliverance from the coming judgment. That was his content of faith, because that was what God had revealed to him. Noah believed and was saved.

Abraham's content of faith was worship God only and believe in the promise God gave to him (Genesis 12:1–3; 15:1–5). That was Abraham's content of faith, because that was what God had revealed to him. "And he [Abraham] believed the Lord, and he counted it to him as righteousness. In every economy, what God required a person to believe—their content of faith—corresponded with what God had revealed in the historical progressive revelation of biblical truth.

Now we must talk about principles. A principle is a fundamental, unchanging truth. A principle is always true and it always applies. For example, "worship the Lord your God and him only shall you serve" is said by Christ at Matthew 4:10. The principle was stated at Deuteronomy 6:13–14, and earlier at Exodus 20:3. But regardless of when in human history that principle was revealed, the principle has always existed. Exodus 20:3 was not just for Israel, but for everyone. Why? Isaiah 45:21 (ESV) restates the principle: "there is no other god besides me, a righteous God and a Savior; there is none besides me."

A different content of faith does not mean a different principle of salvation. The salvation principle, from Genesis through Revelation, is always "saved by grace through faith not by works," Ephesians 2:8–9. A theologian by the name of Charles C. Ryrie explained the salvation principle in this manner.

> The basis of salvation in every age is the death of Christ; the requirement for salvation in every age is faith; the object of faith in every age is God; the content of faith changes in the various dispensations. [Ryrie, *Dispensationalism*, 115.]

When Abraham "believed the Lord, and he counted it to him as righteousness," Abraham was saved from the penalty due sin because 1) he had faith God and the testimony God had given him as his content of faith, and 2) because the death of Christ paid for his sin.

The death of Christ for sin was a yet-future historical event in the Old Testament, but God had decreed in eternity past, Ephesians 1:4, that Christ's death would be the only basis of salvation. The God who "calls into existence the things that do not exist" (Romans 4:17, ESV) accounted the death of Christ for sin to be effective for salvation from eternity past into eternity future. Faith in God and his testimony is always the means by which the merit of Christ's death is applied to save the soul from sin. No work or works can access Christ's merit, because God has decreed faith alone saves.

Most people want to know if salvation under the Mosaic Law was by works—a sacrifice for sin. No, the salvation principle is always "saved by grace through faith not by works."

Salvation is when God rescues a sinner out of the state of spiritual death and delivers him/her into a permanent state of spiritual life. Just bringing a sacrifice did not save (just like being baptized does not save.) What saved a sinner during the Law of Moses, was responding by faith to God's testimony that the proper sacrifice brought with confession and repentance would result in the forgiveness of sin. God by grace accepted the sinner's faith in God and his testimony.

The Old Testament sinner was saved by their faith in God and his testimony, according to the content of faith God had given to them. Because of their faith, God applied Christ's merit by his grace to their sin, and the believing sinner was saved. Salvation is the remission of sin's guilt and penalty by the application of Christ's infinite merit, which is gained by receiving God's gift of grace-faith-salvation through the means of personal faith in God's revealed means (way) of salvation.

Salvation is obtained by grace through faith, not works, and is maintained by grace through faith, not works.

In this New Testament age we have received more revelation: Jesus Christ has been revealed. The content of saving faith in this New Testament economy is faith in God's testimony concerning Jesus Christ. Salvation in this New Testament economy occurs when a sinner repents of his or her sins and believes on Christ as their Savior, Acts 2:38; 3:19–20; 11:18; Romans 3:22–26; 10:9–10, 13; Galatians 3:22; 1 Peter 1:21; 1 John 3:23.

Salvation, therefore, must be defined for both Old Testament and New Testament in a way that always applies the salvation principle, "saved by grace through faith not by works." Salvation in every economy is God by grace forgiving a sinner's sin-guilt and remitting sin's penalty through the application of Christ's infinite merit. Salvation is gained by receiving God's gift of grace-faith-salvation (Ephesians 2:8) and applying that gift by means of personal faith in the content of faith God has revealed in any particular economy. The basis of salvation in every age is the death of Christ; the requirement for salvation in every age is faith; the object of faith in every age is God; the content of faith changes in the various dispensations, according to the progressive revelation given at any point in history. Salvation is obtained only by grace through faith, not by works, and is maintained by grace through faith, not by works. Salvation is always through the sinner's faith in God and God's testimony, as presented in God's historically current testimony as given in the progressive revelation of truth.

What I have explained above is the view of Dispensational theology. Reformed theology teaches the exact same salvation principle as Dispensational theology. The difference between the Reformed and Dispensational view of salvation is in the object of faith and the content of faith.

> Dispensational: the object of faith in every age is God.
> Reformed: the object of faith in every age is Christ.
>
> Dispensational: the content of faith changes in the various dispensations.
> Reformed: the content of faith is always Christ, either coming (Old Testament), or arrived (New Testament).

Regardless of whether a person has a Dispensational or a Reformed view of salvation, the salvation principle applies equally in the Old Testament context as in the New Testament context. On this Dispensational and Reformed theology are in complete agreement.

"What is the relationship between works and faith in the Old Testament context?" Answer: works never play a part in salvation at any time in the past, present, or future history of humankind. The salvation principle is always saved by grace through faith not works.

Why Did Jesus Christ Not Know Some Things?

At Mark 13:32 Jesus said, "Now concerning that day and hour, no one knows, not even the angels in heaven, nor the son, only the Father."

Some have used this to say Jesus Christ was not deity. After all, deity is omniscient. What is the biblical answer?

William Ames (1576–1633) gave the answer in his work, *The Marrow of Theology*, 131 (the standard textbook for seminary studies for many years). Ames said,

> There were in Christ two kinds of understanding: a divine understanding whereby he knew all things, John 21:17, and a human whereby he did not yet know some things, Mark 13:32. So there were two wills, one divine, Luke 5:13, and the other human, with a natural appetite, Matthew 26:39. So Christ has a double presence, but the human presence cannot be everywhere or in many places at once.

So Jesus Christ is, at the same time, both omnipresent and limited to one place at any one moment in time. When he was in the boat on the Sea of Galilee, he was at the same time everywhere at once in space and time.

Jesus Christ is, at the same time, both omnipotent and limited to those acts common to all human nature. When he grew tired, slept, ate, pooped, and walked, he was at the same time governing the entire universe.

Jesus Christ is, at the same time, both omniscient and limited in his understanding. When he did not know the date of his return, he was at the same time omnisciently aware of all things concerning his return.

Jesus Christ is both unlimited deity and limited humanity. The Scripture does not speak of Jesus Christ as the deity nature did this or the human nature did that. Scripture always speaks of the actions of the whole person. But Scripture also always maintains the genuine properties of both natures: Jesus Christ was tired—God does not get tired, but Jesus got tired. Jesus Christ raised the dead—human nature cannot raise the dead, but deity nature can. The Scripture always recognizes and maintains the dual human-deity presence of Jesus the Christ.

Here is why Jesus Christ did not know some things. Christ's

genuine human mind was, and still is, incapable of knowing and accessing everything the deity omnisciently knows. The human nature was perfected in the incarnation with deity, but not exalted. The human nature remained finite, limited, incapable of omni-anything. His mind is genuinely human, and therefore genuinely limited in its knowledge and understanding until informed by his omniscience. Put more plainly, you cannot stuff all the knowledge of the universe into a human mind. His human mind knows what he needs to know when he needs to know, because his omniscience tells him what he needs to know when he needs to know.

Bottom line? Jesus Christ is the God-man, genuine deity and genuine humanity. In the particular instance of Mark 13:32, a particular bit of knowledge concerning the future was withheld from his human mind for reasons that seemed best to God. In this, we see Scripture's testimony that the human nature was genuinely human. Jesus Christ is not only God he is the God-man, and possesses the genuine attributes of each nature.

There was and is in Jesus Christ the kind of understanding in whereby his finite genuine human mind does not know all things, until a thing is made known to his finite genuine human mind by his omniscience.

Translating Scripture: a Literal or Figurative Meaning

As an amateur translator of the scriptures, I try to maintain a balance between formal and dynamic equivalence—as I have learned to do from other translations and translators. I tend to favor a more literal translation more than most, and tend to follow the grammar and syntax of the original language more than most.

As a professional author, I know one must keep the intended reader in mind. The mental reader I keep before me at all times as I translate is always the reader with an average comprehension of English—he or she is functionally literate, but may not be able to grasp the intended meaning from an expressly literal translation. Communication is a partnership between reader and writer. Ideas and concepts are communicated only as well as the words, grammar, and syntax used in their communication, and only as well as the reader's understanding of those words, grammar, and syntax.

I have before me a particular case where one must carefully consider whether the translation should be more literal or more figurative.

At Galatians 5:12, Paul writes, "Would that those unsettling you would *apokóptō*" [Zodhiates, s. v. "609"].

The word apokóptō means "to cut off, amputate." In the context of the Galatian argument, Paul is making a macabre play on words with circumcision. He literally says,

> NIV, I wish they would go the whole way and emasculate themselves!

> HCSB, I wish those who are disturbing you might also get themselves castrated!

> NLT, "I just wish that those troublemakers who want to mutilate you by circumcision would mutilate themselves."

If *apokóptō* is translated literally, Paul has written he wishes those who want the Galatian Christians to be circumcised according to the Law would themselves cut off that part of their body that is circumcised, which means they would become physically emasculated.

Does Paul really desire these Judaizers to physically harm themselves? Is the Holy Spirit teaching Christians that is proper to wish physical harm to others? These are questions the translator must decide.

Some readers may come to just that conclusion from the three translations quoted in the OP. Certainly a literal understanding of certain Old Testament and New Testament passages has led some to cut off the hands of thieves, or gouge out eyes, their own or another's. I have translated such verses literally, because no figurative meaning was available within the semantic range. But I have carefully explained those verses in my commentaries.

Think how much damage has been done through "turn the other cheek" when the meaning is, don't take personal revenge. Yet, I have faithfully translated that turn of phrase exactly as it stands in the text. No other meaning was available in the semantic range, and what was called for was a translation, not a mini-commentary.

Is a literal translation warranted at Galatians 5:12, or is a figurative translation more appropriate? It seems to me very unlikely that Paul wanted these teachers of the Law to be physically harmed. I cannot think of any occasion in Acts or his other letters where Paul had desired physical harm to any person. A spirit of malice or vengeance is not agreeable with the values of Christianity.

In the particular case of Galatians 5:12, a figurative meaning was available within the semantic range, is appropriate to the biblical context, and properly informs the reader of Paul's intent. I explain my reasoning in the commentary I am building on the Galatian letter.

Paul uses *apokóptō*, emasculated, in a figurative sense of being cut off from the Galatians. Paul wishes these people unsettling the Galatian Christians with their requirement to keep the Law of Moses (in order to be a complete Christian) would separate themselves from the Galatians; he wants them to go away.

A better translation: Galatians 5:12, "Would that those unsettling you would separate themselves from you."

A Bible translation is a good faith attempt by men and women of faith to accurately express the ideas and concepts in one language (Hebrew, Greek) in another language. That means the translator must also be an interpreter, because every word has a semantic range (many possible meanings) and most words may be used figuratively. (An example: the word "run" has over 170 possible meanings, from the literal, "I ran a mile," to the idiomatic, "I ran a business," to the figurative, "she ran away with my heart.")

A figurative translation responds to two rules of interpreting figures of speech. One, a figure of speech is based in something literal and teaches something literal. Two, a figure of speech does not teach the literal thing on which it is based.

In Galatians 5:12 the literal something is castration: to emasculate by removing the male genitals from the body. But because it is unlikely Paul wishes physical harm for the teachers of the Law, a literal translation seems inappropriate. A figurative translation seems the best translation: "Would that those unsettling you would separate themselves from you."

The Bible reader must always be aware he/she is reading a translation. The word choices the translator makes are usually appropriate. But one should always be aware of not only the immediate context, but also the larger context—which in this verse is all of Paul's experiences and expressions, oral and written, in Acts and his letters.

Another lesson in "Don't Blindly Follow a Translation."

1 Thessalonians 5:19, "Do not hinder the Spirit." My translation.

This verse is translated by others: Do not quench the Spirit; Don't stifle the Spirit; Do not put out the Spirit's fire.

The word in 5:19 translated "quench, stifle, put out" is *sbénnumi* [Zodhiates, s. v. "4570"]. I have translated this word as "hinder." *Sbénnumi* literally means quench when it refers to a literal fire or a light (such as from a lamp). But the use here is figurative. Can a mere human being stop the Holy Spirit from working? No.

The context of this verse is found in the preceding verses (all my translation).

> 5:15, See that no one to anyone has repaid evil for evil, but always pursue the good toward one another, and toward all.

> 5:16, rejoice always;

> 5:17, pray every time an opportunity presents itself;

> 5:18, in everything give thanks: for this is the will of God in Christ Jesus toward you.

And then, 5:19, "Do not hinder the Spirit," to be understood in the context of the preceding verses. The context is submission to God's will, as expressed in the four preceding exhortations: do good, rejoice, pray, give thanks.

To "do good" is another way to say, "practice love," because love always seeks the best good for another. No one can act for the good of "everyone without exception," but everyone has circles of social contacts: family, close friends, friends, acquaintances, people we know by name, by face, or not at all, and people we meet in the course of daily life. We should pursue the good toward others as opportunities present themselves. The good toward one another and toward all cannot be limited to only physical aid, but must include spiritual aid also.

To "rejoice always" does not mean the believer must always be happy in every circumstance of life. The word translated rejoice, *chaírō* [Zodhiates, s. v. "5463"] has two meanings in Scripture. One meaning is happiness based on circumstances. The other meaning is an attitude of complacency toward God's will. In the sense of complacency, joy is the settled conviction that whatever the outer circumstances might be, one's relationship with God remains one of trust, peace, cheerfulness, contentment, and hope. Joy is inner contentment with God's will that is not unmade when outward circumstances make one unhappy.

Then, the believer is to pray at every appropriate opportunity. (Not pray unceasingly, as some versions state the exhortation, because prayer is only one aspect of the Christian's activities.) Good times or bad, happy or not, the believer is to pray. Prayer is an expression of dependence and worship toward the sovereign God.

Finally, the believer is to give thanks in everything, "for this is the will of God in Christ Jesus toward you." This exhortation corresponds to 1 Corinthians 10:31 (ESV), "whatever you do, do all to the glory of God." James 1:2 also comes to mind, "My brethren, reckon all joy whenever you may encounter various trials." In "everything give thanks" is the companion of "rejoice always." The Christian is not to be a complainer, whether to him or herself or toward God. The will of God is give thanks. Because the Christian is satisfied to trust and be at peace in God's will, then thanks may be given in whatever his or her circumstances might be in the world.

The failure to give thanks is a failure in one's relationship with God to have trust, peace, cheerfulness, contentment, and hope. The failure to give thanks is to allow outward circumstances make one unhappy with God's will. The failure to give thanks is to become discontent with God's will for you. This attitude of thanks is, admittedly, not always easy. But maturity in joy will grow as the attitude of giving thanks matures.

In this context of submission to God's will—do good, rejoice, pray, give thanks—to "hinder the Holy Spirit" is to refuse to submit to God's will. The Holy Spirit's work of teaching, guidance, and blessing turns to conviction of sin to prompt repentance when God's will is resisted. In context, God's will is resisted when the believer fails to pursue the good, fails to find complacency in God's will, fails to give thanks in everything, or fails to pray at every opportunity.

Whenever a word in a translation doesn't make sense in the context, find out what it means.

Critical Thinking on the Incarnation

Critical thinking is not the same as being critical or criticizing. Critical thinking is "the objective analysis and evaluation of an issue in order to form a judgment." In this essay, I am going to do some critical thinking on the question, "Is Jesus God?"

Is Jesus God? Many Christians will firmly state, "Jesus is God." That statement reflects their correct belief in the incarnation of God the Son in Jesus of Nazareth to form the person Jesus the Christ. Jesus the Christ is the God-man, a person of two natures, deity and human. Jesus Christ is God. But is Jesus God? God the Son existed "pre-Jesus," which is to state the biblical fact God the Son is increate (not created) and eternal, but Jesus the human had beginning.

Think about this. Jesus was conceived (by the omnipotent power of the Holy Spirit) in the womb of Mary of Nazareth, Luke 1:31; Matthew 1:21. That means Jesus had a beginning. That means Jesus was and is human. That means Jesus is not God. Jesus was not increate, he was conceived. Jesus is not eternal, because he had a beginning. When we state Jesus had a beginning we are doing what Scripture always does. We are proclaiming the human nature of Jesus Christ the God-man. The humanity of the Christ must be as passionately maintained as the deity of the Christ.

Now, Jesus Christ is God, because he is the God-man, a person of two natures: genuine deity and genuine human. He is God the Son incarnate with Jesus of Nazareth. I state with all the authority of Scripture, Jesus Christ is God. The deity of the Christ must be as passionately maintained as the humanity of the Christ.

Jesus Christ has, as William Ames (1576–1633) stated [131], "a double presence." God the Son is omnipresent, Jesus is not. God the Son is omniscient, Jesus is not. God the Son is omnipotent, Jesus is not. But when we speak of Jesus Christ, we can say with all the authority of Scripture that Jesus Christ is at one and the same time omnipresent, omniscient, omnipotent in his deity nature and is limited in every respect in his human nature. Jesus Christ has, (quoting Ames again), "two kinds of understanding: a divine understanding whereby he knew all things, John 21:17, and a human whereby he did not yet know some things, Mark 13:32. So there were two wills, one divine, Luke 5:13, and the other human, with a natural appetite, Matthew 26:39."

Jesus the man was and is not omniscient. The human mind is finite, limited, incapable of knowing or understanding everything there is to know and understand. The omniscient deity nature informs the human mind what it needs to know when it needs to know it.

The person Jesus Christ is and is not omnipresent. Physically he is present at one moment in time at one place in space. Jesus Christ is physically located wherever he needs to be whenever he needs to be there by the action of the omnipotence of his deity nature.

The same principle applies to his omnipotence. The person is empowered to do whatever he needs to do by his omnipotence.

Both the humanity and the deity of the Christ must passionately maintained, because Jesus Christ is at the same time both God and man, the God-man. Scripture is always careful to maintain both the deity and the humanity. A few examples.

Scripture consistently uses the word "Christ" or "Lord" when it speaks of the actions of deity performed by the God-man Jesus Christ. At Colossians 1:16 Paul teaches "in him all things were created in the heavens and on the earth." Who is the "him" Paul says is the Creator? We must go back a number of verses to find the noun that goes with this pronoun. In 1:13 "him" is identified as "the son of his love." In 1:10 "him" is identified as "the Lord." Let us not make assumptions based on what we know from the rest of the New Testament. Let us pretend we are Colossians who have this letter and no other New Testament writings and are reading this letter for the very first time. How may we Colossians positively identify the person who is "him, son, Lord?" We must begin at the beginning. The entire chapter is about one person. At 1:1, 2, 3, 4, 5 and 7 we see Paul is speaking about Jesus Christ. Jesus Christ is "Lord." Jesus Christ is "the son of his love." We may properly read 1:16 as, "in Jesus Christ all things were created in the heavens and on the earth." Jesus is not the Creator, Jesus Christ the God-man is the Creator. That is the Scripture representation.

Scripture defends the human nature of Jesus Christ. Matthew 2:1, "Now Jesus, having been born." God the Son is increate but Jesus was born. Matthew 3:13, "Then Jesus came from Galilee to the Jordan." God the Son is omnipresent but Jesus walked to get there. Matthew 4:1, "Then Jesus was led up into the wilderness by the Spirit to be tempted by the Devil." God the Son cannot be tempted but Jesus the man could be tempted. The human nature in Jesus Christ could respond to a sales pitch to do evil—a temptation—the deity nature could not, James 1:13. The Scripture always maintains both the human nature and the deity nature of the God-man. Words are important because by them concepts and ideas are communicated. "Jesus" not

"Jesus Christ" was led by the Spirit to be tempted.

The temptations of Jesus by Satan give us the opportunity to understand how the deity nature and the human nature interacted. There were in Jesus Christ two wills. The "will" is the decision-making faculty of the nature. We must be a little technical here. When God the Son became incarnate he did not join with a human person, he joined with the human nature and human body conceived in Mary, joining with it at the very instant of its conception, thereby forming the person Jesus Christ, the God-man. Jesus Christ has one personality, that of God the Son, but he has two natures informing that personality. Jesus Christ has two wills because the "will" is part of the nature: the deity nature has a will and the human nature has a will. (To see a thorough discussion of this subject, please consult my book, *God Became Incarnate*, section, 'The Two Wills of the God-Man,' beginning [in the print version] on page 45.)

When Jesus Christ was confronted with a temptation, the will of the sinless human nature agreed with the will of the sinless deity nature to reject temptation. He experienced temptation because he was genuinely human, but he rejected temptation because he was the God-man. Christ was one person with two different kinds of natures, deity and human. Each nature had a will. Therefore Christ had two wills. But he had one personality because his personality was the sum total of the behavior patterns created by the two natures and two wills. The two wills acted together because he had one personality.

As Ryrie stated [*Basic Theology*, 287–289], "The single person of the incarnate Christ retained the total complex of divine attributes and possessed all the complex of human attributes essential to a perfect human being. Did Christ have two wills? It seems to me that every single decision stemmed from either the 'will' of His divine nature or the 'will' of His human nature or a blending of both, making it proper to think of two 'wills'."

The apostle John believed Jesus Christ was the God-man, proclaiming both the deity and the humanity. At John 1:1 John wrote, "In the beginning was the Word and the Word was with God and God was the Word." Here John tells of two persons—"God was with the Word"—and both of those persons are God—God was the Word. Then, a few sentences later, John wrote, 1:14, "And the Word became flesh." So this Word who was with God and is God, 1:1, joined himself with a human being—the incarnation of the God the Word with Jesus of Nazareth—Jesus the Christ.

Some conclusions.

Jesus is not God. Jesus Christ is God. Jesus Christ is the "Son of God," a biblical term for the God-man.

God the Son is "pre-Jesus." Jesus Christ is both increate (deity) and created (human), both eternal (deity) and immortal (human).

Jesus was virgin born, God the Son was pre-Jesus. Both the deity nature and the human nature were/are sinless: Jesus Christ lived a sinless life.

Jesus did not die a substitutionary death. Jesus could die only for himself. Jesus Christ died a substitutionary death, because only the God-man had the limitless merit to propitiate God for human sin.

Jesus Christ rose from the dead. Jesus Christ ascended to God. Jesus Christ is returning.

Salvation in Jesus Christ is the only way to God. We do not believe on Jesus to be saved. The consistent biblical gospel message for this New Testament age is "believe on the Lord Jesus Christ, and you will be saved." At Romans 10:4–13 the Holy Spirit is careful, through Paul, to attribute salvation to God, not man: confess the "Lord Jesus," a term equivalent to "God-man."

Critical thinking on the incarnation also means we must be careful not to so separate the humanity from the deity that we have a schizophrenic Jesus Christ. Scripture never speaks of the deity nature doing this or the human nature doing that. The whole person acted (as in the temptation, the two wills acting together). The deity nature acted through the human nature. The person Jesus Christ was hungry and sleepy and stilled the storm and raised the dead. But just as important, Scripture is always careful not to attribute the attributes of deity to the human nature. In the incarnation the human nature was perfected, not exalted to deity. Jesus Christ will for eternity be deity and human, unlimited and limited.

Jesus is not God, Jesus Christ is the God-man. For some this is all too technical. For others it is confusing and out of the reach of their understanding: they understand the incarnation as "Jesus is God." Let us remember Christ used Peter the fisherman to teach some, and Paul the theologian to teach others. Peter learned from Paul (2 Peter 3:15), and perhaps some have learned from me (and others who made contributions to this essay.) Do not despise those who cannot understand, but be gentle with them, not judging, not disputing. Christ saves those like Peter and those like Paul: everyone is to be a theologian in some measure, but the depths of theology are not for everyone.

We Must Boldly Go To God

Hebrews 4:16 states, "We should come, therefore, with confidence to the throne of grace, so that we may receive mercy and grace and may find grace for help in time of need."

The Christian can come with confidence to God's throne because he/she has a high priest, Jesus Christ, who always represents his saved people before God the Father, Hebrews 4:14–15. Jesus is a high priest who has endured in the world what you and I are enduring—not the exact same temptations, but the fact of unceasing temptation, and like his saved people, the contradiction of the world's values against the values of faith. He sympathizes with our weaknesses and desires we come to God in prayer for God's help in our times of need.

The Writer of Hebrews tells us in chapter 10 why we can come with confidence to God with our prayers. At Hebrews 10:19 he writes, "Therefore, brothers, having confidence for entering the holy places by the blood of Jesus." The "therefore" is a conjunction connecting 10:19–23 with 10:11–18.

In 10:11–18, the Writer tells us Jesus Christ has made a complete sacrifice for our sins. In 10:11 he tells how the Old Testament priests came daily to offer sacrifices for sins. But at 10:12 he says Jesus Christ offered one perfect sacrifice for all sins—for each and every past, present, and future sin. We know his one sacrifice satisfied God for all our sins because he "sat down."

The Old Testament priests always stood making sacrifices for sins; the need for sacrifice never ended; there was no place to sit in the tabernacle or temple. Jesus sat down after making his sacrifice for our sins, because there were no more sacrifices to be made. His work on our behalf was "finished, completed," John 19:30 (the Greek word for "finished" in that verse is a cry of victory: sin and death had been defeated). The result of Christ's death on the cross is stated in Hebrews 10:16–17.

> This is the covenant that I will make with them after those days," says the Lord, "putting my laws into their hearts and into their minds I will inscribe them," and, "their sins and their lawlessness I will not at all remember.

"Therefore," 10:19, because our sins have been forgiven, 10:12–14, and because God has a covenant of salvation with those who believe on Christ as their Savior, 10:16–17, the believer is able to "have confidence for entering the holy places." Because of what Jesus did for us, "we should," 10:22, "approach with an upright heart in full assurance of faith."

We should also remember God the Father is the believer's father. He is the kind of father who is always kind, who always listens to his saved people, and always answers us in a way that is best for us. God is loving and kind and merciful to his saved people, Psalm 69:16; 119:76–77; 156.

How can we as Christians come with confidence before a holy and righteous God? We see from Hebrews 4:16 and 10:11–22 we are authorized to come with confidence because through our faith in Christ God has forgiven our sins. The way to God is open through our high priest Jesus Christ, giving us the confidence to enter, authorizing us to boldly enter.

How can we come with confidence and not be guilty of sin or disrespect to God? We can come with confidence for two reasons. One we have been authorized to come with confidence, 4:16; 10:19. Therefore to come confidently is not disrespectful. Second, we must always keep in the forefront of our mind that, 1 John 1:7, "the blood of Jesus Christ his Son is continually cleansing us from every sin," so it is not disrespect toward God to come confidently into his presence, because Christ has cleansed us from not only past sins, but also present and future sins.

Will you and I commit acts of sinning? Yes, 1 John 1:8–10, because the sin attribute is still in our born-again saved human nature. But the believer habitually lives a life of righteousness, that is the consequence of his born-again nature. The believer may occasionally commit an act of sinning, but God has a remedy, 1 John 1:9, "If we continue to confess our sins, he is faithful and righteous to forgive us the sins, and to cleanse us from every unrighteousness." How can God forgive our acts of sinning? Because Christ advocates for us at God's throne, 1 John 2:1, and his death on the cross paid for those sins, 1 John 2:2, "Now he is propitiation [satisfaction] for our sins."

But let us suppose we have committed a sin, and are feeling unworthy, disrespectful, of coming to the Father. What says the Scripture? "If we continue to confess our sins, he is faithful and righteous to forgive us the sins, and to cleanse us from every unrighteousness." The exact same faith that resulted in your salvation is the same kind of faith you need when you have sinned.

Christ is the only remedy for sinning, faith is the only means to access forgiveness, God's throne of grace the only place where we may find forgiveness. There we must boldly, confidently go.

When the believer commits an act of sinning, he/she should always, always, always "come, therefore, with confidence to the throne of grace, so that we may receive mercy and grace and may find grace for help in time of need," Hebrews 4:16. God will forgive those sins, because Christ has fully satisfied God's penalty for those sins.

God our Father loves his saved people. They are his children. God's children are never unworthy, because he has made them everlastingly worthy through their salvation. That is something no religion can do. We should always approach him with the respect and affection required toward a father. And if we fail, then we should always come to our heavenly Father for forgiveness, which having received, we come boldly to worship, to ask, and to praise. Philippians 4:6, "Be anxious about not even one thing or person, but in everything by prayer and petition on behalf of yourself and others, with thanksgiving, make your requests known to God."

An Exposition of Genesis 3:15

ESV, "I will put enmity between you and the woman, and between your offspring and her offspring; he shall bruise your head, and you shall bruise his heel."

Let us, for a moment, set aside all other scriptures after this verse and view this one scripture in its context.

The scripture context for Genesis 3:15 is Genesis 1:1–3:14. There is no other revelation to this point. God has created the universe, and all the material things and living things in the universe. This God, YHWH, created one human being, Adam, 2:7. From Adam, YHWH formed a second human being, who was formed body and soul from Adam's body and soul. This being was Adam individualized as a different sexual gender. Adam named her *'Ishshā*, Woman, because she came out of *'îsh*, man. She was his wife, Genesis 2:24.

YHWH, the Creator and Governor of his creation, appointed Adam to manage all the material creation except the fruit of one tree. This one fruit was denied to Adam as a test of his character and faith: would Adam choose to be subordinate to YHWH, or would he choose to be autonomous?

The female Adam, *'Ishshā*, was tempted by a serpent to eat the forbidden fruit to gain, so she believed, a greater likeness to God. She ate. She tempted Adam to eat, and he did eat. The result was each became less like God: through their action they now knew evil experientially; God knows evil only by observation. Eating was an act of rebellion against God.

Genesis 3:15 is part of YHWH's remedial work, 3:9–19, to discipline and correct his saved people, Adam and the Woman, and thereby restore them to fellowship with YHWH.

That is the context.

When Adam and the Woman chose to disobey God, their human nature was permanently altered by the addition of the principle of rebellion against God. The Bible names this principle of rebellion sin. God's remedial work in 3:9–19 consists of their repentance and confession (3:12–13, "I ate") and changes in their environment and manner of life. The purpose of those changes is to help them recognize and cope with the principle of rebellion. They could not return to the beginning and start anew. They must recognize their action had permanent consequences, and learn how to cope with those consequences.

One of those consequences is detailed in 3:15: a continuous

struggle (enmity, conflict) between two different offspring: the offspring of the serpent; the offspring of the Woman.

The Hebrew word the ESV correctly translates "offspring" is *zera* (Strong's #2233). This word is always in the plural, is sometimes properly translated "seed," but when speaking of human beings *zera* always means offspring, descendants. For example, Genesis 21:12, "In Isaac shall your *zera*," offspring, descendants, "be called."

To distinguish between his saved people and the unsaved, God appointed enmity between the serpent's offspring and the Woman's offspring. This verse is both descriptive and prescriptive. It is proscriptive in that there will be enmity between the two offspring. It is descriptive in that the principle of rebellion, sin, is the cause of that enmity. They key to understanding this verse is to understanding the "offspring."

The Woman's offspring seems obvious. Not only the children from her procreation with Adam, but their children as well, and their children, and so on to the end of the world. Every human being is physically the Woman's offspring. (But not spiritually her offspring, which I will explain in a moment.)

Immediately there is a problem in the interpretation. The enmity we see in the world—we cannot deny historical facts—is between the several members of the Woman's offspring: this one is the enemy of that one, beginning with Cain and Abel. But the prophecy is enmity between the Woman's offspring and the serpent's offspring.

Now we must use the spiritual perception the Holy Spirit has given his saved people. Does 3:15 mean every human being is the enemy of every snake and every snake is the enemy of every human being? I know some herpetologists who would dispute both sides of that equation; not to mention Genesis 9:2.

The serpent's offspring cannot be literal snakes. Here we must bring in a later Scripture that shows us how the Woman understood Genesis 3:15. At Genesis 4:25 (ESV), "And Adam knew his wife again, and she bore a son and called his name Seth, for she said, 'God has appointed for me another offspring instead of Abel, for Cain killed him.'"

The first thing we see is the Woman understood *zera* to mean her offspring. The second thing we see is the woman understood the enmity ordained in 3:15 was between her offspring: Cain killed Abel. In 4:25 the Woman makes clear that she now believes Abel and Seth to be her offspring in fulfillment of the promise, implying that she now believes Cain was the offspring of the serpent. We should notice that Moses and the Holy Spirit (the authors of 4:25) carefully do not identify Cain as the Woman's offspring, but do identify Abel and Seth as the Woman's offspring.

Four considerations reveal who are the Woman's seed and who are the serpent's seed.

> One, there is a fundamental difference between each seed that is the cause for continuing enmity. That difference is a relationship with God. Some of the Woman's offspring partake of her characteristics, which are a continuing relationship and fellowship with God. In terms of Genesis 3:15, the Woman's offspring are those who by faith have their sin forgiven and as a result are in a faith-based relationship with God. The difference between faith and no-faith, between a relationship and no relationship, is the cause of the enmity.

> Two, the facts of history reveal that the evil opponents of the Woman's faithful offspring are the Woman's unbelieving offspring: those not in a faith-based relationship with God. Cain killed Abel, and so it has been throughout human history: human beings are the enemy of human beings.

> Three, for the serpent's seed to be literal snakes is ridiculous. An enemy of equal characteristics must be in view.

> Four, in the context of continuing enmity between offspring, the serpent's offspring are the Woman's unbelieving, unsaved descendants who are in conflict with the Woman's believing, saved descendants. Abel and Seth are identified as the Woman's offspring, but Cain is not identified as her offspring; and in a later Scripture is identified as one of the serpent's offspring, 1 John 3:12.

The correct interpretation of Genesis 3:15 *in its scripture context* is continuing enmity between saved and unsaved human beings. That interpretation fits the context, fits the facts of Scripture, and fits the facts of human history.

Now we can bring in other Scripture.

Let us begin with a question. What Scripture or Scriptures quote or allude to Genesis 3:15? Only Romans 16:20 (ESV), "The God of peace will soon crush Satan under your feet." Interpretation? "The God of peace," the same God as at Genesis 3:15, "will soon," future tense, it has not yet happened, "crush Satan under your feet," under the believer's feet.

By alluding to Genesis 3:15, Romans 16:20 informs us the "serpent" of the Genesis 3:15 enmity is actually referring to the fallen angel known as Satan. The fallen angel Satan used a snake to communicate with the Woman. Now we have another one of those "spiritual perception" choices to make. Does Genesis 3:15 mean literal descendants of the fallen angel Satan?

That seems very unlikely. Nothing in Scripture suggests the immortal spirit beings known as angels procreate. In fact, the opposite is suggested, Matthew 22:30; Mark 12:25. Angels do not marry. In the economy that is biblical morality marriage precedes offspring.

Second, angels cannot procreate with human beings. Again Matthew 22:30; Mark 12:25. Angels neither marry, meaning they do not have a human-like male gender, and they are not given in marriage, meaning they do not have a human-like female gender. (Or have you never heard the wedding question, "Who gives this woman in marriage to this man." Males marry, women are given in marriage, at least in the times of the Christ.)

Third, if angels and humans could attempt to procreate, they could not produce viable offspring. That would be a violation of God's unbreakable law of biological reproduction: each kind reproduces its own kind. Angels and human beings are of different kinds in God's biological economy. Human beings cannot reproduce with angel beings.

The inevitable conclusion—from Scripture and history—is Genesis 3:15 is looking to spiritual offspring, not physical offspring. The Woman's spiritual offspring are her believing descendants and the serpent's offspring are the Woman's unbelieving descendants: the serpent's spiritual offspring.

The condition ordained by Genesis 3:15 is ongoing enmity between the Woman's believing and unbelieving offspring. Her unbelieving offspring are motivated by their own unsaved nature, and the influence of fallen angels; hence Romans 16:20, Ephesians 6:12.

Finally let us look back to a little recognized, but important fact. Romans 16:20 is the only place in all the Scripture that alludes to Genesis 3:15. More directly, 3:15 is not about Jesus the Christ. No Scripture in all the Bible applies Genesis 3:15 to Jesus Christ. None. No early church father believed it applied to Christ. Some during Calvin's time thought it applied to Christ, but Calvin did not

[*Commentary*, comments on Genesis 3:15]. The Roman Catholic Church applied it to Mary. But the Bible *never* applies Genesis 3:15 to Christ or Mary, and neither should we. The interpretation the Woman's offspring refers to Jesus Christ is an allegorical interpretation, not a biblical interpretation, and not the Bible's interpretation.

Reformed theology does allegorize Genesis 3:15 to develop what they name the "protoevangelium," a word meaning "first gospel." They allegorize Genesis 3:15 in this way to support their Old Testament soteriology.

Reformed soteriology states Old Testament sinners were saved by believing on a coming messiah (some even say the Old Testament saved believed specifically on Jesus Christ, by name). The Reformed believe a consequence of their covenant of grace requires the object of saving faith be the same for both Old Testament and New Testament: the Messiah coming (Old Testament) or Messiah arrived (New Testament).

They look to Genesis 3:15 to support their soteriology because they know that not until ca. 1000 BC, Psalm 2, is there mention in the Old Testament scriptures of a coming messiah; but that coming messiah in Psalm 2 is Messiah-king, not Messiah-Redeemer.

The only mention of Messiah-Redeemer in the Old Testament, by that name, "messiah," is ca. 539 BC, Daniel 9:26. Yes, there are scriptures about messiah-redeemer, e.g., Isaiah 53, but the word "messiah" (Hebrew: anointed) is not in those passages, so the connection could not be made until the New Testament revelation revealed Messiah-Redeemer; e.g., see Acts 8:34.

We, today, are able to connect certain Old Testament passages to Messiah-Redeemer because we have the New Testament revelation that tells us Jesus Christ is Messiah-Redeemer-King. Reformed theology reads New Testament revelation into the Old Testament revelation to "find Christ in every Scripture."

What Reformed theology is trying to avoid is extra-biblical (not in the Bible) revelation. As an example, Reformed theology teaches Abraham understood the promise of an heir from his own body as the promise of a coming Messiah-Redeemer.

Because there is no mention of a coming Messiah-Redeemer anywhere between Genesis 3:16 to 15:6, Reformed theology either has to allegorize Genesis 3:15 or admit to extra-biblical revelation. And some do in fact say the Holy Spirit gave Abraham knowledge that he (the Spirit) did not record in Scripture.

Ask yourself: Have I (me, the author of this essay) properly interpreted Genesis 3:15 according to the rules of the Literal hermeneutic? (if you are unsure about using the Literal hermeneutic, see my book, *The Literal Hermeneutic, Explained and Illustrated*.)

Where Reformed soteriology and Dispensational soteriology disagree is the object of saving faith and the content of saving faith.

> Dispensational soteriology: the object of faith in every age is God.
>
> Reformed soteriology: the object of faith in every age is Christ.
>
> Dispensational soteriology: the content of faith changes in the various dispensations.
>
> Reformed soteriology: the content of faith is always Christ, either coming (Old Testament), or arrived (New Testament).

Dispensational theology understands the doctrine of progressive revelation applies as much to soteriology as to other doctrines. No one in the Old Testament knew of a coming messiah-redeemer from the Scripture revelation, unless it was from Daniel 9:26, ca. 239 BC; but no Jewish commentary on that passage understands messiah had to die to be the redeemer.

See my book, *Understanding Dispensational Theology*, chapter "Dispensational Soteriology" for an in depth discussion.

Thoughts on 1 Corinthians 10:1–5

(ESV) "I want you to know, brothers, that our fathers were all under the cloud, and all passed through the sea, 2 and all were baptized into Moses in the cloud and in the sea, 3 and all ate the same spiritual food, 4 and all drank the same spiritual drink. For they drank from the spiritual rock that followed them, and the rock was Christ. 5 Nevertheless, with most of them God was not pleased, for they were overthrown in the wilderness." (I have uncapitalized the word "rock.")

As always, the very first thing to consider is context. The context for this section of verses takes a little work to work out. If your Bible has, as mine does, paragraph headings inserted by the publisher, ignore them as best as you can.

The context actually begins at 8:1, compare 10:25–31. But for our purposes the immediate context for 10:1–5 begins at 9:1–14 where Paul speaks to the issue of supporting those who preach the gospel. He concludes the main part of that discussion at 9:14. Those who preach the gospel should live from the gospel.

At 9:15–23 Paul explains why he has chosen not to live by the rule of 9:14. He makes his point at 9:22–23. Those verses correspond with 10:32–33, forming what is known as an inclusio. You won't find this word in most dictionaries because it mostly relates to biblical studies. It was a literary device used in ancient Hebrew and Greek literature, which did not divide sentences into paragraphs. An inclusio is recognized when how a section begins is similar to how it ends. Thus, the inclusio tells us the subject of the bracketed section, in the same way today a paragraph performs that function.

This definition is from Wikipedia. "In biblical studies, inclusio is a literary device based on a concentric principle, also known as bracketing or an envelope structure, which consists of creating a frame by placing similar material at the beginning and end of a section." Everything within the inclusio has some correspondence to the material bracketing the inclusio.

In the inclusio 9:22–10:32, the correspondence might be described as, "How should a Christian behave?" The discussion is specifically oriented toward the behavior of the Corinthian Christians. Here is how it works out. At 9:15–23 Paul tells us how he conducts his Christian life as a minister for Christ: he preaches and teaches the gospel without charge (he will accept gifts, but he does not live by the rule of 9:14).

At 9:24–27 Paul uses his particular choices, 9:20–22, to talk about how and why one should live a certain, Christian, lifestyle. Paul lives in a certain way to further evangelism. Why does he do that? So as to receive the prize. (He spoke about the prize at 3:11–15.) The Christian is to live in a certain way with his or her eyes on an effective ministry and so as to win the prize.

At 10:1–5 Paul's subject remains the same: the believer's manner of living. He is going to use some of the history of Israel as an example of wrong behavior (10:11), to ask the Corinthians if their life leads to an effective ministry and will win the prize. He points out that everyone in the camp of Israel experienced God's works. But "with most of them God was not pleased." Why? See 10:7–10. Those with whom God was not pleased committed idolatry, tempted God, were sexually immoral, and complained against God's mercies. Some of the Corinthians were behaving in a similar manner.

Here is the implied question: Are there any in the Corinthian church with whom "God was not pleased?" See 10:11–12, "Now these things happened to them as an example, but they were written down for our instruction, on whom the end of the ages has come. 12 Therefore let anyone who thinks that he stands take heed lest he fall."

So the point of the analogy Paul makes at 10:1–4 between Israel under the Old covenant and Christians under the New covenant, is this: Just like everyone in Israel at that time had experienced God's works, so also the Corinthians. Every person in the Corinthian church had heard the gospel preached, the Bible taught, had participated in the Lord's supper, and professed a relationship with Christ. Did their behavior justify such confidence? That is the use and application of the analogy at 10:1–4. As Paul said to them in his second letter, 2 Cor. 13:5 (ESV), "Examine yourselves, to see whether you are in the faith. Test yourselves. Or do you not realize this about yourselves, that Jesus Christ is in you?—unless indeed you fail to meet the test!"

Now I must change subjects. Some people isolate 10:4 from the context. At 10:4 Paul wrote, "For they drank from the spiritual rock that followed them, and the rock was Christ." "There," these people say, "the Old Testament people knew about Christ."

Let's look at the history. In Exodus 17 the people of Israel were on their way to the mountain of God (in Midian, which is today Saudi Arabia) and became thirsty. The date is 1445 BC. The people complained. God had Moses use his staff to strike a rock and water flowed out of the rock to save them from their thirst. About 20–30 years later, in a different place, and a different rock, but the same people, God again brought water out of a rock to save them from their thirst.

So, when Paul says the rock followed them, he was not being literal. We know he is not being literal because he says, "the spiritual rock." Paul is also not being literal when he says, "the rock was Christ." He is making an analogy between the literal rock that saved Israel from thirst with the spiritual "rock" that saved the Corinthians from their sin.

The word "rock" is a common Old Testament metaphor for YHWH God. For example, Deuteronomy 32:15 (ESV), "But Jeshurun grew fat, and kicked; you grew fat, stout, and sleek; then he forsook God who made him and scoffed at the Rock of his salvation." See Psalm 78 where YHWH is the rock; 89:26 where YHWH is the rock of salvation. Psalm 144:1, "YHWH my rock."

So Paul, with a number of Old Testament scriptures in mind, makes a salvation analogy between the literal rocks of Exodus 17 and Numbers 20, and Christ the rock of salvation. One satisfied a physical need, the other a spiritual need. Both were satisfied by water: literal water for physical thirst, spiritual water for spiritual thirst. Thus the analogy.

Paul's purpose was not to teach Old Testament soteriology. His purpose was to ask the Corinthians about the state of their salvation, because their behavior up to this point had given Paul serious doubts as to their salvation. Were any of the Corinthians among those with whom God was not pleased?

Looking to the Old Testament, is there any scripture in Exodus, Leviticus, Numbers, or Deuteronomy telling us that any person in the camp of Israel during those forty years understood the rock in Exodus 17, or the different rock in Numbers 20, represented Jesus Christ? If the Scripture doesn't say it, why do you believe 1 Corinthians 10:4 means those Old Testament peoples knew the two rocks were Christ?

That is the main problem with a certain kind of hermeneutic. It, they, read the New Testament revelation back into the Old Testament revelation, in order to change the meaning of the Old Testament revelation, so they can find Christ where he is not mentioned.

Persecutions and Tribulations

An extract from my book, *A Private Commentary on the Bible: Thessalonians*, published 2021.

2 Thessalonians 1:11 "For which also we pray always concerning you, that our God may reckon you worthy of the calling."

How does God, "reckon you worthy of the calling"? What is this calling? Paul began his prayer with "for which," indicating the substance of his prayer concerns what he has written prior to this verse. The immediate context is Christ glorified and admired in his saints, but the circumstances are the judgment of the unsaved and the afflictions of the saints. This calling, then, must be their persecutions and tribulations—that they would be worthy of suffering for Christ, even as Paul said earlier at 1:4–5.

> Your perseverance and faith in all your persecutions, and in the tribulations that you are patiently bearing, proof of the righteous judgment of God, for you have been counted worthy of the kingdom of God, for which you also suffer

Paul prays they would be worthy of suffering for Christ, so that when Christ appears they might be among the saints in whom Christ will be glorified and admired.

An essential truth must be maintained when we speak of persecutions and tribulations in the believer's life. God decides the time, place, circumstances, and kind of persecutions and tribulations. That means persecutions and tribulations do not take place all the time, in every place, under all circumstances in the believer's life, and are not all of the same kind.

Sometimes persecutions and tribulations are physically violent. At other times they may be estrangement from one's friends, co-workers, spouse, children, relatives, etc. At other times, the individual Christian suffers because of persecution directed at the whole Christian community. (For example, right now in China where non-government approved churches are being disbanded, buildings destroyed, and church leaders imprisoned.) The persecutions and tribulations a believer receives from the world and in the world are many and varied, subtle and gross, and sometimes mundane.

Moreover, no believer suffers for Christ's sake all the time, in every moment, under every circumstance. Psalm 103:14 (ESV), "For he [God] knows our frame; he remembers that we are dust," a conclusion from 103:13 (ESV), "As a father shows compassion to his children, so the Lord shows compassion to those who fear him." Two truths must be maintained: Christ makes us able to stand against persecutions and tribulations, and Christ knows just how much we can withstand when he counts us worthy to suffer persecutions and tribulations for his sake. Seasons of trials, seasons of rest, and seasons of refreshing are all from the Lord.

Here we must take a small walk along a side path. Many are constantly looking for a verse here or a verse there that supports their false doctrine a believer is able to lose their salvation. So, this false doctrine would say, if a Christian is not counted worthy to suffer for Christ, then he/she will not be among the saints in whom Christ will be glorified and admired. They will have lost their salvation.

Salvation is not based on a person's works, Ephesians 2:8, but Christ's finished work, Romans 3:14–25; 1 John 2:2. The believer who is unable or unwilling (because not walking with Lord) to endure persecution and tribulation for Christ's sake will suffer loss of reward, not loss of salvation, 1 Corinthians 3:11–15.

Others will look at this one verse and declare if a person claiming to be a believer is not suffering persecution and tribulation for their belief then they are not a genuine believer but a false professor. The general statements in the Scripture about suffering for one's faith are just that, general statements. They are descriptive not prescriptive.

Let me restate that to make sure all understand: the statements about suffering for one's faith in Christ do not prescribe what will happen, they describe what may happen. For example, 2 Timothy 3:12 (ESV), "all who desire to live a godly life in Christ Jesus will be persecuted" describes what happens to the godly in an ungodly world, it is not a prescription for constant, unremitting persecution.

God is sovereign over our life. God determines when and how a believer suffers. When we see the words "persecution and tribulations" we tend to think of physical violence. Not every suffering for the sake of Christ is physically violent. One example: the devoted parents whose child rejects them and the gospel they both preach and live are suffering persecution and tribulations. The believer who is denied worship and fellowship with other believers (e.g., the COVID-19 restrictions) while non-believers are allowed to gather freely is suffering persecution and tribulations.

But no believer is required by God to suffer continuously. There are seasons of trials, seasons of rest, and seasons of refreshing from the Lord.

Can God Contradict Himself

The most interesting question come to me. "If God cannot contradict Himself, does that mean that the law of noncontradiction is somehow 'greater' than God?"

The law of logic known as noncontradiction is actually Aristotle's principle of noncontradiction (*Metaphysics IV* [Gamma] 3–6). I will refer to the Principle of NonContradiction as PNC. (I am using this web site: https://plato.stanford.edu/entries/aristotle-noncontradiction/).

Aristotle stated three versions: an ontological, a doxastic, and a semantic version. The first version concerns things that exist in the world, the second is about what we can believe, and the third relates to assertion and truth.

> First version: "It is impossible for the same thing to belong and not to belong at the same time to the same thing and in the same respect."

There are some qualifications. The "same thing" that belongs must be one and the same thing and it must be the actual thing and not merely its linguistic expression. Example: one cannot be a baseball pitcher and at the same time a pitcher that holds beer.

> Second version: "It is impossible to hold (to suppose) the same thing to be and not to be."

Example: something cannot be "A" and "not "A." You cannot be you and not you.

> Third version: "opposite assertions cannot be true at the same time."

This third version seems to relate to what a person might both affirm and deny. But "the idea that opposite assertions cannot be true at the same time suggests that this third version is better interpreted as a variant of the first formulation."

Aristotle was not clear as to which version he was defending. Aristotle concluded his discussion of the PNC with this statement, "the firmest belief is that opposite assertions are not true at the same time." Thus, the question, "If God cannot contradict Himself, does that mean that the law of noncontradiction is somehow 'greater' than God?"

This question is of a species of questions that seeks to prove the idea of an omnipotent, omniscient, omnipresent deity is preposterous (a silly notion). These kinds of questions seek a contradiction where none exists.

Let us look at a similar question. Is God able to make something so heavy he is unable to lift it? The rational answer is God can do anything that is not logically impossible. The question states a logical impossibility, therefore it has no bearing on God's omnipotence. Looking to Aristotle's PNC, something cannot exist at the same time under the same conditions as light enough to lift and too heavy to lift.

A more in depth answer stems from the essence of God. All the laws of the universe originate in the essence of God. God is the origin and source of every truth, the origin and source of every law, whether physical or metaphysical. Aristotle did not originate the PNC, he observed an aspect of truth that God designed into the universe he created.

The paradox inherent in the question assumes a wrong definition of God's omniscience by rejecting the most basic principles of deity: 1) God can do anything that is possible to his nature; 2) God cannot do anything that is impossible to his nature.

The above is, of course, simply applying the PNC in a specific application. Stated another way, God cannot contradict himself, because God cannot contradict who he is as God. If God could say or do something contrary to who he is as God then he would not be God, because God is truth and God is omniscient. The PNC applies to God because it originates in God, it is an expression of his deity essence. The PNC is the creation of God: God revealing himself to his creatures.

Looking to the PNC, God cannot be right and wrong at the same time. Because of his omniscience God is always right. He himself is the definition and standard of truth. God cannot contradict himself, because God is truth. Again, the PNC, God cannot be truth and not truth at the same time. Hebrews 6:18, "it is impossible for God to lie."

"If God cannot contradict Himself, does that mean that the law of noncontradiction is somehow 'greater' than God?"

Answer: Aristotle's PNC originated in God's character and essence. The PNC is an observable truth in the universe God designed and created. The PNC states a truth about God: God cannot be God and not God at the same time. God cannot contradict himself, God cannot do anything that is impossible to his nature. The very essence and character of God as omniscient, and holy, and just, and true is the sole origin and source for the truth expressed in Aristotle's principle of noncontradiction. Questions about heavy rocks and logical contradictions begin with the assumption God is not God.

My View of Election

As a Dispensational Calvinist Baptist, let me tell you my view of election.

Election: The choice of a sovereign God (Ephesians 1:4), 1) to give the gift of grace-faith-salvation to effect the salvation of some sinners (Ephesians 2:8), and 2) to take no action, positive or negative, to either effect or deny salvation to other sinners (Romans 10:13; Revelation 22:17). The decree of election includes all means necessary to effectuate salvation in those elected. [Quiggle, *Dictionary.*]

My view of election is based on three things: the doctrine of foreordination; Christ's propitiation (aka "atonement"); and the Canons of the Synod of Dort.

Foreordination: The decree of God occurring between his decision to create and his act of creation as to which agents, events, and outcomes, out of all possible agents, events, and outcomes potential in the decision to create, would pass from possible to actual, in which the liberty or contingency of secondary causes is established, in which God is not the author of sin, and in which no violence is done to the free will of his creatures. (Perhaps more simply, God effectuated from possible to actual certain freely made choices, thereby maintaining both his sovereignty and the moral authority he would give his creatures.) [Quiggle, *God's Choices, the Doctrines of Foreordination, Election, and Predestination.*]

Propitiation. The satisfaction Christ made to God for sin by dying on the cross as the sin-bearer, 2 Corinthians 5:21; Romans 3:25; Hebrews 2:17; 1 John 2:2; 4:10, for the crime of sin committed by human beings, suffering in their place and on their behalf. Christ's propitiation fully satisfied God's holiness and justice for the crime of sin. [Quiggle, *Dictionary.*]

The Canons of Dort are much too long to quote here, but a summary of the part applicable to this discussion. "While the death of Christ is abundantly sufficient to expiate the sins of the whole world, its saving efficacy is limited to the elect." The Canons are available in several places on the internet. The applicable sections are Second Head of Doctrine, Articles 3, 8.

A bit about the English word "world" is necessary. In the Greek there is a word for the habitable earth, a word for the inhabited earth, and a word that may be translated "world" but means an ordered system. This last is *kósmos*. The arrangement of hair and makeup on a woman is a *kósmos*. There is a world of artists, a world of Christians, a world of sinners, a world of the elect, and a world of the non-elect. The meaning depends on context. For example, in John 3:16 the meaning of world, *kósmos*, is "the world of sinners."

Some Calvinists, not all, say the word "world" when used in a salvific (salvation) sense in verses like John 3:16 or 1 John 2:2 is limited to the elect. The reason they say this is they don't understand the difference between propitiation (atonement) and redemption. Let me use the familiar terms. Most Calvinists believe in limited atonement because they believe atonement is the same as redemption. Atonement is not the same as redemption.

Christ's atonement (propitiation) was to satisfy God for the crime of human sin—all and every human sin, past, present, and future, see Scripture references, above, under the definition of propitiation. As Dort said, "the death of Christ is abundantly sufficient to expiate the sins of the whole world." God's justice and holiness having been satisfied, God could then act redemptively toward sinners. God applies the limitless merit of Christ's propitiation according to the decree of election, Ephesians 1:4, through the gift of God: grace-faith-salvation, Ephesians 2:8. As Dort said, "the saving efficacy [of Christ's propitiation] is limited to the elect."

The word "world," as in John 3:16, or the word, "whoever desires, Revelation 22:17, or the word "whoever," Romans 10:13 are directed at each and every sinner that ever was, or is, or ever will be. That is because the limitless merit of Christ's propitiation is sufficient to forgive the sins of all. Therefore all are without excuse and are called to obey the gospel.

The direct purpose of the atonement was not redemption, but judicial satisfaction toward God for the crime of sin. Merit must be applied to be effective. That is clear from every Old Testament sacrifice for sin. The merit of the sacrifice (its vicarious death, represented by its blood) must be applied to effect forgiveness. On the first Passover in Egypt, the merit of the lamb's blood was sufficient for each household, but must be applied to each household to be effective for that particular household, Exodus 12:13. The blood of the sin offering, collected at the moment the animal was killed, was sufficient to atone for sin, but must be applied, Leviticus 5:5–7, to be efficient for forgiveness. The blood on the day of atonement was sufficient for all, but must be applied to the Ark of the Covenant to be efficient to forgive sins.

The merit of Christ's propitiation of God for the sins of the whole world, 1 John 2:2, is sufficient for all, so that the call of the gospel and the duty to believe may legitimately be required on all. The preaching of the gospel is legitimately proclaimed to all, because all have the duty to believe, and God prevents no one from coming and believing.

Why, then, do not all believe? Because human nature is infected with the sin attribute, the result of Adam's sin. Adam's sin permanently changed his human nature by adding a principle of rebellion against God. God calls that principle, or attribute, of human nature, sin. Adam propagated his sinful human nature to his descendants, Genesis 5:3; Romans 5:12. The natural response of every human being toward God is to rebel against God and reject his salvation. The sinner desires to maintain his sin. God would act savingly toward any who come to him by faith, the merit is there, but the natural response of the sinner is to desire his or her sin and reject God. Sin is overcome only by the gift of God, Ephesians 2:8.

God prevents no one from coming or willing or choosing to believe, it is their desire for sin—their choice to continue in sin—that prevents them. As I said at the beginning, God takes no action, positive or negative, to either effect or deny salvation to non-elect sinners.

I have an illustration of this doctrine, that sometimes proves useful. "The river of sinful humankind is justly racing toward the waterfall of death emptying into the lake of eternal fire; God reaches into the river and saves many; he prevents no one from swimming to the safety of the heavenly shore; he puts his saved people on the shore encouraging all to believe on Christ and be saved; he saves all that come to him by faith in his testimony of salvation." [Quiggle, *God's Choices.*]

What is a Pastor?

A pastor is Christ's representative to the Lord's congregation. Christ loves his congregation by loving each individual person. The pastor is to have the same attitude of love and exercise the same care for Christ's people which characterized Christ. A pastor is a man who leads the congregation of the Lord as the faithful servant who pays attention to, cares for, feeds, defends, and disciplines his Master's people to promote their physical and spiritual well-being.

A pastor is one spiritually gifted believer among a congregation of spiritually gifted believers. The pastor's spiritual gift is to be a steward managing Christ's household. The pastor-as-steward is to use his Master's goods to ensure everyone is spiritually fed, clothed with righteous works, active in the congregation, able to protect themselves against spiritual evil, and growing and prospering in the Lord, to the end that everyone in the church can use his or her spiritual gifts to accomplish all the necessary work of his Master's household and business, in the church and in the world.

Christian leadership is not supposed to imitate the world. The pastor is an equal among equals. In the local church he is the servant of Christ, and practices ministry as a shared duty and privilege. His greater honor does not come from being the leader, but from the burden of a greater responsibility.

A pastor's duties:

> Help the individual Christian discover, develop, and use his or her spiritual gifts in harmony with other Christians in the church.

> Mentor, train, spiritually feed, and discipline the Christian for his or her individual good.

> Lead Christians to work together to accomplish the ministries of the church.

> Oversee the functioning of the church as a living organism.

> Oversee the functioning of the church as a living organization.

> Recognize each Christian in the church he leads is important, exciting the pastor to spiritually feed, tend, and discipline a Christian for the good of that individual.

> A pastor experiences grief over the injury, wanderings, or loss of one Christian in the church he leads.

A pastor experiences joy over the growth, development, and ministry of even one Christian in the church he leads, knowing that the good of the individual tends to the good of all.

The pastor is part of the church. He leads the church to serve their common Lord and Savior. His professional training is used to mentor some and guide others into effective ministry. He shepherds individual Christians for the good of the whole flock.

Why Is My Pastor Eating The Sheep?

Why is it that some pastors tend the sheep, but others beat the sheep? Why do some pastors feed the sheep, but others eat the sheep? Which is more important, an individual sheep, or the whole flock? This is an attempt to provide a brief but succinct answer to these questions, and others, after four plus decades experience as a bible teacher and church member in more than a dozen churches in the USA and overseas, in six (baptistic) denominations.

Every pastor has three inevitable challenges that are innate to church ministry. How a pastor responds to those challenges will define his view of the office and his approach to ministry.

> The need to always be right: the church expects the pastor to have the right answer for every Bible verse and every life problem.

> The need to always be in charge: the church expects the pastor to lead the church, head every ministry, be involved in every decision.

> The need to avoid conflict: conflict comes to a pastor on its own. A pastor develops the habits of not initiating communication and being hesitant to respond to communication.

Pastors can have four attitudes toward the sheep of their flock (ranked worst to best):

> The sheep are there to be eaten by the shepherd: used and discarded.

> The sheep are the servants of the shepherd to provide for his needs: used and tended for further use.

> The flock is more important than the individual sheep: the loss of one sheep is always acceptable.

> Each sheep is important, exciting the shepherd to feed, tend, and discipline a sheep for the good of that individual. There is grief over the injury, wanderings, or loss of one sheep. There is joy over the growth, development, and ministry of one sheep. The good of the individual sheep tends to the good of the whole flock.

Pastors can have four attitudes toward himself and his ministry (ranked worst to best):

> The pastor is the church. All members are there for his good, his plans, his ministry.

> The pastor is the most important person in the church. Only his ministry can build the church. Without the pastor the church wouldn't know what to do.

> The pastor is the best leader and guide for the church. His professional training is necessary for the church to accomplish its ministries. He shepherds the flock for the good of the whole.

> The pastor is part of the church. He leads the church to serve their common Lord and Savior. His professional training is used to mentor some and guide others into effective ministry. He shepherds individual sheep for the good of the whole flock.

Pastors can develop an attitude of professional snobbery in their relationship with their church members.

> They are the professionals, the ones who went to school, were trained in the knowledge and mysteries of the gospel, were taught how a church is supposed to function, and are absolutely necessary to the success of the church.

> A member of their flock, no matter how spiritually talented, gifted, mature, or experienced, can never overcome the lack of professional training to be as knowledgeable, experienced, or useful as the pastor. The flock would be scattered, weak, and ineffective without their leadership.

> If one sheep does happen to show some training, or knowledge, or spiritual talent, the pastor knows that he himself is the one who is truly called, qualified, and capable to serve Christ the most effectively.

> Church lay leaders (deacons, elders) are acceptable only as he guides the congregation to select men he has previously declared to be qualified for that position.

Pastors can develop an attitude that their personal preaching-teaching ministry is the only truly effective ministry in the church.

> Anyone can fill a children's ministry position, because it is just

baby-sitting until children become old enough to be affected by the professional minister(s) of the church.

Adult bible study-Sunday School ministries performed by church laymen should center on evangelism, or be a sort of lead-in to attract the flock to the main preaching event.

Laymen cannot really, effectively teach the Scriptures, because they are not formally trained professionals.

Some pastors take the position of chief teacher, because in their view no one else is quite as qualified to educate the flock. The ratio between promoting and supporting Sunday School/Bible studies and promoting the preaching event indicates what the pastor believes is important in adult teaching ministries.

All too often a pastor is called by his flock to be their chief evangelist and chief problem solver. Here, the flock is at fault, for the sheep are abdicating their responsibilities to evangelize the lost and take personal responsibility to lead a normal Christian life. When the church places these unrealistic burdens on their pastor, they should expect him to become a ruler rather than an example.

A large part of the blame for pastors who become rulers rather than leaders, for pastors who use rather than tend their flocks, for ministry professionals that discourage others who have spiritual gifts, can be laid at the feet of the Bible college and seminary.

At the Bible college and seminary young servants are taught that only their professional leadership can know what is good for a church. There rulership, versus Christian leadership, is woven into the warp and woof of the prospective pastor's life. The biblical concept of servant leadership finds little practical expression in the bible college or seminary educational process.

If the nation's Bible colleges and seminaries would act for the good of the church, it would be to teach biblically-based servant leadership, theory and practicum of people management, and the proper appreciation and management of volunteer labor. What a wonderfully beneficent revolution this would cause in the churches!

Was Jesus Born December 25?

Although we cannot say with absolute accuracy the year or month Jesus was born, we can be certain it was not December 25. In fact, we can be certain it was late August or early September, between 6 BC–5 BC.

Irenaeus (AD 120–202) said "our Lord was born about the forty-first year of the reign of Augustus," which would be between March, 4 BC to March, 3 BC. It is important to notice Irenaeus "about" because Jesus was born before Herod died between March 29 and April 11, 4 BC. As the new year, 4 BC, began in March, we are safe saying Jesus was born no later than 5 BC. Considering the visit of the Magi and Herod's slaughter of the children of Bethlehem aged two years old and under, Jesus was born several weeks, if not several months, before the end of 5 BC, perhaps in 6 BC.

Second, Quirinius, Luke 2:2, was sent to the Syrian province as the Lieutenant of Augustus sometime between 7–5 BC, in order to conduct a war against local rebels fighting in Galatia and Syria. [See Ramsay, *Was Christ Born in Bethlehem*.] Therefore Jesus could not have been born later than 5 BC.

Third, we must consider the birth of John the Baptist. John and Jesus were born about six months apart—the angel Gabriel told Mary that Elizabeth was six months pregnant. If John Baptist was born between March–May, 5 BC, then Jesus was born between August–October, 5 BC. So we can pin down the latest year of Jesus' birth as 5 BC.

Fourth, the census, Luke 2:1, can be shown, through various Roman and other historical records and events, to have been scheduled for 9 BC. A census was always conducted the year after it was scheduled. Various problems with Herod (he had lost his "Friend of Caesar" status and tried to get it back, involving two trips to Rome by his representatives) indicate the census took place no earlier than 7 BC and no later than 5 BC. Considering administrative and agricultural details (can't have every farmer leave his crops during harvest season), the census was between 6 BC–5 BC, after the wheat harvest, placing it in August or September.

We can be highly accurate as to the time of year. Luke tells us all we need to know at Luke 1:5. Zecharias the priest, the father of John Baptist, served in the temple in the course of Abijah. Regardless of the year, the eighth course served in May. In 6 BC, the priestly course of Abijah served in the temple May 15–22. During that time, the angel

Gabriel met with Zecharias the priest. Zecharias went home the following week and in June Elizabeth became pregnant.

Six months later, in December, Gabriel met with Mary of Nazareth and she became pregnant. She went with her male relatives to the Feast of Dedication (6–13 December) and then went home with Zecharias to visit with her cousin Elizabeth. She stayed about 3 months—until March, 5 BC, when John was born—six months before Jesus was born. Then Mary returned to Nazareth (going with Zecharias to Passover and returning to Nazareth with her male relatives) and married Joseph. Late in her ninth month of pregnancy, which began August 6 or so, Joseph and Mary traveled to Bethlehem, where in late August or early September (depending on when she left Nazareth plus 3–4 days travel time for the very pregnant Mary) she gave birth, in the barn in the cave at the base of the Tower of the Flock, just as Micah 4:8 had predicted.

So, not December, but late August-early September, in 6 BC or 5 BC. [See my book, *God Became Incarnate*, for an extended discussion.]

My list of Essentials of the Christian Faith

These thirty-six essential doctrines of the Christian faith are from the perspective of a Dispensational Calvinist Baptist: me. They are in the order they occurred to me as I was writing.

— Grace is God choosing to bless because he wants to bless. God's grace is undeserved. Therefore God's grace is free and sovereignly given.

— Sinners are saved from the penalty due their sins by God's grace through their faith not by their works. Because salvation is of grace, salvation is free and sovereignly given.

— Only God is the Savior.

— Jesus Christ alone—no other among human or angel kind—propitiated God for the crime of human sin.

— The Scripture says what it means and means what it says.

— What the Scripture says and means is to be interpreted within the historical, cultural, and grammatical contexts of the individual human authors.

— The Scripture is inspired by God: every word in the autographs was inspired and every word was equally inspired.

— The Scripture is accurate, credible, and authentic in every thing it reports.

— The Scripture is God's credible revelation to humankind concerning himself and his purpose, plans, and processes for the things and beings of the immaterial and material domains which God created.

— Only the autographs of Scripture were inspired. Copies and translations of God's Word are not inspired.

— God has protected the copies and translations of his Word in such a manner that in every practical way the Scripture we have today is sufficient as the guide and rule of personal faith and practice.

— The interpretation of Scripture rests on three questions to be answered in the order given here: What does it say? What does it mean? How does it apply to life? Like the legs supporting a three-legged chair, the three questions are co-equal in importance.

— God is increate. Therefore God is eternal. Therefore God is the origin, source, and creator of all that is not God.

— God is sovereign. God foreordained certain (not all) freely made choices of angels and humankind according to his purpose in creating.

— God's purpose in creating was to manifest his own glory in multiple ways.

— This present universe had a beginning, Genesis 1:1, and has an end, 2 Peter 3:10; Revelation 20:11; 21:1.

— This present universe was created ex nihilo by God with immaterial and material domains and is governed by physical laws God created for this present universe.

— The things and persons in the immaterial and material domains of this present universe were formed by God from materials created ex nihilo by God and function according to physical and biological laws God created to govern the universe.

— The person Adam, i.e., his soul, was created ex nihilo. Adam's body was formed from existing materials called into existence in the ex nihilo creation of the universe.

— All human persons were and are derived soul and body from Adam's soul and body. Each human being is Adam individualized into male or female, therefore each possesses the same human nature and human body as Adam, although there are differences in non-essential physical morphology.

— The existence of a human person begins at the moment the human body and human soul are conceived through the union of human male and human female gametes.

— Every human being has inherited Adam's sinful human nature, Genesis 5:3. Therefore all human beings are sinners from the moment of their conception and judicially culpable for their sin.

— God is a Trinity of persons. Each person is co-equal and co-essential with the other persons. God is Father-Son-Spirit. The Father is God, the Son is God, the Holy Spirit is God. The Father is a person, the Son is a person, the Holy Spirit is a person. One Deity essence, three deity persons. God is one God. All that is in God is God.

— Jesus the Christ is the incarnation of God the Son with Jesus of Nazareth. Jesus the Christ is fully deity and fully human.

— Jesus the Christ is returning to the air to remove his New Testament church from the earth.

— Jesus the Christ is returning to the earth to defeat his enemies and establish his kingdom.

— The only living, personal beings in the universe other than God and human beings are those immaterial beings known as God's messengers, aka "angels."

— Every saved person, Old Testament and New Testament, will be conformed to the image of Christ.

— Every sinner saved, both Old Testament and New Testament, was saved by God's grace through the sinner's faith in God, through God's historically current testimony as given in the progressive revelation of truth.

— A sinner saved is permanently positionally justified in Christ: declared by God judicially not guilty of sins through the imputation of Christ's righteousness.

— Every saved person is permanently positionally sanctified in Christ: declared by God holy through the imputation of Christ's righteousness.

— The saved are kept secure in their salvation by the merit of Christ.

— The saved are given the grace of perseverance to overcome all spiritual and physical obstacles to faith so as to persevere in the faith by faith throughout life and death.

— The state of "saved" is confirmed at moment the sinner exercises saving faith. The confirmed state "saved" is the endless state of the saved.

— The state of "unsaved" is confirmed at the physical death of all those who reject God's salvation. The confirmed state "unsaved" is the endless state of the unsaved.

— There is an endless heaven for the saved and an endless hell for the unsaved.

The timing of the rapture of the NT church is not an essential doctrine. Differences in the timing do not rise to the level of false doctrine, are not a reason to break off fellowship. The essential doctrine is the return of Jesus for his church, as Jesus said in the only passage where he speaks of returning for the church, John 14:2-3.

I believe the Scripture teaches the timing of the rapture is prior to the beginning of the Tribulation.

But the timing of the rapture may indeed be at the end of the Tribulation. There are sound scriptural reasons for believing it is not, but it could be at the end.

The timing of the rapture may be in the middle of the Tribulation. There are sound scriptural reasons for believing it is not, but it could be in the middle.

The partial rapture theory violates essential doctrines and is a false doctrine. Those essential doctrines are the propitiation of God's holiness and justice made by Christ on the cross, and the positional justification of the believer in Christ before God the Judge. The partial rapture theory says believers will be raptured as they become worthy. Salvation has made all believers worthy, Jesus paid it all, nothing need be done by the believer to become worthy.

Indeed, Christ's propitiation and the believer's justification in Christ are essential reasons why I believe the NT church will be removed from God's time of judgment upon those who dwell on the earth. None living at the beginning of the Tribulation are saved. We know this because God's judgment during the Tribulation is upon, "those who dwell on the earth," a phrase used 7 times in the Revelation to identify those who God is judging, beginning at 3:10. A simple evaluation of that phrase, "those who dwell on the earth," in each use in its respective context, will reveal the Tribulation is a time when God is judging the unsaved.

But, I suppose the Scripture teaching Jesus paid for all the believer's sins, and every believer is positionally justified (and sanctified) in Christ could be wrong. That everyone from Paul to you and me could be wrong that Jesus paid it all for every believer, and that the tiny part of the NT church physically living at the time of the Tribulation are the only part of the NT church who are not fully justified, not fully sanctified, that Jesus did not pay for the crime of all their sins, and therefore that tiny part of the NT church must suffer God's wrath against those who dwell on the earth. Do you suppose that might be true?

The essential doctrine is Jesus is returning for his church, because Jesus said he was, and because Jesus paid it all for the believer. But even though the timing is not an essential doctrine, our view of the timing depends on essential doctrines. There is much at stake doctrinally in the timing of the rapture.

What Was and Is an Apostle

There is a significant difference between the apostolic office, held only by Paul and the twelve, and the spiritual gift of apostle. Only the twelve and Paul held the apostolic office and possessed the spiritual gift of apostle.

The apostolic office, not the spiritual gift, required the particular work of authoritatively proclaiming revelation. Those thirteen men holding the apostolic office proclaimed "revelation" in its strictest sense of new information revealed by God through chosen men, not in the sense of illumination (knowledge, understanding) of a previously given revelation from God. The apostolic office also required establishing the New Testament church, and authoritatively judging the behavior of believers. Paul established churches on the basis of his apostolic authority, teaching them genuine doctrine through revelation and explanation, and effecting discipline to correct errors in doctrine and practice.

The spiritual gift "apostle" supported the requirements of the apostolic office, but we should be clear that it was the apostolic office itself, not the spiritual gift, that authorized these men to inerrantly deliver revelation concerning Christ and his gospel, inerrantly establish Christianity as a religion, and inerrantly organize and commission the local church as the organism through whom Christ would administer the gospel to the world.

The "apostolic office" is no longer active in the church; the things required by the office were fully accomplished by those men Christ appointed to that office. The apostolic office will not be filled again: the reference to it in Revelation 21:14 is to "the twelve" who held the apostolic office, and to no others.

The spiritual gift of "apostle" is a rare spiritual gift [Quiggle, *Spiritual Gifts*, 9]. This is *not* the office of Apostle, but a spiritual gift of leadership and administration. This spiritual gift is the special ability God gives to chosen individuals to exercise general leadership or oversight over the church at large or a large number of churches, with authority in spiritual matters, to lead and develop the churches by the proclamation and the teaching of true doctrine (illumination not revelation).

The Apostolic office was confined to Paul and the twelve apostles. The New Testament mentions the spiritual gift of apostle in men who did not occupy the Apostolic office: Barnabas, Acts 14:14, James, the Lord's brother, Galatians 1:19; perhaps Apollos, 1 Corinthians 4:6, 9;

Silvanus, 1 Thessalonians 1:1 with 2:6; Titus, 2 Corinthians 8:23; Epaphroditus, Philippians 2:25; possibly Adronicus and Junia, Romans 16:7.

In post-apostolic times one might look to men such as Augustine, Calvin, Martin Luther, and others who lead a significant group of the church, e.g., Wesley, founder of the Methodist church, or more recently, Robert Ketchum, founder of the GARBC, as examples of the apostolic gift.

The duties of the *Apostolic Office* were:

Inerrantly deliver revelation and explanation concerning Christ, his gospel, and the doctrines of Christianity.

Inerrantly establish Christianity as a religion.

Inerrantly organize and commission the local church as the organism through whom Christ would administer the gospel to the world.

Inerrantly discipline other to correct errors in doctrine and practice.

The Scriptures associated with this gift are wherever we read of the Twelve and Paul exercising the duties of the Apostolic office.

The skills associated with the *Spiritual Gift* of apostle are:

Pioneer and establish new ministries or churches and adapt to different surroundings by being culturally sensitive and aware

Desire to minister to unreached people in other communities or countries

Have responsibilities to oversee ministries or groups of churches

Demonstrate authority and vision for the mission of the church.

Scriptures associated with this gift are:

1 Corinthians 12:28–31; Ephesians 4:11–16; 2 Corinthians 12:12; Matthew 10:1–8; Acts 2:42–44.

Beware a Different Gospel

An extract from my book, *A Private Commentary on the Bible: Galatians*, published 2021.

Galatians 1:6–7, "I am astonished that so quickly you have turned away from the one having called you in the grace of Christ to a different gospel, which is not another of the same kind."

The Galatian churches had turned to a different gospel. This word translated "turned" is metatíthēmi [Zodhiates, s. v. "3346"], to transpose, put in another place. They had been living in the right doctrine but now had put themselves in another doctrine: they had turned away from the true gospel to a false gospel. By "gospel" Paul means the simple evangelistic message of salvation. They had believed that message, but now believed something more was required to make that salvific message effective. This is the "gospel plus something" that false Christianity preaches.

For example, Roman Catholicism believes grace saves, but works must be added to maintain salvation. Two of the Canons of the Council of Trent (AD 1545–1563) says this about salvation [Schaff, *Creeds*, 2:112, 115].

> On Justification. Canon 9, If any one saith, that by faith alone the impious is justified, in such wise to mean, that nothing else is required to cooperate in order to the obtaining the grace of Justification [sic], and that it is not in any way necessary, that he be prepared and disposed by the movement of his own will,: let him be anathema.

> Canon 24. If any one saith, that the justice received is not preserved and also increased before God through good works; but that the said works are merely the fruits and signs of Justification [sic] obtained, but not a cause of the increase thereof: let him be anathema.

The Council of Trent was addressing positional justification in Christ as the consequence of salvation. (Experiential justification, how the believer lives his or her life, does wane and wax with one's conformity to God's righteous standards.)

What does the Scripture say about positional justification in Christ?

> Habakkuk 2:4, The just shall live by his faith.

> Romans 1:17, The just shall live by his faith.

Galatians 3:11, The just shall live by faith.

Hebrews 10:38, the just shall live by faith.

Romans 3:24, having been freely justified by his grace through redemption in Christ Jesus.

Romans 3:28, a person is justified by faith not by deeds of the law.

Romans 5:1, Having been justified by faith we have peace with God.

Galatians 2:16, a person is not justified by works of the law, only through the faith of Jesus Christ.

Should the complaint be the Council of Trent was centuries in the past, the answer is the Canons of Trent remain the official doctrine of the Roman Catholic Church.

The same may be said of another religious system that some think of as genuine Christianity. The Church of Jesus Christ of Latter Day Saints, the Mormons, also believe works are required to maintain salvation. [McConkie, 408, 669–670.]

As with all other doctrines of salvation, justification is available because of the atoning sacrifice of Christ, but it becomes operative in the life of an individual only on conditions of personal righteousness.

Conditional or individual salvation . . . comes by grace with gospel obedience . . . this kind of salvation follows faith, repentance, baptism, receipt of the Holy Ghost, and continued righteousness to the end of one's mortal probation.

For more than fifty years McConkie's work defined Mormon doctrine. Then two things happened. The Mormon church began a decades long propaganda campaign to become accepted as genuine Christianity, and in response genuine Christians began using the book to discover Mormon doctrine. Approval of the book was withdrawn and the work is no longer printed (used copies may still be found online). A search of Mormon doctrine on the internet reveals the doctrine stated above is unchanged, although worded with greater subtlety.

I gave these examples to show the "faith plus something" doctrine has continued since Paul's day. But the doctrine also lives on in genuine Christianity. The "Lordship Salvation" gospel, championed by

John MacArthur in his 1988 book *The Gospel According to Jesus*, is a "faith plus something" doctrine. Examples of the doctrine from the book.

> A person must trust Jesus Christ as his Savior from sin and must also commit himself to Christ as Lord [by which MacArthur means Master, not God] of his life, submitting to his sovereign authority. (*The Gospel*, chapter 1, under the heading, "Wrongly Dividing the Word," 3rd paragraph, last sentence.)

> There are many today who hear the truth of Christ and immediately respond like the son who said he would obey but did not. Their positive response to Jesus will not save them. (*The Gospel*, chapter 15, last paragraph.)

In MacArthur's own words, a positive response to the truth of Christ—is that not saving faith?—will not save a person. There must also be a commitment to obey Christ. Lordship salvation requires "the intent to serve to [sic] God" as part of the positive response to the truth of Christ (*The Gospel*, chapter 15, "What is Repentance," 2nd paragraph).

MacArthur's requirement for a commitment to obedience by the sinner as a precondition for salvation is often confused as a works-based salvation; it isn't. But it is another gospel. MacArthur has more subtly stated the doctrine in the intervening years, but has not changed the doctrine.

What saith the Scripture: by grace you are saved through faith; believe on the Lord Jesus Christ and you will be saved; confess with your mouth and believe in your heart and you will be saved. Simple volitional faith is the requirement for salvation. Obedience is the fruit of salvation, not its prerequisite.

Lordship salvation fails to consider the influence of the sin attribute in unsaved human nature. The sinner is incapable of making a commitment to obedience prior to salvation. Only the regenerated, born-again nature is capable of such a commitment. The gift of God (Ephesians 2:8) enlivens spiritual perception and initiates saving faith. Regeneration follows, obedience after regeneration.

Two, Lordship salvation fails to consider the process of spiritual maturity. The newly-saved believer grows in grace, knowledge, and understanding—is led by the Spirit and directed by the Scripture to grow. Lordship salvation considers a lack of obedience a sign the person is unsaved. One would think the fact Scripture acknowledges that believer's do fail to obey, and why they fail to obey (e.g., 1 John 1:8–10) would have had some impact on MacArthur's thesis. Sadly, no. First John 1:8, 10 are not mentioned or considered in MacArthur's book, and 1 John 1:9 mentioned only in the context of "a progressive, life-long process of repentance" (*The Gospel*, chapter 15, "What is Repentance," last paragraph). Sadly, that insight does not apply to those MacArthur thinks must be unsaved.

Lordship salvation may loudly proclaim "salvation by grace through faith," but to the exercise of simple volitional saving faith the doctrine adds a commitment, "the intent to serve God" through obedience to Christ as Master, as the prerequisite for salvation: faith plus the intent to serve God. That is what makes Lordship Salvation "a different gospel, which is not another of the same kind."

Two Common Errors About Salvation

There are two common errors concerning salvation outside of genuine Christianity. These two errors are complementary (they work together) to perpetuate these false doctrines.

The first error is faith plus works are the origin or prerequisite for saving faith. The second error is like it: faith plus works are necessary to maintain salvation. And the corollary follows: faith plus works are necessary to prove salvation. These errors loudly declare, "You are saved by faith plus obedience to God's laws; You must prove by faith plus obedience you are saved; You must maintain your salvation by faith plus obedience."

Paul argues, In Galatians 3:1–3, that belief in "Jesus Christ crucified" wholly and completely saves the soul from the penalty of sin. The demonstrable fact, "you received the Spirit" (the transformation known as born-again), means you were genuinely saved by the obedience of faith to the truth of Christ crucified: "that complete transformation of character which results from the truth when it is allowed to exert its full influence over the mind" [John Brown, "Galatians," 106].

A commitment to obey or an intent to obey God's laws did not save you. A life of obedience to God's laws does not maintain your salvation. Works, even the work of obedience to God's laws, are neither the origin, nor the prerequisite, nor the proof of saving faith, but are the natural consequence of having been saved, Ephesians 2:10; James 1:17.

Salvation is either by grace through faith—a faith originating in God's gift, Ephesians 2:8—or it is not. Salvation is either maintained by God, or it is not: maintained by the limitless merit of Christ (John 10:9; 28); maintained by God's New covenant with Christ (Hebrews 2:11–13; 10:9, 14, 17–18); demonstrated by perseverance (endurance) in the faith by faith, not by works.

The limitless merit of Christ paid the entire judicial debt for all the believer's past, present, and future sins. Christ's obedience to God's law—to be the complete sacrifice, the propitiation, for the crime of human sin—Christ's obedience saved you by his grace through your faith.

Your obedience to God's law did not save you and will not keep you saved. In the words of the old hymn, "Jesus paid it all." His limitless merit as the propitiation for sin endlessly secures the believer's salvation, Hebrews 10:12, 14, and his eternal priestly intercession in heaven endlessly maintains the believer's salvation, Hebrews 7:25; 1 John 2:1. He will never leave us nor forsake us. Hebrews 13:5, and none can take us out of his hand, John 10:27–30.

Denominations are Inevitable and Important

Saw this meme, again: "Jesus didn't call you to be Catholic, Pentecostal, Baptist or any other denomination. He called you to be born again."

Sounds smart and biblical, doesn't it? Let's just all be born-again. Seems as though it has a kernel of biblical truth. Jesus did not call me to be part of a denomination, that's true.

Well, it's not true. How could Jesus tell his saved people to associate with a particular Christian denomination? None existed! Christianity did not exist! This oft repeated meme is a spiritually-sounding but irrationally anachronistic comment that serves no good purpose.

What Jesus did tell us to do was to associate with the truth, to gather together with others of like precious faith. That is why believers and local churches belong to a denomination: to fulfill the biblical responsibility to gather together with those of like precious faith. A believer associates with a particular local church and denomination because they believe that particular church and denomination is aligned with biblical truth.

We have a biblical example of nascent denominational beliefs and practices: 1 Corinthians 1:11, "I am of Paul, I am of Apollos, I am of Cephas, I am of Christ." The desire to belong, to stand for something, to be loyal to the leader is natural; but that natural desire so easily becomes misguided.

In the same passage, 1:10, we are told what to do about it: "that there be no divisions among you." As time passed the meaning of that exhortation became clear. As time passed divisions continued and became more significant. Separation from false doctrines and wrong practices became necessary. The division between truth and false is always necessary, so that there will be no divisions among those who hold fast to biblical truth.

Here is the value of denominations: they let us know at a glance who is aligned with biblical truth and who is not.

Indeed, that is why denominations began, over 1,500 years ago: to need to withdraw from unscriptural beliefs and practices in order to gather together with others of like faith and proclaim the truth. They were known as Dissenters. They separated from the growing worldliness and doctrinal errors of Roman Catholicism. These Dissenters were criticized for being divisive, for departing from the one true church: for creating denominations.

The Roman Church held so strongly to the principle of "no denominations" that they executed every Dissenter they could lay hands on. Millions—men, women, children, babies—were tortured and murdered in an effort to stop the denominational spirit. But the Holy Spirit prevailed, and truth prevailed, and the Dissenter denominations survived.

Do you see how something biblically sound can so easily be turned into something without biblical value? The division between truth and false is always necessary, so that there will be no divisions among those who hold fast to biblical truth. Those who hold to the false will always violently persecute those who hold to the truth. Violence in the name of truth is a true sign of false beliefs.

The Dissenters were right to separate. They had some doctrinal peculiarities of their own, but they kept biblical truth alive for over a thousand years, persecuted and murdered until the Reformation took up the cause. But keep in mind the Reformers were not trying to separate, they were trying to reform their error-riddled non-denominational church. They also despised the Dissenters, and persecuted them, and encouraged the civil government to violently contain them.

The Holy Spirit was the one who forced the Reformers to form denominations, so the truth would be clearly separated from error. We owe both Dissenters and Reformers a debt of gratitude. We owe the Holy Spirit worship and praise for separating truth from error.

Whatever local church and denomination you associate with, don't just accept what it says and what it does, but carefully measure its beliefs, and doctrines, and values, and practices by the Scripture. Then associate yourself with one that you can prove from Scripture has the most scriptural beliefs, doctrines, values, practices.

There is an irony in the meme I mentioned at the beginning. The author of that meme is advising believers to create a denomination: Born-Again Followers of Christ. Catchy name.

Watch out for those biblically-sounding memes.

Or You Cannot Be Saved

An extract from my book, *A Private Commentary on the Bible: Galatians*, published 2021.

Galatians 2:3, "But not even Titus, who was with me, being Greek, was compelled to be circumcised."

A bit of context is required to understand this verse. The verse is part of the letter Paul is writing to the Galatians concerning the introduction of obedience to the law of circumcision as necessary to salvation. Certain had come and were teaching, "unless you are circumcised according to the custom of Moses, you cannot be saved" (this teaching is revealed at Acts 15:1).

In this section of the Galatian letter, Paul is rehearsing the history of this, "gospel plus obedience" to be saved. Certain men had come to Antioch, Syria, from Jerusalem and were teaching circumcision was necessary to be saved. Paul and Silas and others disputed this teaching. The church decided to send Paul and Silas and others to the apostles and elders in Jerusalem to decide the issue. See Acts 15:6 ff.

We know the result: the council decided no act of obedience was to be added to the gospel of saved by grace through faith. A letter was sent to the churches stating this fact. The Galatians had received this letter, Acts 16:4.

Galatians 2:3 refers to the time before the council had reached its verdict, see Acts 15:4–5. Luke doesn't say anything about Titus. The incident was not relevant to the story Luke was telling in Acts. Here in Galatians the story becomes relevant.

Paul refused to allow Titus to be circumcised. Paul was not opposed to circumcision in and of itself. He circumcised Timothy, Acts 16:3. He did that because the Jews in Lystra knew Timothy had a Greek father and suspected Timothy was not circumcised. They would not meet with Paul and would not let him in the synagogue. Timothy's uncircumcision was a hindrance to preaching the gospel. There was no salvation principle at stake, so Paul followed the rule he stated years later in the first letter to the Corinthians, 9:22 (NKJV), "I have become all things to all men, that I might by all means save some."

But seventeen years before the Corinthian letter, at the council of Jerusalem, certain Christians of Jewish heritage demanded Titus be circumcised. Why? The Jewish law—not the Law of Moses—said gentiles were unclean and therefore physical contact was to be avoided. The only way a gentile could become clean was to convert to Judaism and go through the cleansing rituals, one of which was circumcision. But obviously gentiles were being saved apart from the law. What to do to make these saved gentiles religiously clean?

The covenants of God with Israel, the Abrahamic and Mosaic covenants, required circumcision as a sign of the covenant. No circumcision meant one was outside the covenant. Salvation in Christ was a covenant with God, therefore circumcision must be required. That conclusion was yet another theological construct without a shred of Scripture proof, just a logical argument.

The conclusion logic derives depends on the premise: is it true or false. The premise of this construct was "the covenant of salvation by faith in the Messiah was the same as the former covenants." It wasn't. The sign of the covenant of salvation in Christ is the indwelling Holy Spirit who has made the believer his temple by cleansing the believer's human nature (regeneration; born-again). The only demonstration of that sign is a changed life of obedience to God. But that obedience is the fruit of salvation, not its prerequisite.

Thus the belief, "unless you are circumcised according to the custom of Moses, you cannot be saved," though logical, is false, because the premise underlying the conclusion is false. The Jerusalem council would decide this issue for all the churches. They decided there is no requirement for obedience in order to be saved. They decided for faith plus nothing.

Prior to that decision, some Jewish Christians at the council protested the presence of an uncircumcised believer, Titus. Paul refused to circumcise Titus because the salvation principle, "saved by grace through faith," was at stake. To add any act or action to the gospel is to become enslaved to a law of men, because the gospel principle is simple volitional faith in order to be saved. "Believe on the Lord Jesus Christ and you will be saved," Acts 16:2, and "There is no distinction between Jew and Greek . . . Whoever calls on the name of the Lord shall be saved," Romans 10:12–13.

That principle is what Paul argues in Galatians. That principle is what the uncircumcised Titus represented at the council of Jerusalem. Those Jewish Christians had created "the gospel plus obedience" in order to be saved. Their intent was good. They were zealous for the Law, that God be properly worshiped and obeyed. They were zealous for their gentile Christian brethren, that they be properly saved and escape the judgment of God. But their sincerity was not a proof their doctrine was right.

The gospel is God's grace plus faith in the risen Savior and nothing added. The gospel frees the sinner from the misapprehension that salvation comes by righteousness gained through obedience. This is what is so pernicious in those religions systems—falsely known by the world as Christianity—that require obedience after (what they name) salvation, "or you cannot be saved" (e.g., Mormonism, Roman Catholicism). That is what is so pernicious about "Lordship" salvation: it adds the "intent to serve God" prior to salvation or you cannot be saved [MacArthur, *The Gospel*, chapter 15]. But the salvation principle is solely and simply, "Saved by grace through faith," Ephesians 2:8.

The salvation principle is saved by God's grace alone through the sinner's faith alone in Jesus Christ alone. Paul was zealous for that principle. We should be just as zealous.

When Does a Human Being Become a Person?

A recent candidate for the USA Senate, claiming to be a Christian Pastor, said abortion is consistent with his biblical values.

He responded (to a question about his biblical values): "I think that human agency and freedom is consistent with my view as a minister."

Human agency that is not exercised under God's authority is sin—the very sin that Adam chose. Freedom without authority is rebellion. God has not given humankind the authority to murder human beings.

The candidate was unable to cite or quote a Scripture verse or passage that supported his biblical values.

A human being is a person from the moment of conception. Attributes such as individuality, sentience, reason, morality, self-consciousness do not make a human being a person, they are the result of being a person. Those attributes, and others, manifest as a human being develops because present from conception. The newly-conceived human being is therefore a person, no matter how rudimentary the physical form.

To deny the newly-conceived human being is a person is to deny the human being in the womb has a soul from the moment of conception. The soul is the person. The soul is formed at conception. The animating principle known as "life" is contained in the soul, therefore if the newly-conceived form is alive it must have a soul that makes he or she a living soul, a person.

The authority for the belief the soul is life, the soul is the person is (partly) from Genesis 2:7. God breathed the breath of life into the inert physical form he had molded from the dust of the ground, and that inert, physically dead, physical form became Adam, a living being.

Some think because God breathed a soul into Adam then a human being is not a person—does not have a soul—until the first breath of atmospheric gases is drawn into the physical body. God did not breath atmosphere into Adam—God does not breath—God placed into Adam the soul he had created from nothing.

Adam became physically alive after receiving his soul; the human being in the womb is alive; therefore the human being in the womb has a soul from the moment of conception, not from the first breath, for conception is when the life of the unborn person begins.

That act of God implanting a soul in Adam's physical form was not repeated with the Woman (Eve). She was formed body and soul from Adam. Nor was that act of God repeated at the conception of

Cain, or Abel, or Seth. Life reproduces life, an undeniable law of biology. Life is in the soul, not the body, an undeniable fact of God's creation of living beings.

The human soul possesses all the attributes of a person from the moment the soul begins, demonstrated by Adam's sentience, reasoning, self-consciousness, and other attributes from the moment his life began. For he was created on the sixth day, and on that day received the commands to tend the garden, maintain himself by eating the fruit thereof, given laws to obey, understood the difference between himself and other living beings, and understood the creation of the Woman in relation to himself, Genesis 2:7–8, 16–23.

The soul is a person: the newly-conceived human being has life; therefore the newly-conceived human being has a soul; therefore the newly-conceived human being is a person. Abortion is the premeditated murder of a human person.

The Person Jesus the Christ

In two earlier essays I have discussed that the newly-conceived human being, technically known as a zygote, is a human person: an independent substantive entity. But the incarnation of God the Son in Jesus Christ presents an unusual and irregular circumstance. Does the incarnation of God the Son with Jesus of Nazareth prove a newly-conceived normal human being, the zygote, is a human person?

No. The incarnation presents a special case. The incarnation of God the Son does not prove the newly-conceived, non-incarnational, regular, everyday, normal and expected result of human conception, the human zygote, is a human person.

The human soul the Holy Spirit formed for the purpose of the incarnation was similar to all human souls, but unlike other human souls that particular human soul was not an independent human person. God the Son assumed a human nature—material and immaterial—to himself, joining with the human essence and body and human nature, not with an independent person.

We know all the above: Jesus the Christ was one person with two natures. The person was informed by and acted out of the two natures. But the person did not exist as a person until the incarnation. The incarnation was instantaneous upon conception, forming a person. The council of Chalcedon, AD 451, in what became the definitive statement on the incarnation, said this about the person formed by the incarnation.

> Christ, Son, Lord, Only-Begotten, recognized in two natures, without confusion, without change, without division, without separation; the distinction of natures being in no way annulled by the union, but rather the characteristics of each nature being preserved and coming together to form one Person and subsistence, not as parted or separated into two persons, but one and the same Son and only-begotten God the Word, Lord Jesus Christ

The incarnation was simultaneous with the human conception, but the human conception did not produce an independent human person, else Jesus Christ would be two persons with two natures. The complex of attributes that compose human nature is not the person but is part of the person. God the Son did not merge with a person, but assumed human nature to his deity nature, becoming one person with two natures [Buswell, *Theology*, 2:52]. Looking again at Buswell.

A person is a non-material substantive entity, and is not to be confused with a nature. A nature is not a part of a person in the substantive sense.

A nature is a complex of attributes, and is not to be confused with a substantive entity. [A nature is not a person.]

A will is a certain kind of behavior pattern and is not to be confused with a substantive entity. [A will is not a person.]

We may draw conclusions:

A person has an independent existence as an immaterial soul. A person is a substantive entity.

A nature is not a person. A nature has no independent existence; it is not a substantive entity in any sense. A nature is a complex of attributes or life-principles which must be attached to the soul.

A will is not a person. The will has no independent existence; it is not a substantive entity in any sense. The "will" is a term representing decisions made by the nature.

The personality is not a person, but is the sum total of the attributes and the behavior patterns created by the nature and its decision-making process. The personality has no independent existence; it is not a substantive entity in any sense.

Of the four essential aspects of a sentient entity (person, nature, will, personality), only the person is a substantive entity.

Berkhof [*Theology*, 321–322] provides a similar explanation tending to the same conclusion.

The term "nature" denotes the sum-total of all the essential qualities of a thing, that which makes it what it is. A nature is a substance possessed in common, with all the essential qualities of such a substance. The term "person" denotes a complete substance endowed with reason, and, consequently, a responsible subject of its own actions. Personality is not an essential and integral part of a nature, but is, as it were, the terminus to which it tends. A person is a nature with something added, namely, independent subsistence, individuality. Now the Logos [God the Son] assumed a human nature that was not personalized, that did not exist by itself.

Berkhof concludes that God the Son did not adopt a human person but assumed a human nature, so that there are not two persons in Christ, but the human nature had its personal existence and individuality in the person of the Son of God. The human nature of Christ is not a person but is part of the one Person—the Christ, the Son of God—formed by the incarnation.

A newly-conceived human being is a human person. But the newly-conceived body and soul of Jesus of Nazareth was a special case prepared by the Holy Spirit for incarnation with God the Son. That newly-conceived soul had all the attributes of all human souls, but it was not an independent substantive entity; it was not a person.

Therefore, we should not point to the incarnation to demonstrate the newly-conceived zygote in the mother's womb is a person: an independent substantive entity. The newly-conceived soul to which God joined himself was a human soul, with a human nature, but not a personality, and not a person. Person and personality were from God the Son as informed by the two natures.

[Parts of the above are from Quiggle, *God Became Incarnate*, chapter: His Incarnation; section: The Two Wills of the God-Man.]

Christ Was Born Under The Law

Christ was "born under the Law," that is, the Law of Moses, for several reasons.

One, it was the time of the Law of Moses in Israel.

Two, like the Passover lamb, selected four days before the Passover celebration, Exodus 12:3, he might prove himself to be "without blemish," the requirement for any and every sacrifice.

Three, by living under the Law, Christ qualified himself as that sinless sacrifice who could propitiate God, Hebrews 5:8.

Four, he could die, Philippians 2:8; Hebrews 2:9.

Some teach Christ's obedience to the Law of Moses made the believing sinner obedient to the Law of Moses, through the biblical principle of representation. But neither Paul, nor any other New Testament writer, nor Jesus himself, ever said or implied Christ's obedience to the Law made the believing sinner obedient to the Law of Moses.

If through Christ's sinless, perfect obedience to the Law, the sinner believing on Christ is found obedient to the Law, then the believing sinner was justified by obedience to the Law. God forbid, for then Christ need not have died, and our faith would be in Christ the Law-keeper, not Christ crucified. Christ saved the believer from the Law of Moses by enduring the Law's penalty against the believer. Christ represented the believing sinner on the cross, not through his daily obedience to the Law.

You Cannot Save Yourself.

The self-righteous man or woman will say, "I'm not as bad as I could be. After all, I have not murdered."

Indeed, if you have not murdered you have done well. God's law says, "Do not murder." God's law also says do not commit adultery, do not steal, honor your mother and father, worship God only, do not lie.

If you do not commit adultery, do not steal, you do honor you mother and father, but you do tell a lie, even one lie, then you have violated God's law. Though it has many parts, the law is one law. To violate one part is to be guilty of violating the law. The righteousness you gained by obeying some commandments is lost because you disobeyed one.

God's law is composed of 1,050 individual commandments, including the Ten we tend to think of as God's only commandments. To keep 1,049 of those commandments, but violate one, is to be guilty before God as a lawbreaker. To violate even one commandment is a crime against the holy, just, and righteous God.

God's justice does not add up your good works against your bad works to see which wins the day. God's law has one simple requirement: whoever may keep the whole Law, but in one point may fail in that duty, has become guilty of all, James 2:10.

You have failed to keep all parts of God's law. You violated the law, a crime against God, a sin. The Law-Giver's just sentence against you is, "Guilty of a crime against God."

Every crime has a penalty. God requires complete obedience to his law to gain the righteousness that saves from the penalty for breaking the law. You broke the law. You have no righteousness with which to pay the penalty. Therefore your judicial guilt is endless and the punishment endless. The penalty for a crime against God is physical death and endless separation of your soul from God, in a prison known as hell.

God, in mercy toward you, has delayed your punishment until your physical death. In love God provided a judicial payment for your crime. God came to earth and became man, the God-man Jesus Christ.

Jesus Christ alone has the righteousness to pay the penalty for your crime. Being God he is endlessly righteous. Being man he could die on your behalf for the penalty. He alone was willing to suffer the penalty for you. Jesus Christ suffered for your sin on the cross: he endured God's wrath against your sin and he died for your sin. He was raised from the dead because he fully and completely satisfied God's justice for the crime.

God presents this testimony to every lawbreaker: "*In my love for you, Christ suffered the penalty due to you for your crime, to redeem you out of your guilt and death.*" God's love met your crime of sin by sending his Son to die for your sin.

How do you, the guilty sinner, have Christ's righteousness applied to your need? By faith. If you will believe that you are a sinner needing salvation; that no efforts of your own can save your soul; that Jesus Christ died for your sins; then God will save your soul by applying Christ's payment for sin to the spiritual need of your soul. God will forgive your sins and give you eternal life.

Faith is believing that God's testimony is true; faith is taking action just because you do believe. Faith is the hand of your soul reaching out to take God's gift of salvation and apply it to your soul to take away the guilt and penalty of your crimes against God.

Right now, and once for all, take the keeping of your soul out of your hands, and place the eternal destiny and well-being of your soul into the hands of Christ, for him to keep it safe for eternity. Only by faith in God and God's testimony of Christ the only Savior can you be delivered from the penalty for your crimes against a holy God.

Believe on the Lord Jesus Christ and be saved. Call upon Christ by faith and be saved.

Today's Word Study: *ággelos*

For those who do not know, there is a great gulf fixed between transliteration and translation: they are not the same. To translate a foreign word is to give the meaning of that word in another language. The Greek *epistolé* is translated "letter." To transliterate a foreign word is to replace the foreign alphabet characters with the corresponding alphabet characters in the target language. The Greek *epistolé* is transliterated into English as "epistle." The transliteration of a word is not the meaning of that word.

The Greek word *ággelos* (the double gamma, "gg" is sometimes transliterated into English as "ng", *ángelos*) means "messenger." The word does not mean "angel." The word means "messenger." Sometimes God's messengers were angels. Most of the time God's messengers were human beings. (See my book, *Angelology, A True History of Angels*, Appendices 1–5, for a complete list of all angel appearances and mentions.)

The same is true for the Hebrew word *ma'lāk*, which means "messenger," which is not always translated by Bible versions as "messenger" but is too many times replaced with the transliterated Greek *ággelos*, "angel."

The consistent transliteration of *ággelos* with the transliterated *ággelos*, and the consistent replacement of the Hebrew *ma'lāk* with the transliterated *ággelos* is just wrong. To do so violates the very purpose of a translation, and subverts the interpretive process.

Translators, ancient and modern, knew and know they were doing wrong, but the need to preserve tradition was and is strong. The earliest Bible in my library is a reprint of the AD 1535 Tyndale New Testament. Here is an example of an early misuse of transliteration. Hebrews 2:2, "For if the word spoken by angels was sure." Every version from the KJV to the ESV wrongly preserves this transliteration of *ággelos* (except Young's Literal Translation).

The actual translation of Hebrew's 2:2 is "For if the word having been spoken by messengers." The translators turned into bad interpreters when they transliterated instead of translating. The translators assume the Hebrews Writer was referring to the giving of the Law at Mount Sinai, based on the comparison of Christ to genuine angels in Chapter 1. But the writer changes subjects beginning at 2:1. Neither chapters 1 or 2 mention the Mosaic Law. Moreover, there is no mention of the spirit beings angels in the Exodus 20–23 passage, where the Law was given.

The transliteration of *ággelos* as "angels" at Hebrews 2:2 is based on a false interpretation of the passage by the translators, which has led generations of Bible students to misunderstand Hebrews 2:2. In Hebrews 2:2 the writer looks at all of God's word (the Old Testament). That word spoken through God's messengers has proven to be trustworthy, and every transgression and disobedience of that word received a just punishment—such was Israel's history.

Therefore, Hebrews 2:3, how shall we [the Writer's readers, and you and me] escape a just punishment, if we neglect so great a salvation, that at the first (implying later messengers) began to be spoken by another of God's messengers, the Lord Jesus Christ, a message which was confirmed by those later messengers, the New Testament writers, who heard the Lord Jesus Christ, and 2:4, and confirmed by God himself with signs and wonders (just like the Old Testament revelation was confirmed)?

Now the passage beginning at 2:1 makes sense. Those neglecting the Word of God—not merely, not only, the Mosaic Law, but the entire Old Testament revelation—received a just punishment. So also those who neglect the Word of God spoken by Christ. The comparison is between two revelations of God, because some doubted the validity of this new revelation. If the Old revelation spoken by God through messengers required obedience, so also the New revelation, which was given by a better messenger, the Lord Jesus Christ, and was confirmed by God (just like the older revelation) and confirmed by those messengers whom Christ appointed. don't neglect that Word of God.

Occasionally, translators realized they could not transliterate *ággelos* everywhere. For example, at 2 Corinthians 2:7 *ággelos* is properly translated: "a thorn in the flesh was given to me [Paul], a messenger [*ággelos*] of Satan." The thorn might have been harassment by a fallen angel, but Paul does not define his thorn, so "messenger" is the appropriate translation.

In the Old Testament *ma'lāk* occurs 213 times in 196 verses. About 120 of those times the context indicates an angel is present or mentioned. In the New Testament *ággelos* occurs 186 times in 181 verses. About 150 of those times the context indicates an angel is present or mentioned. God's word was given through many messengers, most of them human. A few messengers were genuinely angels.

In some scriptures, based on context, the proper interpretation of *ma'lāk* or *ággelos* is the spirit beings angels. In those places the word "angel" could be inserted into the translation for clarity. But should not that choice be left to the reader and interpreter, not the translator? In both the Old Testament and New Testament, *ma'lāk* and *ággelos* should be translated "messenger," every time.

What to do? Every time you come across the word "angel" in either the Old Testament or the New Testament, check the context. Understand, don't merely read.

Always Consult the Context

2 Corinthians 9:7, "For God loves the one who gives willingly." My translation.

Once again the English translations do the believer a disservice. Other versions universally translate "God loves a cheerful giver." "Cheerful" is not the meaning of *hilarós* [Zodhiates, s. v. "2431"] in context. The word appears only here in the New Testament.

Some pulpit expositions make this word to mean "hilarious" (which is derived from *hilarós*) but that is not the correct meaning. The word does mean a happy, glad, or cheerful state of mind, but does not mean overcome with laughter or mirth, or humorously affected.

The correct meaning of *hilarós* is seen in the contrast Paul makes in 9:7 between the one who gives "grudgingly or of necessity" versus the one who gives *hilarós*. The meaning of *hilarós* in its contrast with "grudgingly or of necessity" is willingly, voluntarily.

The point is not the sentiment of joy or happiness, but the inclination to act agreeable to God's will in giving: voluntarily yielding the intent of the soul to the needs of others according to the will of God.

The decision formed by *hilarós* is to give eagerly, out of the desire to please God and submit to his will. Giving is delight to the *hilarós* person because it is an honor and joy to give to God by giving to meet the necessities of his people.

The reason for giving, which is doing God's will, means a person is not giving with regret as unwilling to let the money go, nor of necessity, as though pressured to give, but from delight, because the righteous person delights him or herself in the will of God.

The emotion happiness can accompany *hilarós*, but it is the attitude of willingly and voluntarily responding to the will of God that is the foundation that happy emotion, and thereby the root of becoming a happy, generous, willing giver.

God loves the one who gives willingly. [Source: James D. Quiggle, *Why Christians Should Not Tithe*, 86.]

Canons of the Synod of Dort, AD 1619

The Official Definition of the Reformed Doctrine of Soteriology, accepted by Reformed and Dispensational alike. From the Canons of Dort.

Second Head of Doctrine. Article 3.

> The death of the Son of God is the only and most perfect sacrifice and satisfaction for sin, and is of infinite worth and value, abundantly sufficient to expiate the sins of the whole world.

My discussion. The limitless merit of Christ's "perfect sacrifice and satisfaction for sin" was and is of "abundantly sufficient" value in the sight of God "to expiate" (make atonement for, propitiate God for) "the sins of the whole world," even as 1 John 2:2 states. There remains no sin past, present, or future for which Christ did not atone. As will be seen in Article 8, this atonement for all sins is not universal salvation. The Bible teaches some are endlessly saved and others will suffer endless punishment because not saved. The conclusion is Christ's "abundantly sufficient" atonement, Christ's propitiation of God for "the sins of the whole world" is not the same as redemption, because only some are saved, not all.

Second Head of Doctrine. Article 8. (Emphasis mine.)

> For this was the sovereign counsel, and most gracious will and purpose of God the Father, that the quickening *saving efficacy of the most precious death of His Son should extend to all the elect, for bestowing upon them alone the gift of justifying faith,* thereby to bring them infallibly to salvation: that is, it was the will of God, that Christ by the blood of the cross, whereby He confirmed the new covenant, should effectually redeem out of every people, tribe, nation, and language, all those, and those only, who were from eternity chosen to salvation and given to Him by the Father; that He should confer upon them faith, which together with all the other saving gifts of the Holy Spirit, He purchased for them by His death; should purge them from all sin, both original and actual, whether committed before or after believing; and having faithfully preserved them even to the end, should at last bring them free from every spot and blemish to the enjoyment of glory in His own presence forever.

My discussion: The limitless merit of Christ's "perfect sacrifice and satisfaction for sin" (article 3), was of "abundantly sufficient" value in the sight of God "to expiate" (to make atonement for, propitiate God for) "the sins of the whole world" (article 3) even as 1 John 2:2 states. The "saving efficiency" of that limitless merit to effect a sinner's redemption is applied to "extend to all the elect," and only the elect.

Conclusion: Christ's propitiation of God for sin was of sufficient merit to satisfy God's justice for the crime of all sins past, present, and future. That propitiation of God's justice is not in itself redemptive. The merit of Christ's propitiation must be applied to effect redemption.

That is what the Old Testament sacrifices for sin taught. Forgiveness was a two-step process: the sacrifice for sin was killed; the merit of that sacrifice, that is, its blood, representing its vicarious death on behalf of the sinner, must be presented to God—in the OT applied at the altar—to effect forgiveness. Without a sacrificial death there was no merit; without application there was no forgiveness. Atonement is not forgiveness, atonement powers forgiveness.

The merit of a sacrifice for sin must be applied to be effective. Even so, God applies the merit of Christ's propitiation to individual sinners according to his decree of election, Ephesians 1:4, through his gift of grace-faith-salvation, Ephesians 2:8. As the Canons of Dort teach, the merit of Christ's propitiation was sufficient for all the sins of the whole world, efficient only to save the elect. Atonement is not redemption, atonement powers redemption.

Atonement-Propitiation-Merit is sufficient for all sins; Redemption-Salvation is applied to the elect alone. The death of Christ is abundantly sufficient to expiate the sins of the whole world, its saving efficacy is limited to the elect. The doctrine is Unlimited Atonement, Limited Redemption.

The unlimited sufficiency of Christ's propitiation is why the gospel call may be legitimately proclaimed to all. Any sinner, elect or non-elect, who rejects his or her sin and believes on God and God's testimony as to the way of salvation may be saved.

But Christ's merit saves only those who do believe, and only the elect do believe. Why? The sinner loves his or her sin more than salvation. That is why the sinner must be given by God his gift of grace-faith-salvation, that overcomes sin's dominion and convicts the sinner of sin, the Savior, and salvation. Thereby the sinner is made willing to believe and be saved, and thereby he/she does infallibly believe and is saved.

The complete satisfaction of God's justice through Christ's propitiation also allows God to righteously interact with all the world by delaying justice and dispensing mercy.

To summarize: the merit of Christ's atonement (propitiation) of God for sins was sufficient for all the sins of all the world past, present, and future, and efficient to redeem only those to whom it is applied, which are those whom God has elected.

There are six conclusions that may be derived from the Canons of the Synod of Dort, Second Head of Doctrine, Articles 3 and 8.

1. The TULIP, developed after the Synod of Dort, does not quite reflect the Canons of Dort, but the opinions of other Reformed theologians. Instead of the "L" representing "Limited Atonement," the "L" should represent "Limited Redemption." The Canons teach Unlimited Atonement, Limited Redemption.

2. The limitless merit of Christ's Atonement-Propitiation must be applied to be efficient to save. The limitless merit is applied individually through the decree of election via the gift of God.

3. Atonement is not redemption. Christ's Atonement-Propitiation was not redemptive in itself. The purpose was to satisfy God's justice so God could act redemptively. Christ's Atonement-Propitiation is not redemption, it powers redemption.

4. Christ did not die for the elect. Christ died to propitiate (completely satisfy) God's justice for the crime of human sin. Having been satisfied, God may act justly in mercy toward the world and in redemption toward the elect. God applies the limitless merit of the atonement according to his decree of election in order to effect the redemption of the elect.

5. The strawman argument that unlimited atonement means universal salvation is false. Salvation is effected by God according to his decree of election, Ephesians 1:4, through God's gift of grace-faith-salvation, Ephesians 2:8, thereby applying the merit of Christ's propitiation only to those individuals whom he elected, and to the elect only.

6. The gospel of salvation may be legitimately proclaimed to all, and saving belief required of all, because there is all-sufficient merit to save all. God could and would act savingly toward any non-elect who rejected their sin and believed on God and God's testimony as to the way of salvation. But the non-elect desire their sin more than their salvation, and by nature reject God. The dominion of sin cannot be overcome except by God's gift, Ephesians 2:8, which convicts the

sinner of sin, the Savior, and salvation, thereby making the sinner willing to exercise saving faith, which he/she will infallibly do upon receiving God's gift.

The Merit of the Atonement

I am regularly in a discussion about the limit or intent of Christ's propitiation of God for sin. Was Christ's propitiation the same as redemption: purposefully of limited sufficiency to redeem the elect (Limited Atonement, Limited Redemption)?

Or is propitiation not redemption but intended to power redemption, by being unlimited in its sufficiency to satisfy God's justice against sin, so God could justly act in mercy toward the world of sinners and act in redemption toward certain sinners (Unlimited Atonement, Limited Redemption)?

If the merit Christ gained on the Cross to save sinners is limited to a select few (the doctrine of Limited Atonement, the "L" in the TULIP), then we had better change a few scriptures. A small sampling:

> John 3:15, Whoever believes in Him should not perish but have eternal life.

> Acts 2:21, Whoever calls on the name of the Lord Shall be saved.

> Acts 10:43, Whoever believes in Him will receive remission of sins.

> Rom 10:13, Whoever calls on the name of the Lord shall be saved.

> Rev 22:17, Whoever desires, let him take the water of life freely.

After all, we don't want to call God a liar. But fortunately a sound hermeneutic and proper exegesis does not require us to remove or change any scriptures.

If the merit to save is unlimited, then the proclamation of sin, the Savior, and salvation may be legitimately, honestly, and with the authority of Scripture given to "Whoever." Which, after all, is the commandment to the NT Church. Because the merit is unlimited, the moral obligation to believe legitimately falls on all who are told, "Whoever calls on the name of the Lord shall be saved."

How it works: the unlimited merit of Christ's atonement is the complete satisfaction Christ made to God by dying on the cross as the sin-bearer, 2 Corinthians 5:21; Romans 3:25; Hebrews 2:17; 1 John 2:2; 4:10, for the crime of sin committed by human beings, suffering in their place and on their behalf. Christ's propitiation fully satisfied

God's holiness and justice for the crime of sin.

How God applies that merit: The choice of a sovereign God (Ephesians 1:4), one) to give the gift of grace-faith-salvation to effect the salvation of some sinners (Ephesians 2:8), and two) to take no action, positive or negative, to either effect or deny salvation to other sinners (Romans 10:13; Revelation 22:17).

A simple illustration of Unlimited Atonement, Limited Redemption: The river of sinful humankind is justly racing toward the waterfall of death emptying into the lake of eternal fire; God reaches into the river and saves many; he prevents no one from swimming to the safety of the heavenly shore; he puts his saved people on the shore encouraging all to believe on Christ and be saved; he saves all that come to him by faith in his testimony of salvation.

The correct doctrine is Unlimited Atonement, Limited Redemption. "Whoever calls on the name of the Lord shall be saved" also means "Whoever does not call on the name of the Lord shall not be saved."

The Reformed doctrine of Christ's atonement is: "abundantly sufficient [unlimited] to expiate the sins of the whole world, its saving efficacy is limited to the elect" (Canons of the Synod of Dort," Second head of Doctrine, Articles 3, 8). Some disagree, but, ironically, they still proclaim the gospel to "Whoever."

But (always a "but") someone will say, if Christ propitiated God for all sin, then why are all sinners not saved, and how is God just in punishing sin? The answer is twofold. One, as discussed above, propitiation is not redemption but intended to power redemption. The propitiation was directed toward God to satisfy his justice so he could act in redemption.

> "Satisfaction or expiation does not awaken love in the divine mind. It only renders it consistent with his justice that God should exercise his love towards transgressors of this law" [Hodge, 2:478].

By being unlimited in its sufficiency to satisfy God's justice against sin, God could justly act in mercy toward the world of sinners and act in redemption toward certain sinners: those whom he elected to salvation (Ephesians 1:4; 2 Thessalonians 2:13; 1 Peter 1:2).

The second part of the answer is the merit of the propitiation must be applied by faith, else there is no salvation. The merit of a propitiation must be applied to redeem. That is an elementary teaching of Scripture. The Old Testament teaches us. The sacrifice for sin was slain away from the altar. Then the merit of the sacrifice, the blood and body representing its substitutionary death for sin, were presented on the altar to effect forgiveness. Propitiation, then redemption.

The New Testament doctrine is the same. Christ vicarious suffered for the imputed sins (the judicial guilt of those sins) of the world, was slain as punishment for the crime of those sins, buried, went to heaven to present the merit, and resurrected because his propitiation had satisfied God's justice and therefore was effective to redeem. Then the disciples received the Holy Spirit, John 20:22. Then salvation was preached in Jesus' name, Acts 2:38.

Without the application of Christ's merit there is no salvation. How is that application made? That is also an elementary teaching: by faith alone. No faith = no application of Christ's merit = no salvation.

The reason the unsaved remain unsaved is not because the merit for salvation is lacking (it is limitless), but the unsaved never apply that limitless merit to their spiritual need by faith. The unbreakable rule of salvation is just this: saved by grace *through faith*.

The NIV, An Interpretive Translation

Ah, the NIV. A blessing because more people own Bibles because of it, and presumably (hopefully) more people read their Bibles because of the NIV.

But, the NIV has a problem (No, I don't want to hear the KJV is better, or the NIV leaves out verses. Go write your own essay).

The NIV has a problem. The NIV often, way too often, gives an interpretive translation. A translation is when you use a word or words that faithfully represents the meaning of the word as defined or used in the original language. An interpretive translation is when the translator says, "Well the original word means this, but I am going to translate it with a word that doesn't mean that but better fits the context, as I interpret the verse." (Oversimplified, but essentially correct.)

The NIV's interpretive translations are not all bad. I use the NIV in my studies, and from time to time quote it in my commentaries. Sometimes the NIV makes a relatively harmless interpretive translation. For example, 1 Samuel 15:33, KJV, "Samuel hewed Agag in pieces"; NKJV, "Samuel hacked Agag to pieces"; HCSB, "he hacked Agag to pieces"; ESV, "Samuel hacked Agag to pieces"; NIV, "Samuel put Agag to death." The NIV communicates the meaning, if not the details.

But sometime the NIV goes too far. Their translation really is an interpretation. I am of late working in Galatians, and 3:22–35 is a good example.

In 3:22–25 Paul uses three Greek words that must be considered synergistically, not individually, if the meaning is to be brought out in translation. I have highlighted the critical words, and give the reference numbers from Zodhiates *Dictionary* (which are also the Strong's numbers). First, my translation.

> 22 But the Scripture *included* [4788] the whole under sin, so that the promise by faith of Jesus Christ may be given to those believing. 23 Now before faith came we were being *guarded* [5432] under the Law, *enclosed* [4788] until the faith about to be revealed. 24 So that the Law became our *guardian* [3807], unto Christ, so that by faith we may be justified. 25 But faith having come we are no longer under a *guardian* [3807].

The passage in the NIV.

> 22 But the Scripture declares that the whole world is a *prisoner* [4788] of sin, so that what was promised, being given through faith in Jesus Christ, might be given to those who believe. 23 Before this faith came, we were *held prisoners* [5432] by the law, *locked up* [4788] until faith should be revealed. 24 So the law was *put in charge* [3708] to lead us to Christ that we might be justified by faith. 25 Now that faith has come, we are no longer under *the supervision of the law* [3807].

The NIV translation "whole world" in 3:22 is also quite wrong, as the Greek word there is simply "all" (and wrong interpretively, as Paul is referring to the Mosaic Law), but we will focus on the highlighted words.

Word number 4788 in 3:22 and 3:23 is *sugkleíō*, "to shut up or enclose together." In no use does the word mean "prisoner" or "locked up" as in the NIV translation. All occurrences: Luke 5:6; Romans 11:32; Galatians 3:22, 23.

The word number 5432 in 3:23 is *phrouréō*, "to watch, guard, keep." In no use does this word mean "held prisoner" as in the NIV translation. All occurrences: 2 Corinthians 11:32; Galatians 3:23; Philippians 4:7; 1 Peter 1:5.

The word number 3807 in 3:24, 25 is *paidagōgós*. The *paidagōgós* was a domestic slave responsible for the moral and physical safety of the minor heir. One of the duties of the *paidagōgós* was to accompany the minor heir to and from home and school. Over time the original meaning was lost by a metonymy of the effect for the cause: the cause, accompany the heir to protect from physical or moral harm along the way, was substituted for the effect, taking the heir to the teacher, and that further evolved into the later meaning of *paidagōgós*, which is, "teacher."

In no use does the word mean "put in charge" or "supervision of the Law" as in the NIV translation. All occurrences: 1 Corinthians 4:15; Galatians 3:24, 25.

The interplay of these words indicates Paul's intent. At 3:23, every person in OT Israel was included under the Law's accusation of sin, "so that the promise by faith of Jesus Christ may be given to those believing," not to those being obedient to the Law. At 3:24–25, during the era of the Law, everyone was guarded by the Law, until the era of faith in Christ arrived, which, having come we who believe are no longer under a guardian.

(Paul's argument about the Law does apply to the gentiles, who show a law written in their conscience, Romans 2:14–15, indicating God also gave the gentiles a law as a guardian. But Paul does not make that argument here in the Galatian letter. Paul's focus in Galatians is on those teachers of the Law who are trying to place the saved gentiles under the Law of Moses.)

What to do? If you read the NIV devotionally, or as part of reading plan, incorporate another versions into your reading. I suggest (no particular order of preference) the ESV, HCSB, or NKJV. When the NIV has something not in essential agreement other versions, go with another version for that day's reading.

If you use a commentary based on the NIV, compare it with another (it is always a good idea to compare commentaries). Most commentators merely using the NIV will call it out when its interpretive translation does not agree with the majority view of a Scripture passage. The guy on the fringe is seldom the guy you want to listen to.

If you use a commentary that was specifically commissioned to use only the NIV text, meaning the commentary author is obligated to defend the NIV translation, well, the advice on using multiple commentaries takes on greater importance. The *NIV Application Commentary* (NIVAC) is one of those where the author of each individual volume is obligated to use and defend the NIV translation. The author's comments in the NIVAC volume on Galatians prompted this essay. Be a smart reader and consumer.

We never did it that way before.

This question was asked: "Is online Christianity an assembly of God?"

The answer is, "What are the functions of a church?"

If the functions of a NT church may only be met by people meeting daily in the Jerusalem temple and in many houses, the earliest form of the NT church, Acts 2:46, then when the NT church began meeting in fields, and later in graveyards and catacombs filled with graves, and in prisons, and then later in buildings dedicated to the purpose, then very shortly after the beginning the NT church has failed and continued to fail to be a church.

But thank God the NT church is not defined by where it meets, but by what it does.

If the functions of a NT church may be performed in a house, a field, graveyards, a catacomb, a prison, a building, then there are no limits to where and how a NT church may meet, as it adapts to times, cultures, and circumstances—as long as the functions of a NT church are performed.

History, like any other tool, when wrongly used produces wrong results. The history of the NT church, considered in all the places in the world where the Holy Spirit has formed NT churches, is not limited to a building.

What are the functions of a New Testament church? It is a small list.

— Preach the Word, 2 Timothy 4:2.

— Teach the word, 2 Timothy 2:2

— Assemble together, regularly, Hebrews 10:25.

— Baptize new believers, Matthew 28:19; Acts 10:47.

— Communion, Luke 22:17–20; 1 Corinthians 11:24–25

— Financial support to ministers of the gospel, 1 Corinthians 9:14.

— Minister to one another, 1 Peter 4:10.

Which of these require a building?

— Preaching and teaching maybe done online.

— An online community is assembling together.

— Financial support may be given online

— Ministering to one another maybe done online.

What about baptism? Answer: the New Testament church does not have a priesthood, and water in sufficient quantity for dunking is required. If a sufficient amount of water is not available, if baptism may be done only by pouring or sprinkling, the New Testament church has done that too, in its long history (see the Didache). A river, a stream, a bathtub, a shower, a pitcher of water will do. Is it the quantity of water that counts, or the obedience of the believer?

What about communion? Answer: the New Testament church does not have a priesthood. The elements may be self-administered. If an online community has gathered for that purpose, then have they not shared in that experience? Communion is a remembrance of the Lord, not one another.

Brethren, my preference is the assembly of the saints meet in person. But that preference is based on decades of personal experience reinforced by centuries of Christian tradition.

Times have changed, and the New Testament church must be willing to adapt. The early church regularly met in homes, and when under persecution met in graveyards, catacombs and open areas in small groups of a few individual believers. They also met as a congregation from time to time, when it was allowed (see Governor Pliny's letter to emperor Trajan), or when it was safe.

Traditions are wonderful servants, but terrible masters. Every hallowed tradition of today was at one time a new practice, to which many objected, because it was not tradition. So also meeting in buildings weekly to do "church." There is no place in the scriptures requiring we meet in a building.

I believe the New Testament church must adapt. I believe that in some places in the world, the USA for example, the Holy Spirit has in fact begun that process of creating new traditions to meet current circumstances. We should—we must—with the power and guidance of the Holy Spirit, continue to find ways to meet as a congregation in person, as did the early, persecuted church. But we must not object to new ways of meeting just because "we never did it that way before."

Free Will

God has given human beings the moral authority to make choices (free will), he allows his saved people to exercise that authority to cooperate, or to resist, the Spirit's work in their life.

> Free will is the moral authority to make choices within the physical, moral, and spiritual boundaries of human nature, as further influenced by internal and external motivations and consequences. [Quiggle, *Dictionary.*]

Jonathan Edwards, his treatise, "A Careful and Strict Inquiry Into the Prevailing Notions of the Freedom of the Will," [*Works*, 1:4–5], agrees (emphasis Edwards).

> The faculty of the *Will*, is that power, or principle of mind, by which it is capable of choosing . . .. A man never, in any instance, wills anything contrary to his desires, or desires anything contrary to his will . . .. in every act of *Will* there is an act of choice; that in every *volition* there is a *preference*, or a prevailing inclination of the soul.

This preference (desires, inclination), is just the same as what I describe as the physical, moral, and spiritual boundaries of human nature. We choose out of what we can do, not out of what we cannot do. Though a person might prefer to fly to than walk (Edward's illustration), he cannot choose to fly because that preference is not within the capability of his human nature.

R. C. Sproul agrees, saying, "Edwards declares that free moral agents always act according to the strongest inclination they have at the moment of choice. To say it another way, we always choose according to our inclinations, and we always choose according to our strongest inclination at a given moment." External forces also incline the will. "Coercion involves external forces coming into our lives that seek to force us to do things, that, all things being equal, we would not choose to do," giving us the inclination to choose one course of action or another. [https://www.ligonier.org/learn/series/chosen_by_god/what-is-free-will/].

Sproul also addressed the effect of sin in relation to choice and salvation. "Calvin, in examining the question of free will, says that if we mean by free will that fallen man has the ability to choose what he wants, then of course fallen man has free will. But if we mean by that term that man in his fallen state has the moral power and ability to choose righteousness, then, said Calvin, "free will is far too grandiose a term to apply to fallen man." And with that sentiment I would agree." [Same reference as above.]

Sproul summarizes Edwards and Calvin with his view of Free will [same reference].

> What I'm saying, along with Edwards and Calvin, is that if my choices flow out of my disposition and out of my desires, and if my actions are effects that have causes and reasons behind them, then my personal desire in a very real sense determines my personal choice.
>
> If my desires determine my choice, how then can I be free? Remember I said that, in every choice, our choice is both free and determined. But what determines it is me, and this we call self-determination. Self-determination is not the denial of freedom, but the essence of freedom. For the self to be able to determine its own choices is what free will is all about.
>
> The simple point I'm trying to make is that not only may we choose according to our own desires but, in fact, we always choose according to our desires. I'll take it even to the superlative degree and say that we must always choose according to the strongest inclination at the moment. That is the essence of free choice—to be able to choose what you want.

Both the sinner and the saint choose to cooperate, or not, with the Holy Spirit. In the issue of salvation, the sinner refuses to cooperate, unless the Holy Spirit applies to his spiritual state God's gift of grace-faith-salvation, Ephesians 2:8.

That the Holy Spirit may be resisted is clear from Scripture. Acts 7:51 (NKJV), "You always resist the Holy Spirit; as your fathers did, so do you." Though Stephen is speaking of the unsaved in Israel, that same sin attribute that prompts the unsaved sinner to reject God prompts the saved sinner to resist God. That is one reason why there is such a wide variance in spiritual maturity within any Christian community.

Recommending the Works of A. W. Pink

I have all (or the vast majority) of Pink's republished works, and his biography by Iain Murray. I haven't read out of Pink in quite a while, but I still use him now and then. Pink was a good teacher, and remains useful in that respect, especially for the fundamental Calvinistic doctrines of sin, the Savior, salvation, and the Puritan emphasis on the normal Christian profession and life.

Pink was prone to excessive typology in some of his OT expositions, but that was a characteristic of many writers of his times. He was anti-Dispensational, but most of his reading in the Dispensationalists was from the hyper-dispensationalist's; and he was very well read in the Puritans and Neo-puritans, which contributed to his rejection of dispensationalism. But his books on the Antichrist and the Rapture ("The Redeemer's Return") should be required reading; as should his work, "Why Four Gospels," a work as worthy as Juke's book on that subject.

One cannot deny Pink's basic argument against those Dispensationalists with whom he was familiar, who, much in the same way as the Mid-Acts Dispensationalists of today, wrongly divided the scriptures as applicable only to this group or that group, whereas Pink taught all the Scripture is for every believer.

One cannot find a better argument or exposition for God's sovereignty than Pink, not only in the book that bears that name ("The Sovereignty of God"), but as a characteristic in all his writings. I vividly remember his comments on Judas (in his exposition of John's Gospel), which give all the glory to God.

One cannot find a better argument and exposition of the sin attribute in human nature than "Gleanings From the Scripture" (Moody Press) a book that changed my entire perception of the human condition and the necessity for salvation. That exposition, read early in my Christian life, remains the core of my hamartiology, unchanged by decades of subsequent study on the subject.

One cannot find a more soul-searching book on the Christian profession and life than "Practical Christianity (Baker Books). Nor a more sound exposition of the prayers in the NT epistles of than "Gleanings From Paul" (Moody Press) and "Effectual Fervent Prayer (Baker Books).

Pink's works on the revelation and interpretation of Scripture were very valuable to me as a young Christian, especially, "Interpretation of the Scriptures" (Baker Books). The other two works were, "The Divine

Inspiration of the Bible" (Guardian Press), and "The Doctrine of Revelation" (Baker Books). These three will set you on the right course to always respect the Scripture.

I don't always agree with Pink. For example, the short studies on tithing and Sabbath-keeping (which reflect both the Puritans he read and majority views of his times). His excessive typology in "Gleanings in Exodus" and "Gleanings in Genesis" (both Moody press) mar the usefulness of both books (*without* rendering them useless).

On the other hand, I learned how to do scripture biography from "The Life of Elijah" (Banner of Truth), and some good life-lessons as well.

My experience with those who are "anti-Pink" is their prejudice is informed (or mal-informed) by this or that particular work(s). As someone who has read the republished works of A.W. Pink, and as a young Christian looking for biblical answers, I found him practical and informative. As with any author on the Scripture, I recommend him with the usual cautions.

Prayer.

Whatever God has decreed to happen, he decrees means as well as ends. Prayer is one of the means God has decreed to accomplish his ends—prayer is one of the processes that accomplish God's plans that fulfill God's purpose.

Prayer is the believer asking God for such things that are within God's will to give the believer. As such, prayer is an act of dependence upon and submission to God. The first step in prayer is worship, the second is submission, the third is dependence, the fourth is giving thanks and praise, the fifth is asking for one's self and then for others.

God answers prayer in many ways for five reasons.

No. You are asking amiss that you may spend it on your pleasures (James 4:3). I will never give you these things. Stop asking.

No. You are asking for something you may have, but what you are asking for is not right for you, at least not now. I love you too much to give you what you are requesting.

Yes. I want you to understand this thing you want so desperately is not the best for you, so you become wise and stop wanting to have it.

Yes. Here is what you have requested. Use it wisely.

Yes, and here is more for you to use wisely.

Here is what we must learn about prayer. Ask in faith for the things God has promised. Receive by faith whatever God gives. Receive a "Yes" or "No" with equal praise and thankfulness.

I believe there are some things in our life that are conditioned upon our prayers, and other things that are not. Regardless, we are to pray, the exhortation occurs several times in Scripture.

When you come to God in prayer, are you demanding or are you asking? Don't push God to do what you want and call it faith or prayer. Follow in faith where God is leading, even though you can't get all you want.

To repeat: the first step in prayer is worship, the second is submission, the third is dependence, the fourth is giving thanks, the fifth is asking for one's self, and then for others.

Marriage: Patriarchalism or Egalitarianism?

A simple definition of egalitarianism is "the doctrine that all people are equal and deserve equal rights and opportunities." Patriarchalism is a bit more complicated. "Patriarchy is a social system in which men hold primary power and predominate in roles of political leadership, moral authority, social privilege and control of property."

The fact Eve was a comparable helper to Adam must mean Adam was a comparable helper to Eve. God designed a partnership. The word translated "comparable" is *neged*, whose basic meaning is "before," in the sense of "in front of." The Hebrew word suggests that what God creates for Adam will correspond to him. Thus the new creation will be neither a superior nor an inferior, but an equal. If, as is the case, each is equal to the other, then each is the *'ēzer*, helper, of the other. Adam immediately understands. His *'ēzer* neged is the same as he is: the source of her physical nature was his body; the source of her soul was his soul.

A man and a woman bear God's image, so they complement (complete) each other and can unite to complete each other. A woman is man's equal and must be treated with respect and love. Adam's authority was a delegated and therefore limited authority. He had dominion, but he must exercise his dominion responsibly, in accordance with God's sovereign rule over all things, living and non-living. Adam could not treat, use, or abuse the Woman in any way. As Paul says in Ephesians 5:24, "But even as the church is in submission to Christ, even so the wives to their husbands in all things" (my translation). Christ never exercises his dominion to abuse the church in any way, or tell the church to do something morally or ethnically wrong, degrading, or demeaning. So too the husband in his headship and dominion of his wife and family. The husband exercises his dominion through responsible leadership, he is not to be a king, a tyrant, or a dictator. His dominion is not sovereign but a partnership with his *'ēzer neged*.

At Genesis 1:26 both man and woman were to "have dominion" over the earthly creation, but it is never said men were given dominion over women. Men and women equally share their dominion over the earthly creation, for both were created in the image of God. That image was deranged but not erased by their sin; they each remained equally made in God's image, therefore equal respect was due to each from the other. Adam's "rule," at Genesis 3:16 (*māshal*) cannot mean a woman is to be subjugated to a man in the manner the other living creatures are subjugated to humankind. In most uses in Scripture *māshal* simply means to exercise authority. Considering the "comparable helper" relationship between husband and wife, the word has the idea of leadership.

The Woman was formed to be a comparable helper for man: a helper suitable for life, not merely for projects, or labor, or house work, or bearing children, or having sex, or cooking dinner. No other living creature was suitable to be man's helper. For the woman to be formed suitable for the man means she must be like the man, and the man must be like her: each is to be a comparable helper for the other. The words *'ēzer neged* invoke partnership and companionship, not dominion and oppression, and certainly not patriarchalism, which was created by sinful human beings, not by God.

The Problem of Complementarianism in Marriage

It is simply a fact the man was formed first, Genesis 2:7, then the woman from the man, 2:21–22. A fact God gave Adam the prohibition against the tree, 2:17, and Adam told it to the Woman. A fact the man named the animals, 2:19–20, and gave the woman her name, Woman, 2:24. A fact that after sin the Woman's position under the man's leadership was affirmed, 3:16, and the man chastised for following the Woman's leadership, 3:17. And a fact we see Adam exercise his leadership authority by renaming the Woman, 3:20, Eve.

The leadership authority and responsibility was vested in the man, not the woman. But the man's leadership is not dominion, Genesis 1:26, "Let *them* have dominion over" the earth and its creatures, but not the man over the woman, or the woman over the man. Thus, men and women are partners in their joint dominion and in their relationships, including the marriage relationship. Marriage is a partnership of equals. If the Woman was formed to be the comparable helper to the man, which she was, then the man must be comparable to her, and thereby her helper also.

The man's function in marriage is to be the managing partner: leadership, not ruling. The woman's function as the man's partner in marriage is to advise her partner and support his leadership. Neither is restricted from performing any function a marriage may require, they just need to work out who does what. The man, as the leader, bears the responsibility for the decision and its consequences.

The problem is how the man's leadership and the woman's advice and support are worked out in a marriage. The answer to that question for most is Complementarianism. But that is not really the answer. Let me explain.

A marriage is either egalitarian, a partnership of equals, or patriarchal, man rules, woman submits. The basis for egalitarianism in marriage is "Who are you?' The basis for patriarchalism in marriage is, "What is your function."

Here is what most do not know: Complementarianism works in both egalitarian marriages and in patriarchal marriages.

Complementarianism is a theological view in Christianity, Judaism, and Islam, that men and women have different but complementary roles and responsibilities in marriage, family life, and religious leadership. One need merely compare how complementarianism functions in Christianity, Judaism, and Islam to see that Complementarianism easily fits under both patriarchalism and egalitarianism. Complementarianism is a man-made (literally made by males) social construct designed to justify both patriarchalism and egalitarianism. That is the problem of complementarianism in marriage

In the patriarchal view of marriage, men hold primary power and predominate in roles of leadership, moral authority, social privilege and control of property. Marriage is not a partnership under patriarchalism. The wife's complementary role is to submit, the husbands complementary role is to rule. Complimentary marriage under patriarchalism says, "this is your function" because of who you are: a man or a woman. Under patriarchalism the woman is never right unless the man says she is right. The woman's advice is useless unless the man adopts it as his own idea. The man rules, the woman submits.

Under the patriarchal view of marriage, the woman can never be responsible for any function. The man decides what is or is not to be done; the woman's responsibility is to do as she is told, to be responsible when she does not, and to be responsible for her failure. The man rules, the woman submits.

In the egalitarianism view of marriage, husband and wife are equal and deserve equal rights and opportunities. Both have responsible roles in leadership, moral authority, social privilege and control of property. Marriage in the egalitarianism view is a partnership of equals. The husband's complementary role is to provide leadership, the woman's complementary role is to provide advice and support the husband's leadership.

In marriage under egalitarianism, the man says to the woman, "You are my equal and your role in the partnership is the supporting partner, because the Bible says the man is the managing partner." Under egalitarianism the woman's advice may be right or wrong. The woman's advice may be useful, whether adopted or not. As the managing partner, the man may adopt the woman's advice without injuring his status as the managing partner. As the managing partner the man has the ultimate responsibility for the consequences of any course of action he may chose for his family, whether his own or the woman's advice.

Under the egalitarianism view of marriage, the man may have the woman take responsibility for certain functions or duties of the household; e.g., finances. She is responsible for her own actions, success or failure, the husband is responsible with her for success or failure.

Obviously, under real world conditions, all marriages are

complementary, and most marriages are a combination, greater or lesser, of egalitarianism and patriarchalism. But one or the other will predominate. Certainly we can go to any point in history, and look at any religious or cultural situation, and find one or the other carried to the logical extreme.

In Christianity, both man and woman are equal in Christ. In Genesis 1:26 both men and woman are given dominion over the earth and its creatures, Neither is given dominion over the other. This did not change after their sin. Genesis 3:16 reiterates the leadership role given to the husband by reason of his primacy in the creation. Notice nothing similar is said to the man. Indeed, at 3:17 he is chastised for abandoning his leadership responsibilities. At 3:20 he exercises his leadership: he renames his wife from "the Woman" (2:24), to "Eve." The man is the managing partner, the woman the supporting partner. Each was designed to be helper to the other.

Your task, as husband and wife, is to keep your marriage relationship in proper biblical balance between authority, function, and responsibility. In my view, the better marriages decide "what is your function" based on "who are you": egalitarianism not patriarchalism. Each is either a partner to the other, or not.

Abuse in Marriage

The wife is to submit willingly to her husband's leadership authority, but within the limits of her own relationship with Jesus Christ.

Just as all believers are to submit to governmental authority until it crosses the line between sin and righteousness set by God, even so the wife toward the husband, and the husband toward the wife. The submission of the wife to the husband is not unlimited, the authority of the husband over the wife is not unlimited. Both "submit to one another" (Ephesians 5:21) in the Lord. Each must meet his or her own responsibilities to Christ first, spouse second. This applies whether married to a believer or an unbeliever.

Godly virtues do not include submission to abuse of any kind. A spouse is not to be afraid, but rather to stand firm in their faith. Their wife's submission to the husband is built upon the foundation of her submission to Christ. Just as she would not receive abuse from Christ, she is not to submit to abuse from her husband.

A husband is to love his wife as Christ loves the church, Ephesians 5:25. Christ has authority over the church. The leadership authority of the husband toward the wife is like Christ's headship over the church, but the authority of the husband is not absolute, for he is not Christ. Moreover, he does not stand apart from his wife, but the two form one-flesh, a union at once physical and spiritual.

Christ's authority over the church is used to lead the church into righteousness, by responding to the needs of the church for spiritual leadership and power. Christ is the head of the church through his servant-leadership over the church, by which he rules the church, so that through his body (the church) Christ can fulfill his various offices. But the husband's leadership compared to Christ's headship has limits: the husband is not Christ, he is not sovereign in authority, his authority has limits. Christ's headship applied to the husband's leadership expresses care rather than control, responsibility rather than rule, leadership not dominion.

The husband must not abuse his leadership authority as a means to command his wife to rebel against God, and the wife must resist any such abuse. The wife is to submit to her husband as to the Lord, but this does not mean the wife's submission violates her responsibility to love, obey, and serve her Lord and God Jesus Christ.

The biblical commandment to the husband to love his wife as Christ loves his church, means his leadership authority is to be used properly for the benefit of his wife, not to abuse his wife in any way. If the husband would have the wife respect and support his leadership, then he must give to her the same respect and care and love as Christ for his church. The commandment to the wife to respect her husband recognizes the honor due the one who has the authority.

Therefore, a wife is not required to submit to abuse. She is not required to allow her children to be abused. She is not to be an emotional or physical "doormat" for her husband's immoral behavior, physical abuse, or emotional abuse.

A Christian wife may take many good and proper actions if she or her children are physically, sexually, verbally, or emotionally abused. These actions range from prayer and counseling, to seeking shelter outside the home, to involving police and lawyers. The same may be said of the Christian husband who finds himself or his children in an abusive situation.

Small Reflections and Ruminations

On Various Subjects

Repentance

Repentance is not to be a continuous act by the Christian, but its occurrence is to be inversely proportional to his or her life of practical righteousness. That's why we are called to holiness. That's why we are exhorted to righteousness.

Repentance is the New Testament equivalent of the Old Testament sacrifice for sin. To borrow from the Old Testament, 1 Sam. 15:22; Psalm 51:6; Isaiah 1:11. "Have I as great a delight in your repentance as in a life of righteousness?"

As Augustine said, "Insofar as a believer abides in Christ, insofar he does not sin." (Homily IV, Epistle of John)

Abide more often than you repent.

Worldly Solutions to Worldly Problems

Not every issue is a spiritual issue to be resolved by spiritual means. I don't turn to the Bible when my car won't start or my clothes washer needs replacing. I look for a worldly solution to a worldly problem.

Do I pray about the problem? Yes. Do I ask for guidance to the best solution? Yes. But I look to the world to help me find a mechanic, or advise me on the best replacement for the washer. Do I follow biblical principles in spending that $$$? Yes. But I spend worldly $$$ to get a worldly solution to a worldly problem.

Various Christians have identified the spiritual issues facing us in the USA today, and the spiritual actions required to resolve the spiritual issues. But they one and all seem determined to convince Christians not to vote.

That's just wrong. We live in the world, and those worldly issues require worldly solutions. Therefore I vote. Do I pray about my vote? Yes. Do I ask for guidance to the best vote? Yes. Do I seek biblical principles and values to guide my vote? Yes. But I still get out there and apply the worldly solution to the worldly problem. I vote.

Example: the worldly problem is abortion. The biblical value is life. The biblical solution is prayer. The worldly solution is peaceful protest and voting.

Do both. Don't let your Christianity become so idealistic that you cannot act pragmatically. Be salt and light: preserve moral values and expose wrong values. Vote.

God Works With Us Not For Us

Our Christian life is a product of God's grace, but a lot of effort must be expended in living that life. God will work with us, but he will not work for us. When we turn a problem over to God, we are trusting in him to make all our circumstances work out for our good. His usual way of doing that is to help us work through the circumstances.

In other words, God does not resolve our problems apart from us, but through us as we work our way through the problem, trusting in him and using the power and wisdom he supplies (or has supplied through our past experience). He gives empowering grace that enables us, but grace is useless unless we use it. He supplies all the grace needed to overcome the problem, but we have to use that grace to overcome the problem: a lot of hard work is required on our part.

You and I flip a switch and power is supplied to our clothes washer. The washer uses our power to do its hard work. So it is with empowering grace and the believer. In most cases and under most circumstances, God doesn't solve our problems with a divine word to make them go away, he manages our circumstances and provides us working power so that they can be satisfactorily resolved through our faith and good works.

"Give your problems to me," says God, "and then work with me as together we resolve these issues, for I am the empowering God, and you are my servant who accomplishes my will." Isn't this how Jesus lived? God supplied, Jesus worked. Jesus believed, God empowered. God required, Jesus obeyed. Jesus obeyed, God blessed. Jesus was a genuine believer: Be, Go, and Do likewise.

In Times Like These

God makes the rain to fall on the godly and ungodly alike (Matthew 5:45), which is to say, the goodness of God blesses in a general way. But that also means both godly and ungodly are alike affected when God withholds his blessing.

A believer may respond in two ways. He/she may remain and endure the trials. Or he/she may move away from the arena of trials and suffering, as Elimelech (Book of Ruth) did. Whatever the choice, a believer is always responsible to live a godly life. Some believers will endure, by necessity or by choice, and demonstrate their godliness through a trial. Other believers will choose to remove themselves from the trial; they remain responsible to live godly lives.

God is an ever present help in times of trouble and blessing. The life of faith is not that God keeps his saved people out of difficult times, but in how his people respond when God withholds the rain.

Love One Another

Christ commanded his saved people to love one another. The kind of love he requires is not affection. This kind of love is a choice of the will to seek the best good for another without expectation of recompense, reciprocity, or recognition for one's self, and without consideration of merit or demerit in the one so loved. This love is willing to experience self-sacrifice for the benefit of a fellow believer. This love causes the believer to be long suffering toward others, to treat others kindly, to actively seek the welfare of the one loved, the best good for his or her sake alone, without seeking any return for one's self, without jealousy or pride or vanity, bearing all things, believing all things, hoping all things, and enduring all things which achieve the goal of loving another. This love is to be pure, i.e., without ulterior motive, and in its application it is to be earnest, constant, and fervent. This kind of love cares for others more than self. This kind of love, i.e., its application throughout one's Christian life, is mandatory: Jesus said, "This is my commandment for you." Its exercise is not natural to the human soul, but can only be achieved through a relationship with Christ as Savior.

The Persistence of the Death Cult

The old ways never truly die or fade away; they just change clothes and names. Killing unwanted children has always been the way of the world. Molech was an ancient false god whose form was a brass bull with outstretched arms. The interior was hollow; a fire was kindled inside the brass form; children were tied to the arms and burned to death in worship to the god. The ancient Egyptians set their children on the banks of the Nile to be eaten by their crocodile gods. All societies practiced abortion in the womb, and a form of late term abortion known as exposure: leaving an unwanted new-born outside to be killed by dehydration, starvation, foul weather, or wild animals.

From the earliest days Christians condemned abortion and exposure (e.g., Justin Martyr, *First Apology*, AD 150), and saved as many exposed children as they could.

Predating Justin, the Didache 2:2, "You shall not murder a child by abortion nor kill them when born." The "Didache" or "Teaching of the Apostles" was a Christian text, dated mid to late 1st century AD. Some date it to the 2nd century. The Christians regarded abortion and infanticide a crime. The Romans thought that point of view was strange.

Brothers and sisters in Christ, We have been fighting this battle for a very long time. Our spiritual ancestors did not stop fighting. Neither should we.

Today, the religion of abortion-on-demand names their gods "convenience" and "pro-choice," but it is still the same old gods and practices, just dressed up in new clothes and modern euphemisms.

Can I do All Things?

Philippians 4:13, "I can do all things through Christ which strengtheneth me." (KJV, NKJV, NLT).

Interestingly, the word "Christ" is not in the vast majority of manuscripts. The word appears to have been added (at the end of the verse) in some manuscripts to supply a noun for the definite article *tó*, the, (in the Dative masculine singular, thus, the one.) Applying a little common sense, if Christ had been in the original text, there would have been no reason to omit it.

Philippians 4:13 actually reads, "In everything I have strength in the one [*tó*] strengthening me."

The one strengthening me does so in order that I may do all those things which he has purposed for me to do.

Thus, interpretively, "I can do all the things God requires of me, because he strengthens me to do those things."

Through the more accurate text one eliminates the abuse and misuse caused by the Textus Receptus and the KJV translation. You cannot do all things, but you can do those things for which you have been strengthened.

You are able to do all those things God requires of you. Within the context of the passage, the "all things" Paul refers to are those things he has previously mentioned: "4:12 And I know how to be low, and I know how to have more than enough. In everything and in all things I have learned also to be filled and to be hungry, and to have more than enough and to suffer need."

Whatever God brings into your life, those are the things you can do, because those are the things he has given you strength to do. Philippians 4:13 brings us back to the most basic element of the Christian life: submission to and dependence upon God in Christ.

With so many language tools available today (most coded to Strong's numbering), no one should depend solely on an English translation.

Persistent Faith

I sit on the edge of personal disaster, my feet dangling over the precipice of destruction, weak—all too weak—in body and soul. "Lord, where are you?" I whisper. "Lord where are you?" I demand.

"I am here, answering your prayers. Did you not ask to have your faith made strong? Did you not ask to depend on me more? I know you, my child. If you are well enough to depend on yourself, then you will forget to depend on me."

I sit on the edge of my destruction, weak in body and soul, all my devices and plans useless, restrained from falling into the abyss of despair by the mercy and kindness of Jesus alone. So foolish was I. The Lord keeps his people nearby to disaster so they can hear the noise and feel the heat, but not so close that their faith may be destroyed. There, in that middle ground between comfort and destruction, they remain sensible of Christ's guiding, empowering, protecting presence.

To the worldling this seems cruel. They want a god who will keep them from every trial and bless them with success in every endeavour—a god whom they will abandon at the first sight or sense of trouble. But the wise Christian understands the mercy in Christ's loving providence that makes us weak in the world but strong in the Lord.

1 John 1:7

I was thinking on this part of 1 John 1:7, "The blood of Jesus Christ his Son cleanses us from all sin." The sentence reads about the same in any translation from any denomination, whether Protestant, Dissenter, or Roman Catholic. The Greek "cleanse" in this context means the same in any language: to purify from the moral pollution and judicial guilt of sin. No more is required to cleanse from sin than faith in risen Christ who shed his blood on the cross, who imputed sin to himself (2 Corinthians 5:21) and paid the penalty—death—on behalf of and in the place of sinners.

If one is cleansed by the blood, what other acts or works, here or hereafter, can be required? Moreover the grammar requires a continuing act of cleansing: the blood was shed once but constantly cleanses the believing soul. "All" is the Greek *pas*, "all, every." Every sin brings death without the blood, no sin is so minor but that it needs the blood, and no sin is excluded from the cleansing power of the blood. The blood is "continually cleansing us from every sin" so that no human intervention in this life, and no extra remedy in the next life, are required. "The apostle joins nothing with this blood. It hath the sole and sovereign virtue" (Charnock).

Not a Building

The other day I saw an article on China's government using zoning laws to remove crosses and destroy buildings used by local churches. Some congregations had disbanded because they didn't have a building in which to meet.

Friends, this is just wrong. A church is not a building, and it had better be identified by words and actions more tangible than a symbol. The Christian church prospered for about 300 years without buildings. They used worship, evangelistic, and missionary models that fit their circumstances. They multiplied throughout the world and we are their heirs. Christians of generations past prospered as they met in secret on the outskirts of a town, in a farmer's field, someone's home, a cemetery, an abandoned or condemned building, underground storm drains, or ancient catacombs.

Christian, what would you do if the government razed your building? It is happening today throughout the world. Obedience to the command to "not forsake the assembling of ourselves together" (Hebrews 10:25), doesn't require a building or a symbol, just a church willing to love Christ and be obedient.

Ask For Help

Even the very best of Believers need help from other Believers. The holy angel in Daniel 10 said he struggled for 21 days against a fallen angel. He did his best, he persevered in his task, but the fallen angel was too powerful for him to overcome. So he asked God for help and God sent Michael, a more powerful angel. With Michael's help the angel overcame his problem. If a holy angel can ask for help, so can I; so can you.

Basics

The basics of the Christian life are read, study, and understand the word; pray for spiritual guidance, understanding, and power; obey God's rules for living; serve one another in the name of Christ; and testify to the lost about Jesus. Some of these things can be and should be done individually, daily, and life-long. However, these "musts" of the Christian life are also meant to be done corporately, that is to say, together, in a local church, with fellow brothers and sisters in Christ of like faith. The Believer, then, has two critical choices. One, he/she must be a participating member of a local church. Two, he/she must be a member of a local church where the majority believe and practice the "do this" and don't do that" doctrines and practices of the Christian faith. As Jude said, contend for the faith, build yourselves up in the faith, pray in the Holy Spirit, keep yourselves in the love of God, look for Jesus, give the gospel of salvation. Are you doing the basics?

A Little Strength

In Jesus' letter to the church at Philadelphia he commended them for having "a little strength." That may not seem like a great commendation, but look what they did with a little strength. They "kept my word," meaning they did not mix their faith with worldly practices or compromises. They did not "deny my name," meaning they publicly confessed Christ as Lord and Savior, regardless of the outcome.

Because they had a little strength, Christ "opened a door" to them of opportunities to serve and testify. It wasn't their strength that opened the door and it wasn't their strength that kept it open. What gave them opportunities to serve and testify was the "little strength" they consistently used to worship, obey, serve, testify, and fellowship with Christ. Be encouraged! Be faithful to the basics—do what Scripture says, witness about the Savoir—and Christ will empower you to do the rest.

Tell Them the Gospel

When witnessing to the unsaved, do you invite them to your church? Or do you tell them about your Savior? Inviting an unsaved person to your church may seem like a good idea—they can hear the gospel there from the preacher. Well, why can't they hear the gospel from you? Jesus didn't say, "I am the door of the sheepfold" (the local church) he said, John 10:7, "I am the door of the sheep. If anyone enter in by me, he/she will be saved." The Christian's first witness to the lost should be about how to be saved. Tell the lost about Jesus, because he is the only door by which the lost become Christ's sheep and enter into eternal life.

Partnership

The life of testimony and service in Christianity is one of partnership with Christ. He is the managing and empowering partner and we are the working partner: the channel of communication through which his wisdom and strength are applied in the world. It is not the strength of the hammer that drives the nail; it is the strength and skill of the builder that causes the hammer to accomplish the purpose of its existence. The hammer needs be strong enough to withstand the impact; it must be stronger than the circumstances of its life.

The "little strength" our Lord requires of us is to endure the trial—and he provides each believer with the endurance and wisdom to endure and prosper (James 1:2–4). When that happens, when the will of God is accomplished with the power of God through the instrument of God—when the believer is made perfect (by God) in his or her weakness, then all the glory goes to God, 2 Corinthians 12:9, 10.

Always Uphill

The Christian's path in life winds uphill all the way. We come to no point in our lives where we can cease our earnest striving to be less like the world and more like Christ. The path is not reformation, which is all of self, but transformation, which is the believer and the Holy Spirit working together to worship, obey, serve, and have fellowship with God in Christ. Everything of significance begins with worship;

obedience is the key that turns on every spiritual power; serving Christ brings glory to God through his good works performed with us; intimate fellowship is the result of depending on his guidance and power in every aspect of life. The Christian's path in life winds uphill all the way, until we are face to face with Christ our Savior.

Important Verses

Important verses in my life. "For if I build again the things which I destroyed, I make myself a transgressor" (Galatians 2:16). "Also I heard the voice of YHWH saying, 'Who will I send, and who will go for us?' Then I said, 'See me! Send me!' " (Isaiah 6:8). "Go, stand in the temple and speak unto the people all the words of this life" (Acts 5:20). "Your statutes have been my songs in the house of my pilgrimage" (Psalm 119:54).

Therefore my prayer: teach me that I might teach others also" (from 2 Timothy 2:2); and my purpose: to teach the Scripture to faithful men and women, who will then be able to teach others also; and my process: to explain the Scriptures and answer the questions for those who want to understand.

Then A Miracle Happens

I once saw a cartoon in which a scientist was working out a new process on his marker board. After many calculations he had reached an impasse, so he had drawn a box and written in it, "Then a miracle happens," and then his process continued with actions to take once he had his "miracle."

I want to use that cartoon in a serious way to talk about the gospel and salvation. The Christian is a witness: he or she gives a witness of sin, the Savior, and salvation. Then a miracle happens. It is the supranatural action of Jesus and the Holy Spirit that saves the sinner, and we dare not forget that fact.

The Christian is not a salesperson pitching the product "salvation" for the coin of faith; he or she is not supposed to teach sinners how to act like Christians before Christ acts to save the sinner. The Christian is to be a faithful witness, "then a miracle happens," and after the sinner is saved the Christian's work of making disciples—followers of Jesus—begins.

Let us always remember the biblical order of the gospel: we

testify; Jesus saves.

Tokens of His Love

When Christ's saved people experience his chastisement, the lack of his blessing, and the withholding of his grace, these are tokens of Christ's love calling out, "You have done wrong, return to me. I will receive you with mercy and forgiveness, I will restore you to your place at my side."

Christ will hold out his hands in love, grace, mercy, and forgiveness to any of his people who will turn again to the Lord in confession and repentance from their sins. "We have sinned, we have not obeyed, we have done wickedly, and we have rebelled." Our restoration from sinning is grounded in the merciful character and forgiving nature of Christ.

"O Lord, hear! O Lord, forgive! O Lord, listen and act! Do not delay for your own sake, my God, for your people who are called by your name" (Daniel 9:19).

The Gospel In Terrible Times

We see a world rejecting Christ and moan that we live in terrible times. We pray Christ would return to punish his enemies and reward his people. But these modern conditions are not unlike what faced the earliest Christians. Like it was for them, so also us: this time of moral and spiritual emptiness is a call for Christians to take action.

First, by counting the cost and living righteous lives which reveal true faith in Christ, honoring him and his commandments for holy living. Second, by testifying to individuals sinners about sin, the Savior, and salvation. The Holy Spirit will use the moral and spiritual emptiness of the culture to bring some to saving faith in Christ through Christian lives and testimony.

No matter how desperate and morally defiled a culture may become, God will always glorify himself by saving souls for himself. The early Christians didn't have programs and ministries to evangelize the lost. Each Christian lived the Word, preached the gospel, suffered for Christ, and entered into His glory. Go and do likewise. We cannot change the culture—2000 years of experience tells us that; but through us Christ can change individual lives.

Fixing Problems

I have small problems, big problems, and huge insurmountable problems. So I worry and stress and try to fix them the best I can. THEN I remember that to God all my problems are small. THEN I go to God. I need to remember to take the shortcut around all my problems, big or small: go to God first!

But that's not the whole story. God is in the faith building business. That is why God won't fix all our problems. We have to learn to accept that. Loved ones get sick, or die, or become disabled, or . . . something we don't want. Bad decisions lead to worse consequences and outcomes. When God doesn't help us escape he will help us endure, by giving us grace to cope with circumstances and outcomes. That is how he teaches us faith and trust and dependence on him, not on self and the world. That is the whole story.

Are you pushing God to do what you want and calling it faith? Or will you follow in faith where God is leading, even though you can't get all you want?

Not My Ministry

"When I became the AWANA director at [a particular church] many people quit, hoping I would fail. I went to God and said, 'God, this is your ministry. If you want it to succeed I ask you to convict people to come and serve.' People came. They were the irregular people on the fringe of the fellowship that the former leaders had not wanted. God gave his ministry success in the changed lives of leaders and children. The ministry was never easy, there were always challenges, but that is how faith grows. A little at a time God gave us a few more children and a few more leaders, until we grew into the resources he was willing to provide, because in my mind it never stopped being his ministry. Having had this experience more than once, I am convinced it is the way to run any Christian ministry. Keep asking God for what he wants to give. Keep praising God for what he chooses to give. Keep doing only what God wants to do." — Linda Quiggle

One Guy

The Holy Spirit sent Philip the evangelist to a meeting in Gaza about sixty miles south of Jerusalem (Acts 8:26). It was a long walk, about two to three days, and he (not the church) paid for his food and lodging. When Philip got to Gaza the Holy Spirit said to him, "See that Ethiopian man over there? Go give him the gospel." That was Philip's evangelistic meeting. One guy. Today's leaders measure success in tens, hundreds, and thousands. God measures success one saved soul at a time. The Ethiopian evangelized northern Africa. God changes the world one saved soul at a time. Let's stop trying to get tens and hundreds and thousands, and ask the Holy Spirit what it is he wants us to do.

A Lot Like Farming

Christian ministry is a lot like farming. Sometimes people throw out lots of gospel seed over large crowds willy-nilly, hoping some of it will grow. But that's not the best way. The best way is to plant it one soul at a time. God the Holy Spirit is seeking the lost and telling the story, "Jesus Saves." He mostly does that through his saved people: 1 Corinthians 3:6–7, one person plants the gospel seed, another person waters the gospel seed, and God is the one causes the gospel seed to grow into salvation. Ask the Holy Spirit to take you with him as he goes out witnessing to the lost. He knows just where to plant, water, grow, and harvest the gospel seed.

Called to do What?

The Holy Spirit calls all believers to do something, but he never calls any one believer to do everything, whether that believer is a leader or a follower. To insist leaders must do what their followers are doing (or vice versa) ignores the biblical fact the Holy Spirit is the chief administrator of the church who calls, and gifts, and convicts, and empowers as he chooses.
A church is like a puzzle, every member, from Pastor to newly saved, is a part—but only a part—of the whole. The Spirit is the puzzle master who puts the pieces together, this one with that one, to accomplish the evangelism, discipleship, and fellowship ministries of the church. We can trust the Holy Spirit to use his people when and where they are needed. He knows what he is doing.

The Fringe People

Every local church has what I call the fringe people: the people who are different, the one's that make us uncomfortable, the ones always at the edges of fellowship.

Often they are the ones doing the work around the church no one else wants to do. Usually they are the ones left out of church ministries.

Get to know the fringe people. Both you and they will benefit from the fellowship.

Small Thoughts

> There is a scriptural order to doing God's will: ask, receive, do. Ask God what he wants you to do. Receive what he is willing to give. Do his will according to his giving.

> Don't do something permanently stupid because you are temporarily upset.

> Great gain creates neither godliness nor contentment. Nowhere is this more true than a Christian ministry which uses the size of the crowd as the measure of success.

> Do you submit to the sovereignty of the Holy Spirit? If you ask for five and he gives you five, you are thankful. If you ask for five and he gives you three, are you thankful?

> Do you run ahead of the Holy Spirit and then ask him to bless you? Or will you ask him to bless you and run only as far as he has provided?

> I resolved not to make my needs known, but with faith in God to move men through prayer alone. — J. Hudson Taylor (1832–1905), Founder of the China Inland Mission (now OMF International).

> "All those stones that the Davids of God have flung at the Goliaths of error, they have been taken out of the brook of the Scriptures." — John Collins, Puritan Minister and Pastor, 1632–1687

"The Word of God and your faith must run parallel." — John Collins, 1632–1687

Using the world's methods in the church are not so much designed to create success, as to measure success: attendance, money, baptisms, salvations, ministries, and programs—the list goes on. God's successes are different: the gospel presented; a new life in Christ; a marriage saved; a child fed; an addict delivered; an increase in knowledge, understanding, and wisdom gained over many years; and more. What God has done is not easy to quantify and measure, but God knows. He remembers and will reward our part in his successes in due time.

Most of the time when we seek God's will we are asking about the future. But God's will is pretty much in the every-day "Do this" and "Don't do that" commandments in the Bible. He gives wisdom to understand his commandments, James 1:5, and power to do them, Philippians 4:11–13.

The Empty Mind

Some seek an empty mind so as to clearly hear the voice of their God.

An empty mind is a tenet of eastern religions such as Buddhism, which seeks to become empty so as to be one with their pantheistic god, of which all things, including human life, are nothing more than a mode or manifestation. The Buddhist "heaven," Nirvana, is nothingness, it is non-existence as the loss of individuality, it is the termination of being a distinct person by rejoining with their god through return to the substance of which all things are but a manifestation.

Human beings are not a manifestation of any god or gods. Each human being is distinct person and personality, each with a distinct future with God or separated from God. An empty mind is like a vacuum. Anything—good or evil or mundane—will rush in to fill the void.

How much better is faith in Jesus Christ and meditation on the living Word and the written Word. The genuine Christian fills his or her mind with Christ and the Word of God. When the mind is filled with the Word and his Word, then and only then is one able to clearly hear the voice of God.

The Sabbath Day

A seventh day was not identified for worship from the beginning of the world, but from ca. 1445 BC, for a particular people, in a particular covenant, the Law covenant, a covenant the New Testament apostles say the Christian is not under.

The first day of the week, Sunday, is never identified as "the Lord's Day" in the Scripture. On the contrary, there is historical evidence the term was applied to Sunday after the apostolic age.

The New Testament never denotes any particular day as "the Christian Sabbath." The serious Bible student can trace the repetition of the other nine (of the ten) commandments in the New Testament, but the fourth commandment, the Sabbath day commandment, is never repeated in the New Testament.

Based on the available Scripture evidence, Acts 2:46; Acts 20:7; 1 Corinthians 16:2, we may say meeting for worship, instruction, and Lord's Supper on the first day of the week was a practice of two local churches in the apostolic age—possibly all the local churches Paul founded—but he was not the only apostle who founded local churches.

Church history tells us meeting on the first day of the week became a tradition among most of the post-apostolic church, but not all.

But meeting on the first day of the week is not and never was a commandment to the New Testament church. Any day is usable for worship, instruction, and Lord's Supper, and the church should maintain the principle on which the commandment is based: a local New Testament church should meet regularly by devoting a specific day specifically to God.

Choices and Foreordination

I have spent a great deal of time and thought on the doctrine of foreordination. Looking at human beings only, God, out of all possible freely made choices, effectuated from actual to possible those free choices that would accomplish his purpose in creating. So every choice you make is certain, but not necessary. Certain because effectuated, not necessary (not fate, not destiny) because freely made.

That being said, I suspect that God's purpose, plans, and processes sometimes allow multiple choices that tend to fulfill the plans that accomplish his purpose. (Processes fulfill plans that accomplish the purpose. Human beings are among the processes.) So, your choices, for example, to eat well or eat unhealthily, thereby affecting the date of your death, may be more significant than you believe.

How Does Faith Grow?

Faith grows in three ways: knowledge, understanding, and practice. In knowledge by knowing the facts of Scripture. In understanding by correct interpretation of the facts. In practice by applying the understanding of the facts to the manner of living.

A simple example, both ancient and modern, common to everyone.

> The fact, 1 Corinthians 6:18, "Flee from sexual immorality."
>
> The understanding: sexual immorality covers every possible sexual action outside a believer's personal marriage covenant, for the married, and every possible sexual action for the unmarried.
>
> The practice: turn away from all forms of sexual immorality, take all steps possible to prevent such from entering into your manner of life. In our modern world that includes all manner of audio-visual-literary display of acts of sexuality.

In religious terms the practice means the married are to be chaste and the unmarried chaste and celibate in their thoughts and actions. Like Job, every male believer is to "make a covenant with my eyes that I should not look upon a woman," with sexual desire other than one's spouse, and every female to make a similar covenant that she should not look upon a man with sexual desire, other than one's spouse.

It probably goes without saying, but needs to be said, that the problem is not knowledge and understanding, but application, because that requires obedience toward God.

The Gospel Plus Nothing

The gospel is God's grace plus faith in the risen Savior and nothing added. The gospel frees the sinner from the misapprehension that salvation comes by righteousness gained through obedience. This is what is so pernicious in those religions systems—falsely known by the world as Christianity—that require obedience after (what they name) salvation, "or you cannot be saved" (e.g., Mormonism, Roman Catholicism). That is what is so pernicious about "Lordship" salvation: it adds the "intent to serve God" prior to salvation or you cannot be saved [MacArthur, *The Gospel*, chapter 15]. But the salvation principle is solely and simply, "Saved by grace through faith," Ephesians 2:8. Obedience follows salvation just as a flower grows from the seed.

The Mosaic Law

The Mosaic Law had three functions.

One, to make known God's moral values—God's rules for living—that he requires of all human beings, through the moral values, principles, and precepts of the Law.

Two, to protect his saved people from moral harm by their keeping the moral values, principles, and applicable precepts of the Law.

Three, to reveal the sinner's inability to keep God's commandments without grace from God, thereby condemning the person unable to keep the Law.

None of these functions has expired.

Passive Righteousness

The righteousness that effects salvation is a passive righteousness. By passive I mean we cannot create it, but only receive it from God in Christ.

There are many kinds of active righteousness in the world. We should obey the laws of men and God. We should do morally right toward ourselves and others. We should teach our children how to properly behave in the world.

But the active righteousness that proceeds from daily life does not save from sin. Only passive righteousness, that which we can only receive from another, even from God in Christ, by his sovereign grace, only righteousness freely given and freely received is able to forgive sins and give eternal life.

Like the thirsty ground that needs the rain, even so the sinner needs the grace of God that gives his righteousness to the believing sinner. The ground can do nothing to produce the rain; no strength or labor or effort will create the rain or make the rain fall. The ground must wait for the rain to fall of its own accord, and then the ground may receive it and bear fruit.

Like the ground waiting passively for the rain, even so the sinner cannot produce the righteousness that saves. No strength, no labor, no effort, no good intent, no penance, no confession, no obedience, no tangible work of one's hands, no intangible work of one's soul will create, bring, or give the righteousness that saves the soul. The sinner must wait for God to give the righteousness gained for him by Christ on the cross, and then receive it by faith alone, and then only will it bear the fruit of his salvation.

The biblical rule of representation.

Adam legally represented his physical descendants, the result of his seminal representation: all human beings were in potential in his loins.

Christ legally represents his spiritual descendants: all human beings elected by God the Father to salvation and predestined to be adopted as God's sons and conformed to Christ's image.

Therefore, as Paul states in Romans 5, the sin of the one was imputed to the many, just as the righteousness of the other is imputed to many.

Salvation Secured

Jesus Christ's limitless merit as the propitiation for sin endlessly secures the believer's salvation, Hebrews 10:12, 14, and his eternal priestly intercession in heaven endlessly maintains the believer's salvation, Hebrews 7:25; 1 John 2:1. He will never leave us or forsake us, Hebrews 13:5, and none can take us out of his hand, John 10:27-30.

I was asked, "Do you believe regeneration proceeds belief?"

I believe that question, which is at the center of a vigorous and on-going debate, is simplistic.

I believe that in the sinner, the soul's faculty of spiritual perception, which is grossly dulled by the sin attribute, must be enlivened by the Holy Spirit, through application of the gift of God, before the sinner is able to understand the spiritual issues of sin, the Savior, and salvation.

Without that spiritual understanding there could not be conviction of personal sin and the appropriation of truth by the sinner to his or her spiritual need. That personal appropriation of truth to satisfy the spiritual need for salvation is the exercise of saving faith.

Upon the exercise of saving faith, the sinner's human nature is regenerated. The regeneration of human nature is God sharing the communicable aspects of his eternal life, and the attributes of human nature prioritized to serve God not self.

Some in the aforementioned debate would consider the enlivening of spiritual perception to be regeneration; others would see it as conviction.

I see enlivening the faculty of spiritual perception as the first act of a regeneration that results in conviction, faith, and salvation, that in turn results in the completed regeneration of human nature, as I have defined regeneration.

I believe that in some persons the Holy Spirit enlivens the faculty of spiritual perception all at once, resulting in an inevitable and immediate conviction, faith, and salvation. I believe in others the Holy Spirit enlivens spiritual perception as a process, a process of indeterminate length suited to each individual, resulting in a growing conviction, that ultimately reaches its inevitable climax, resulting in completed conviction, with immediate faith and salvation.

The tendency in popular theology is to overly simplify complex issues—to turn a ten course meal into a bologna sandwich. There is a time and place for a sandwich, but I usually prefer the meal.

The Gospel Call

The gospel call to believe and be saved is directed toward "whoever desires," Revelation 22:17; whoever believes on him, John 3:16; Romans 10:11; 1 John 5:1; whoever calls on the name of the Lord, Acts 2:21; Romans 10:13. How do we find those people? Go and proclaim the gospel call to all.

The Law and Human Nature

Before Christ came, the Law of Moses (and the law in the

conscience for the gentiles, Romans 2:14) served to convict of sin and protect from moral and spiritual harm. That function continues today as the Law of Christ.

But no Law can effect that change in human nature which eliminates the need for the Law: "the law is not made for a righteous person, but for the lawless and insubordinate, for the ungodly and for sinners," 1 Timothy 1:9.

The spiritual power to change human nature is through faith in God and God's testimony of the means to salvation. You will not see the kingdom of God by obedience to the laws of any religion, man-made or God-given. "If a law had been given able to give life, truly from out of the Law there would have been righteousness," Galatians 3:21.

What is faith?

Faith has two aspects, each of equal importance.

Saving and Sanctifying faith is inwardly believing the testimony of God through the infallible conviction given by the Holy Spirit, and outwardly acting through the power given by the Holy Spirit to conform one's thoughts and actions to that conviction.

Persevering faith is "the title deed of the things of which we are assured, the objective evidence of the things not yet seen" (Hebrews 11:1, my translation).

Through the one we are saved and conformed to be like Christ.

Through the other we persevere in the faith by faith through all the difficulties of life, in expectation of heaven at physical death or rapture, and our resurrection and reward at Christ's return for his New Testament church.

Grace For Salvation

Every theology that looks to the Bible for understanding believes every human being is a sinner. Every theology that looks to the Bible for understanding believes God must give grace for a sinner to be saved. Everyone, Arminian and Reformed and Dispensationalist, agree this is the case: every one is a sinner; everyone needs grace from God to be saved.

The term for that grace God gives for salvation is called "prevenient grace," meaning "grace given before." Without prevenient grace no one can believe and be saved, because all are sinners.

Arminianism teaches God gives prevenient grace to everyone, no exceptions (how God gives that grace varies in Arminian theology), so that every sinner is able to overcome their sin and either choose to believe or choose to not believe.

Calvinistic-Reformed-Dispensational theology teaches God gives prevenient grace according to his choices in election, and gives that grace only through his gift of grace-faith-salvation, Ephesians 2:8, only to the elect. Those elect sinners receiving the gift are made willing to believe by the gift, and do believe. Those sinners not receiving the gift are unwilling to believe and don't believe.

(Note: some Dispensationalists are Arminian in their doctrine of salvation.)

Grace and Duty

Praying? Rebuking your sins in Jesus' name? Be sure and follow through. God's graces require man's duty. God gives, the believer receives *and* puts to use. Otherwise you are just spouting nonsense and dishonoring God.

The Poor

The Greeks had two words to describe the poor. One word was *pénēs* [Zodhiates, s. v. "3993"]. That word described the person who earned just enough to meet his or her daily needs for food and shelter. In modern terms, they were the "living paycheck-to-paycheck" poor.

The other word was *ptōchós* [Zodhiates, s. v. "4434"], which referred to those who must beg to earn their daily needs for food and shelter. If they did not receive sufficient money by begging, they went without one or more or all of those daily needs. The ptōchós poor were in abject poverty, utter helplessness, complete destitution, and therefore a helpless beggar. In modern terms, the homeless depending on the kindness of strangers for their survival.

The Macedonian Christians at 2 Corinthians 8:2–5 were *ptōchós* poor: they sacrificed their daily needs to make a contribution to Paul's ministry. The rich young ruler of Luke 18:22 was to sell his goods and distribute the proceeds to the *ptōchós* poor: the helpless beggars in Jerusalem.

In the New Testament, except for 2 Corinthians 9:9, the word translated "poor" (34 occurrences) is always the *ptōchós* poor.

Inerrant or Trustworthy?

If Scripture is not inerrant, but merely trustworthy, then what is the standard for trust? Stated more simply, who decides what in the Bible is or is not Scripture? Who decides what Scripture actually teaches? Answer: every person does what is right in his own eyes.

The Grain of Doubt

Our cultural presuppositions teach us that one grain of doubt destroys a mountain of evidence. That cultural attitude is highly destructive to understanding the Bible.

Understanding the Bible is always a progression from what is possible, to what is plausible, to what is probable, to what is certain.

The essentials of the faith are certain. Other things, such as when does the rapture take place, are within that range of interpretation from possible, to plausible, to probable.

Understanding the Bible is not so much a matter of an explicit scripture, nor lack of doubt, but "what does the Bible as a whole teach?"

That is why one of the rules of Bible interpretation is this: do not reinterpret a clear scripture(s) with an unclear, doubtful scripture.

More simply, in Bible study, a mountain—even a hill—of evidence crushes a grain of doubt.

Books

Some books are like a well-stocked pantry, in which there may be an item here or an item there I do not like or want. Those books I keep, I read, I study.

Other books are like pouring water through a colander: little of interest or profit sticks. Those books I discard.

The books do not make my learning true to Scripture. My intent is to understand the truth in Scripture, guided by the Holy Spirit, as I seek to fulfill and improve my spiritual gift, Bible Teacher. That is why I read books and study the Scripture.

Three Things

The three things to look for in a NT church are these: do its teachers and preachers teach and preach the gospel of salvation, Christian doctrine, and the normal Christian life.

If all three are not present in a balanced way, from week to week, over a sufficient period of time in which to evaluate the preaching and teaching ministry of that church, keep looking.

Praying?

Praying? Rebuking your sins in Jesus' name? Be sure and follow though. God's graces require man's duty. God gives, the believer receives *and* puts to use. Otherwise you are just spouting nonsense and dishonoring God.

Becoming a Dispensationalist

Read for yourself the Scripture in the plain and normal sense of its words and you will inevitably arrive at the Dispensational view of Scripture. All non-dispensational views have to be taught.

Refuting modern-day prophets

Refuting modern-day prophets is a matter of looking at the whole teaching of Scripture, and using rational reasoning. The Scripture intimates God's revelation to humankind is completed, e.g., Rev. 22:18–19; 1 Cor 13:10, John 16:12–13.

The New Testament uses "prophet" in two ways: a preacher of things present; a preacher of things to come. An argument may be made 1 Cor 14:37–39 is speaking of a preacher of things present, but that argument will not convince any who believes otherwise.

Here is the main point. Is the modern-day preacher of things to come giving new revelation from God? If so, then three things must take place: one, that prophecy must not conflict with any other revelation from God in the 66 canonical books; two, that prophecy should come true exactly as given (if the time period allows); three, every Bible on the face of the earth must be revised to include that prophecy, for the prophet is claiming this is new revelation from God.

Let us bear in mind that Joseph Smith did number three (above), because he understood his (supposed) new revelation required adding to existing revelation. Yet, his revelation failed to meet numbers one and two. So, too, all so-called prophets after the New Testament apostles died.

If the "prophecy" is not new revelation from God, then it is preaching things present, not things to come. If a new prophecy about things to come agrees with existing Scripture but adds no new information to scripture, then it is not a revelation from God, it is not preaching things to come, and it is useless as prophecy.

Finally, the apostles did not accept any revelation from any person other than themselves as new revelation from God. All warned against false prophets and false teachers. As the apostles were limited to the 12 plus Paul, then all others are false prophets.

Worship and Fellowship

I pity those whose worship requires a building and a worship leader and a priest or a pastor.

If this year-long pandemic and quarantine has taught us Christians anything, it should have reminded us worship is not in a building, but by the believer toward his God and Savior.

No church leaders can require me to wear a mask or get a vaccine in order to engage in worship. They can only make those requirements for me to gather together with them.

Nothing can stop the believer from worshiping. Only imprisonment can stop believers from gathering together for worship and fellowship; and even then the Spirit usually makes a way. If the people in the "church building" will not worship with me, others will.

My 47 years of Christian experience have taught me the Holy Spirit always satisfies the believer's desire to worship and fellowship with others of like precious faith. Always.

Genesis 3:15

I was asked, "How do you interpret Genesis 3:15?" Certainly not about Christ, of whom there is no mention in the verse; and no Scripture in the Bible associates Genesis 3:15 with Christ.

Genesis 3:15 speaks of the continuing conflict between those of faith and those not of faith. That is how Paul interpreted it, Romans 16:20—and note the outcome is yet-future. Eve interpreted 3:15 to mean Cain was of the serpent's offspring: those who are not of faith, an interpretation confirmed at 1 John 3:12. Eve interpreted 3:15 to mean Able and Seth were of her offspring: those who are of faith.

In biblical usage, the phrases "sons of, seed of, offspring of, daughters of," etc., indicate descendants or followers who have the characteristics of the person or thing of whom they are the "son of, seed of" etc.

The "sons of rebellion," at 2 Samuel 23:6 were the rebellious. The "sons of the prophets," 2 Kings 2:3, were those men who were faithful to God and preached his Word. The sons of fools, and the sons of vile men, Job 30:8, were fools and vile. The "sons of God" (Hebrew: *benê 'ĕlōhîm;* Greek: *huiós theós*), are those who are like God because they are in a faith-based relationship with God, Genesis 6:2, 4; Job 1:6; 2:1; 38:7; Matthew 5:9; Luke 20:36; Romans 8:14, 19; Galatians 3:26.

The offspring of the Woman are those of her descendants with her characteristic of faith. The offspring of the serpent are those of the Woman's descendants without her characteristic of faith. There will be continuing struggle between the two kinds of offspring; the Woman's offspring may lose battles but will win the war.

Through the New Testament revelation, we understand serpent's offspring—Eve's descendants without faith—are motivated to oppose those of faith by their own sinful nature and fallen angels, Ephesians 6:12. Through the New Testament revelation, we understand the Woman's offspring—Eve's descendants with faith—will win the war because of the victory over sin accomplished by Christ on the cross.

That is the interpretation in context: the continuing conflict between those of faith and those of no-faith.

(I have a longer and in depth discussion in my book, *Adam and Eve, A Biography and Theology.*)

Freedom to Lose Your Salvation?

Can a saved person decide not to be saved? Can a saved person decide to give up his or her salvation and become unsaved, again? The answer does not lie within the choices of the saved human being, but within the character of God.

If, as is the case, God makes unsaved sinners willing to be saved through his gift of grace-faith-salvation (Eph 2:8), does God make them unwilling to continue in salvation by withdrawing his gift of grace-faith-salvation, making them unsaved sinners, again?

If, as is the case, God's gift enlivens the unsaved sinner's spiritual perception (1 Corinthians 2:10–16), so as to understand the issues of his or her sin, Christ the only Savior, and the necessity for salvation, does God take away that spiritual perception from some, and withdraw his communion and fellowship, thereby denying his word, "Never no never will I leave you, never no never will I forsake you," Hebrews 13:5?

Does God's arm become so shortened, that having saved, he is unable to maintain a person's salvation?

Will God withdraw that eternal life he gives to the saved, so that one who was saved will perish?

Does the limitless merit Christ gained in his propitiation of God have a time limit, or perhaps an expiration date, for some who are saved?

I think God does none of these things. To do any one of those things would be to deny himself as God. When we speak about the maintenance and security of salvation, the issue is not about the possibility of human choices, but God's holy and righteous character.

When God stops being holy and righteous and loving and just and faithful and eternal, then the saved person will be able to decide to discard his or her salvation. Until God ceases to be God, God will continue to sustain the believer through his eternal life that he communicates to every saved person without ceasing.

Keep on loving Me.

John 14:15 (JQT), "If you keep on loving me you will obey my commandments."

Someone has counted 1,050 NT commandments; that's twice the number in the Mosaic Law. That is more than one person can remember at any one time. So how can we do what God wants? There are three ways God has provided for us.

First, when God created human beings he designed a conscience and informed it with an understanding or right and wrong. The conscience can be damaged (and have to be retrained).

Second, God makes the believer born-again. When the believer is born again God writes his laws on our heart and mind and gives is the disposition and inclination to obey him. But we still need to know what to do.

So three, the Holy Spirit will guide the believer into what is right. But, the Spirit does not work apart from the Scripture, so your responsibility is to read and learn and then the Spirit will give you power to do what the Scripture says. (And it we don't always obey, 1 John 1:9 restores our fellowship with Christ.)

How to obey God? Read the Scripture to inform your conscience. Read the Scripture so the Holy Spirit can bring God's commandments to your remembrance. Trust the Spirit to guide you into righteousness.

Th real key to obedience is exactly what Jesus said: keep on loving me. The person in love with Christ always seeks to do what Christ desires.

Over a Lifetime

Over his or her lifetime, the Christian should know the Bible as well as the master carpenter knows woods and tools, as well as feet in the dark know the path from bed to bathroom, as well as penguins know how to swim, and babes know how to suckle nourishment from their mother's beast.

Over a lifetime as a believer there should be no mountain not climbed, no river not fished, not a meadow in which you have not camped and collected wildflowers, not a path you have not walked from beginning to end, not a page you have not turned, not a word you have not read, eaten, and digested.

If taken blindfolded and dropped somewhere in the scriptures, upon uncovering your eyes you should know at a glance exactly where you are: the lay of the land, the people you will meet, the trees and their fruit, and the grain in the fields. You should know the people in every city, the way of its streets and alleys, the sights and smells of its marketplaces and shops. Each should be as familiar to you as your fingers are to your hand.

You should be able to list the books in forward and reverse order, from Genesis to Revelation, from Revelation to Genesis. If you hear a verse you should recognize it. If asked to explain a doctrine you should know it. The scriptures are your light on the path of life, the furniture in your house of faith, food on your pantry shelves, your meat and drink prepared and waiting to be consumed for your spiritual health.

Over a lifetime you should come to know the Bible chronologically, biographically, and doctrinally from "In the beginning" to the final "Amen." If you don't, yet, what are you waiting for? Read, study, learn, grow, mature.

I don't need theology/doctrine, I just need Jesus?

Which Jesus?

Jesus the teacher? Jesus the poor man from Nazareth who lived a life of charity? Jesus who was executed as a criminal? Jesus the healer? Jesus the miracle-worker? Jesus the revolutionary? Jesus the Son of God? Jesus the God-man? Jesus the one in whom faith in him redeems from the penalty of sin?

Perhaps the incarnate God the Son, Jesus the Christ, the God-man, the Son of God who died for your sin according to the Scripture, was buried, and rose out from the dead the third day, according to the Scripture?

The moment you choose, or do not choose, the Jesus you need, you have made a statement of your theology, your doctrine, or lack thereof.

Don't be deceived by the anti-intellectualism of a Christianity (so-called) that believes Christianity is a feeling, not an objective revelation of truth. That believes Christianity is a life, not a doctrine. Don't be deceived by a Christianity that is "just Jesus" and knows nothing—and does not want to know—of the apostolic doctrine that defines genuine Christianity.

Truth minus the doctrine that explains the truth will always degenerate into heresy, and heresy into apostasy.

Sources

Alexander, Joseph Addison. *Commentary on the Gospel of Mark*. 1864, Reprinted, Minneapolis, MN: Klock and Klock Christian Publishers, 1980.

Ames, William. *The Marrow of Theology*. 1648. Reprinted, Durham, PA: The Labyrinth Press, 1983.

Anderson, Sir Robert. *The Silence of God*. 1907. Reprinted, Grand Rapids, MI: Kregel Publications, 1978.

Beale, G. K. and D. A. Carson. *Commentary on the New Testament use of the Old Testament*. Grand Rapids, MI: Baker Academic, 2007.

Berkhoff, Louis. *Systematic Theology*. London: Banner of Truth Trust, 1959.

Boettner, Loraine. *The Millennium*. Philadelphia, PA: Presbyterian And Reformed, 1957.

Burton, Ernest De Witt. *The Ancient Synagogue Service*. "The Biblical World," August 1896, Vol. 8, No. 2 (Aug., 1896), pp. 143–148. PDF accessed from http://www.jstor.com/stable/3140264.

Charnock, Stephen. *The Doctrine of Regeneration*. Grand Rapids, MI: Baker Book House, 1980.

Cohick, Lynn H. *Women in the World of the Earliest Christians*. Grand Rapids, MI: Baker Academic, 2009.

Dana, H. E., and Julius R. Mantey. *A Manual Grammar of the Greek New Testament*. New York, NY: The Macmillan Company, 1927.

Danby, Herbert. *The Mishnah*. Oxford, England: Oxford University Press, 1933.

Davenant, John. *An Exposition of the Epistle of St. Paul to the Colossians*. 1627. Reprinted, Carlisle, PA: Banner of Truth Trust, 2005.

Davids, Peter H. *The First Epistle of Peter*. New International Commentary on the New Testament. Grand Rapids, MI: Eerdmans Publishing, 1990.

Fee, Gordon, D. *Paul's Letter to the Philippians*. The New International Commentary on the New Testament. Grand Rapids, MI: William B. Eerdmans Publishing Company, 1995.

Grudem, Wayne. *Systematic Theology*. Grand Rapids, MI: Zondervan, 1994.

Harris, R. Laird; Gleason L. Archer, Jr.; and Bruce K. Waltke. *Theological Wordbook of the Old Testament*. 2 vols. Chicago,

IL: Moody Press, 1980.

Hodge, Charles. *Systematic Theology*. Grand Rapids, MI: Eerdmans Publishing, 1981.

Martin, Luther H. *Hellenistic Religions, An Introduction*. Oxford, England: Oxford University Press, 1987.

Morris, Leon. *The Gospel According to Matthew*. The New International Commentary on the New Testament. Grand Rapids, MI: Eerdmans Publishing, 1992.

Murray, Iain, H. *The Life of Arthur W. Pink*. Carlisle, PA: Banner of Truth Trust, 1981.

Nisbet, Alexander. *An Exposition of 1 & 2 Peter*. Carlisle, PA: The Banner of Truth Trust, 1982.

O'Brien, Peter T. *The Letter to the Ephesians*. The Pillar New Testament Commentary. Grand Rapids, MI: Eerdmans Publishing, 1999.

Owen, John. *Biblical Theology*. Trans., Stephen P. Westcott. 1661. Reprinted, Grand Rapids, MI: Soli Deo Gloria Publications, 1994.

Pentecost J. Dwight. *Things to Come. A Study in Biblical Eschatology* Grand Rapids, MI: Zondervan, 1958.

Perowne, Stewart, J. J. *The Book of Psalms*. 1878. Reprinted, Grand Rapids, MI: Zondervan, 1976.

Quiggle, James D. *A Private Commentary on the Bible: Colossians*, Amazon/KDP, 2018.

______. *A Private Commentary on the Book of Hebrews*, 2012. Revised, Amazon/KDP, 2020.

______. *A Private Commentary on the Bible: Philippians*, Amazon/KDP, 2020.

______. *Adam and Eve, A Biography and Theology*. Amazon/KDP, 2011.

______. *Dictionary of Doctrinal Words*. Amazon/KDP, 2018.

______. *God Became Incarnate*. Amazon/KDP, 2014.

______. *God's Choices, The Doctrines of Foreordination, Election, and Predestination*. Amazon/KDP, 2012.

______. *Life, Death, Eternity*. Amazon/KDP, 2019.

______. *The Epistle of Jesus to the Church: A Commentary on the Revelation*. Eugene, OR: Resource Publications, 2007.

______. *The Literal Hermeneutic, Explained and Illustrated*. Amazon/KDP 2018.

______. *Translations of Select Bible Books*. Amazon/KDP, 2018, rev. 2020.

Ramm, Bernard. *Protestant Biblical Interpretation.* 3rd Revised Edition Grand Rapids, MI: Baker Book House, 1995.

Ramsay, Sir William. *Was Christ Born in Bethlehem.* 1898. Reprinted, Minneapolis, MN: James Family Publishing, 1978.

Ramsey, James. *The Book of Revelation, an Exposition of the First Eleven Chapters.* 1873. Reprinted, Carlisle, PA: Banner of Truth Trust, 1977

Ryrie, Charles C. *Basic Theology.* Chicago, IL: Moody Publishers, 1999.

______. *Dispensationalism.* 1966. Revised, Chicago, IL: Moody Press, 1995.

______. *So Great Salvation, What it means to Believe in Jesus Christ.* USA: Victor Books (A Division of Scripture Press Publications), 1989.

Shedd, W. G. T. *Dogmatic Theology.* 1863. 3 vols. Reprinted, Nashville, TN: Thomas Nelson Publishers, 1980.

Schaff, Philip. *Nicene and Post–Nicene Fathers, First Series.* Vol. 1. *The Confessions and Letters of Augustin, with a Sketch of his Life and Work.* 1886. Reprinted, Peabody, MA: Hendrickson Publishers, 1999.

______. *The Creeds of Christendom.* Vol. 2, *The Greek and Latin Creeds.* 1889. Reprinted from the 1931 ed., Grand Rapids, MI: Baker Book House, 1983.

Thomas, Robert L. *Revelation 1–7, An Exegetical Commentary.* Chicago, IL: Moody Press, 1992.

Thomson, William M. *The Land and the Book.* 1880. Reprinted, Hartford, CN: The S. S. Scranton Company, 1910.

Trench, Richard Chenevix. *Commentary on the Seven Churches in Asia.* London: 1897.

Vlach, Michael J. *Dispensationalism, Essential Beliefs and Common Myths.* 2008. Revised, Los Angeles, CA: Theological Studies Press, 2017.

Waltke, Bruce K. *A Commentary on Micah.* Grand Rapids, MI: Eerdmans Publishing, 2007.

Westcott, B. F. *The Gospel According to St. John.* 1881, Reprinted, Grand Rapids, MI: Eerdmans Publishing, 1978.

Wilken, Robert L. *The Christians As the Romans Saw Them.* New Haven, CN: Yale University Press, 1984.

Zodhiates, Spiros. *The Complete Word Study Dictionary New Testament.* Revised. Chattanooga, TN: AMG Publishers, 1993.

www.ingramcontent.com/pod-product-compliance
Lightning Source LLC
Chambersburg PA
CBHW050312160726
48002CB00001B/2